Praise for *The Practitioner*

Picasso once remarked that "art is the elimination of the unnecessary." Ernest L. Rossi's Mirroring Hands method is brilliant in its simplicity and elimination of the unnecessary, yet is complex beyond belief in the results it can engender. This method can eliminate any resistance you may encounter in the change process and can evoke deep inner wisdom, often in a very short time.

Richard Hill has facilitated and expanded this guide to using Mirroring Hands in such a way that makes it accessible for all.

Bill O'Hanlon, author of *Solution-Oriented Hypnosis* and *Do One Thing Different*

In *The Practitioner's Guide to Mirroring Hands*, Richard Hill and Ernest L. Rossi honor the wisdom of the courageous people who come to us seeking healing. They offer deep wisdom about the inherent health that lies within our clients and the support we can provide to allow that health to come forward. A wonderful contribution!

Bonnie Badenoch, Ph.D., marriage and family therapist, author of *Being a Brain-Wise Therapist* and *The Heart of Trauma*

Within the crucible of a technique Hill and Rossi call Mirroring Hands, *The Practitioner's Guide to Mirroring Hands* shares a storehouse of practical insight, scientific theory, and clinical wisdom. In the process they challenge accepted assumptions and synthesize complex principles, all the while encouraging clinicians to learn to listen to their inner voice.

The Practitioner's Guide to Mirroring Hands is a warm and fascinating adventure in which you get to know two explorers of the mind and learn about the history of psychotherapy while gaining practical knowledge. You may not agree with everything the authors say, but I suspect that you will respect and enjoy their unique blend of complexity, depth, and self-insight – so often missing from contemporary discussions.

Louis Cozolino, Ph.D., author of *The Neuroscience of Psychotherapy, The Neuroscience of Human Relationships, The Making of a Therapist,* and *Why Therapy Works*

What a fascinating book! Starting as an easy read, it gently descends to deep levels. Richard Hill brings straightforward clarity to Ernest L. Rossi's genius, and their combined work brings contemporary insight into ideas pioneered by my father, Milton H. Erickson.

The Practitioner's Guide to Mirroring Hands will inspire ongoing discoveries by others and carry this important work into tomorrow.

Roxanna Erickson-Klein, Ph.D., R.N., author of *Hope and Resiliency* and *Engage the Group, Engage the Brain,* editor of *The Collected Works of Milton H. Erickson*

Have you ever wondered how to help a client access their unconscious? Building on the work of Milton H. Erickson, Ernest L. Rossi developed Mirroring Hands to do just that, and, along with Richard Hill, he has now brought it to you. Not only do Hill and Rossi give clear step-by-step instructions for how to use Mirroring Hands, but they also lay out the framework for understanding the dynamic power of this tool.

The Practitioner's Guide to Mirroring Hands is a well-rounded resource full of practical applications and illustrative casebook studies. Readers will find themselves both informed and empowered by this guide.

**Ruth Buczynski, Ph.D., licensed psychologist,
President, National Institute for the Clinical Application of Behavioral Medicine**

Providing extensive research background for the theories on which the Mirroring Hands technique is based, *The Practitioner's Guide to Mirroring Hands* is an outstanding manual accomplished with precision and clarity. It takes readers on a journey through neurophysiological and genomic discoveries and offers intriguing speculations on quantum influences which may give readers a glimpse of the inevitable future of psychotherapy.

**Stephen Lankton, M.S.W., D.A.H.B., editor-in-chief, *American Journal of Clinical Hypnosis*,
author of *The Answer Within* and *Tools of Intention***

There is plenty of research and ideas presented here that made me think new thoughts, and you can't ask much more from a book. I'm sure *The Practitioner's Guide to Mirroring Hands* will be one I return to repeatedly.

**Trevor Silvester, Q.C.H.P.A. (Reg), N.C.H. (Fellow), H.P.D.,
Training Director, The Quest Institute Ltd, author of *Cognitive Hypnotherapy*, *Wordweaving*, and *The Question is the Answer***

The Practitioner's Guide to Mirroring Hands really does do magnificent credit to Richard Hill's documentation and to his dedication in uncovering the genius of Rossi and Erickson, and will provide you with a never-ending source of wisdom on your professional journey in the therapy room. The authors should be commended for this text, which obviously sets out to achieve a quite remarkable feat in its presentation of the Mirroring Hands process, and it doesn't disappoint. It is indeed a tour de force which will – and should – become a classic.

**Dr. Tom Barber, founder, Contemporary College of Therapeutic Studies,
educator, psychotherapist, coach, and bestselling author**

The Practitioner's Guide to

MIRRORING HANDS

A Client-Responsive Therapy That Facilitates Natural Problem-Solving and Mind–Body Healing

Richard Hill and Ernest L. Rossi

Crown House Publishing Limited
www.crownhouse.co.uk

First published by

Crown House Publishing Ltd
Crown Buildings, Bancyfelin, Carmarthen,
Wales, SA33 5ND, UK
www.crownhouse.co.uk

and

Crown House Publishing Company LLC
PO Box 2223, Williston, VT 05495, USA
www.crownhousepublishing.com

British Library Cataloguing-in-Publication Data

A catalogue entry for this book is available from the British Library.

Print ISBN 978-178583246-8
Mobi ISBN 978-178583290-1
ePub ISBN 978-178583291-8
ePDF ISBN 978-178583292-5

LCCN 2017955324

Printed and bound in the UK by TJ International, Padstow, Cornwall

This book honors two extraordinary women: Kathryn Lane Rossi and Susan Jamie Louise Davis who have not only made our lives an immeasurable pleasure, but have also been a source of healing for many thousands of people.

Acknowledgments

This volume spans many decades of growth and change, so acknowledging everyone who has made a contribution is probably impossible. We would like to begin with a heartfelt thank you to all our patients and clients over the years who have been, in a very special way, co-creators in the emergence and development of Mirroring Hands. It almost goes without saying that we equally acknowledge the numinous, and continuing, presence of Milton H. Erickson.

Richard Hill extends the first acknowledgment and his unqualified gratitude to Ernest Rossi, who has facilitated his becoming as a therapist for more than a decade. Starting a new career in midlife is so much more possible when surrounded by the best.

We must, again, thank our wives, Kathryn Rossi and Susan Davis, for their enormous contribution, on both professional and personal levels. Almost as dedicated has been Michael Hoyt, in San Francisco, who has generously read and re-read progressive drafts, providing invaluable guidance and advice. Many thanks to Nick Kuys, from Tasmania, Australia, for his kindly role play as our "quintessential practitioner," helping us to appreciate what was interesting and important. A very special thanks to Jeff Zeig for contributing the foreword. He is an icon of professional excellence throughout the world and tireless in his work as founder and board member of the Milton H. Erickson Foundation.

We have been befriended and gently encouraged by wonderful people, including John Arden, Bonnie Badenoch, Rubin Battino, Steve Carey, Giovanna Cilia, Lou Cozolino, Mauro Cozzolino, Matthew Dahlitz, Jan Dyba, Roxanna Erickson-Klein, John Falcon, Bruce and Brigitta Gregory, Salvatore Iannotti, Paul Lange, Stephen Lankton, Paul Leslie, Scott Miller, Michael Munion, Carmen Nicotra, Bill O'Hanlon, Kirk Olson, Debra Pearce-McCall, Susan Sandy, Dan Siegel, Lawrence Sugarman, Reid Wilson, Michael and Diane Yapko, and Shane Warren. There are more we hold dear to our hearts, including colleagues and friends at the Global Association for Interpersonal Neurobiology Studies (GAINS) who are more family than just friends; the wonderful people at the Milton H. Erickson Foundation; and Venkat Pulla and our Strengths Based Practice Social Work community in Australia, Asia, and the Subcontinent. It has been a wonderful journey. Thank you all.

Our appreciation goes to the whole team at Crown House Publishing who have believed in the value of this book and done so much to make it possible. Thanks to Mark Tracten for being an annual presence for many years, David and Karen Bowman, Tom Fitton, Rosalie Williams, and all the hard-working Crown House team around the globe.

Contents

Foreword

Ernest Rossi has been a seminal contributor to and a historical figure in the evolution of psychotherapy. He is blessed to have Richard Hill as a collaborator.

Rossi has contributed in many professional arenas, including advancing Jungian perspectives and the work of Milton H. Erickson, M.D., who was the dean of 20th century medical hypnosis. Rossi was Erickson's Boswell and the person who was primary in making Erickson's work available to the world. But Rossi's own groundbreaking contributions have been in psycho-neuro-biology. He pioneered the use of hypnotic techniques in mind–body therapy, including the way in which hypnotic suggestion alters gene expression. How the mind creates the brain and the body is a door that Rossi has unlocked so that other investigators can enter and explore.

Contributions to hypnosis have also been central to Rossi's work. He is a specialist in ideodynamic activity – the way in which associations and mental representations alter behavior and sensory experience. When you think vividly about a lemon, you salivate. If you're a passenger in a car, and you want it to stop quickly, you stomp on the imaginary brake. These ideodynamic principles can guide psychotherapy and are the foundation of this important book.

Rossi invented the Mirroring Hands technique, which can be used both for hypnotic induction and hypnotherapy. The protocol and accompanying theory are presented and enriched with clear clinical examples. Variations are explained and limitations are offered. Therapists who want to advance their technique can now learn from a psychotherapeutic master.

Richard Hill is a co-author, not merely an expositor. He expounds on the importance of curiosity as a palliative factor and enriches perspectives on using the brain to alter the body. Orientations are developed to aid clinicians to avoid burnout.

Not only is this book an important resource for those who practice hypnosis, it can also be an important introduction for any psychotherapist who wants to learn about mind–body therapy. This manual provides keys to the solutions to problems that have previously evaded psychotherapeutic technique.

Ernest Rossi and Richard Hill are to be commended for their vibrant exposition. They have cleared previous undergrowth and created a path that others will be wise to follow.

Jeffrey K. Zeig, Ph.D.
Milton H. Erickson Foundation

Introduction

Richard Hill Meets Ernest Rossi

I first saw Ernest Rossi demonstrate Mirroring Hands in December 2005. My reaction to Dr. Rossi's undeniable intellect and broad ranging ideas was to be, simply, blown away. I knew this was a turning point, a phase shift, in my life. There had to be a reason why I had flown 7,500 miles to attend the Evolution of Psychotherapy conference. I did not ever imagine I was embarking on a journey that would lead to a decade long engagement with Ernest Rossi, culminating in this book.

But things happen, and they have a way of telling you what you need to know. Sometimes you notice quickly and easily, other times you need to be smacked in the face more than once before it all falls into place. So, what were the smacks in my face? Frankly, there have been quite a few over the past decade. Let me share an experience from a few years ago which absolutely convinced me why I was so drawn to Mirroring Hands. I hope that in describing a case, you can more easily "walk in my shoes" for a while.

RH's Casebook: A "Walk-In"

I answered an unexpected knock on the door of my clinic. A woman in her mid to late thirties asked if I could see her straight away. That is a little unusual but, as it happened, I was available and I invited her in. She spoke quickly and had a way of gazing intently that was a little unnerving, but I didn't feel she was psychotic, just intense. In something of a machine-gun delivery she set up the conditions for the session.

> *Your sign says counseling and brain training. I don't know what brain training is. (She didn't pause for an explanation.) I've just come from seeing another psychiatrist. In fact, I've seen a lot of different therapists, had just about every therapy … and read everything. You reckon you can do something different? I'll give you 60 minutes.*

Well, it was nothing if not a challenge, and so we began. She sat down and I went through my standard intake process. She wasn't all that keen on telling her story in detail, again, to another therapist.

Then she looked at her watch:

> *You have 45 minutes left.*

No pressure! In the tradition of Milton H. Erickson, I was looking for her to show me some clues as to how to proceed.[1] She had been clear so far: don't do any of the standard treatments. She almost seemed to be saying, don't treat me at all. Wow! This was such a unique experience and, to be honest, I really didn't know what to do. So I watched her. She was very expressive with her hands, pushing them toward me to highlight things as she spoke. I was suddenly transported to my workshops with Ernest Rossi. This looked something like what happens during a Mirroring Hands experience. I took the gamble that no other therapist had used this technique with her.

> *I'm noticing that you are very expressive with your hands. Have you ever really looked at your hands ... noticed what is really interesting about them?*

She was surprisingly cooperative and stared at her hands for about 30 seconds, then flicked her gaze back to me.

> *What are you doing?*

Well, she had basically told me that she didn't think much of what therapists thought. She was also sick and tired of them forcing different therapies down her throat. Feigning a surprised confusion, I replied:

> *I don't know, but you said you'd done everything. So ... have you ever done anything like this before?*

She stared intently at me for a moment, looked at her watch and told me as a matter of fact:

> *You have 35 minutes.*

I began to facilitate Mirroring Hands. We will learn the details of the procedure later in the book, but, suffice it to say, as the experience unfolded, she told me, with some surprise, that she felt her hands were representing two aspects of her persona. One hand was representing a part of herself she keeps private and the other hand was representing her public face. It was like watching someone open doors to rooms she had not seen for a long time. Sometimes she shared what was happening and other times she just explored her "rooms" privately. Many things happened over the next 30

1 Erickson, M. H. (2008). *The Collected Works of Milton H. Erickson, M.D.* Vol. 1: *The Nature of Therapeutic Hypnosis*, ed. E. L. Rossi, R. Erickson-Klein & K. L. Rossi. Phoenix, AZ: Milton H. Erickson Foundation Press, p. xii.

minutes that are not vital to replay here, but finally her hands settled together, with her "public self" hand totally covering her "private self" hand.

She was quiet for a little while, then looked up. Her eyes had softened their intense gaze. Her voice was slower and more contemplative. It was clear that she knew something now that she did not know 30 minutes ago. Over the next 15 minutes – yes, she stayed beyond her 60 minute deadline – she told me how she had created this "public self" as a protector against early family difficulties. Now she knew why she felt so frustrated and had resisted previous therapy. Everyone was trying to "fix" her public face, but that was her protector. To take away her protector would be disastrous for her private self.

After all those years of therapy, when she had only allowed people to see her *protector self*, today she had allowed her hands to become mirrors into her deeper self. In this Mirroring Hands experience she was able explore "rooms" that were usually locked or avoided. She was able to tend to her vulnerable "private" self and begin the process of letting her protective "guardian" self take a well-earned rest. The most amazing thing is that she did the bulk of this work without my interference, imposition, or direction. She found what she was searching for: how to begin her own healing. I expect she might say that was 60 minutes that truly changed her life. Equally, that was 60 minutes that truly set my sails.

What Is This Book About?

We will show how to create and facilitate therapeutic experiences like this, utilizing the Mirroring Hands technique. We will also show how to integrate our therapeutic approach across all therapies, and even into daily life. The woman found natural "inner" and "between" connections on numerous levels that literally changed her psycho-neuro-biology. The realizations and changes that happened to her indicate a variety of implicit activities, including brain plasticity and neural integrations, cognitive perceptions entering and altering conscious awareness, the necessary gene expression and protein synthesis to enable these processes, and the possibility of epigenetic changes to her DNA.[2] On the observable level, she clearly experienced new thoughts and a deeper self-understanding. It was evident that she had connected with her own capacities for problem-solving and was ready to begin her own healing. We will describe and show how Mirroring Hands is conducted, but equally, if not more importantly, we will explore the framework of knowledge and understanding that surrounds and supports the process. We have differentiated seven variations of Mirroring Hands. These are punctuated with chapters that reveal different aspects of the surrounding and supporting framework. The

2 Rossi, E. L., Iannotti, S., Cozzolino, M., Castiglione, S., Cicatelli, A., & Rossi, K. L. (2008). A pilot study of positive expectations and focused attention via a new protocol for optimizing therapeutic hypnosis and psychotherapy assessed with DNA microarrays: the creative psychosocial genomic healing experience. *Sleep and Hypnosis,* 10(2), 39–44; Simpkins, C. A. & Simpkins, A. M. (2010). *Neuro-Hypnosis: Using Self-Hypnosis to Activate the Brain for Change.* New York: W.W. Norton.

complete picture gradually emerges over the course of the book as we guide you around the activities of the technique and into the foundational frameworks of the Mirroring Hands approach.

When, Where, and Why?

It is important to clarify at the very beginning that we are not presenting Mirroring Hands as *the therapy* for everything and everyone. It is not a magic bullet, any more than is any other therapy. In fact, current research is concluding that no one therapy is necessarily more effective than any other.[3] As if to confuse and confound, practitioners know from their personal cases that a particular therapy *can* be much more successful with a particular client. Equally, with another client, a different therapy is more effective. The conundrum is resolved when we position the client as central to the therapeutic process, when the experience and efficacy of the therapist and the therapies they utilize are taken into account, and when there is a comfortable and collaborative relationship between the therapist and the client (the therapeutic alliance).[4] A pragmatic definition of *evidence based practice* has created a pressure toward determining preferable therapies or perhaps permissible therapies that *should* be applied to clients only by available, research based evidence. This appears to be a growing construct in agencies, insurance funded therapies and other funded institutions, as well as many educational institutions. Although we appreciate the responsibility to produce predictably successful outcomes, we feel that these limiting determinations are not the right path to follow.

You may be surprised that the American Psychological Association's Presidential Task Force produced and published a formal definition in 2006 that is not evidence centric: "Evidence-based practice in psychology (EBPP) is the integration of the best available research with clinical expertise in the context of patient characteristics, culture, and preferences."[5] It is quite clear that the *client* is the context, and the therapy, intervention, or technique utilized is only one part of an integration of reliable practice, practitioner expertise, and how the client responds. A client centered approach is hardly new. It was first introduced by Carl Rogers in the latter half of the 20th

---

3 Wampold, B., Flückiger, C., Del Re, A., Yulish, N., Frost, N., Pace, B. et al. (2016). In pursuit of truth: a critical examination of meta-analyses of cognitive behavior therapy. *Psychotherapy Research*, 27(1), 14–32; Connolly Gibbons, M. B., Mack, R., Lee, J., Gallop, R., Thompson, D., Burock, D. & Crits-Christoph, P. (2014). Comparative effectiveness of cognitive and dynamic therapies for major depressive disorder in a community mental health setting: study protocol for a randomized non-inferiority trial. *BMC Psychology*, 2(1), 47.

4 Ardito, R. B. & Rabellino, D. (2011). Therapeutic alliance and outcome of psychotherapy: historical excursus, measurements, and prospects for research. *Frontiers in Psychology*, 2, 270; Miller, S. D., Hubble, M. A., Chow, D. L. & Seidel, J. A. (2013). The outcome of psychotherapy: yesterday, today, and tomorrow. *Psychotherapy*, 50(1), 88–97.

5 American Psychological Association Presidential Task Force on Evidence-Based Practice (2006). Evidence-based practice in psychology. *American Psychology*, 61(4), 271–285 at 273.

century.[6] We suggest that it is possible to create an even deeper degree of engagement with the client in their pursuit of effective therapy by asking the therapist to take one more step back from the client once they are "centered," and allow the therapy to emerge in a *client-responsive* way. So, the answer to *when, where,* and *why* is much more about the client than it is about prescribed or usual treatment and predetermined therapeutic programs or plans. Again, it is important to qualify this by acknowledging that there are times when a therapist *needs* to do much of the work and perhaps impose a therapeutic program on a particular client. On close examination, however, even those situations can be seen as client-responsive because the client is showing they need help to get to a place where they can start to work for themselves.

Mirroring Hands is introduced at the best time, in the best place, and with the best intention – when, where, and why – in response to the client's indications of need. We suggest this is possible for all therapy because the best therapy *emerges* from the interaction between the client and the therapist.[7] It is, therefore, not our desire to predetermine the conditions in which you should utilize Mirroring Hands, but, having said that, we would like to give some guidance based on our experience.

When You Just Don't Know

Mirroring Hands is often utilized to break through the impasse of the client's "I don't know" or even "We don't know," when both client *and* therapist are unsure. You saw this dual "not knowing" in the case at the beginning of this introduction. Admittedly, this is why people come to therapy – because they don't know what to do or they don't know what their problem is really all about. Sometimes clients talk of a feeling that they know there is something to know, but that knowledge just can't be reached or there is something blocking access to it.

Regardless of the techniques or processes that emerge during a session, the first task is always to create and build the therapeutic alliance.[8] This often starts with talking things through. This is a very familiar beginning for most therapists. This conversation largely comes from *explicit awareness,* where both client and therapist can verbalize or, in some other way, consciously express what they are thinking or feeling. Establishing and building an interpersonal rapport is essential to earn the

---

6 Rogers, C. R. (1957a). A note on the "nature of man." *Journal of Counseling Psychology*, 4(3), 199–203; Rogers, C. R. (2007). The necessary and sufficient conditions of therapeutic personality change. *Psychotherapy: Theory, Research, Practice, Training*, 44(3), 240–248.

7 Stiles, W. B., Honos-Webb, L. and Surko, M. (1998). Responsiveness in psychotherapy. *Clinical Psychology: Science and Practice*, 5, 439–458; Hatcher, R. L. (2015). Interpersonal competencies: responsiveness, technique, and training in psychotherapy. *American Psychologist*, 70(8), 747–757.

8 Lambert, M. J. & Barley, D. E. (2001). Research summary on the therapeutic relationship and psychotherapy outcome. *Psychotherapy: Theory, Research, Practice, Training*, 38(4), 357–361.

trust of the client and for the client to feel safe. From trust and safety, it is possible to deal with the issue that has moved the client to come for therapy.

Beneath conscious control there is an inner, implicit world which does not have direct access to vocalization or consciously directed behavior. It is hidden, elusive, and abstract. Memories and feeling that are too difficult to bear are often "purposefully" hidden in the implicit, inner world. Behaviors and emotions can appear on the surface almost as if arising from somewhere unknown. These are usually called symptoms, but, equally, they are how the implicit makes itself known in the explicit. Symptoms create feelings of disconnection and disintegration, creating a disharmony that triggers a client to seek therapy. Mirroring Hands is a *natural* and *responsive* way to enable the client to repair those connections. We will show how this can be done safely and with natural comfort, even when the therapeutic experience is difficult and testing.

Exactly how therapy proceeds depends on what the client is able to do, is expecting to do, and is prepared to do. It can also depend on what the client knows about you and your practice. Clients who have come specifically for Mirroring Hands might want to start with that process almost straight away. That doesn't mean that we always do. We still work carefully with *all* the messages coming from the client. We discuss this sensitivity of the therapist to the client's many levels of communication in Chapter 7 (Natural, Comfortable, and Sensitive Observation).

Although we describe a number of variations, Mirroring Hands can be utilized in countless ways. The interplay between client and therapist creates whatever is needed in that moment. We discuss this in Chapter 12 (Improvising, Drama, and Mirroring Hands). Improvising is, fundamentally, the unplanned utilization of your knowledge base and skill set. The exact therapeutic experience that emerges is the hallmark of the artisan nature of psychotherapy.[9] Think of a pianist who shifts away from the predetermined melody and begins to improvise. The musical notes that emerge are qualities from the musician's skills, experience, and expertise, as well as the interplay with other musicians, the audience, and the marvels of the player's own imagination. A poorly educated, technically weak, or inexperienced player is simply not able to improvise as well. This is a capacity that develops over time. Because we want each therapist to add their own unique qualities to their Mirroring Hands experience, we strongly encourage and highlight the importance of learning all that interests you. *We really want you to be interested.* We also encourage you to seek feedback about your work through regular supervision, and regularly ask your client what is working well for them.[10] We will explore different ways that you can receive client feedback, and check on therapeutic effectiveness, as we work through the variations and some of our case examples. We hope this brings you, as a practitioner, confidence and comfort in your ability to flow within and around all your possibilities. Surely that is why the client has sought to bring you into their experience!

9 Schore, A. N. (2012). *The Science of the Art of Psychotherapy.* New York: W.W. Norton; Storr, A. & Holmes, J. (2012). *The Art of Psychotherapy,* 3rd rev. edn. London: Taylor & Francis.

10 Miller, S. D., Duncan, B. L., Brown, J., Sorrell, R. & Chalk, M. B. (2006). Using formal client feedback to improve retention and outcome: making ongoing, real-time assessment feasible. *Journal of Brief Therapy,* 5(1), 5–22.

Where Do We Begin?

It is not unusual to begin a book with a historical reflection and evaluation. In that tradition, our first chapter explores the history of mirroring hands and how the approach emerged from psychotherapy, therapeutic hypnosis, and Ernest Rossi's years with Milton H. Erickson. It *is* unusual, however, to have access to a central player in that history. Chapter 1 (The History of Mirroring Hands) reproduces an interview, a conversation really, between Ernest Rossi and Richard Hill. You will find that the conversation introduces information that has never been revealed before, and also challenges some of the established ways in which psychotherapy is approached, and our personal approach to health and well-being.

That conversation sets up the first challenge which is addressed in Chapter 2 (Thinking *IN* the Systems of Life). We begin our exploration with a fresh look at how we think. We have an educational tradition of logic based around the principle of cause and effect, but the reality of the world in which we live is somewhat different. This chapter explores the wonders and seemingly mysterious processes that occur in systems, complexity, and chaos. Complexity theory is, simply, a way of explaining what happens when many things make connections, interact, integrate, and produce outcomes. At any given moment, most of us can see that we are involved and engaged with all kinds of influences and it is hard to know exactly what is going to happen. It would be great if things were as simple as one cause and one predictable outcome, but our life experience tells us it is more unpredictable than that.

The very latest brain research occurring as part of the Brain Initiative, launched by President Obama in 2013 in the United States, is shifting research focus from individual brain components and processing mechanisms to looking at the brain as a complex system that shifts and changes as a function of energy and information flow.[11] As you work through the book, you will see we also seek to create a shift away from the way we have been taught to think. Rather than being the therapist who sits with but outside the client, introducing interventions that will produce a resolution, we will show you how it is possible to be a therapist who enters into a *therapeutic system with the client*. We will show how being *in* the system (instead of acting *on* the system) produces a very different engagement with the client. The therapist naturally becomes client-responsive, and the client is able to shift from *following* the therapist to being in the center of the therapeutic process. The client becomes the source of their own therapeutic change.[12]

---

11 See: https://www.braininitiative.nih.gov/.

12 Rossi, E. L. (2004b). *A Discourse with Our Genes: The Psychosocial and Cultural Genomics of Therapeutic Hypnosis and Psychotherapy*. San Lorenzo Maggiore: Editris S.A.S.; Scheel, M. J., Davis, C. K. & Henderson, J. D. (2013). Therapist use of client strengths: a qualitative study of positive processes. *Counseling Psychologist*, 41(3), 392–427.

A Framework for All Therapies?

Although we are committed to concepts and principles that are well founded in science, each of the theoretical chapters is not delivered as dry academic theory. These chapters describe and explore what is natural to the practice of all psychotherapy. We hope you will find that you can apply the framework and foundations we set out here for Mirroring Hands to everything you practice, both professionally and in your daily life. These chapters establish how systems function, how they self-organize, and how we can – as practitioners, clients, or private individuals – be comfortable and creative participants in the experience. We are trying to shift thinking away from being the conscious controller or the dominating influence, to embracing a state of participation in the natural qualities of our being that do not need control or domination. Instead, we can participate in a creative integration of our whole system. Our argument is that this very control and domination of the experience can make therapy *less effective* and *harder* for both practitioner and client.[13] Again, it is important to qualify that we are well aware that sometimes it may be necessary to be pragmatic, controlling, and even dominant, but this is rarely being done as a therapy. This is, most often, to stabilize the client or their situation *before therapy can begin*.

This book is largely addressing situations that are receptive to therapy. Having said that, you will be able to apply the knowledge about our natural rhythms and cycles to the most difficult of cases. You may discover wider applications when we explore the deeper elements of curiosity, what turns it on and what might be turning it off, in Chapter 9 (Curiosity and the Elephant in the Room). Chapter 5 (The Rhythms and Cycles of Life in Therapy) will explain what we mean by natural rhythms and cycles. We believe this puts the practice of psychotherapy in the context of what is natural about us, about the way the world functions around us, and the ways in which we function in the world.

Is There More?

The final two chapters might be considered more like an addendum or appendix, but we feel that we have not finished our guided tour yet. Anyone who has participated in Mirroring Hands has had the felt experience of an energetic difference and shift occurring in the hands. Is this just a cognitive invention or is something really happening? In Chapter 14 (Research and Experiments) we review the research of Leonard Ravitz and our current updates. This fascinating work produces a graphical electrodynamic recording, in real time, of the millivolt changes in the left and right hands.

13 Rosenfeld, B. D. (1992). Court ordered treatment of spouse abuse. *Clinical Psychology Review*, 12(2), 205–226; Hopps, J. G., Pinderhughes, E. & Shankar, R. (1995). *The Power to Care: Clinical Practice Effectiveness with Overwhelmed Clients*. New York: Free Press.

The recordings show not only the energetic changes, but also that there is a difference between the left and right sides. Having established that these are energetic processes which occur at the micro-particle level, we have opened the door to quantum field theory. We feel incumbent to provide a sketch, at least, of this fascinating topic to give you some foundation and open your curiosity to seek out more detailed information elsewhere. In Chapter 15 (Down the Rabbit Hole), we explore the quantum world and also speculate on what the future might hold. Finally, we have kept the hard science for two special papers, added as appendices, in which you can dive as deeply as you wish.

The Creative, Growing Edge

We conclude this introduction as we began, with a personal perspective from Richard Hill:

> Despite my great good fortune and privilege of being mentored by Ernest Rossi, it has always been about where the experience takes me – how I change, where I grow. This book is an expression of what has emerged over the past decade of exploring new ideas and techniques with Ernest Rossi. Something certainly began on that auspicious day in December 2005, but the burden of responsibility for my development, however, has always been mine. It was my task to create effective and productive growth at the most exciting region of my being – my growing edge.[14]

The growing edge is the edge of your known space, your known capacities, your known comfortableness. From the growing edge you step into a creative space where everything is new and unknown. When you step out it is not a rupture or disconnection from who and what you are. It is just as it sounds – a point of growth. Always keep in your mind that you remain connected to everything *you are*. This adventure is growth into a space where you become more – more than you are right now. I (RH) am still expanding at my growing edge and Ernest Rossi tells me that, even in his mid-eighties, he also continues to push outward at his growing edge.

The creative, growing edge can be a difficult place to be. By its nature, you are there on your own. Even though you may be supported on many fronts, cheered on and encouraged, it is an unknown space. Our unique expression of what we learn, and the way we integrate that learning into daily life, is our expansion at our growing edge. Every therapeutic technique, process, and protocol is the expression of someone's movement outward at *their* creative growing edge. In this context, there is no therapy, technique, or process that is ever entirely a perfect fit for you, because they have all been created at someone else's growing edge. Some may well be a close fit, but this is why *Ericksonian psychotherapy* is so hard to reproduce exactly, because the only perfect Ericksonian practitioner was

14 Rossi, E. L. (1992). The wave nature of consciousness. In J. K. Zeig (Ed.), *The Evolution of Psychotherapy: The Second Conference*, 216–238. New York: Routledge.

Erickson himself. We each must find our own best form and expression in order to be natural, comfortable, and unburdened as we practice.

We genuinely wonder where you will take this. What you might do with our words and ideas. How this book might enable, encourage, or inspire you to explore *your* growing edge. What will you create? It may be something very small. It may be a radical diversion. Chapter 9 (Curiosity and the Elephant in the Room) developed out of Richard Hill's years with Ernest Rossi, but also out of his own life. What does this say to *you?* What do you have in your mind that may spill out beyond your growing edge? The intention of this book is to show you how we have done it, so that you can explore how you will do it.

> *One doesn't discover new lands without consenting to lose sight, for a very long time, of the shore.*
>
> **André Gide, *Les faux-monnayeurs* [The Counterfeiters] (1925)**

To get to where we are now, however, there has already been a journey. It is natural to wonder about the history, about how things changed, and how they grew. It is natural, therefore, to begin this book with a historic review, and we are able to tap into the source, Ernest Rossi himself. Let's ask him how it all began.

Chapter 1

The History of Mirroring Hands

Ernest Rossi in Conversation with Richard Hill

Figure 1.1. Richard Hill and Ernest Rossi in conversation, June 2016

In June 2016, I met with Ernest Rossi and his wife, Kathryn Rossi, at their home in California. The main reason for the visit was to explore the writing of this book. We met every day over seven days, recording over 25 hours of interviews and conversations. In the second session on day 1 of my week with the Rossis, I asked Ernest Rossi, "What is the history of the Mirroring Hands approach? How did it emerge from your 'apprenticeship' with Milton Erickson?" I have reproduced the bulk of the answer. The transcript has been edited for clarity and some additional commentary has been added. *Italicized* words indicate emphasis.

In this transcript, and throughout the book, Richard Hill is represented by RH and Ernest Rossi by ER.

From the Rossi/Hill Conversations, 2016

Los Osos, California, June 1, 2016, 2pm

RH: Maybe this is the opportunity, what do you think, in among all the questions that I have, one was, really, to hear from you about the emergence of this Mirroring Hands approach.

ER: Oh ... what's the essence, profoundly the essence ...

RH: Yes!

ER: I remember once being introduced from the lectern, "And now Ernie Rossi will show his approach with the hands" (we laugh). Isn't that silly?

RH: And that was ... that?

ER: I think, "He doesn't get it." So, what doesn't he get? We have two sides ... you know all this stuff about the left and right hemisphere? It's all true from the quantum field theory perspective of consciousness and cognition, empathy, personality, brain plasticity, molecules, and gene expression. all the way down to the quantum level. It's built in here (ER indicates his head).

RH: Yes, I'm very familiar with much of that ...

(ER pauses as he contemplates where to begin.)

ER: I was with Milton Erickson many times when David Cheek was there, so it was a three-way conversation between us ... just like I was there many times when Ravitz was there ... and I learned in these informal shop-talk trialogues a lot that the public's perception of therapeutic hypnosis seemed to have no appreciation of ...

* * *

Erickson might reasonably be considered one of the major thinkers about modern psychotherapy and therapeutic hypnosis. He qualified as a psychiatrist in the 1920s and conducted extensive research in the field of therapeutic hypnosis. The Milton H. Erickson Foundation, led by Jeffrey Zeig, Ph.D., continues the legacy of Erickson through education, a huge archive, and the organization of an annual conference to celebrate his work and the ongoing evolution of psychotherapy.[1] Erickson's publications are best recorded in the 16 volumes of *The Collected Works of Milton H. Erickson, M.D.* (2008–2015) edited by Ernest Rossi, Kathryn Rossi, and Roxanna Erickson-Klein.[2] He was a master teacher. The people who spent time with him, learned from him, and developed their work in association with him are a "who's who" of modern psychotherapy.

1 See: http://www.erickson-foundation.org/.

2 Erickson, M. H. (2008–2015). *The Collected Works of Milton H. Erickson, M.D.*, ed. E. L. Rossi, R. Erickson-Klein & K. L. Rossi, 16 vols. Phoenix, AZ: Milton H. Erickson Foundation Press.

Ernest Rossi regularly visited Erickson, often monthly, and usually for about a week, beginning in 1972 until Erickson's passing in 1980. Many significant people would visit Erickson, so being in the Erickson household was a fertile ground for any developing student, researcher, or writer. Leonard Ravitz, a psychiatrist from Yale, was a student of Erickson from around 1945. Ravitz was involved in the pioneering work of the measurement of human electrodynamic fields and the variations between the left and right sides of the body. In the 1950s, he and Erickson applied this technique to subjects during hypnosis. Let it suffice to say that the apparatus had similarities to other electrodynamic measuring apparatus such as an electroencephalogram (EEG), which measures brain activity, or an electrocardiogram (EKG/ECG) machine, which measures the electrical activity of the heart. He and Erickson mentored Rossi in the use of the measuring apparatus and they conducted a number of experiments with patients, on themselves, and with family members during the mid-1970s, much of which is documented in Ravitz's book *Electrodynamic Man.*[3] During my visit with Rossi, we conducted several experiments, including the first ever measurement of two people in trance, using a modern version of the apparatus. Rossi and I became the "left" and "right" sides of a dyad connected by the holding of hands to create the circuit. The details of our solo experiments and other experiments conducted previously are detailed in Chapter 14.[4] The important aspect to note is that the measuring electrodes were adhered to the palms of each hand. The voltage was recorded as a line on a strip of paper that showed the variations over the time of the experiment. The right and left sides were recorded as different lines, so it was possible to see the variations happening in each side and the differences in activity between the two sides of the body.

Dr. David Cheek was also an important mentor for Rossi. He began his medical career as a specialist in gynecology and obstetrics. He became very interested in hypnosis and developed the process of "ideomotor signalling."[5] Cheek first learned this from hypnosis training seminars presented by Erickson in the 1950s. In essence, the positive, or "yes," attribution was given to one finger and the negative, or "no," to another. The subject is trained to raise one finger or the other as a response. During trance, it was found that one or the other of these fingers would rise or move in a non-conscious way – "almost by themselves" – indicating a connection with implicit, unconscious regions of the subject. These movements may agree with the conscious dialogue or may disagree to indicate discord or incongruence between the conscious and non-conscious worlds of the subject. The non-conscious, or non-self-directed, action is similar to hand levitation which is also an ideomotor response that occurs "by itself" and is a behavior during hypnosis that can indicate a state of trance. The important aspect to note is that the different finger responses reflect opposite and mirror aspects of the situation being investigated.

* * *

3 Ravitz, L. J. (2002). *Electrodynamic Man: Electromagnetic Field Measurements in Biology, Medicine, Hypnosis and Psychiatry.* Danbury, CT: Rutledge.

4 See also: Rossi, E. L. & Rossi, K. L. (2016a). How quantum field theory optimizes neuropsychotherapy. *The Neuropsychotherapist*, 4(4), 14–25; Rossi, E. L., & Rossi, K. L. (2016b). A quantum field theory of neuropsychotherapy: semantic mind–brain maps and the quantum qualia of consciousness. *International Journal of Neuropsychotherapy*, 4(1), 47–68. doi:10.12744/ijnpt.2016.0047-0068.

5 Cheek, D. B. (1994). *Hypnosis: The Application of Ideomotor Techniques*. Boston, MA: Allyn & Bacon.

ER: So, I'm reading the literature and sitting with these guys and I realize that in the literature, there is a term – the ideomotor – the idea gives rise to a push, an activity … that's what I connected with. I'm intrinsically a top-down person. It's the idea that evokes (ER indicates with his hands a movement down the body from his head).

This was one of the things I found brilliant about Cheek that the rest of the hypnosis world did not understand. Apparently, there were some high science guys who pride themselves on their "science" and "experiment" and "research" in the field of hypnosis who demolished Cheek.

What they found was unreliability in the movement of the fingers. Cheek says, "This is your 'yes' finger and this is your 'no' finger and this is your 'I don't know' finger." These guys did some experiments and found the subjects to be unreliable, "Cheek is not *scientific*!" (ER describes this with high pantomime.) They turned the whole world of hypnosis and psychotherapy against the idea of the "ideodynamic."

But … if you stop to think about it … ideo means "idea," but it also means "the individual." So, what kind of simple-minded mechanism would it be if every time I say, "Yay," your yay finger goes up, and every time I say "Nay," your nay finger goes up? In other words, *human complexity* is involved, not human unreliability.

These scientific types were looking for some objective science, just like in the 1890s – the beginning of experimental psychology in Würzburg, in Germany – and they said, "Ah, psychology is a science, an experimental science" and it's been futzing around with the subjective humanities ever since … Really, these so-called scientists were talking about the experience of the world only from their left hemisphere – the verbal, the mathematical – rather than the right hemisphere – the episodic and experiential. So, it was an effort to see the truth. I saw the truth in Erickson and I saw the truth in Cheek. But, I saw that the finger signals could be unreliable and it concerned me too.

So, I did a book with Cheek,[6] and I developed all those paradigms, all those techniques, all those boxes in the book, and they really are still good. I haven't used them that much because I moved on to other things, but I was looking for something else because there was one thing that did bother me – the finger signals – as some people just didn't show them.

Somehow, when you were in the atmosphere of Cheek, he carried such an authority that the subject's finger really did go up by itself. Other people, the scientific types, said it wasn't by itself, Cheek was "programming" you. So, I was looking for something that was less programmable, so to speak …

You're really asking what were the steps that led to my inventing the Mirroring Hands technique … It was the idea of the ideodynamic – the essence of that so-called "trance" thing – it was also the ideodynamic that was a split between my point of view and Cheek's. He called

6 Rossi, E. L. & Cheek, D. B. (1988). *Mind–Body Therapy: Methods of Ideodynamic Healing in Hypnosis*. New York: W.W. Norton.

it "ideomotor," but if there is ideomotor, there must be ideosensory, and I thought the word "ideodynamic" included both of them. When I wrote the book, I used the word ideodynamic, but he really never went for that.

RH: How did you get to using the hands?

ER: I think it really just came out of body language. (ER demonstrates the use of one hand and then the other while in discussion.)

So, I thought, "Why not use the whole hand?" Now, that's the connection with Erickson, who invented the hand levitation approach in therapeutic hypnosis. I'm not exactly sure of when, in my memory, but I believe that I put the ideas of Erickson and Cheek together to create the mind–hand mirroring approach to therapeutic hypnosis. Erickson did this (ER raises his arm off the chair like a hand levitation) but, actually, this was kind of hard for a lot of people, but maybe ...

(ER's eyes sparkle in a numinous a-ha moment of discovery) ... Oh, now I recall the connection ...

This was one of the earliest ideas about what hypnosis was – that it was a manifestation of *electromagnetism*. I think ... I don't know if it was me or somebody else ... sometimes I really do think, "Was that really me or did I read that somewhere?" Anyway, those old historical books on hypnosis show pictures of old guys with big eyes ... and so-called magical gestures ... I know I've seen in these historical documents the idea of magnetic movements, but I found, somehow, a connection between magnetic and hands and fascination in what I call the "novelty-numinosum-neurogenesis-effect," which is the scientific basis of therapeutic hypnosis.[7]

So, if you put your hands together like this (placing his hands in front and separated) you can feel – ideosensory – you actually feel it subjectively ... Now, as I closed my eyes when I demonstrated that I was really feeling it ... (acts out his thinking processes) ... Was I really feeling the pulling together? Yes! But could I also feel a "no" response, where the hands come apart? Right now with you, Richard, I am experiencing that pushing apart ...

Now, when I did this, I put together the ideomotor with ideosensory ... Now I'm speculating that this very fragile subjective experience is *a quantum quale of inner sensation and perception that can only be felt and realized by me, myself, and I*. It is the essence of the self, a secret sense of my aliveness that no one else can possibly experience! Shall we call it the "Quantum Sense of Being" or the "Uncertainty of Self"? I wonder ... is this the essence of the very fragile and numinous experiences of empathy, compassion, relationship, and healing during mind mirroring between people in love in real life, as well as in the psychotherapeutic relationship? I've never written about this, have I?

---

7 Rossi, E. L. (2004b). Gene expression and brain plasticity in stroke rehabilitation: a personal memoir of mind-body healing dreams. *American Journal of Clinical Hypnosis*, 46(3), 215–227.

RH: Not really ... no.

ER: So, here was Rossi "doubling down" so to speak. I'm trying to increase the person's hypnotizability – I don't like that word – I want to say, instead of hypnotizability, a quantum hypersensitivity to one's inner ideodynamic ... a quantum quale of inner sensation and perception. Part of my shift now, by the way, to the quantum field theory is that finally somebody got it. There was an article in the *American Journal of Clinical Hypnosis* and they said, "Ernie Rossi said that it was not so much suggestion ..." and they say correctly, "Erickson was not a genius of manipulation ... Rossi said it was more correct to say that Erickson was a genius of observation."[8]

RH: You say this in volume 6 of the *Collected Works* ...[9]

ER: Now that heartened me. Somebody's got it! Yes, that's what I really think. That's the new connection to the quantum level of human experience ...

RH: ... the observation ...

ER: ... and the deeper quantum level of sensitivity. Quantum and hypnosis are not strange and weird. They are another dimension of being hypersensitive to your inner world.

The problem of psychotherapy is: people have problems. Why? Because they don't know how to listen to themselves and their own impulses, their own truth, their own myth. Why don't people all follow their inner passion? Because the outside world overwhelms them.

RH: Following your bliss is what Joseph Campbell was saying ...[10]

ER: Yes! The typical teacher says, "Now you are going to make an 'a' like this, not like that ..." and the kid has to practice making an "a" – a small "a" and then a big "A". So, a lot of learning that is taught to kids is learning how "not to." There are a million ways, infinite ways, of "not to," but apparently only one way that is "correct."

RH: This is the winner/loser idea of mine that is based on the idea that there is a winning – a way that wins – and everything else loses ...[11]

ER: Yes ...

RH: ... and losing is bad.

ER: ... and so, we see the "power" instinct ...

RH: Yeah ...

---

8 Hope, A. E. & Sugarman, L. I. (2015). Orienting hypnosis. *American Journal of Clinical Hypnosis*, 57(3), 212–229.

9 Erickson, M. H. (2010). *The Collected Works of Milton H. Erickson, M.D.* Vol. 6: *Classical Hypnotic Phenomena, Part 2*, ed. E. L. Rossi, R. Erickson-Klein & K. L. Rossi. Phoenix, AZ: Milton H. Erickson Foundation Press.

10 Campbell, J. & Moyers, B. (1991). *The Power of Myth*, ed. B. S. Flowers. New York: Anchor Publishing.

11 Hill, R. (2006). *How the "Real World" is Driving Us Crazy! Solving the Winner/Loser World Problem.* Sydney: Hill & Hill; Berne, E. (1996 [1970]). *Games People Play: The Basic Handbook of Transactional Analysis.* New York: Ballantine Books.

ER: … aggression, rather than sensitivity and positive empathy. That is what I am exploring – can humans educate themselves to the values of quantum level sensitivity and well-being, rather than stress, anxiety, addictions, and depression?

RH: Yes.

ER: I was about to say "subjective awareness," but subjective awareness can be your finest quantum quale level of sensitivity. So fine that many people don't get it because it is directly dependent on your particular brain structures and the classical as well as quantum contingencies environment. All of us have infinitely different possibilities in life …

Basically, people have problems because they are overwhelmed by the outside world saying "it's my way or the highway." By saying we have to do it in only one way it just deepens the pathology. So, a politician is truly great when you have someone like Lincoln, say, give voice to something that is emerging in the fragile shadows of human consciousness and cognition …

RH: The zeitgeist?

ER: Yes, we should not make slaves of each other, and so forth. So, I don't think I ever wrote it, but the basic human problem is that you've lost your voice. No one told you to be a poet when you were a child … it's the educational system … reliance on group testing and competition … the competition for who is going to be the dominant voice, rather than who has the most sensitive understanding … who is going to see the world in a new light, like Einstein.

You know that Einstein was a "duffer"? He wasn't that good at mathematics and he was an inspector third class in the patent office.

So, people have problems not because they have problems, but because nobody taught them how to respect their own genius. Everybody has a genius when they learn how to optimize their best self! How do we help each other to find our own opportunities in self-development? That's the real problem of nation building for politicians – not perpetual self-aggrandizement, which is a crime …

So, now it's quantum sensitivity, observation, empathy, and compassion for yourself and others that are the important things, not suggestion …

RH: And certainly not direction …

ER: You bet … And so, when I wrote *The Symptom Path to Enlightenment* in 1996, it suddenly came as a great insight to me that the symptoms, really, are your guide.[12] Symptoms show where you are bumping against consensual reality, and so you've got to learn to work on that … But, of course, the outside world isn't fair. It doesn't say, "Oh yes, that's right. You're

12 Rossi, E. L. (1996). *The Symptom Path to Enlightenment: The New Dynamics of Self-Organization in Hypnotherapy. An Advanced Manual for Beginners*, ed. K. L. Rossi. Los Osos, CA: Palisades Gateway Press.

really right after all, Richard ..." I know a politician currently fighting for dominance who would never say that to you.

So, this is how I made the connection between hypnosis and quantum self-sensitivity and the NNNE. The dominant outside world said, "It's not your self-sensitivity and self-creation that's important, it's my direction that's making everything good for you."

My struggle has always been: how do I get the person to be more sensitive to themselves, to explore their own best experience, to find their own unique truth, and then when they find their truth, their passion, so to speak, how do they develop more skills to share their truth with the world around them? This is stage 4 of the creative cycle[13] – you do your inner work, using the NNNE to create the best of yourself and give back something of value.

This became a very important transition from Cheek, who pointed out which finger would say "yes" and which "no." My first shift away from this was to move the focus to "Let's see which will be your 'yes' finger and which will be your 'no' finger." We would get the client to say "yes, yes, yes, yes ..." and see which finger moved. This is a sensitive process. When Cheek would work with me, though, my finger would *really go* ... But that didn't happen for everyone. Did you ever meet Dr. Cheek?

RH: No.

ER: He was a rather large presence – a wonderfully benign family doctor. You'd love just looking at him. He'd smile and you'd feel comfortably, confidently contained – wrapped in the wings of his well-being ...

Then I went through a phase where those fingers could be like magnets. I went through all those transitional things and finally I came up with the importance of inner awareness and self-care in daily life (ER demonstrates by making a large sweeping circle with his arms, with his hands very slowly swirling in the surrounding space) ... I found that in my personal experience, even though I am not particularly "suggestible," even I can feel something. When I'm working with someone, I'm habitually in deep empathy and rapport. I try to extend my sense of union with the person by asking, "Can you feel how one part of you is pushing away what you no longer need and another part of you is pulling together what you need to receive?" And the person would look and see their hands slowly going together, and I would ask, "Are they really going together or are you just doing that deliberately?" and they would say "No, I'm not doing it!"

And then, one day, after a person's fingers touched, I dared to ask, "OK, now what would happen if the magnets, the inner forces, reversed? Could you feel, sense, the hands pushing apart?" and sure enough the hands would draw apart. I would say, "Are you just trying to be a good subject for me or is that really happening all by itself?" So, *happening by itself*, what some hypnotherapists would call "a mild sense of dissociation," became a very important thing for

13 For more on the four-stage creative cycle see Chapter 5.

me in conceptualizing changing novel states of consciousness and cognition. I now speculate that such heightened states of inner ideosensory dynamics may be a currently evolving dimension of consciousness at the quantum level of the NNNE.

So, if the NNNE is happening by itself, well, of course, everything in nature is unconscious on a quantum level of uncertainty, probability, and potentiality for creative change. This is how we are making contact – a connection between newly evolving consciousness, cognition, dreams, and the probabilistic nature of the quantum unconscious. So, for many years, this is how it was – facilitating essential "yes" or "no" states of emotional transition through my Mirroring Hands technique, drawing brain/mind states together or pushing them apart via the NNNE. Then came the final switch: I discovered I could do this without using the hypnotic metaphor. I could say, "Place your hands together, about chest height and the palms facing each other – just like *mirroring* each other – and let's see what starts to happen – all by itself."

I think that the first time I said this it was a mistake, I forgot to use the term "magnetic." I just forgot to use the term. Maybe I was tired that day, but I said, "Let's see if those hands come together or maybe push apart." Of course, I meant like a magnet, but I forgot to say "magnet" and I found that it was really happening all by itself without the magnetic metaphor which was from historical, classical therapeutic hypnosis.

RH: So, no suggestion?

ER: Right. Then came the next step which was … I'm trying to remember how I made the jump … "Can you get a sense of which hand feels like it is expressing your problem?" And that was *very* easy for people, whether they believed they were experiencing hypnosis or not! Hand levitation had its problems – not everyone can do it. Fingers weren't reliable, but everyone could suddenly experience, "Oh yeah, this hand feels like the problem …"

Then later I would generalize it: "If you have your problem in one hand, what do you have in the opposite hand?" What's the opposite of a problem? Well, obviously, a solution! So, if this is the problem, what is happening in the other hand is the opposite – a cure or a-ha experience of psychological insight, or stage 3 of the creative cycle. Then the word "opposite" became very important in my mind, just as it was for Carl Jung.

So, I'm finding a path – an idiosyncratic path between the problem and its solution – a "symptom path to enlightenment" – and that's how that book got written.

RH: Oh, wow. Everything fits together.

ER: Yes, that's my daily and hourly work! I had found a way of doing what people were doing with hypnosis without calling it hypnosis, without calling it magnetic, without even calling it suggestion. What was I doing? Facilitating ideodynamic consciousness and cognition. Purely ideodynamic – ideosensory and ideomotor. Hey, let's go wild with this … we could call it ideo-pleasure and write a book about mindful positive psychology! Ideo-pain? So, with pain patients and perhaps post-traumatic stress disorder (PTSD), "Let's see which hand expresses the pain and what's the opposite? Keep the pain in that hand for a

> moment and then let yourself experience the opposite." Here I am reinforcing the ideosensory: "And let's see what the opposite of pain would be ..."
>
> So, instead of pain, it's going to be some sort of pleasure. So, what I'm doing is shifting the focus of sensory/perceptual consciousness and cognition from the pain spot in the brain to the pleasure spot. This can now be called the quantum experiential essence of neuroscience and neuropsychotherapy.

We talked for a while about the recent *Nature* paper which maps the position of words and how they are globally distributed, indicating that communication requires global interactivity – an interplay of the whole brain.[14]

> ER: This may be the origin of the ideosensory. I've got to look at that *Nature* paper more carefully to see if they use the term ideosensory. This gives me a new insight into the neuroscientific basis for therapeutic hypnosis. When I say a word – say, "puppy" – you're going to get an image, a feeling about "puppy": the image – verbal, the feeling – sensory, associations to gentleness, sweetness, and the puppy side to your personality ... and you can start being the puppy within you. There is an ideosensory dynamic within your brain. In fact, this is an issue for all schools of psychotherapy. Now we have all these modern multi-million dollar machines with scientists showing what is going on in the brain. Is this the new neuropsychotherapy? You could write a book on that!
>
> RH: I have just written as you suggested – "A New Approach to Psychotherapy." I suppose you had experiences with Erickson where you thought, "Gosh, am I in this room?" because for me to write that on a piece of paper, "Yeah, sure, Richard will do that ..." that's extraordinary! I will get past that limitation, but 12 years ago I was nothing in the world of psychotherapy ...
>
> ER: You're still searching for some kind of foundation?
>
> RH: This is the beginning of a surprising shift in what is happening to me ...

You will see when you read on that Rossi has perceived that I am realizing and releasing something that is important for me. Suddenly the conversation is no longer about Rossi's recollections, but something very real and present in *my* inner world. The shift seems effortless, perhaps better described as an *effortless effort*, but it is also a reflection of Rossi's *personal naturalness* as a facilitator for others – in this case, me.

> RH: Well, I'm in a room with Ernie Rossi who says, "You can write that book." Yeah, that's pretty good. It satisfies my confidence ...

14 Huth, A. G., de Heer, W. A., Griffiths, T. L., Theunissen, F. E. & Gallant, J. L. (2016). Natural speech reveals the semantic maps that tile the human cerebral cortex. *Nature*, 532, 453–458.

ER: Confidence. You're feeling confidence now?

RH: Well, you make me feel confident.

ER: Let's pause for a few moments and feel your confidence ...

We sit quietly for a couple of minutes.

ER: See how sensitive I was and how self-sensitive you are right now? You've finally come out with the word "confidence" and you are smiling and animated, so I shut off my own thoughts and say to myself, "Shut up, you damned fool ... just listen." Then I say to you, "OK, let's be quiet for a couple of moments to enjoy your confidence." You closed your eyes and you immediately said, "Yes, yes!" That was my sensitivity – our quantum level of rapport, our mind mirroring. We finally got a spot where Richard reached for something at his growing edge, his very own NNNE, without me asking, "Well, what's your growing edge, Richard? What's your passion?" You were manifesting your passion, and I saw this tiny manifestation and that's my therapeutic sensitivity as a "quantum field theory psychotherapist" (gentle laughter, because we both know neither of us really know what that means yet). I'm very sensitive to growing edges, your passions – where you need to go. I'm very sensitive to stage 2 of the creative process – your difficulty, where you get stuck, where you can't experience your confidence.

And at that crucial moment I have the wit to say, "Let's be quiet about this for a couple of minutes," and let you go with a natural inner search, an exploration about that. That got a hit! You said, "Yeah, yeah." You immediately felt something good inside; warm and self-confident as your own self-generated motivation for writing a book. This is an ideal example of how I work. If you want to use a hypnotic metaphor, you can call it a hypnotic induction, but you went down into yourself near your growing edge. Of course, I'm ruining it now by analyzing and talking about it, but I wanted to give you an example. See how simple that was? That was Ericksonian sensitivity, not manipulative genius. You felt very good when I reflected, mirrored back to you your hunger for your own confidence, which is what you needed to manifest your own best self. You made another shift. Confidence is not just like that politician (laughs). You are confident because it vibrates well. It feels well within you and you are on the right path – from symptom to security on your current path to enlightenment ... and it's happening in you, now!

This is the secret behind Erickson teaching therapists that their task is to *shift the burden of responsibility for effective psychotherapy back to the person.*[15] It's old-fashioned language and sounds simple, but this has been an example of how Erickson would shift your burden back to yourself and that inner task naturally evokes the four-stage creative cycle and the NNNE, so you automatically go into a so-called "private therapeutic trance." You need to go into trance to self-facilitate the sometimes difficult transition between stage 2 and stage 3 of the

15 Erickson, M. H. (1964). The burden of responsibility in effective psychotherapy. *American Journal of Clinical Hypnosis,* 6 (3), 269–271.

creative cycle, then you can take time to pause and enjoy. Because you are motivated to make this interview a part of your personal development …

We pause for half a minute in another spontaneous state of inner focus and rapport – a feeling of accomplishment in shifting to stage 4 of the creative cycle.

RH: When I teach, I use a piece of footage I found of you on YouTube where you tell the therapist to "Get out of the way …"

ER: Yes! Exactly where therapy begins.

RH: … and having you say it before I say it helps. Maybe it is old-fashioned language, but I like it. I think it is good language and some people say I have an old style of language in the way I speak … I don't know …

ER: The therapist's focus of attention is to be very interested in what the experience is rather than focus on the therapy. The best answer that is going to come from the therapist is for the therapist to work out how to get more sensitive to what's *really* going on in the ideodynamic within their client – what warms their heart and soul.

RH: So, everyone operates with this dynamic, and this is motor and sensory which can also be a bottom-up. We need to trigger … This is where I'm suggesting that *curiosity* energizes the motion in a particular and helpful way. Then an idea comes, or maybe it's a motor action that comes …

ER: … or it might be a pleasure of some sort …

RH: … a sensation …

ER: Yes, you've made a connection between curiosity and the essence of therapy, so write something about that now …

I write in my notepad: "Novelty – something catching your 'notice': Curiosity for Information; Numinosum – wondering and amazement at this novel stimulus – Curiosity for Play; and Neurogenesis – the facilitation of gene activity, protein synthesis and brain plasticity – Curiosity for Possibility."

Numinosum is a word that is a key element in Rossi's teaching and practice. The term was coined by the German theologian, Rudolph Otto, in his famous book, *The Idea of the Holy* from 1923, which is still in print.[16] It is a term often used by Carl Jung. It describes an "indescribable" feeling that arises, almost independent of will, a feeling that is more than oneself – fascination, mysterious, wondrous, amazing, tremendous.

16 Otto, R. (1950 [1923]). *The Idea of the Holy: An Inquiry into the Non-Rational Factor in the Idea of the Divine and its Relation to the Rational*, tr. J. W. Harvey. New York: Oxford University Press.

ER: Yes. This is what I now call the novelty-numinosum-neurogenesis-effect (NNNE). Something is novel to you – and this is basic neuroscience – something in the environment caught your interest. The numinosum is your sense of fascination and wonder about something very important to you. You're entranced by that novel stimulus and that is what turns on the spiritual sense of Otto's numinosum. I believe it's the essential neuroscience dynamic of gene expression, protein formation, and brain plasticity that potentially underpins the generation of new consciousness, cognition, and mind–body healing every 90–120 minutes, the basic rest–activity cycle, about 12 times a day.[17]

RH: The dynamic flow of activity that occurs on many levels in a complex response to what seems like such a simple behavior or emotion on the surface …

ER: Now we've gone from a sensory perceptual – ideodynamic – to emotions – to turning on genes that actually make new proteins and new cells, heightening appropriate neural and immune systems and healing factors. You get more engaged in the "opposite of the pain" which is pleasure – the opposite of the problem which is a therapeutic consciousness. I'm using the phrase "facilitating therapeutic consciousness and cognition." That's my name for my daily work. I'm a facilitator of optimizing consciousness and cognition …

RH: … through sensitivity …

ER: Yes, through sensitivity and your curiosity. Curiosity leads to the numinosum when you are really sensitive, not just behaving in the ordinary way. When you are entranced by the novel you are able to enter a new space in your mind-gene-brain and you are actually recreating yourself. That's the simple neuroscience statement of all this.

RH: Curiosity for possibility!

ER: Yes! – possibility thinking …

RH: … and I see a difference between the general understanding of curiosity. I'm keen to show there is the generally thought of *curiosity for information* and then there is also curiosity for unexpected information – *curiosity for play* – which become the starting points for possibility because curiosity for information and play only function during and until the information is found. Curiosity for possibility is open ended – as is numinosum – because it is on the growing edge, to which there is no limitation.

ER: Yes! Have you got that written there?

RH: Yes, I have this recorded …

ER: Good.

RH: To put it simply, curiosity turns on the "good stuff" by putting you in the best state of being to start with. I think there is a "curiosity system" based around all those nuclei in

17 Kleitman, N. (1982). Basic rest–activity cycle – 22 years later. *Journal of Sleep Research & Sleep Medicine*, 5(4), 311–317.

what looks like a small gathering at the top of the brainstem and base of the midbrain (see Chapter 9) that I'm calling the *nuntius nuclei*. It seems to me that this is just a nice little way of describing physically and neurobiologically what we've just said. We like it! – it turns on good stuff.

ER: Yes! That's right.

RH: And we can all be confident. I mean more than just emotional confidence; I am also meaning body confidence …

ER: Yes … and comfort – that's a *big* word!

RH: … and that allows you to *feel* the numinosum and the curiosity …

ER: … wonder, fascination, and tremendousness.

RH: Novelty is a trigger – novelty/surprise/interest – which the outside world, the winner/loser world as I call it, this dominating outside world, suppresses. If you are not sensitive to the novelty, the system may not begin …

ER: Yeah …

RH: So, sensitive is the big word for me today. A very important word …

(We pause for a moment, enjoying these revelations.)

RH: I've been sitting here looking across at the bookshelf to a book edited by a friend of mine, Michael Hoyt, *Creating the Moment* …

The actual title of the book is *Capturing the Moment*, edited by Michael Hoyt and Moshe Talmon.[18] I spoke to Michael about misspeaking the title. His reply was that I should mention the correct title, but to leave the "error" because it was relevant to the moment. Indeed, he felt we were *creating a moment* and we should leave the serendipity to speak for itself.

ER: Exactly, that's the most important thing. The "creative moment" is stage 3 – the a-ha, the positive – and that's what a lot of therapists don't know how to do – to grab the moment …

(We both enjoy a contemplative pause.)

RH: I'm wondering … there is so much here for me to consider … I'm wondering if there is any more that we could do today?

ER: You can carry some of this away with you and perhaps write this afternoon?

RH: Yes … that I will do. We've shared so many wonderful ideas … lots of interesting terms, concepts, and principles that need more explanation. We'll be using these throughout the book so we really need to begin by establishing the basics. I think we need to do a section

18 Hoyt, M. F. & Talmon, M. (Eds.) (2014). *Capturing the Moment: Single Session Therapy and Walk-In Services*. Carmarthen: Crown House Publishing.

on these fundamentals … I mean, these fundamentals aren't things that we "do," they're the things that lie *beneath* and *within* the things we do. What we do *emerges* from these fundamental principles, so I think we should start there, be clear, and have everyone understanding … that's a good plan. I'd better go and do some work!

Chapter 2

Thinking *IN* the Systems of Life

Preparing the Therapeutic Mind

ER: Did you find the story about van Leeuwenhoek in the books I left you?

RH: I did, Ernie! He developed the microscope and was the first to see red blood cells and bacteria … How amazing to look into the body for the first time.

ER: What do you make of that?

RH: They could see what we were made of.

ER: Ah, there's more to us than meets the eye?

RH: And we've gone much deeper since then … right down to the DNA.

ER: What do you make of that?

RH: Well, we've been changing the way we deal with all kinds of health treatments, medicines and psychotherapy too …

ER: Sure …

RH: So, we should know more about what we are made of.

ER: And how the whole system works …

RH: The system?

ER: OK, just a moment … (Ernie goes to the shelf and pulls out a book). Read this …

From the Rossi/Hill conversations, June 2016

A new client comes to the clinic, and once the introduction formalities are completed, the therapist and client settle down to what will be about an hour or so of talk. Regardless of what methods you use, the client eventually reveals something about why they have come to see you: the *something* that bothers them; the *something* that is not right; the *something* that is not good or feels bad. No one visits a therapist to tell them that all is well, that they feel great, that there is nothing in their life that needs to change. They come to figure out, and fix, whatever it is that is making them *not* feel OK.

How is it that we know we are *not OK*? There is, clearly, something about us that knows. Equally, there is something about us that *prefers* to be OK and will try to move us toward being OK: toward health, feeling positive, loved, connected, and part of something meaningful. We are *attracted* to these ways of being. When someone comes for therapy, they are responding to these natural needs, tendencies, inclinations, and preferences. Unfortunately, what they are doing in their current life isn't working, and is possibly making things worse. Frankly, who knows. At this point, not the client or the therapist.

Something needs to break the impasse. There are dozens, in fact hundreds, of therapeutic methods designed to *fix* the client's problem. But could we just put all those to the side for the moment and consider the natural capacities *within* the client? If we can turn them on and activate them, then maybe the system that seems keen to make us OK will kick into gear. Can the client access those inner capacities that they either don't know about or perhaps have lost faith in?

In this book we call those processes our *natural problem-solving* and *mind–body healing*. In order to access these inner self-healing capacities, we need to be in a *therapeutic consciousness*. By that we mean the *mindset* that knows you are not OK, but is willing and able to engage in the necessary processes to become OK. Not being OK is a different state of consciousness where it is hard to connect with problem-solving and healing. In this state of being we are *un-well* or in *dis-ease*. This is a *disrupting consciousness*. Therapy is intended to take us through processes that produce beneficial change toward a state of wellness and well-being. This occurs when we not only make the connections to our better self, but also when we are able to integrate those changes into our whole system from neurons to genes. This is an *integrating consciousness*. Mirroring Hands takes us from disruption into the therapeutic and from there to integration, resolution, and a state of well-being. Mirroring Hands seeks to open the connections to our inner capacities for problem-solving, and our mind–body healing, to find our best self.

All By Itself

Have you ever experienced a client who declares they are feeling better, or has solved something, or has had an amazing insight or recovery, and you are not exactly sure what caused the problem to be solved – what part of the therapy, what you said or did, that was the breakthrough for the client? This might seem strange in one sense but to be expected in another. That is what we would like to explore with you now. How is it normal for there to be an unexpected response that seems to have come from no direct cause and is a major breakthrough for the client? The answer is found in the physics of how complex systems function.

The rest of this chapter will explore the nature of systems and show what non-linear dynamics, self-organizing, adaptive complexity, and chaos theory are all about and why they are important. We will be succinct and put theory into context within therapeutic practice where we can. We will also take it slowly and carefully, because these theories and concepts challenge many of society's familiar approaches toward how to think about the way things work. This is particularly relevant when trying to understand the processes of psychotherapy. How do we know we are doing what is needed to effect change and growth? There are so many aspects to a person's life and to the problem that brought them to therapy. How do we know what to do to fix the problem and let the client go with a much brighter future? How do we find the cause and implement the most effective therapy? To answer these questions it is necessary to show why these are not the right questions to ask. They come from thinking *about* the system. We will show how any human system that you can think *about* is a system that you are *in*. In therapy, the therapist is unquestionably *IN* the system, and this notion radically changes the way we approach therapy and approach life. We begin this exploration with a journey.

Birds Know How

In the skies over Newquay, Cornwall in England, or Olevoortseweg, Nijkerk in the Netherlands, or Sacramento, California in the United States, you can witness tens of thousands of starlings taking to the air in a spectacle that defies logic. The birds form a fluid display that ebbs and flows across the sky.[1] There is, however, no conductor, no leader, no organizer; just a very special set of conditions and factors from which this extraordinary shape shifting display emerges. It is impossible to predict exactly the shape and flow in any given moment, other than that there *will be* a shape and flow.

The flock of birds is self-organizing. The ebb and flow of the birds is something that emerges from a set of parameters that is inextricably woven into their existence. This display happens almost "all by itself," which may seem an odd suggestion because humans generally think that for complex things to function successfully they need to be directed, organized, and led. In our modern world, it seems a little crazy to suggest that a business could organize itself, or that children could learn in an undirected education system, or that a community could function with no rules and no police to enforce right and wrong. It is a logical step to imagine that psychotherapy requires organized techniques with predictable outcomes. The technical term for such organized approaches is *linear causation*, which means that there is a cause and effect relationship, in a step-by-step process, which has predictable results.[2] More pertinently, this suggests that we – and by we, we mean humans – are

1 Watch a video of a murmuration of starlings at: https://www.youtube.com/watch?v=eakKfY5aHmY.

2 Hardesty, L. (2010). Explained: linear and nonlinear systems. *MIT News* (February 26). http://news.mit.edu/2010/explained-linear-0226.

able to exert a direct cause–effect control on the world around us. Linear causation has become the central focus of scientific inquiry and analytical process. Linear causality has been the dominant paradigm in education,[3] scientific research,[4] and industrialized corporate thinking[5] for the better part of the past century. This can be traced back to ancient Greece, but was firmly established by Isaac Newton in his *Principia* in 1687.[6]

Yet a flock of starlings, a school of fish, the flow of people passing by each other on a crowded crosswalk, DNA, planets, solar systems and galaxies, and the functioning of the human brain all emerge from a collective group of parts that self-organize, in concert with principles and intentions, to produce health and well-being, which creates something more than just the parts themselves, without any guidance, direction, or instruction from anyone. How is that possible? The answer is that self-organization and non-linear dynamics are the natural stuff of life. We have just shifted our attention to linear causation and lost sight of the whole picture. It is important to note that this is not to suggest that linear causality does not exist or is not important. Linear processes occur between elements *within* non-linear systems. They do not cancel each other out. They are complementary aspects of nature and natural experience. It's how we think about them that makes the difference. It is very difficult to think about non-linear systems from a linear perspective, but it is not at all difficult to see linear processes occurring within non-linear systems. Perhaps linear systems are dominant in our thinking because a lot of things we deal with day to day have a basis in Newtonian, linear physics. Learning how to appreciate the complex, non-linear world, you will be pleased to know, is not that complicated.

3 Koopmans, M. (2014). Change, self-organization and the search for causality in educational research and practice. *Complicity: An International Journal of Complexity and Education*, 11(1), 20–39.

4 Galea, S., Riddle, M. & Kaplan, G. A. (2010). Causal thinking and complex system approaches in epidemiology. *International Journal of Epidemiology*, 39(1), 97–106.

5 de Langhe, B., Puntoni, S. & Larrick, R. (2017). Linear thinking in a nonlinear world. *Harvard Business Review* (May–June). https://hbr.org/2017/05/linear-thinking-in-a-nonlinear-world.

6 Cohen, I., Whitman, A. & Budenz, J. (1999). *Isaac Newton: The Principia. Mathematical Principles of Natural Philosophy.* Berkeley, CA: University of California Press. http://www.jstor.org/stable/10.1525/j.ctt9qh28z.

Complex Systems

A *complex system*[7] is simply where there is a number of different but interconnected and interdependent elements[8] or parts. Open complex systems tend to become more complex over time. A human being is certainly an open complex system. It is possible to differentiate a complex system into autonomous parts. Our body is made from trillions of individual cells. These cells are also parts of subsystems like the heart, liver, or brain. These subsystems can interconnect or be interdependent with other parts and become larger subsystems like the digestive system or the limbic system. The message here is that there is a lot going on within the whole human body "system", and although it is possible to discern some parts separately, they are all integral to the outcome, or emergent property, of the system – a human being. The parts give rise to something that is more than just the parts and these parts give no clear indication of what the whole system will become.

Clients are often experiencing disruption and disconnection in the complex system of their psyche. There are lots of ways that a system can be disrupted and disorganized. Trauma, negative attachments, negative criticism, social rejection, and many more affective and biological insults can cause disruptions to a healthy psyche. Clients come to therapy seeking to understand why and how they have become disconnected and disrupted, to solve the problem and repair the damage, and to reintegrate into a whole and healthy psyche.

Complex system: Many parts are interconnected and interdependent and the whole that arises from the complexity is *more* than the individual parts of the system.

---

7 These books have excellent definitions of complexity in relation to psychotherapy: Rossi, E. L. (1996). *The Symptom Path to Enlightenment: The New Dynamics of Self-Organization in Hypnotherapy. An Advanced Manual for Beginners*, ed. K. L. Rossi. Los Osos, CA: Palisades Gateway Press; Marks-Tarlow, T. (2008). *Psyche's Veil: Psychotherapy, Fractals and Complexity*. Abingdon & New York: Routledge; Siegel, D. J. (2016). *Mind: A Journey to the Heart of Being Human*. New York: W.W. Norton.

8 Chan, S. (2001). Complex adaptive systems. www.web.mit.edu/esd.83/www/notebook/Complex%20Adaptive%20Systems.pdf.

Non-Linear Systems

A *non-linear system* is, of course, very different from the linear system we have discussed. A non-linear system is a system whose output is not directly proportional to its input due to the interconnections and interdependencies within the system. In a linear system, the energy that goes in is equal to the energy that comes out, and is therefore predictable. Newtonian physics tells us that if you hit a ball with a bat, then the force of the bat will determine how far the ball will travel, and this can be predicted by a mathematical formula. This is true if you isolate the ball and the bat from everything else around it. Systems that have no physical interaction with anything else are called closed systems.

In scientific research, a lot of effort is made to exclude all the variables and confounders to produce a reliable, repeatable result. In reality, the ball and bat are a non-linear, complex system that is interdependent and interactive with the air, the weather, the skill of the batsman, the part of the bat that hits the ball, the angle at which the ball is struck, and maybe even whether a bird flies by and is struck by the ball. In a natural (complex) system that ball could go anywhere. It is unpredictable. A big swing might get a small result and a small swing might get a large result, especially if a dog catches the ball and runs away with it. But you will know the result when it happens. This is what it is like when working with a client. The same task given to different people can produce a very different result. In fact, the same task given to the same person at a different time or in a different way can have a very different result.

Non-linear system: The output, outcome, or resulting experience is not directly proportional to the input because of the unknowable combined effect of the interconnections and interdependencies of all the other parts of the system.

Chaos

Chaos theory takes us a little bit further into the unusual and more counter-intuitive aspects of complex systems. Chaos in a complex system has two relevant fundamental properties. First, it is *sensitive to initial conditions* and, second, there is a struggle between *order and disorder*. Sensitivity to initial conditions is what is commonly known as the "butterfly effect." This was an analogy used by the originator of chaos theory, Edward Lorenz, as a subtitle for a lecture on predictability at MIT, in Cambridge, Massachusetts, in 1972.[9] The question was that if a butterfly flaps its wings in Brazil, does this set off a tornado in Texas? This is not to say that the butterfly was the *cause* of the tornado, but that the butterfly wings were the initial condition that set up a cascade of interactive events that made a big change in another part of the system. Whenever we add something new into the therapeutic experience, we are potentially altering the initial conditions from which surprising changes might occur. Drawing a client's attention to a different viewpoint or perspective is one example, but what is more effective is if the client changes their viewpoint or perspective. Effective therapeutic change always lies within the client, so small changes can have large effects.

Chaos in a complex system is sensitive to the initial conditions. When the initial conditions change by even a small amount, large effects can be felt elsewhere in the system.

Order and Disorder

When the system is so overactive that it has no order, it is unable to exhibit useful form or behavior. Mania and rage might be considered a chaotic condition. At the other end, when there is too much order, activity is constrained and stuck in rigidity and the system is unable to exhibit functional forms or behaviors. Depression and obsessive compulsive disorder (OCD) might be seen as rigid conditions. Daniel Siegel suggests that almost all mental health conditions described in DSM-5 can be categorized as chaotic or rigid conditions.[10] There is, however, a natural inclination toward order, especially in open living systems, because chaos and rigidity can lead to an inability to function successfully and to ceasing to function. We are naturally inclined toward a manageable degree of order for survival. At the edge of chaos or rigidity there is an abstract boundary between order and disorder. This is a space where transition from a chaotic or rigid phase to a more ordered and successfully functioning phase can occur.

This is called a point of phase transition at the space between the edges of chaos or rigidity. This is a natural period for effective therapy because the client's system is under the most "pressure" to move toward a more ordered, or disordered, state. This means that there is enough volatility for change to occur. You can see this play out in the behavior of water. We know that water boils at 100°C (212°F)

9 Follow this link to see the original paper of the 1972 MIT meeting: http://eaps4.mit.edu/research/Lorenz/Butterfly_1972.pdf.

10 Siegel, D. J. (2007). *The Mindful Brain: Reflection and Attunement in the Cultivation of Well-Being*, 198–199. New York: W.W. Norton; American Psychiatric Association (2013). *Diagnostic and Statistical Manual of Mental Disorders, Fifth Edition* (DSM-5). Washington, DC: APA.

and freezes at 0°C (32°F). Although the temperature of water changes gradually between the states of being ice, fluid, or gas, the transitional change does not begin to occur until water is within just a few degrees of state change. Then the change is rapid and dramatic. This small temperature range is the region of phase transition.[11] For all the temperatures between the phase transitions, water is stable because it is able to adjust and adapt to the temperature changes to maintain its current state (i.e. water is a stable liquid between about 2°C and 98°C). Water is in a harmonious balance with being in a liquid state between those temperatures, even though the temperature has a range of change. If liquid water comes close to freezing, all you need is some stimulating heat to maintain the harmonious liquid state. Equally, near boiling, all that is needed is for the heat to be turned down for the water molecules to calm back into a harmonious liquid state. The harmonious state is not that liquid water stays the same temperature. The harmonious state is that the water remains a liquid. Now, that has been a lengthy analogy, but just replace the compound of "water" with the human condition of "health and well-being" and the human story is comparable. So, the experiential field between regions of phase shift or phase transition is the "field of harmony." The "temperature" may vary, but the state of being is relatively stable (see Figure 2.1).

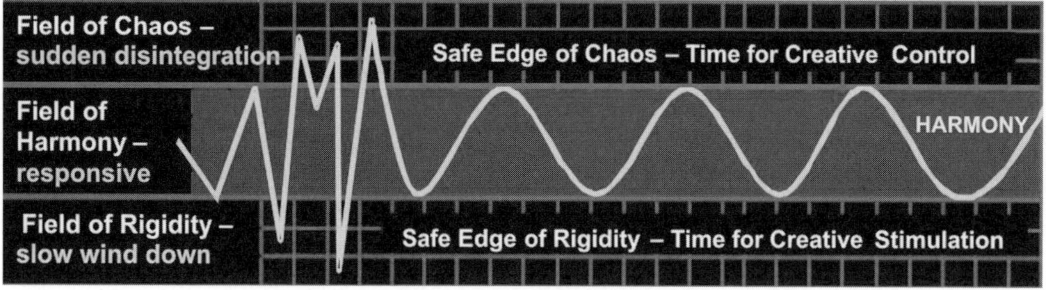

Figure 2.1. This figure represents our proposed "field of harmony" that exists between disintegrating chaos and dissipating rigidity. Harmony is not a straight line but a flow of activity that moves between the safe edges of chaos and rigidity. At times of chaos there needs to be some creative restraint, calming and turning expansive creativity into something practical. At times of rigidity there needs to be creative stimulation to energize and activate. When the white line is nearing the edge, the need for change is called a "phase shift." When very close to the edge it can be a "critical phase shift." An adaptive response will maintain the flow of harmony. A maladaptive response will create excessive chaos or rigidity. Excessive chaos or rigidity produces problems and difficulties that are often experienced as mental or emotional disorders.

11 Rosen, J. (2004). *Encyclopedia of Physics,* 243–245. New York: Facts on File; Olander, D. (2007). *General Thermodynamics*. Boca Raton, FL: CRC Press.

Clients often come for therapy when they are near, or in, the conditions of phase shift. They might experience a phase transition during therapy. Reaching a phase transition is expressed in the client's behaviors. This could be tears or some rise in energy such as stress or anxiety in the session. It is not unhealthy or unnatural to wander close to the edge of chaos or rigidity because it is through being sensitive to, and responding to, points of phase transition that enables living systems to react to the world, to be spontaneous, adaptive, and maintain life.

Order and **disorder** meet at an abstract boundary at the edge of chaos (or rigidity) where a phase transition from disorder to order, or vice versa, can occur. Periods of phase transition are where therapeutic change can most effectively be made; equally, so can disruptive shifts into disorder occur.

Attractors

An *attractor* is something that draws a complex adaptive system toward a particular outcome or state, especially when the system is unstable or under stress.[12] An attractor is not the same as an organizing principle, which is a fundamental aspect of self-organization. An attractor influences the state of a system by drawing the system toward specific types of patterns. They can be a restriction on the system but can also stimulate creative shifts. This gives us some insight into those repetitive but puzzling aspects of mind and behavior that don't seem to make sense. Why do we repeat the same mistake, choose the wrong job again, or think the same thoughts? Why do we repetitively experience compulsions, addictions, and habits we would rather not have? On the positive side, what drives some creative people to explore and make new discoveries? Attractors are points of energy and information that have become embedded in the system. They can be past experiences that are embedded in memory; thoughts and actions that have been encoded into neural structures like the amygdala and basal ganglia; social attitudes, family traditions, or religious doctrines and rituals. The Freudian *unconscious complex*, Jungian *archetypal patterns*, and *cognitive schemas* are, roughly speaking, forms of cognitive attractors in the complex system of the psyche.

12 Boeing, G. (2016). Visual analysis of nonlinear dynamical systems: chaos, fractals, self-similarity and the limits of prediction. *Systems*, 4(4), 37; Pascale, R. T., Millemann, M. & Gioja, L. (2001). *Surfing the Edge of Chaos: The Laws of Nature and the New Laws of Business*. New York: Three Rivers Press.

There are four main types of attractor:

1 The *fixed point or steady state attractor* draws a system toward a final resting place: a rock that rolls down a cliff to a final resting place has reached a fixed point attractor.

2 The *periodic or limit cycle attractor* is most common in biological and ecological systems as a continuous but isolated state: the swing of a pendulum or the orbit of a planet.

3 The *quasi-periodic cycle attractor* is found when two or more rhythms of different periods interact to produce oscillations that never repeat themselves exactly: a pendulum with two hinged swinging arms or natural systems like air turbulence.

4 The *chaotic or strange attractor* produces an adaptive, fractal pattern of response that can change the initial conditions. Systems can shift radically when initial conditions change. Examples include the weather, fluid turbulence, electric circuits, chemical systems, molecular dynamics at the cellular genetic level, social dynamics, and the personal dynamics of mind, personality, emotions, and behavior.

The therapist seeks to help the client find their courage and capacity to move out of the stagnant fixed points and outmoded limit cycles that are producing problems and symptoms. Getting out of a stuck or repetitive state will change the client's *initial conditions*, effectively creating a new starting point. This systemic change can be heard in colloquial expressions like, "I have turned over a new leaf," "I have turned a corner," or "I am ready to start over." The whole system is then at a creative period of phase shift where effective problem-solving and mind–body healing can occur.

Attractors are points of influence in a system that can alter the pattern of flow within the system and the predictability of the system's end state.

Natural Problem-Solving and Mind–Body Healing

So, how do we create the order that is needed to survive, be stable, be healthy, and be well? What can the client do when they are suffering from the fragmentation of chaos or the stuckness of rigidity in their lives? How can they escape the restrictive grasp of attractors that past experiences have locked into the system? Perhaps it is not so much what the therapist and the client *do*, but how well they work together to give the system the opportunity to resolve itself. This next section is not about magic. It is about natural problem-solving and mind–body healing which can be utilized in all therapies.

Emergence, self-organization, and feedback are the very important properties of complex systems which help to explain the effectiveness of Mirroring Hands. These are, essentially, what happens when the elements of a complex system interact, spontaneously resolve problems, and naturally move toward healing and well-being.

Emergence

Emergence is when properties and qualities arise from the interactions of the elements of the system. New properties and features are naturally created when separate elements come together. Emergence is a product of the synergies between those elements. In our previous description of the flock of starlings, the emergent property was the flowing cloud of birds. The cloud is not a quality of an individual bird, but is something that arises, or emerges, from the collective, synergetic activity of the birds. Emergent properties and qualities alter in relation to the scale of the complex system. As you might imagine, a hundred birds will create a different flowing cloud to a thousand birds. The important message is that what emerges is not the same as the parts themselves.[13]

Insight is a human example. The interaction of a variety of elements – which might include neuronal potentiation, brain associations, thoughts and ideas coming from others, and seemingly unrelated things in the environment – can suddenly and unexpectedly coalesce into a radical and transformational cognitive realization. In the television show *House*, a brilliant doctor was challenged with finding diagnoses for patients with completely mysterious complaints.[14] Dr. Gregory House would often struggle with logic and scour his brain for information. Just when he was about to give up, he would be inspired by something as mundane as an empty chip packet rolling across the floor or some unrelated comment made in conversation. Like magic, the answer emerged. Equally, as we work with a client, we might be introducing all kinds of educated, evidence based therapy, but when the client improves they tell us it was something they saw in the way the flowers were arranged in the vase behind us that triggered their recovery.

Emotions, sensations, affective states, thoughts, behaviors, and intuitions are all emergent properties and qualities. Affective states like depression, anxiety, panic, anger, love, happiness, joy, and so many more, are all emergent properties and qualities from the interactions, both positive and negative, within the complex human system. Why these emotional states have emerged is the therapeutic

13 Berrondo, M. & Sandoval, M. (2016). Defining emergence: learning from flock behavior. *Complexity*, 21(S1), 69–78.

14 *House* (2004–2012) was created by David Shore for the Fox network.

question we need to ask. What is going on in the system that is driving those emotions to arise? What is the message about the client's inner world that is being heralded by these emergent emotions, thoughts, or behaviors? This is how to think *IN* the system. Emergence, in some form, is inevitable, but exactly what the emergent property or quality *means* is the therapeutic question.

Emergence is when new properties, qualities, and features are actualized through natural self-organization where elements of a complex system interact and interconnect.

Self-organization

The most interesting emergent quality from complex systems is *self-organization*. The mathematics of complex systems tells us that closed complex systems become more complex and more disordered over time in a process called entropy. Living systems, however, are open systems that may become more complex over time, but move toward order in response to internal rules and regulating processes. Self-organization is the emergent process of a complex system that acts to find a balance between lack of order and too much order. The great astrophysicist, Murray Gell-Mann, described emergence and self-organization as "fundamental properties plus lots of accidents."[15] Complex systems have an internal set of rules and principles that affect the nature of order within the system. This explains why complexity and non-linear dynamics do not mean that systems are totally unpredictable. There are parameters that seem to move systems toward certain sets of probabilities. In living systems, survival is, obviously, a fundamental principle. A living system is naturally inclined to move toward states of order that prolong and promote life. You may be surprised to learn that for all those thousands of starlings to produce a flowing cloud, called a murmuration, there are only three fundamental rules of organization. Over time, these have become encoded into starling biology in various ways:

1 When a neighbor moves, so do you.

2 Fly away from danger, like a hawk or peregrine falcon.

3 Act together, almost instantaneously, with seven neighboring birds.

That's it. When you add some essential fundamentals, like the nature of flight, air in which to fly, chemistry, and biology, then you have a system that is ready to self-organize. Humans, of course, have many more "parts" and have a much more complex set of environmental factors, but the process

15 Gell-Mann, M. (2007). Beauty, truth and … physics [video]. *TED.com* (March). https://www.ted.com/talks/murray_gell_mann_on_beauty_and_truth_in_physics.

of self-organization is the same. We suggest that it is reasonable to assume that a fundamental organizing principle in humans is to naturally self-organize toward health and well-being. The most obvious evidence is our immune system. When we get sick our immune system is triggered into a host of activities, from cell to gene, with the intention and purpose of returning us to health. We know from gene expression research into the Mirroring Hands therapeutic experience[16] that there is an ongoing genetic cascade that includes anti-inflammatory proteins and stem cell activation, which are positive for physical and mental health.[17]

Self-organization is the spontaneous creation of order in a complex system. Order arises from an initially disordered system in relation to fundamental and organizing principles. The process is spontaneous and occurs without needing control by any external agent.

Feedback

Self-organization results in emergent properties and qualities arising as additions to the system. These new properties are then included in the next phase of self-organization through a feedback loop. In this way, the new state of the system, created by emergence (whether it is order or disorder), feeds back into the system to interact with the existing elements. In effect, the principles of emergence and self-organization mean that a system changes itself. The feedback loop enables systems to change over time in relation to the nature of what is emerging from within the system, as well as those things being added from outside of the system. This means that negative emergent properties can cause the system to become more negative. This is why people can remain in disrupted, damaged, and disintegrated mental and emotional states for many years, repeating the same errors and placing themselves in the same destructive situations. It is difficult to recover from within a disrupting consciousness while in a damaging environment. Equally, adding positive things to the system – be that a safe therapeutic environment, a caring therapeutic rapport, or a helpful therapeutic

16 Cozzolino, M., Cicatelli, A., Fortino, V., Guarino, F., Tagliaferri, R., Castiglione et al. (2015). The mind–body healing experience (MHE) is associated with gene expression in human leukocytes. *International Journal of Physical and Social Sciences*, 5(5), 1–31. http://www.ijmra.us/2015ijpss_may.php.

17 Rossi, E. L., Iannotti, S., Cozzolino, M., Castiglione, S., Cicatelli, A., & Rossi, K. L. (2008). A pilot study of positive expectations and focused attention via a new protocol for optimizing therapeutic hypnosis and psychotherapy assessed with DNA microarrays: the creative psychosocial genomic healing experience. *Sleep and Hypnosis*, 10(2), 39–44; Atkinson, D., Iannotti, S., Cozzolino, M., Castiglione, S., Cicatelli, A., Vyas, B. et al. (2010). A new bioinformatics paradigm for the theory, research, and practice of therapeutic hypnosis. *American Journal of Clinical Hypnosis*, 53(1), 27–46.

approach – not only feeds back to create positive change, but also the positive changes that emerge feed back to generate more positive change.

The therapeutic process can be quite a roller coaster ride for a client. Negative and positive influences will competitively feed back, and flow through, a client's complex therapeutic experience. As we will discuss later, therapy can be a "dark night of the soul," but that "night" can be worth the effort if there is a bright light of positive possibility swirling through and feeding back into the whole system. The flowing pattern created by the starlings, which we consider to be so beautiful, is not just for their own aerobatic pleasure, but because the flock is constantly reorganizing itself in reaction to the negative disruption of swooping attacks by hawks and peregrine falcons. The beautiful pattern is the visual expression of self-organization resolving problems, difficulties, and disruptions in order to maintain the health and well-being of the flock. That is the true beauty of our natural, inner processes of problem-solving and mind–body healing.

Feedback is a circular process in which a system's emergent output, in addition to external introductions, is returned or "fed back" into the system as "new" input.

The Mind Is Not Just the Brain

A client's mental activity can be imagined as similar to the many birds that populate the flock of starlings. The mind, however, is something different. The mind is more like the shape-shifting aerial pattern that is the self-organized, emergent property of the flock. The murmuration of starlings is not simply an emergent property of the activity of the birds. There are many more elements involved. The whole system includes the hawks and falcons, the wind direction, and the fixed objects such as trees, buildings, and the terrain. Alter any of those components and the magical ebb and flow of the starlings is different. Many describe the mind as simply an emergent quality of the brain, but it is more logical to think of the mind as an emergent property of not only our neurobiology, but also our biology, the surrounding environment, and the influence of other people, including their minds.

As with the movements of the flock of starlings, the mind is an emergent property that feeds back to the system from which it emerged. It may test our rational thinking, but in a complex self-organizing system, the mind is actively creating itself every moment. This challenging concept is thoroughly explored by Daniel Siegel in his book, *Mind*, so we won't expand further here, but this gives us some insight into how mind–body healing works. This wider concept of mind means that the therapist becomes an element in the mind of the client simply by being present. The therapist does not need to overtly impose, direct, intervene, or try to control the client's brain. The therapist can effectively facilitate an engagement with the client's mind–body processes simply by adding gentle, client-responsive, positive input into the therapeutic experience. The Mirroring Hands practice prevents the therapist from dominating the client's experience or adding anything that removes the client from the locus of control.

What a therapist adds to the "client's system" is very important. We suggest that the more the therapist imposes and directs, the more the client can be disrupted from connecting with their own problem-solving and mind–body healing – their own natural self-organizing processes. Finding the right balance can be very difficult and the therapist needs to progress carefully and with sensitive observation of the client. We will discuss sensitive observation more in Chapter 7, but for now it will suffice to say that there is a time to hold and be still with the client, there is a time to help them into a therapeutic consciousness, and there is a time to be present with the client lightly, only facilitating *their* process and acting in concert with *their* problem-solving and mind–body healing activity.

Review

The concept of complex, non-linear systems that self-organize, producing problem-solving and mind–body healing without overt direction or control, may challenge how we think about therapy and the world. We hope it also stimulates a sense of wonder about the world. From the very early years of education, we are taught to think in a logical way that builds our understanding of the world in a set of linear, step by step progressions – this leads to that, which leads to the next thing, and so on. We are told that having the right knowledge is what we need to reliably predict future outcomes and to provide a sense of security about the future. Unfortunately, complex systems are not conducive to predictability and control, but complex systems *will* move toward an order that is regulated by organizing principles, attractors, disruptors, and other systemic influencers. Affecting those regulators is what enables the client to move through the phase shifts to return themselves to a harmonious state of well-being.

As soon as a client enters the room, the therapist and client become part of a complex therapeutic system. What the therapist says and does will have an impact. Our presence changes the initial conditions of the client's system, and that alone can trigger surprising outcomes. What the therapist and client add into the system, as a relationship, will feed back into their self-organizing processes to facilitate the activation of the client's own inner healing capacity.

In this chapter, we have explored the terms and definitions, and put these into the therapeutic context where we could. This chapter is by no means exhaustive. We expect it to stimulate further inquiry, but now we have prepared your mind for thinking *IN* the system, we move on to the next step – preparing the client for a Mirroring Hands experience.

Chapter 3

Unlocking Natural Connections

How We Begin

RH: There's so much to observe and share and sense …

ER: Where is the client at today? They sit, "How is it today?" What were their dreams, their early morning thoughts? Sometimes you sit there and wait and see, but always looking to see … Where is the client? … Do they really want to talk to me? Something is growing in them …

RH: Sometimes they teach us too …

ER: Yes, that's always a great place to begin …

From the Rossi/Hill conversations, June 2016

Preparing the Client

The most effective healing is when someone is able to access and activate their own *natural* problem-solving capacities and mind–body healing. As we described in Chapter 2, this requires the client to be in a state of being that allows healing to occur – a *therapeutic consciousness*. The client usually enters the therapy room in a consciousness that is fractured and troubled by their personal difficulty and disturbance – a *disrupting consciousness*. At the other end of the scale, there is a state of well-being that emerges as problems are recognized, resolved, repaired, and reintegrated back into the system, enabling a phase shift to well-being – an *integrating consciousness*. That is the ideal goal.

Creating a Therapeutic Consciousness

The work of therapy is achieved in-between the disrupting (or *unhealed*) state, and the integrated (or *healed*) state. Therapeutic consciousness is where realization, resolution, repair, reintegration, and the process of *healing* is possible. The first task of the therapist is to facilitate a shift from a disrupted (disengaged) to a therapeutic (engaged) consciousness. This can be facilitated through a surprisingly simple set of actions. The three key elements are:

1 Focused attention.

2 Curiosity – for information, playfulness and meaning.

3 Nascent confidence (confidence in the potential of the process).

Focused attention is an important component in a number of mind and mind–body processes, including therapeutic hypnosis, meditation, and mindfulness.[1] By drawing the attention to something specific, preferably something calming, benign, or safe, it is possible to change the way energy and information flow in the brain, which is reflected in the neural and biochemical processes that inform and alter body state. Change in energy and information flow affects us on many levels, all the way to gene expression and to changes in quantum probability fields, but we will leave that fascinating discussion until Chapter 15. For those familiar with our work to date in relation to gene expression and quantum theory, you will already have some insight into what is being suggested. For practical purposes now, it is relevant to know that focused attention facilitates an altered quality of consciousness.

Curiosity will be explored in greater depth in Chapter 9, but the essence of curiosity is that the curious mind is, by nature, a "moving toward" state. The client is often in a "moving away" or a "stuck" state, which is a barrier and a resistance to opening up to a curious moving toward state. It is difficult, if not impossible, to be in a moving away or stuck state at the same time as being in a curious state, so moving into a curious state initiates a radical shift toward a therapeutic consciousness. Curiosity both triggers and requires the mental and physical biology to change. As curiosity is stimulated there is, among other responses, a reduction in fear and fearfulness, a shift of intention from a constrained to a more adventurous or exploratory mode, a broadening of positive emotions, and an increase in sensitive awareness.[2] These are qualities that are very helpful, if not fundamentally vital, for effective therapy – in both client *and* therapist.

---

1 Lifshitz, M. & Raz. A. (2012). Hypnosis and meditation: vehicles for attention and suggestion. *Journal of Mind–Body Regulation*, 2(1), 3–11.

2 Kang, M. J., Hsu, M., Krajbich, I. M., Loewenstein, G., McClure, S. M., Wang, J. T. & Camerer, C. F. (2008). The hunger for knowledge: neural correlates of curiosity. *Semantic Scholar*. https://www.semanticscholar.org/paper/The-Hunger-for-Knowledge-Neural-Correlates-of-Kang-Hsu/43b06df4bcef7435a12e22dc8bbfb9891e3e3bf7; Spielberger, C. D. & Reheiser, E. C. (2009). Assessment of emotions: anxiety, anger, depression, and curiosity. *Applied Psychology: Health and Well-Being*, 1(3), 271–302; Alcaro, A. & Panksepp, J. (2011). The SEEKING mind: primal neuro-affective substrates for appetitive incentive states and their pathological dynamics in addictions and depression. *Neuroscience and Biobehavioral Reviews*, 35(9), 1805–1820.

Nascent confidence is the feeling that what is happening is worth the effort of continuing – that there is potential and possibility worth pursuing. This harks back to Albert Bandura's "self-efficacy"[3] which has been adopted into positive psychology: when there is some evidence that you are able to do something, and it is working, then it amplifies the inclination to follow that line of action. Nascent confidence interacts with curiosity to support and amplify this inclination, enabling the client to feel progressively more willing and able to effectively participate in the therapeutic experience.

Unlocking Therapeutic Consciousness with the Three Keys

You may already be thinking about the ways in which you can activate these three key elements in your usual practice. We suggest this because we know that these key elements are present in many therapeutic techniques, sometimes intentionally included in the method, at other times as a serendipitous outcome. Although the order and timing of activation and/or implementation may well vary, the three keys are fundamental organizing principles within a therapeutic consciousness.

In Mirroring Hands, we activate and utilize these keys at the very beginning in order to move directly toward a therapeutic space. This is not, however, an irreversible drive into therapy. The client-responsive nature of the Mirroring Hands process can help the therapist and client to realize that the time might not yet be right, or the client is not yet ready, to move into a therapeutic space. The client may need more "first aid" to stabilize their situation. For the therapist, it can mean that this may not be the most appropriate therapy and/or not the most appropriate time to begin. This is one of the ways in which preparation for Mirroring Hands has a "fail-safe" mechanism inherent in the process. We will discuss this further in the next section.

We wondered whether to write an objective description of the process or a transcript of the words spoken to the client. We have chosen the spoken transcript, with some objective commentary. We feel this to be a more experiential model. Again, however, we want to stress that these are not formal scripts to be repeated word for word. We appreciate that while you are learning you may feel safer using our words, but you will soon discover that the words you naturally choose to speak will emerge as a response to the individual "therapeutic system" at the time.

Our final recommendation is that we find it best for the therapist to perform the actions *with* the client, like a mirror – not leading but co-creating. This models the movements for the client and helps if they are unsure how to interpret your verbal instructions. This also stimulates mirror neurons in

3 Bandura, A. (1977). Self-efficacy: toward a unifying theory of behavioral change. *Psychological Review,* 84(2), 191–215.

both client and therapist, which helps to create a deeper awareness of each other on both explicit and implicit levels.[4]

Induction to Therapeutic Consciousness

Step 1: Inducing Focused Attention

There are numerous practices that ask the client to focus their attention on the body. Meditation often begins with focus on the breath or the heartbeat. Some relaxation practices begin with the feet and move slowly up the body releasing muscle tension. Mirroring Hands asks the client to focus on the hands. The hands have the added safety of being both close and at a distance from the body, which the client can vary in accordance with their needs.

Some people have difficulty focusing on breathing because it draws their attention inward, where many feel their implicit painfulness, trauma, and distress reside.

We start by asking the client's permission to begin:

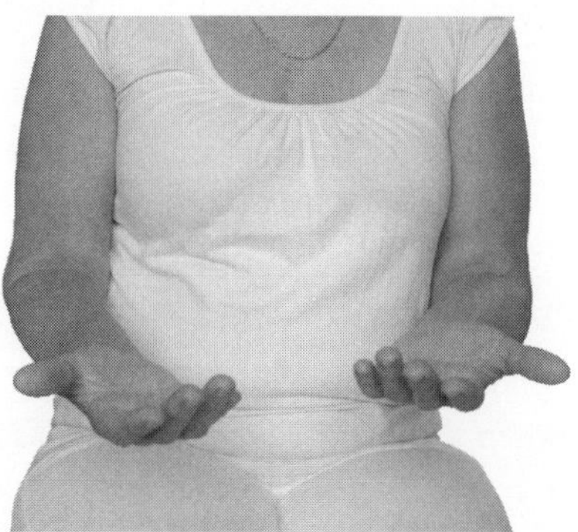

> *Is it OK if you sit upright, as comfortably as you can, so that you can raise your hands in front of you, about chest height, your elbows not resting anywhere, somewhere above your lap? Hold your hands maybe a foot (30 centimeters) or so apart. I wonder if you can look at your hands. I mean, really look at them, carefully, as if you have never looked at those hands quite so carefully and closely*

4 Iacoboni, M. (2008). *Mirroring People: The Science of Empathy and How We Connect with Others*. New York: Farrar, Straus and Giroux.

> *before. Notice the different sizes of your fingers and the shape of your palm … I want to tell you that every time I do this I notice more lines. I must be getting older …*

The non-directive tone is established in the opening words. Even the request to look at the hands is framed as a curiosity. This shows that you are not instructing; you are *interested* in what the client may or may not do. The client is at the center and in control. Performing the actions with the client helps them to both hear and see what to do. We have also found that sharing our own experience helps the client to feel that we are doing this together in a playful way. In addition, this gives them some suggestions of what they might look for if they are unsure. It is important to allow the client to work silently at times during the process. You are facilitating, but it is their experience. How long you remain silent is intuited by your sensitive observation of the client. This sensitivity builds over time and will be discussed more in Chapter 7.

You may feel that it is helpful to add supportive general comments:

> *How extraordinary hands can be. So easily taken for granted …*

Although we are not seeking to make suggestions or give directions, these sorts of phrases can be added to seed the situation with ideas and concepts that might expand the client's awareness. In this example, we use the words "extraordinary" and "taken for granted" which are words you might use with a client who has shown they have become blasé and habituated to their discomforts. The most appropriate words to use are those that emerge unrehearsed and unplanned in response to your sensitive observation of the client.

Being responsive and supportive:

> *That's wonderful … I see you are very focused … you have relaxed your shoulders … your breathing is easier … (Again, allow an appropriate time for the client to continue in silence, as you carefully observe.)*

The description of body changes obviously depends on what the client is actually doing. Your description is only a word or two to help show that you are paying attention. You are not trying to be clever and describe every subtlety; it is only necessary to show that you are there with them. There will be a natural moment to shift into the next step. The timing will differ for each client, but to give you some indication, this first step might take less than a couple of minutes.

Hands

Our hands are extraordinary things. There are no muscles in the fingers and only a bare minimum in the palms. The majority of the muscles that operate the hand's complex and intricate movements are in the forearm. The engineering of our arms – the hinges in our elbows and the ball and socket joints in our shoulders – enables us to move our hands in and around our immediate spatial environment. The ability to touch each finger with our thumb has enabled our species to achieve an almost miraculous acceleration in evolutionary development both physically and socially. Our ability to grasp, hold, and manipulate objects has given human beings the ability to become both creators and masters of tools, more so than any other species.

Although only a small part of our anatomy, the hands occupy large areas of "real estate" in the brain. The somatosensory cortex and motor cortex, which regulate activity and sensitivity, dedicate nearly 25% of their neurons to the hands. Avatar models of our sensory and motor homunculus, based on these neuron counts, produce a strange looking person with very large hands at the end of tiny arms, supported by tiny legs, with a very large head and protruding lips and tongue. We explore and test the world around us more with lips, tongue, and hands than anything else. Mirroring Hands taps into that neural disproportion and our subsequent heightened awareness of the hands.

Not only are the hands ideally suited to focus and capture our attention, they can also be moved through our spatial environment by the arms. We can twist and turn at the wrist, as well as move all the fingers. The hands are sensitive, noticeable, mobile, and flexible. This means our hands can have a dynamic relationship with our surrounding environment. Although connected to our body at the end of our arms, it is possible for the hands to feel distant from the rest of the body, and even disconnected in some circumstances. From the therapeutic perspective, this is very useful. We are able to utilize the hands to hold things away from the body, including abstract things like fears and problems. Externalizing fears and problems into the hands creates a sense of distance from the vulnerable spaces of the inner self, protecting the client from re-traumatizing through internalizing recall of trauma or other potentially disturbing memories during therapy. At the same time, the client is able to hold the therapeutic experience within their spatial sense of self, so they continue to be the locus of control.

Step 2: Introducing Curiosity

Curiosity is, by its nature, exploratory, playful, and open to the unexpected. Several words are very evocative for curiosity. Our favorite words are *wonder, wonderful,* and *interesting.* There are also words/phrases that support and encourage progress such as, "*Yes, can you keep going?*" and the ubiquitous "*OK.*" You are seeking to trigger the client's curiosity to find an inner connection. The method we utilize to do this invites the client to create a "sensation" in their hands. Below, we describe the three most effective sensations that have emerged over the years of Mirroring Hands practice. The client will settle into the sensation that suits them best. The therapist facilitates by offering reflections that are responding to the client, not leading. If you find that your reflections are not in sync with the client, simply shift the invitation to another option. Sensitive observation will pick up cues from the client. Remember, it is never a bad idea to simply ask the client. The three sensations are *energy sensation, contrasting sensation,* and *conceptual sensation.*

1. Energy Sensation

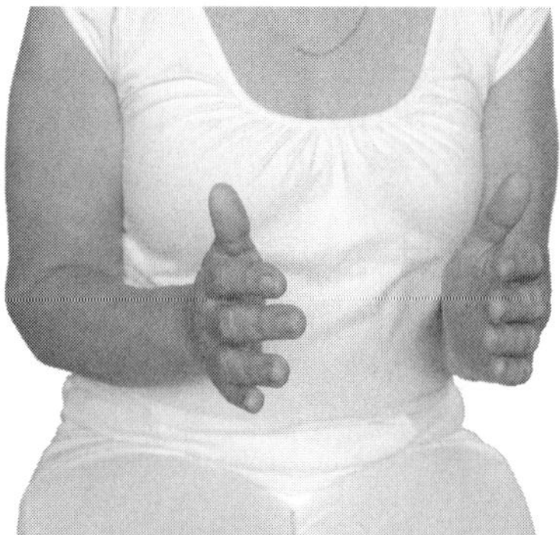

> *I wonder if it is comfortable for you to move your hands so that the palms are facing each other, about body width apart, still at around chest height? Will you feel an energy between the hands ... (Allow time for the client to engage, test, and play with the experience.)*
>
> *Wonderful! I wonder if those hands feel like they are being drawn together, or perhaps pushed apart, or maybe held in the same place ... almost all by themselves ...*

These requests are not suggestions or directives, just curious wondering about whether the client is able to feel anything energetic happening between their hands.

2. Contrasting Sensation

This variation invites the client to determine a contrast between the hands. There are probably countless examples but we most often use temperature or weight.

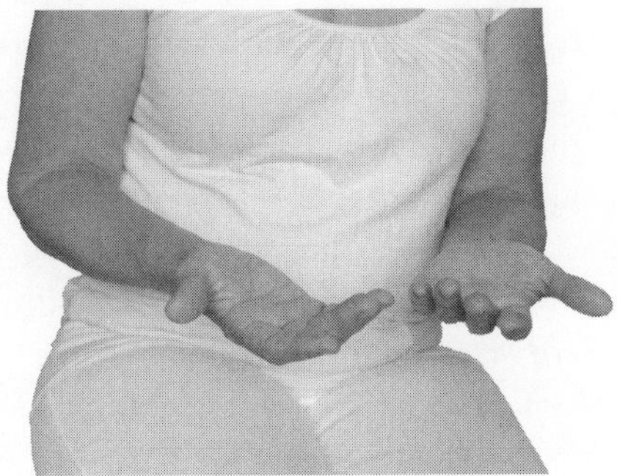

> *I wonder if you can tell me which hand feels cooler? (Another version is to ask which is heavier.) Just allow your conscious mind to become aware of this feeling, as if it is happening all by itself… (Allow time for the client to engage, test, and play with the experience.)*

If the client is having trouble with the sensation you have nominated, then simply change to the opposite form – *warmer* or *lighter*. If the client is not responding to your specific invitation, but they still seem to be comfortable with the process, then it is perfectly acceptable to ask the client if they feel some difference of their own. In many respects this is an excellent sign that the client is fully engaged as the operator of the experience and is also observing their experience at the same time.

3. Conceptual Sensation

This variation invites the client to feel a conceptual difference between the hands. Again, there may be countless examples but we most often use periods of time or a sense of inner strength.

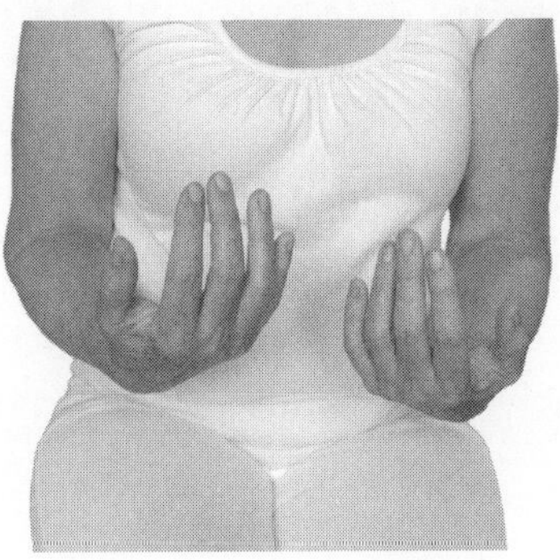

I wonder if one hand represents an earlier time in your life … perhaps your childhood or school years – your young self – and the other hand represents a different time – your later years, your adult self? (Another version is to ask which hand represents their strengths and which their weaknesses.) Just allow your conscious mind to become aware of this feeling, as if it is emerging in your hands all by itself … (Allow time for the client to engage, test, and play with the experience.)

Now we are ready to seek some evidence that something is happening in the client's hands that is unusual, unexpected, and outside of their direct conscious control.

Step 3: Validating Nascent Confidence

The words below can apply to all three variations above, with some changes to suit the specific scenario.

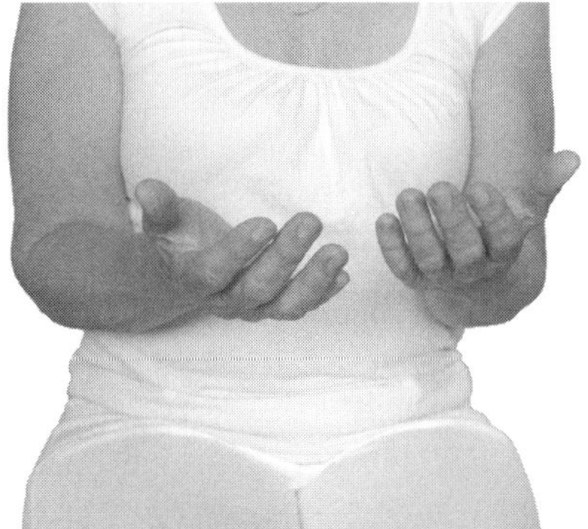

Yes … wonderful … Is it possible, with just a little movement of the hand, and a word or two if you wish, to share with me … (whichever of the three sensations the client has chosen to work with, e.g. (1) that you feel the energy between your hands, (2) which hand is feeling cooler/heavier, or (3) which hand is holding your younger self/your strengths. Wait patiently until one of the hands moves in some way.) Wonderful … yes … that's the hand that feels (whatever the sensation is) … How interesting …

The response is not always immediate or obvious. Depending on their level of focused attention, the client may move their hand consciously or may stare intently at their hands waiting for something to happen. It is a matter of the therapist having the patience and the confidence to wait and allow the movement of the client's hand to emerge in whatever way the client wishes. The client may not wish to speak much at this time. It is also not uncommon for there to be just a twitch or two in the fingers. You can assist the client by noticing, commenting, and asking if that is the hand they wish to indicate – but only the client knows. Always try to follow the client's lead. It is important for the therapist to keep out of the way and not interfere with the client as they build connections within themself.

Review

We have now explored the preparation stage of Mirroring Hands where the client has some evidence that they have made connections to their inner self and has reached a point where they are in, or can readily shift into, a therapeutic consciousness. The client can feel and see that they have created a reality based on something *within*. We can say this because the client observes that one or the other hand is experiencing a sensation, which has appeared independently of their conscious thinking – *all by itself* – and they have confirmed the sensation with a movement that identifies the appropriate hand. It is a reasonable conclusion that this sensation is being created by inner, non-conscious, implicit processes because there is no external explanation for the sensation. The client has been a witness to their own capacity to alter their perception of reality from somewhere within themselves. We suggest that: (1) the client has held an explicit thought, (2) a connection is made with the implicit world, (3) implicit processes have generated a sensation in the hand, (4) that is consciously observed, (5) which explicitly confirms that a mind–body connection has been established. This is a mind-to-body experience. The client is now consciously aware that they are connecting to their inner, non-conscious, implicit world *and* that they can continue safely to observe this unusual experience.

We now represent the preparation dialogue without the commentary. This should help you to appreciate the flow. We invite you to speak the words out loud, so that you fully appreciate the natural, easy progression of the process. The preparation process is often only about four or five minutes in duration, depending on the client's use of silent, private work, but it can be a little quicker or much longer. In this version, we will use the scenario of the cooler/warmer hand.

> *Is it OK if you sit upright, as comfortably as you can, so that you can raise your hands in front of you, about chest height, your elbows not resting anywhere, somewhere above your lap? Hold your hands maybe a foot (30 centimeters) or so apart … I wonder if you can look at your hands. I mean, really look at them, carefully, as if you have never looked at those hands quite so carefully and closely before. Notice the different sizes of your fingers and the shape of your palm … I have to tell you that every time I do this I notice more lines. I must be getting older …*
>
> *How extraordinary hands can be … So easily taken for granted …*

> *That's wonderful … I see you are very focused … you have relaxed your shoulders … your breathing is easier …*
>
> *I wonder if you can tell me which hand feels cooler? Just allow your conscious mind to become aware of this feeling, as if it is happening all by itself …*
>
> *Yes … wonderful … Is it possible, with just a little movement of the hand, and a word or two if you wish, to share with me which hand is feeling cooler … (one of the hands moves in some way) … Wonderful … yes … that's the hand that feels cooler … How interesting …*

Quite short when you see it as a single piece. Did you sense how the pauses might be different for each client? How long did you feel *you* needed, as the therapist, during those pauses? Did you feel that you might like to add more pauses? Being sensitive to the silent periods is important. That is where the client works privately, establishing and exploring their inner connections.

There are a number of different practical forms of Mirroring Hands and these will be explored in the chapters to come. With experience, the most suitable form often emerges spontaneously – almost all by itself. Learning to trust, notice, and respond to emerging properties and qualities comes with experience. This is not to say that you should abandon established forms of assessing the client's, and the therapy's, progress. Sometimes it is effective to openly ask the client how things are going, especially if they give indications that they are losing connection with the process. You can then make adjustments and alterations accordingly. As much as possible, however, the therapist needs to allow things to emerge; be sensitive, notice what emerges, and be mindful about responding in a way that benefits the client.

We will leave the client for now, albeit the client is in a prepared state to move forward to the next stage. It is equally important for the other person in the room to feel prepared. In the next chapter, we will show you, the therapist, how to speak in a non-directive, client-responsive manner. We will describe the "language principles" that best support the Mirroring Hands approach and maintain the integrity of the process. We have found that many therapists find it surprisingly difficult to move out of the way of the client's process. We will show you how it is possible to share your knowledge, wisdom, and reflections without imposing your opinion; to invite and encourage, rather than direct or advise; and how to be silent, observing, and responsive.

Chapter 4

Language Principles

Client-Responsive Language

ER: … being in sync, yes … as the client walks in from their car, they are beginning to synchronize. When they sit in the waiting room, even for a few minutes, I don't know where their conscious mind is, but I know where their unconscious mind is – getting in sync with me … So I need only be as humble and observing and as sensitive as I can be … to feel and then facilitate our synchrony … These are the natural fluctuations of the world that are fundamental to the quantum space … but just to notice and be genuinely interested … they know you are sincere.

From the Rossi/Hill conversations, June 2016

Preparing the Therapist

Over the years of using Mirroring Hands, it is not surprising that a unique language style emerged. At the same time, words in the therapeutic dialogue have shifted to more humanistic forms. Words like manipulate have been replaced with facilitate, control with evoke, and technique with approach.[1] Having shown how to prepare the client in Chapter 3, we would now like to prepare the therapist for working in a non-directive, client-responsive manner. The following language principles, or you might prefer to describe them as language styles, are particularly effective in allowing the client to express themselves without undue interference and interruption by the therapist. We will explore:

- Incomplete sentences
- Supportive responses
- Surprise and wonder
- The double bind
- Ideodynamic questions
- The basic accessing question

1 An audio recording of Paul Watzlawick talking about his systemic/communications perspective (Ernest Rossi is the discussant) at the Evolution of Psychotherapy Conference, organized by the Milton H. Erickson Foundation in 1985, is available at: https://ce21.blob.core.windows.net/global/huxrbwnpguyjjoqp3ofkgg.mp3.

The Mirroring Hands approach is for the therapist to facilitate the client's connection to their own natural problem-solving capacities and a deeper relationship with their inner self. The important message from our understanding of self-organization is that whatever is added to the system can have a strong effect. When a therapist introduces something new into the system – an idea, an opinion, a direction, a suggestion – it will become part of a feedback dynamic that potentially impacts all the other elements of the system. To facilitate healing and recovery, the therapist needs to introduce elements that produce positive feedback. This creates amplification of beneficial activity within the system, whereas negative feedback dampens or restricts the flow. Each of the language principles here seeks to limit the amount of interference and interruption, or negative feedback, the therapist adds to the system.

Selective language and non-direct approaches are certainly found in other methods. Carl Rogers employed the principles of minimal responses and engaged reflection to foster non-directive, client-centered practice.[2] It is clear in the work of Erickson that being responsive to the client is a fundamental therapeutic skill. We, as therapists, can sometimes lose sight of the balance of who is doing the work during therapy. Ultimately it is the client who will resolve their problems. Even in successful therapy, the therapist may never truly know the deeper implicit processes occurring within the client and, on a conscious level, neither may the client.

Incomplete Sentences

Utilizing incomplete sentences can be surprisingly challenging. Reflecting what you feel the client has been saying is common to a number of therapeutic methods. In the incomplete sentence, you halt *before* stating your main observation. It might be argued that the therapist's job is to be able to reflect back to the client. We agree. The therapist must be sensitive and aware of their client. This is how rapport is built and trust developed. We wish to be clear in our support for therapists to establish rapport and build trust, but we also urge therapists to be thoughtful about not doing anything that risks the client's autonomy or shifts them from their central role in the therapeutic journey.

The therapist is the *facilitator* of the client's process, not the controller. We are not suggesting that controls and impositions are never appropriate. There is no "never" in client-responsive therapy. We are saying that if the therapist's actions interfere with the client's process, then that can disrupt the connections the client is creating to activate problem-solving and mind–body healing. This is counterproductive to the client's goal of achieving resolution, recovery, and reintegration to an integrating consciousness.

2 Rogers, C. R. (1957b). The necessary and sufficient conditions of therapeutic personality change. *Journal of Consulting Psychology*, 21(2), 95–103.

The incomplete sentence is one of the most effective tools in client-responsive therapy. The client is moved – emotionally activated – to fill the verbal vacuum with a comment. Be aware that the client may not have anything come into conscious awareness, and so it is equally important to be patient and give the client time for their realization to emerge. A client may also "respond" with facial expressions or body movements instead of words. Whichever way the client manifests conscious awareness of their inner process, simply continue to observe, be aware, sensitively respond, and, as much as possible, stay out of the client's way.

Here are some examples of incomplete sentences:

I wonder if you are starting to feel the ...

Yes ... I wonder if you will have the courage to continue on, all by yourself, for a little while longer, until ...

Ah, I see you taking a deep breath as you continue your important inner work and as you ... Wonderful ...

Note that the incomplete sentence is not a question. There is no upward vocal inflection at the ellipsis (...). You are not questioning the client as if you don't know. You are just not sharing everything you are thinking. Instead, you are indicating that you are much more interested in what the *client* is thinking and feeling. When a therapist completes the sentence, they are speaking as an expert. The client is inclined to acquiesce to the therapist's opinion, even if it is not how they feel. Equally, the client might rebel against the therapist's opinion, even if it is a good one. The primary effect is that the client must pause their mental processes to consider what the therapist is saying. The client may hold only a fragile grasp of their inner connection. It is a little like daydreaming and being distracted by someone talking. The daydream is lost, but worse, any possible meaning or inspiration from the daydream is lost.

An Incomplete Sentence as a Creative Implication

An implication is different from a directive in that it only *indicates* something significant or worthy of notice. Because it is not a directive, the client is not being asked to do anything in particular. The client is free to create what they need from your words. The keywords of the creative implication emerge in response to something you see or feel in the client in that moment. It is similar to a reflective comment, but is delivered in such a way that the client is able to use your words to create something helpful for themself.

The following examples add a creative implication. The bold words are the keywords.

Sometimes it's OK just to **simply experience** *what you're feeling …*

It takes **courage** *to* **explore** *what is really happening …*

Maybe your **obsessing** *is how you can* **explore your growing edge** …

You can truly **wonder** *about the* **nature** *of your problem …*

As you can see, these are not instructions or directions, but a way of introducing alternative possibilities. The keywords are reflective of comments and issues that the client has brought up in the moment and/or during earlier conversations. You may find that your body position will intuitively shift in relation to the client. There is no predetermined rule for anything you might do. It is all in sensitive response to the client (this is discussed in greater depth in Chapter 7).

Supportive Responses

Supportive responses give the client encouragement to continue with their inner therapeutic work. We seek to show the client support without trying to modify or condition the experience. Empathetic responsiveness follows the client's lead. The therapist is seeking to assure the client that the therapeutic relationship is secure and they are continuing to provide a safe space. The client knows and feels this when the therapist is watching, listening, and responding to them.

Part of the effect is in the words, but the intention behind the words is also important. If the therapist says something that unfortunately disturbs the client, that is not a disaster but an opportunity to reassess what is being done and where the intentions are based. A good therapist is one who continually assesses and adjusts their actions.

Here is a small selection:

That's right …

Yes …

Wonderful …

Please continue in your own way …

I can see your courage as you work through this …

You can also give support through verbal reflection of the client's physical activity. This gives the client confirmation of your close attention and supportive intention.

That deep breath … yes … allowing you to go deeper into your private inner work …

Ah … you swallow just a little as you relax more and …

Wonderful … adjusting and relaxing your shoulders as you create comfort and …

Your observant comments are, of course, based on what the client is actually doing. The purpose is to describe enough of the picture for the client to feel emboldened to continue with their own process, but not so much as to take their self-observer role away.

Surprise and Wonder

Surprise and wonder help to both maintain an energetic level during the process and reflect the energetic processes happening within the client. These words might be similar to supportive responses, but the intention is different because you are adding curiosity, wonder, and the feeling that something tremendous is happening.

Here is a selection:

Wow … amazing … I saw/felt/heard that …

You seem to be receiving/doing/feeling something wonderful/surprising/satisfying … are you not?

Wow, I can see that something is happening in your face/breathing/legs …

I wonder if you are … Marvelous … yes …

Comments of surprise and wonder will also help the therapist to feel encouraged and enlivened. This is one of the many ways in which Mirroring Hands acts as a preventative for therapist burnout and emotional fatigue.

The Double Bind

Although the broad principle is not to direct the client, there are times when a client might need to be guided toward a particular outcome. Giving directions or instructions can, at times, be helpful, but care must be taken to remain client-responsive. Getting the client into a place where they are able to begin work can be a challenge, especially with court mandated clients or those pressed into therapy by family or partners.[3] Can we do this without being directive? The problem with directives, and even suggestions, is what to do if the client does not follow the direction. Not following, or not being able to follow, a directive can negatively impact the therapeutic relationship and even create a division between therapist and client. Erickson found that he could bypass these problems with what he called the *double bind*. The concept was first named by Gregory Bateson and co-authors in the 1950s.[4] The idea of the double bind is to create a situation in which the client feels they are making the choice but the desired outcome is still achieved. This is done by creating options where the desired outcome is *bound* to all the choices.

This is a very helpful technique when working with resistance. For example, a parent dealing with a child who does not wish to go to bed might suggest, "Will you go to bed now and I'll read you a story or will you stay up for another 10 minutes watching TV and then go to bed without a story?" The choice in the situation has now been shifted from going to bed to whether the child gets a story or watches a little more TV. Going to bed has been *bound* to both options, so the child is still able to feel they are making the choice and the parent is getting the desired result without resistance or discomfort. If there are more than two options the principle is the same, but you will create a triple bind or a quadruple bind.

Starting a Process with a Double Bind

There can be many reasons why a client may be having difficulty beginning, other than just obstinate resistance. Perhaps they are not focused or are distracted in relation to conditions like attention deficit hyperactivity disorder (ADHD) or compulsive disorders. Lethargic conditions can arise from affective disorders or concentration disorders. Some people are simply anxious or shy. The following triple bind helps the client to feel they are back in the driver's seat by empowering them to choose when they might begin therapy, but at the same time binding the fact that therapy *will* begin at some time.

---

3 Rosenfeld, B. D. (1992). Court ordered treatment of spouse abuse. *Clinical Psychology Review*, 12(2), 205–226.

4 Bateson, G., Jackson, D. D., Haley, J. & Weakland, J. (1956). Towards a theory of schizophrenia. *Behavioral Science*, 1(4), 251–264.

> *Will we begin our important work right now … or will we wait a little while before we begin our work … or will we continue working with your conscious thoughts before beginning that important inner work …?*

There is a deliberate pause at the end of each bind to allow the client the opportunity to agree. Once the first question is put, it is not uncommon for clients to agree to begin the inner work right away. If the client chooses to wait, it is reasonable to return to the question, "*Will we begin now …*" because *starting the inner work at some time* is a bound part of the choice made by the client.

Ending the Session with a Double Bind

At the conclusion of Mirroring Hands it is necessary to bring the client's attention back from their deep inner work to normal awareness. More often than not, clients will close their eyes at some stage during a Mirroring Hands process. They will need to open their eyes eventually, but this doesn't have to be a directive.

> *I wonder if you will open your eyes as you become fully awake … or will your eyes stay closed as you return to feeling fully awake … or will you find your own way to open your eyes and become fully awake …? Yes … I wonder …*

Double binds, as with most language elements, vary in response to the client. If you are inviting something and there is no response, you can simply invite something else. All you need to do is bind the desired outcome to whatever options you create.

Ideodynamic Questions

Ideodynamic questions open the client to their inner dynamics for self-exploration. Opening a doorway to the client's own phenomenological world can be a valuable prelude to problem-solving. Ideodynamic questions are open ended and have no right or wrong answer. They evoke curiosity, wonder, emotional arousal, sensing, and inner search. They are usually asked with the implication that they may be reviewed privately and do not require an answer, or at least not one that needs to be spoken aloud to the therapist. They may be so non-directive that they may be nothing more than "psychological noise" – the type of chaotic/strange attractor that creates arousal and problem-solving in an almost random way. Ideodynamic questions can deepen the general waking trance as the client becomes more connected to their deeper, inner self and begins hypnotherapeutic work.

For example:

Would you like to do some important inner work now?

What are you experiencing within yourself right now that requires attention?

What is really most curious about what you are privately feeling at this moment?

I wonder how your unconscious (inner mind, guide, spirit, body, etc.) might deal with that issue right now?

Does that make you wonder, be curious?

Do you feel OK about exploring that within yourself right now?

Where is that problem (issue, symptom, worry, etc.) taking you?

Where do you experience that tension (anxiety, concern, etc.) within yourself?

Do you feel that confusion (depression, anxiety, headaches, or whatever symptom) may be an invitation to learn something new?

Do you ever wonder what kind of inner work you would need to do to solve that problem?

How are you experiencing the hidden part of you that needs aid and support?

The Basic Accessing Question

The basic accessing question is a template for constructing therapeutic questions that allow client and therapist to know if the client is ready and able to continue. It is important that it is safe to access the client's inner, implicit world. The full history of the basic accessing question is found in the work done with Erickson and can be read elsewhere.[5] In a brief summary, as Rossi developed his own approaches, he realized that the more the therapist got out of the way, the more the client was able to do beneficial work within and for themself. It was Erickson's genius to realize that indirect suggestions were most effective when utilizing the client's own belief system and inner resources. This idea developed over time, away from overt imposition and toward the subtle approach of indirect suggestion and the implied directive. The implied directive is a form of expression that shifts the locus of control away from what the therapist says and toward what the patient *does* with what the therapist says. It is not about determining what the client *should* do, but giving the client the

5 Erickson, M. H. & Rossi, E. L. (1979). *Hypnotherapy: An Exploratory Casebook*. New York: Irvington Publishers.

opportunity to utilize what the therapist is making available in order to activate their own problem-solving capacities. This is what we mean by *facilitation.*

Erickson's implied directive had three parts:

1 A time-binding introduction.

2 The implied (or assumed) suggestion.

3 A behavioral response that signaled when the implied suggestion has been accomplished.

For example:

> *(1) As soon as you know (2) you are able to begin working with your inner thoughts (3) your hand will descend to your thigh.*

In the 1980s, Rossi made a simple change to create a curious question. The basic accessing question has almost the same three elements but with a question as the third aspect:

> *(1) As soon as you know (2) you are able to begin working with your inner thoughts (3) will your hand descend to your thigh?*

The change is deceptively simple but it has a strong effect. As we know, changing the initial conditions of a complex system can lead to surprising outcomes throughout the system. You may recognize that some elements of the basic accessing question were used in our description of the preparation phase, especially asking a question with client-centered options: "I wonder if you can tell me which hand feels cooler?" rather than a specific directive, "Now, tell me which hand feels cooler."

The basic accessing question facilitates confidence in the client, and the therapist, that the client's implicit connection is now able to engage in therapeutic activity: we have accessed a basic indication of what is possible at this time.

Practical Application

Your client has been prepared comfortably and they are feeling an energy between the hands. The first question is if the client is *able* to make an inner connection and implicitly explore their inner world to solve their problem. The following invitation will inform both of you that the client is ready to move toward solving their problem. This is the first question that connects progressively, in four stages, with the client's inner self.

Stage 1

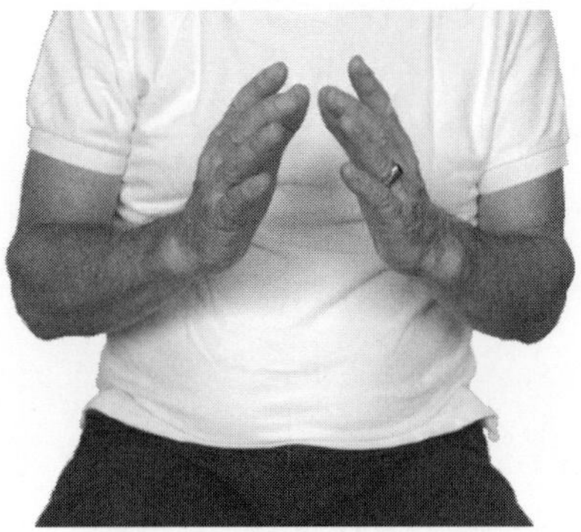

(1) When (2) your inner mind is ready to solve your problem (3) will those hands move together all by themselves to signal yes?

If the hands do move together, then both therapist and client know they are ready to continue. If there is no movement, then we utilize the fail-safe quality of the process by responding positively to the client about there being no response. There is no failure in Mirroring Hands; even no answer is an answer. The client and the therapist can take a "no" response to simply mean that the *inner mind* is not yet ready to *solve the problem*. There are still many options available. For example, it might be decided, together, that more time is needed to feel safe about opening up to their inner world. You might decide to utilize a different therapeutic approach. The therapist might even ask the client if they have become aware of something interesting or surprising that was *different* from the therapist's request. Did they feel something in another part of their body? Did they have an unusual thought or visualization, or hear something, or perhaps notice an aroma? What happens to the client is the absolute center of the process. The basic accessing question thus relieves both the therapist and the client of the stress of "fear of failure" in therapy.

Let us assume that there was a movement response to that first basic accessing question. The client is often surprised that their hands moved all by themselves. Sometimes it is helpful for the therapist to give a little reassurance that it is quite normal for movements to occur outside of our conscious control, even though it does feel strange. The important thing is for the client to feel confident that a connection has been created between their inner implicit operator-self and their conscious observer-self. That means they are ready to solve problems.

The next stage is to ask if the client is *able to explore* what their implicit, inner world knows and remembers. Accessing information that has been held, or perhaps even hidden, in the inner space needs to be done carefully. It may not be safe to just jump in recklessly. Using a basic accessing question is a sensitive way for a therapist to gently ask the client for permission to proceed. Even more important, the client is discovering the feeling of their outer self asking their inner self if it is safe to proceed.

Stage 2

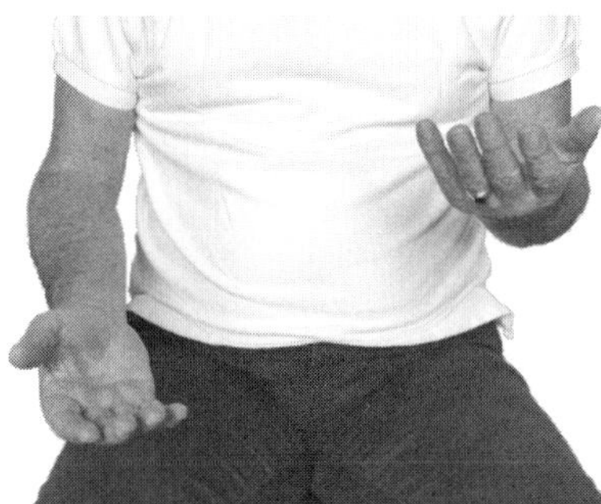

> *(1) When (2) the inner you is able to experience all the sources, memories, and emotions related to your problem (3) will one hand drift down toward your lap … all by itself?*

If there is a positive response to this question about accessing information held in their inner world, the next stage is to explore whether the client will be *able to access* problem-solving capacities and abilities in their inner, implicit space.

Stage 3

> *(1) As soon as it is appropriate (2) to review all the options for solving that problem in the best manner (3) will that other hand go down, or perhaps rise up, or even stay just where it is?*

This is a simplified and idealized example that does not include all the options that can emerge when working with a client. It is always good to offer the client other alternatives, so that every response is seen, by both therapist and client, as a positive response: "Will that other hand rise up?" or "Will that other hand feel like staying just where it is?" You could offer this as a double or triple bind. The purpose is not necessarily to have the hands move, but for the client to *feel* a confirming sensation or activity, so they are *confident* to continue the process on the assumption that something helpful is happening.

The final stage is to bring the client to a conclusion, prepare them for future work, and enable the natural, implicit problem-solving and mind–body healing processes to begin their activity.

Stage 4

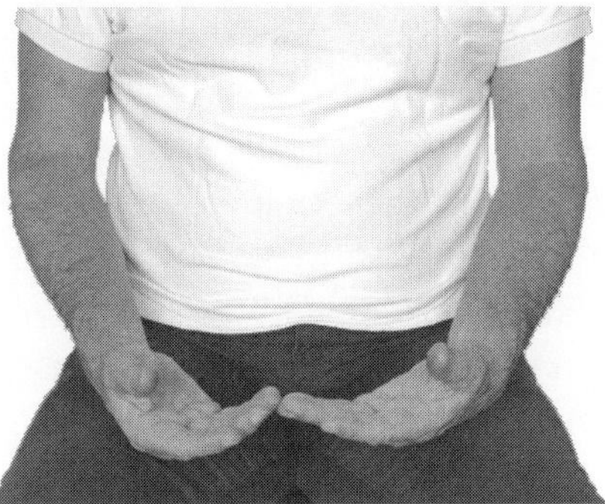

> *(1) When (2) your unconscious knows it can continue with that inner healing you are feeling now, at the appropriate times during the day, and (1) when (2) your conscious mind knows it can cooperate by helping you recognize those periods during the day, (3) will you find yourself awakening?*

We now repeat the four questions without commentary. You might like to read them aloud to see how simple they are and also to appreciate the opportunity the client is being given to *feel* their own inner voice.

Stage 1

> *(1)When (2) your inner mind is ready to solve your problem (3) will those hands move together all by themselves to signal yes?*

Stage 2

(1) When (2) the inner you is able to experience all the sources, memories, and emotions related to your problem (3) will one hand drift down all by itself?

Stage 3

(1) As soon as it is appropriate (2) to review all the options for solving that problem in the best manner (3) will that other hand go down (or whatever)?

Stage 4

(1) When (2) your unconscious knows it can continue that inner healing hypnosis, and (1) when (2) your conscious mind knows it can cooperate by helping you recognize those periods during the day, (3) will you find yourself awakening?

Casebook Examples

The following cases show the effect of basic accessing questions when working with a client who finds it difficult to speak about their issue. It is an effective strategy when dealing with shame; when the client is bound by religious/cultural barriers; has restrictions in cognitive functions; or has concerns about what might be "hiding" in their inner world.

ER's Casebook: Memory and Sexual Molestation

A rather conservative corporate executive officer presented himself for hypnotherapy to help him remember if he had really sexually molested his son and daughter more than 25 years ago as they were now accusing him in a court of law. He insisted with some indignation he had no memories of molesting his own children. After discussing with him the ambiguous legal status of hypnosis as evidence in legal cases, he then made it clear that he wanted hypnosis for his own benefit and curiosity. He decided he would not make use of his hypnotic experience in the lawsuit he was facing.

Because of his sense of urgency, and my surmise that this might be a single session case, I proceeded immediately:

> *[Stage 1] If your unconscious has some valid information regarding this urgent question about sexual molestation of your children, will those hands signal yes by moving together all by themselves as if a magnet were pulling them together?*

After five long minutes of staring at his apparently fixed and unmoving hands I suspected we might have an inconclusive fail-safe outcome wherein nothing much happens. Out of habit, I attempted to turn the situation into a therapeutic double bind by adding:

> *Or will those hands be pushed apart to signal that there is no reliable information available to answer your question?*

Paradoxically, he responded to this by slowly closing his eyes as his hands hesitantly moved together with that very fine and slight but rapid vibratory movement that is so characteristic of involuntary finger and hand signaling.[6] As soon as the hands touched together, I continued:

> *[Stage 2] When your unconscious knows it can make available privately ... to you alone ... the simple truth, and only the truth, will one of those hands slowly drift down all by itself?*

Tears slowly welled up as one hand began drifting down. When his hand finally reached his lap after a few minutes he gave a deep sigh and much quiet weeping. I had no way of knowing the details of what he was really going through but I suspected that his continuing privacy was necessary to obviate "resistance" that could easily rupture his experience. So I proceeded methodically:

> *[Stage 3] And when your unconscious is ready to explore how you can now proceed with the situation ... will that other hand now drift down more or less by itself to signal that you are sorting through options for dealing fairly and appropriately with your personal issues?*

As the other hand drifted down, he gradually composed himself so that he apparently recovered his acumen by the time it reached his lap. After a moment or two, I continued:

> *[Stage 4] And when you become aware that you can awaken with a full memory of all you need to know about your situation, will your eyes open as you come fully alert with a comfortable stretch?*

After another moment or two he shuffled his feet, stretched, opened his eyes, and casually touched himself a bit about his lap, arms, face, and head as is highly characteristic of patients reorienting themselves to their fully awakened state after a trance experience. Without any prompting, he

---

6 Rossi, E. L. & Cheek, D. B. (1988). *Mind–Body Therapy: Ideodynamic Healing in Hypnosis*. New York: W.W. Norton.

reported how he had recovered long forgotten memories of playing and romping about naked on a bed and running about the house with his children when they were about 3, or at the most 4, years old. But he thought it was play, not sexual molestation.

Would his children believe his version of what really happened? He asked if he could bring his son and daughter to a family therapy session with me to discuss it all. I assured him that I thought that was an excellent idea. I never heard from him again, however.

RH's Casebook: "Not Knowing" in a Relationship

A client presented with relationship issues. He had just begun a trial separation from his partner of several years and was unable to decide in which direction to turn. He wanted to know whether they would be able to recover the relationship from this upset. Whatever the outcome, he wanted to be sure to do all he could to work it out.

All of these concerns were about what he did not know. I wondered to myself whether he felt he did know, but was afraid to be conscious of what he really felt. At our third session, I suggested using a process that might help him connect with this inner knowing. Although he said that he wasn't usually into "that sort of thing," he was prepared to see what would happen.

I took him through the preparation process and he felt, quite clearly, that one hand was heavier than the other. He told me that he found this to be strange, but he agreed this was a clear indication that something unusual was happening and he was keen to proceed.

> *[Stage 1] As you think about your partner and all the things you don't know, will one of your hands move in some way to show you are safe to explore what you know inside?*

The fingers of his "heavy" hand twitched noticeably.

> *... Wonderful ...*
>
> *[Stage 2] And now, as you explore that "not knowing," will your heavy hand drift down to your lap?*

His "heavy" hand began to slowly descend. His eyes had spontaneously closed and he seemed deeply engrossed in private work. After about 10 or 15 seconds of his hand drifting downwards he spoke, "This is weird!" but continued the process. His hand finally settled in his lap. Some supportive and a few encouraging surprise comments were all that was spoken during the nearly two minutes in which his hand descended.

> *[Stage 3] And now, as you explore what you can know, what your inner mind can tell you, will your other hand, the "not heavy" hand, drift down toward your lap?*

After just a moment we both realized that his hand was drifting upward and I simply responded with a confirming incomplete sentence.

> *Ah … moving upwards … all by itself … continuing to work through … yes …*

His hand eventually came to rest on his shoulder. His face was very relaxed and calm for the first time that I had seen.

> *[Stage 4] And when you feel that you can create that comfort at appropriate times during the day, will you find yourself opening your eyes, stretching a little, or whatever you need to do right now …*

He took only a few moments to return his focus to me and the room. He repeated that it felt weird and that he usually didn't like those sorts of things, but he had really liked this experience. He stated simply, "I know what I need to know."

It is important to note that I did not ask him what he had discovered. I didn't want to interrupt his thoughts or feelings by shifting his focus to an explanation for me. I waited for him to decide what he wanted to do next. As it happened, he chose to volunteer more about what he learned: "I now know that I don't need to know what is going to happen. I need to let what is going to happen happen, without expectations." We continue to work together and the client's relationship is still repairing.

Review

When the client creates a connection with their inner self, an opportunity, a doorway of possibility, opens for access and activation of the client's own problem-solving and mind–body healing capacities. The therapist is charged with helping the client to facilitate that connection, but then deftly keeps out of the way while the client effectively works on solving their difficulties through processes of realization, resolution, and repair. Everything that a therapist adds into the client's therapeutic experience circulates in dynamic feedback that affects the entire complex system of the client. To that end, the best way to create a positive experience for the client is to *follow* the client and act in *response* to the client. It is not always possible to be responsive, but if the therapist firmly establishes that as their intention, then responsiveness will be the natural priority.

The language principles in this chapter have emerged from this intention. Over our many years of practicing Mirroring Hands these language principles have come to feel natural and comfortable, but experience has shown that not everyone finds it easy to adjust to these principles. We recommend, as with any new skill, that these language principles be practiced and reviewed regularly. Each therapist will find their most comfortable expressions in their own time. We know, and expect, each therapist to gradually formulate their own best words and phrases to convey the intentions of these language principles. As we have said before, this chapter shows you how the language of Mirroring Hands is done, so that you can, eventually, evolve how *you* will do it.

These four stages are very important and fundamental to Mirroring Hands. The next chapter will explore this four-stage cycle, along with another fundamental rhythm of life, as we continue to embrace not only the practice of Mirroring Hands, but also the broader Mirroring Hands approach.

Chapter 5

The Rhythms and Cycles of Life in Therapy

The Natural Foundations of Mirroring Hands

ER: Every couple of hours we go through an activity cycle. The resting part – about 20 minutes – is when we sink close to the quantum, the energetic shifts, in concert with our intentional frame of creating development and transformation … Unfortunately, in the modern world, we take another gulp of coffee, stimulate ourselves to satisfy the "real world," which is only the shadows in Plato's cave …[1]

RH: … and it drives us crazy![2]

ER: Yeah …

RH: … and people mistake the shadows for their essence, but they're only the shallow surface of what is possible.

ER: We give away our self-possibilities to Plato's "puppeteers" to manipulate the essence of our lives for us, denying our access to those natural things that are wonderful and enlightening.

From the Rossi/Hill conversations, June 2016

This chapter explores the natural psychobiological processes that underpin the psychodynamics of Mirroring Hands. Two volumes of international research, edited by David Lloyd and Ernest Rossi, provide the deep biological and mathematical scientific data basis for these key concepts of life and well-being which document how these rhythms and cycles are fundamental to all effective therapies.[3] Understanding and attuning to these natural rhythms and cycles creates a common bond and exchange of truth between therapist and client. This is what therapeutic consciousness, cognition, and rapport in effective therapy is really all about. The therapist and client engage in something that is natural, healing, and mutually accessible. We will describe and explore:

- The natural 90–120 minute basic rest–activity cycle (BRAC), which is the basis of the ultradian rhythm.

1 Plato (1968). *The Republic of Plato*, tr. A. Bloom. New York: Basic Books.

2 Hill, R. (2006). *How the "Real World" Is Driving Us Crazy! Solving the Winner/Loser World Problem*. Sydney: Hill & Hill.

3 Lloyd, D. & Rossi, E. L. (Eds.) (1992). *Ultradian Rhythms in Life Processes: An Inquiry into Fundamental Principles of Chronobiology and Psychobiology*. New York: Springer-Verlag; Lloyd, D. & Rossi, E. L. (Eds.) (2008). *Ultradian Rhythms from Molecules to Mind: A New Vision of Life*. New York: Springer.

- The four-stage creative cycle, originally outlined by Ernest Rossi in 1967 and 1968 as the basis of humanistic psychotherapy,[4] which has been noted throughout human history in many independent autobiographical accounts by scholars, scientists, mathematicians, creative artists, and philosophers.

The Ultradian Rhythm: The Natural 90–120 Minute Cycle of Rest and Activity

When Erickson conducted therapy, the sessions would regularly extend beyond the standard hour. When asked why he did this, he replied that it just seemed to take that long to get something done![5] Because Erickson's focus was on the client, he would continue to work until the client gave some implicitly motivated indication that they had done enough for that session. This might be a body movement, a deep sigh, or a shift in focus and attention, such as the client's eyes flicking away from the therapist or looking down. The signal varied but the message was clear: the client had completed their work for now. This shift would most regularly occur at around 90–120 minutes.

An exploration of the literature for research that might shed light on this phenomenon uncovered work by a sleep researcher named Nathaniel Kleitman. He found that there was a discernible cycle of behavioral and cognitive activity throughout the night. He described it as a 90–120 minute cycle, which he called the basic rest–activity cycle (BRAC).[6] The stages of sleep, from early deep sleep to dreaming (rapid eye movement or REM), occur within a single BRAC, collectively forming a nightly rhythm of around four or five BRACs. Further research showed that this rhythm existed throughout the day as well. While we are awake, the first part of the BRAC exhibits faster brainwave activity so we feel more alert and focused. In the second half, brainwaves slow, alertness reduces, and in the final 20 minutes we feel calmer and even sleepy as our system prepares for the next up-regulation of energy in the following BRAC.

We refer to this flow of cycles throughout a 24 hour period, as the *ultradian rhythm*.[7] Ultradian simply means a period of time less than one day. A rhythm is a cycle that progresses in a repetitive

---

4 Rossi, E. L. (1967). Game and growth: two dimensions of our psychotherapeutic zeitgeist. *Journal of Humanistic Psychology*, 7(2), 139–154; Rossi, E. L. (1968). The breakout heuristic: a phenomenology of growth therapy with college students. *Journal of Humanistic Psychology*, 8(1), 16–28.

5 Erickson, M. H. (2015). *The Collected Works of Milton H. Erickson, M.D.* Vol. 15: *Mind–Body Communication in Hypnosis*, ed. E. L. Rossi, R. Erickson-Klein & K. L. Rossi, 67–71. Phoenix, AZ: Milton H. Erickson Foundation Press.

6 Kleitman, N. (1957). Sleep, wakefulness, and consciousness. *Psychological Bulletin*, 54, 354–359; Kleitman, N. (1982). Basic rest–activity cycle – 22 years later. *Journal of Sleep Research & Sleep Medicine*, 5, 311–317.

7 Rossi, E. L. & Nimmons, D. (1991). *The Twenty-Minute Break: Using the New Science of Ultradian Rhythms*. Los Angeles, CA: Jeremy Tarcher.

flow. We do have other rhythms. Our daily rhythm is called the *circadian rhythm* and is related to repetitions over a 24 hour cycle. There are other natural rhythms that are shorter than 90–120 minutes, such as heartbeat and eye blink. The 90–120 minute rhythm, however, is most relevant to human behavior because it relates to our mental activity. Each cycle in the ultradian rhythm has its unique variation in relation to the natural energy changes throughout each 24 hours.

It is not difficult to find expressions of the 90–120 minute ultradian rhythm in daily life. Movies are generally between 90 and 120 minutes. Many sports are played for 90 minutes with a half-time break, and in quite a few of those that are not, there is still an expression of an ultradian rhythm.[8] Cricket, which is often played over five days, is segmented into sessions of 120 minutes. The captain's tactics can be seen to take advantage of the energetic ebb and flow of the ultradian rhythm throughout the day. Baseball, which is played over nine innings, averages out at about three and a half hours, but some tacticians say the fifth inning is the most important and can determine the game. This is partly because the pitcher often begins to tire at about 100–120 minutes.[9] Mealtimes follow the ultradian rhythm and we'll discuss that further shortly. Daily energy levels ebb and flow in the ultradian rhythm. In a psychotherapy session it is important to pay attention to this energetic ebb and flow and work with it. The ultradian rhythm begins with a rise into a high phase of mental activity and then eases down to a low phase that includes a period of mental rest. During Mirroring Hands, it is important for the therapist to be aware of and responsive to the fluctuations of energy and the subsequent shifts in the therapeutic process as the client flows along with their ultradian rhythm.

Ultradian Healing Response

Figure 5.1 shows the rise and fall of energy and activity during the BRAC and how this continues as the ultradian rhythm. The 20 minute rest phase at the end of the BRAC is a normal low phase of mental activity that is often the best time to experience a nap or practice naturalistic forms of meditation, prayer, deep self-reflection, and holistic healing. This is a very important period of time in daily life which we call the *ultradian healing response*.[10] We are naturally organized to take something of a pause or shift of activity about every couple of hours in order to maximize our learning, engage in reflection, and open our psycho-neuro-biology to integrate the benefits of recent experience. Pushing through these periods of natural pause interferes with the processes of brain plasticity which enable learning and memory as well as adaptation – that is, the integration of newly formed ideas and realizations. Brain plasticity is generated by a complex set of implicit biochemical

8 This article shows that 90 minutes plus 15 minutes at half time is usual: Tuckey, I. (2017). In good time: why are football matches 90 minutes long? Here's everything we know. *The Sun* (January 4). https://www.thesun.co.uk/sport/football/2526687/why-are-football-matches-90-minutes-long-heres-everything-we-know/.

9 Bell, E. (2012). *Winning in Baseball and Business: Transforming Little League Into Major League Profits for Your Company.* Lake Placid, NY: Aviva Publishing, p. 115.

10 Rossi & Nimmons, *The Twenty-Minute Break.*

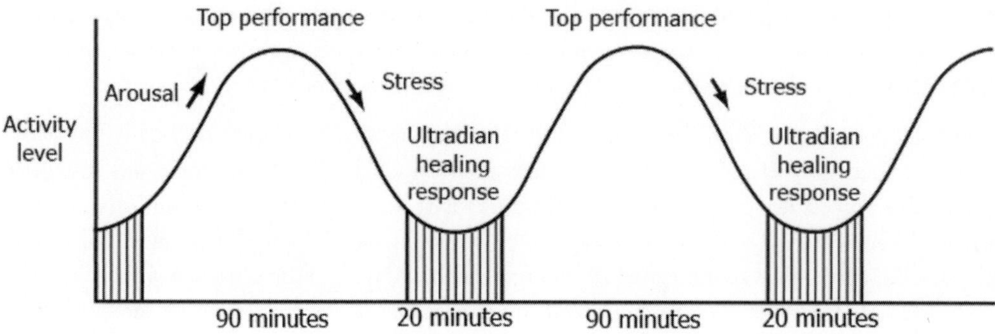

Figure 5.1. The ultradian healing response

processes that include gene expression for the protein synthesis that produces the building blocks for new neural connections.[11] Fortunately, we don't need to be consciously aware of all these processes. All we need is to be aware of the natural call to enjoy a period of ultradian healing response for 10–20 minutes every two hours or so, or at least as often as we can.

As clients enter this period of pause and reflection there are a variety of indicators. Clients might show a loss of focus or attention. They could look away, blink slowly, or adjust their body position. During the Mirroring Hands process, the client might indicate they are entering the ultradian healing response period by relaxing their face and body. The client might begin to speak quietly about their experience or become quite calm and quiet in a state of private inner reflection. The down-regulation of energy, animation, and stress indicates to the therapist that the client has done all the active work they can for now. The therapist need only facilitate the client's return to present awareness or perhaps leave them to enjoy the quiet, regenerative healing space they have opened within themselves for a little while.

11 Rosenberg, T., Gal-Ben-Ari, S., Dieterich, D. C., Kreutz, M. R., Ziv, N. E., Gundelfinger, E. D. & Rosenblum, K. (2014). The roles of protein expression in synaptic plasticity and memory consolidation. *Frontiers in Molecular Neuroscience*, 7, 86. http://doi.org/10.3389/fnmol.2014.00086.

Ultradian Stress Syndrome

If the client, or therapist, persistently chooses to ignore nature's call for rest and restoration, they will fall into the *ultradian stress syndrome* where the disruption and disturbance to these natural healing processes can lead to psychosomatic symptoms and the development of affective disorders such as depression or anxiety. In our current world, there is a constant pressure to push through the ultradian pause. It is now common in business, and even in schools, to work through meals and breaks and constantly try to be stimulated and energized in the drive for success.[12] There is now another powerful external distraction in online devices and social media. Curiously, modern business culture is now encouraging a "power nap," which, although it may be an intuitive response to the ultradian rhythm, is a somewhat desperate compensation for disruptions to both daily and nightly ultradian cycles.[13] Modern society suffers from sleep debt and a desperate need to find relief from the pressured stress of daily expectation and demand, whether it is school, work, family, or even social engagements.[14] However, the power nap is better than nothing.

The rise in mindfulness is therefore hardly surprising in such a driven world. The value and benefit of mindfulness is well researched,[15] but there is little written about the relationship between mindfulness and the ultradian pause. Like the ultradian rhythm, mindfulness is a natural emergent activity that has evolved into an implicit quality of human health and well-being. Mindfulness is likely to have emerged as a beneficial activity in relation to the ultradian healing response. The ultradian healing response has been our natural opportunity to enjoy a change, shift, or pause in activity as many as seven or eight times a day, and four or five times each night, for a very long time. Some of these ultradian pauses have become the pauses taken to eat and engage with others in the family and village. Some have been for distractions such as play, dancing, music, story-telling, and spontaneous enjoyment through laughter and comedy. Other pauses are ideal for mindfulness type experiences, such as meditation, self-reflection, and trance inducing dance, music, and rituals.

We would like to suggest a natural daily experience that may account for why mindfulness, meditation, and contemplation have evolved into an important activity for our well-being. At the end of each day sunset heralds the time to stop work as light fades; a wondrous, spectacular, and numinous vision appears on the horizon, producing a sense of grandeur that overwhelms personal issues. As the daylight shifts to evening there is an opportunity to contemplate the activities of the day, talk, eat, share stories, and explore the day's experience for learning, meaning, and purpose.

---

12 This National Public Radio article quotes that only one in five working Americans step away from their desk for meal breaks: http://www.npr.org/sections/thesalt/2015/03/05/390726886/were-not-taking-enough-lunch-breaks-why-thats-bad-for-business.

13 Weir, K. (2016). The science of naps. *Monitor on Psychology*, 47(7), 48.

14 Andersen, M. L. & Tufik, S. (2015). Sleep and the modern society. *Journal of Sleep Disorders and Therapy*, 4: e131. doi:10.4172/2167-0277.1000e131.

15 Davis, D. M. & Hayes, J. A. (2011). What are the benefits of mindfulness? A practice review of psychotherapy-related research. *Psychotherapy*, 48(2), 198–208.

So, at the very least, sunset has given humans the opportunity to experience at least one daily, natural, ultradian healing response for the entire evolutionary span of our species, and before. Unfortunately, our modern, time-pressured, constantly rushing, and now device-distracted society has increased the prevalence of ultradian stress. Informing and assisting clients to function in concert with their natural ultradian rhythm is fundamental for well-being. Engaging in the ultradian healing response, even if only a few times in the day, utilizing any or all of the forms previously suggested – including Mirroring Hands, of course – is a wonderful and simple way for the client to reduce ultradian stresses and benefit from regular daily engagement with their own natural problem-solving and mind–body healing.

In Practice

Unfortunately, we must conclude that the generally practiced "50 minute hour" therapy session is not in concert with the 90–120 minute ultradian rhythm. Therapists are no doubt familiar with the experience of a client who suddenly begins to open up just as we usher them to the door. Our compensation is the promise of another meeting in a week. On the other hand, have you ever gone beyond the hour, as did Erickson, and noticed the client was not only happy to continue working, but also making important progress? Both authors have found that some of the most productive and effective work can occur between the 65 and 80 minute mark. If another 10 or 15 minutes can be allowed for the client to enter a quiet phase, or a short period of pause, then they can complete a single cycle of their ultradian rhythm. Sometimes this quiet contemplation can be conducted privately by the client as they travel home. Recently, a client declared as he left that he wanted to go for a long walk. Another texted that he enjoyed the session very much, but ended up needing to sleep when he arrived home. Both these clients intuitively engaged in the ultradian healing response period as it naturally occurred, but it is so often ignored or overridden.

If it is simply not possible to extend the therapy session, then we suggest that you could say something that at least acknowledges the client's "unfinished" state. It can be very helpful to give the client a task or something to contemplate. This is not so much "homework" as it is an opportunity to remain connected with their ongoing processes, capture them in some way, and continue the work without feeling such an abrupt end to the session. For example:

> *I can see/hear that you are suddenly aware of some wonderful thoughts and feelings you wish to share, but unfortunately our session has to conclude. I wonder if you might be able to take a few moments before you head home to write these down or perhaps do a voice recording on your phone? It's a great idea to journal your thoughts between sessions, anyway. Not only can we look at these when you arrive for the next session, but you can review them yourself when you have a quiet moment. Maybe next session you can begin by telling me the amazing things that emerged into your mind, just because you listened to or re-read your own thoughts.*

The exact dialogue will vary, of course, depending on the client. The important thing we are putting forward is that when you and the client tap into the ultradian rhythm, this begins a natural mental energy flow, both in sessions and between. Between sessions, the client has the opportunity to take advantage of ultradian healing responses up to 12 times each day. If the next session is in one week, then there are 84 opportunities between sessions for the client to pause, consciously or non-consciously, to allow natural, implicit, self-organizing problem-solving processes to occur.

The Interplay of Systems and Cycles

Noticing, tuning in, and engaging with the ultradian rhythm, which includes enjoying the ultradian healing response several times each day, is the ideal, but mental processes are not the only way to tune into our ultradian rhythm. Kleitman's original research was about ultradian rhythms during sleep. If a client has poor sleep, and many who present for therapy do, then turning attention to improving sleep with various sleep hygiene practices can improve the positive function of their daily ultradian rhythm.[16] Another daily activity that is in sync with the 90–120 minute daily ultradian rhythm, as we mentioned earlier, is eating: specifically mealtimes and eating habits. Feeling hungry and taking a meal is the experiential emergence of our inner, implicit, self-organizing nutrition system that is timed to the ultradian rhythm. There are usually two cycles between meals. The biology of digestion is complex, but basically we digest for one ultradian cycle and then store excess food and use existing adipose tissue (fat cells) for the second cycle when we feel hungry again.[17] Mealtimes ideally involve social engagement, story-telling, laughter, and the pleasure of taste, smell, and touch.[18]

Encouraging clients to make mealtimes a time of pause and engagement is another way to refresh the flow of their natural ultradian rhythm. Many more systems are likely to be a part of this interplay because feeling hungry emerges as a result of implicit changes in the endocrine system, neurobiology, energy production, and more.[19] This interplay of systems partly explains why some symptoms of mental and affective health can emerge as digestive disorders, sleep problems, immune system dysfunction, and endocrine system dysfunction. We are not divisible between what happens in our head and what happens in our body. Everything is connected in the interplay of living. Repairing

16 A good website with lots of sleep information is: http://www.sleephealthfoundation.org.au/fact-sheets-a-z/187-good-sleep-habits.html. Also see https://www.betterhealth.vic.gov.au/health/conditionsandtreatments/sleep-hygiene.

17 Both these articles by Kerry Grens in *The Scientist* explore natural eating patterns and timing, and the subsequent problems that occur: Feeding time (February 1, 2013). http://www.the-scientist.com/?articles.view/articleNo/34153/title/Feeding-Time/; Out of sync (September 1, 2013). http://www.the-scientist.com/?articles.view/articleNo/37269/title/Out-of-Sync/.

18 Reese, E. (2013). Fathers and storytelling – a natural fit. *Psychology Today* (June 15). https://www.psychologytoday.com/blog/tell-me-story/201306/fathers-and-family-storytelling-natural-fit.

19 Conger, C. (2008). How food cravings work. *HowStuffWorks.com* (August 18). http://science.howstuffworks.com/innovation/edible-innovations/food-craving.htm.

disruptions to other 90–120 minute ultradian rhythms can be an effective side door to facilitating effective therapy.

The Four-Stage Creative Cycle

The ultradian rhythm is an emergent property of biological and mental function. The four-stage creative cycle is not so much a specific function, as a fundamental organizing principle that affects all creative processes. Creativity is, at its heart, the process of utilizing what is available in this moment to make something new, or something more, in the next. Creativity involves a sense of personal engagement and self-relevance: the ability to perceive the world in new ways, to find patterns, and make connections between seemingly unrelated phenomena in order to generate something that did not exist before. The four-stage creative cycle is a universal pattern that underlies creative activity and is evident in just about everything from the stimulation of gene expression to the emergence of the universe. In the human experience, this is how the four stages play out:[20]

Stage 1: Information. Gathering information and data – *what is this all about?*

Stage 2: Incubation. Working out what the problem is *really* all about – *how does this affect me? What does this mean to me?*

Stage 3: Breakthrough and illumination. A flash of insight, resolution, or revelation (an a-ha moment) followed by an expansive and creative response to change – *things makes sense now and I can create something better in my life!*

Stage 4: Verification. The whole experience is quietly reviewed, considered, and the benefits integrated into everyday life – *I understand, appreciate, and accept what I have learned.*

Let us expand a little more.

Stage 1: Information

Whenever we encounter something new, we first need to check it out – see what it is, what it is made of, how each sense reacts – and answer the question, "What have we got here?" This might also be termed a preparation stage when we define the problem, need, or desire, and gather as much

20 Rossi, E. L. (2005). Einstein's eternal mystery of epistemology explained: the four-stage creative process in art, science, myth, and psychotherapy. *Annals of the American Psychotherapy Association*, 8, 4–11.

information as possible, both pre-existing and new, that might help us to not only understand the situation, but also to resolve or improve the situation later.

Stage 2: Incubation

Information is not enough on its own, so we need to dig deeper to find what might be the meaning and purpose behind the new information. We often need to take a step back from the problem and let our minds contemplate and work it through. Incubation can last minutes, weeks, and even years, especially if there is some form of dissociation or avoidance of working with the information as might be seen in a trauma case. The questions in stage 2 are: *How does this situation or this problem relate to me? How do I relate to it? What is it that I don't understand? What is it that I don't know or understand? What is it that I don't want to know or understand?* This stage is the struggle to try to make sense of the new experience and figure out what to do with it. It can be very challenging and confronting and is sometimes likened to "the dark night of the soul."

Stage 3: Breakthrough and Illumination

The breakthrough is usually sudden and short. It can be an insight, a surprising realization, the shifting of a barrier, or a sudden change in perception that creates a burst of excitement and a release. The intensity of the breakthrough varies in relation to the context and the individuals involved.

The breakthrough is followed by a period of creativity, celebration, relief, openness, engagement with others, and ideas that generate new plans, hopes, and expectations. This is a sudden and rapidly expansive stage which reflects the extent to which the breakthrough has created a shift in the person. Stage 3 acknowledges, appreciates, and utilizes the insight that emerged at the breakthrough to create beneficial change and growth. After an initial energetic arousal in response to the breakthrough, there is a winding down of energy toward relaxation, calm, and a satisfying sense of relief, resolution, and renewal.

Stage 4: Verification

This is a quiet time when the experience, learning, and new frame of being is contemplated, most importantly, to verify the value and benefit of both the breakthrough and the flurry of mental activity in stage 3. This is a time to consider how these new revelations, realizations, and resolutions can be incorporated into daily living. On an implicit level, the new state of mind is transformationally integrated into our being through various biological encoding processes. New memories and new neural connections are encoded through brain plasticity; endocrine activity and immune system responses begin natural mind–body healing; and biomolecular changes in the DNA, as well as epigenetic changes, self-organize to reflect the new state. We literally become a new being. These integrations will continue to occur during sleep and during future daily ultradian healing responses.

Timelessness, Entrainment, and Stuck Stages

The four-stage creative cycle entrains to the varied timing of each and every creative process. In evolution, the four stages might play out over geological time. In the ultradian rhythm, the four stages are expressed across the 90–120 minutes of the cycle. This is why we purposefully differentiate Mirroring Hands into the four stages. It would be folly to ignore or be unaware of this fundamental principle of life's self-organizing processes. We expect you will be able to see the four stages being expressed in whatever therapy or activity you utilize.

Because the four stages are not time limited, clients can get stuck in one of the stages. Many clients come to therapy having been stuck in stage 1 or stage 2 for years. Clients commonly arrive for therapy stuck in stage 2 but primed for a phase shift. In recent years, we have found that many people have a near addiction to stage 1 – new, new, new! – with very little motivation or inclination to seek out what might be the personal meaning and purpose. This contributes to a shallowness of character, due to a resistance to personal growth and to an increased sense of isolation and disengagement as people get caught up in the distraction of the outside world (we discuss this more in Chapter 9). Mirroring Hands is an excellent approach to help move clients on from stuck conditions because we are actively turning on and engaging them in their natural rhythms and cycles. The most important thing to remember is that once the client connects to their natural problem-solving and mind–body healing, the client is both consciously and implicitly in a place where *they are able to* continue working through the four stages of their creative process, in concert with their ultradian rhythm and their ultradian healing responses.

A Little History

Creative cycles can be found in the literature as far back as the Pyramid texts of Ancient Egypt from over 4,500 years ago.[21] The German philosopher and physician Hermann von Helmholtz described three stages of creativity in his *Lectures and Papers* in 1896.[22] The mathematician, Henri Poincaré, was fascinated to notice that after studying a subject it was often when you *stopped thinking about it* that the realization would come to mind. He described the process of non-conscious incubation of ideas and the subsequent stages of thought in his essay, "Mathematical Creation," in 1908.[23] These writings were a foundation in the thinking of professor of political science at the London School of Economics Graham Wallas, who described the four stages of control in his seminal book *The Art of Thought* in 1926.[24] Wallas' framework has been prevalent for more than century and the four-stage creative cycle has been adopted and adapted on many occasions. It is evident in David Kolb's experiential learning cycle,[25] Goleman and Boyatzis' intentional change theory,[26] and Scharmer's Theory U.[27] Ernest Rossi also saw these stages reflected in Joseph Campbell's *The Hero's Journey*.[28] Campbell described 17 elements of the "monomyth" which were grouped into three stages that reflect the natural, organizing principle of the four-stage creative cycle. Whether considering the problem-solving activity of a human being, the movement of a worm, or even something inanimate like the developing flow pattern of rainwater, the four stages play out.

---

21 van den Dungen, W. (2016). *Ancient Egyptian Readings*. Brasschaart: Taurus Press.

22 Helmholtz, H. von (1896). *Vorträge und Reden*. Brunswick: Friedrich Viewig und Sohn.

23 Poincaré, H. (2000 [1908]). Mathematical creation [reprinted from *Science et méthode*], *Resonance*, 5(2), 85–94.

24 Wallas, G. (1926). *The Art of Thought*. New York: Harcourt, Brace, and World.

25 Kolb, D. A, Boyatzis, R. E. & Mainemelis, C. (2000). Experiential learning theory: previous research and new directions. In R. J. Sternberg and L. F. Zhang (Eds.), *Perspectives on Cognitive, Learning, and Thinking Styles*, 227–248. Mahwah, NJ: Lawrence Erlbaum.

26 Boyatzis, R. E. (2006). An overview of intentional change from a complexity perspective. *Journal of Management Development*, 25(7), 607–623.

27 Scharmer, C. O. (2016). *Theory U: Leading from the Future As It Emerges*. Oakland, CA: Berret-Koehler.

28 Campbell, J. (2014 [1990]). *The Hero's Journey: Joseph Campbell on His Life and Work*, ed. P. Cousineau. Novato, CA: New World Library.

The Four Stages in Pictures

As we have already shown, learning to recognize where the client is in the four-stage creative cycle is a key skill that assists the therapist to heighten engagement with the client's current experience and understand how to best facilitate their natural progress. It is also key for the therapist to understand their own state of mind and progress. The therapeutic experience itself is flowing through the stages. Tracking the different stage progressions is a challenge for the therapist, but it makes all the difference in successfully facilitating the client's capacity to access their natural problem-solving and mind–body healing.

The following figures (5.2–5.4) show the four-stage creative cycle from different perspectives and in relation to different experiences to assist your understanding of how the four stages entrain to life's creative processes.

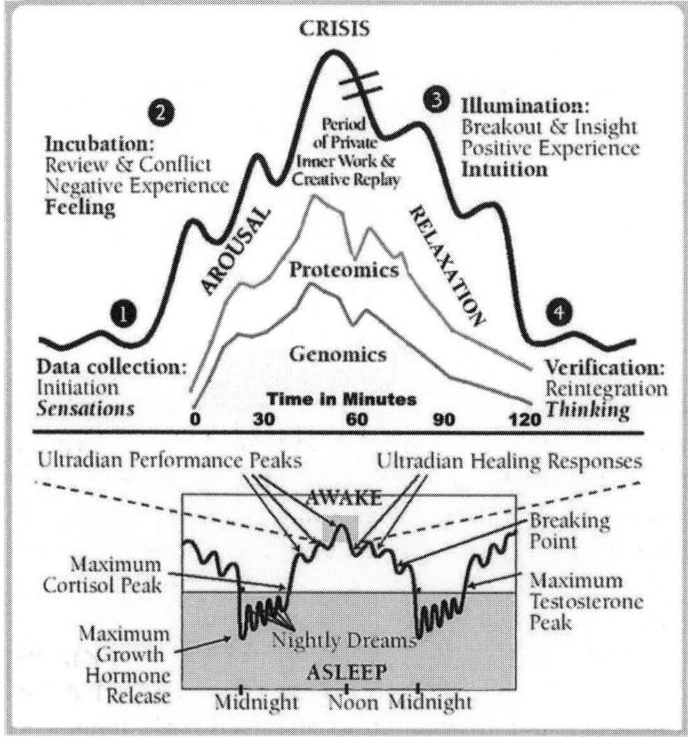

Figure 5.2. The four stages and the ultradian rhythm

Figure 5.2 is ER's integration of the four stages and the ultradian rhythm. The top part of the figure is a single unit of the cycle which is highlighted from the 24 hours of the cycle in the bottom part. The inner lines are related to the co-occurring implicit biological processes in our proteomics (protein building) and genomics (gene expression). The lower part also indicates some of the peaks of cortisol and growth hormone.

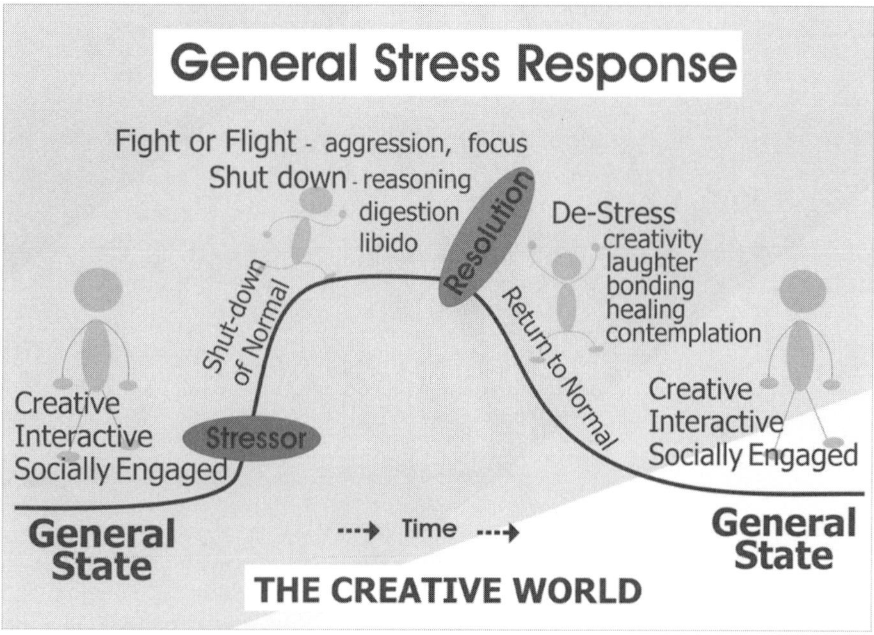

Figure 5.3. General stress response

Figure 5.3 is RH's linear depiction of the four stages in response to a threatening stressor. In a danger based stress response we close our attention around resolving the problem. At the cellular level, a danger warning is responded to in the same way, regardless of whether it is a physical threat or an emotional one.

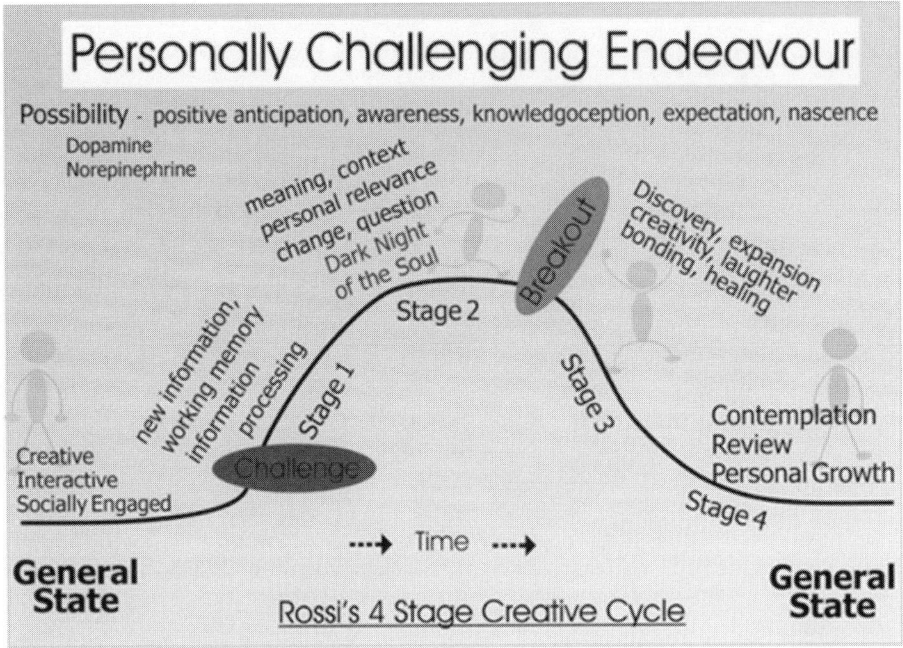

Figure 5.4. Personally challenging endeavor

Figure 5.4 is the four-stage creative cycle in the context of a challenge (i.e. not a distressing situation, but a positive experience). This doesn't mean that stage 2 is an easy stage. Even when voluntarily exploring there are still major issues to be resolved. In the challenge mindset, however, there is an openness to possibility at the growing edge.

Practical Application of the Four-Stage Creative Cycle During Mirroring Hands

We will now focus on the therapeutic experience of Mirroring Hands, differentiating what is happening for the client *and* therapist. Some scripted dialogue is included, but only as a guide to the language style you might choose to suit your specific client.

Stage 1: Information

The Client

When the client attends therapy for the first time they are often in stage 2 of the problem, but the therapeutic experience is beginning in stage 1. New information is shared in the first conversations. Client responses vary from positive to difficult and can range between curiosity, hope, expectancy, confusion, uncertainty, and resistance. There can also be a vacillation between an exploratory attitude and a fearful attitude. These are typical experiences in this initial stage. The client's major task is to identify what issues or problems are most pressing in the here and now. It is not surprising that clients might express stress, anxiety, anger, hopelessness, frustration, and a variety of negative attitudes about themselves and the therapeutic process. The client usually accepts that revealing their information is a difficult process, but they do this in the hope that the therapist will guide them into a therapeutic consciousness so they can move toward productive and beneficial work.

The Therapist

The typical therapeutic session ideally begins with client and therapist cooperating in a search for the problems and issues that the client hopes to resolve. Stage 1 includes the establishment of rapport, building the therapeutic alliance, and may, at the appropriate time, include the preparation for Mirroring Hands and utilization of some basic accessing questions. Mirroring Hands may not even be mentioned as an option during stage 1. This all depends on the client. Fundamentally, though, the therapist's role in this initial stage is to facilitate the client's search for a place to start. Open ended questions allow the client the latitude they need to reveal themselves, while maintaining a feeling of safety.

What's most important on your mind today?

What issue is absorbing your attention today?

What is most interesting to you right now?

What is the most important emotional problem right now?

What would you like to tell me about what has brought you here today?

Just start with whatever feels OK for you right now.

Stage 2: Incubation

The Client

Stage 2 is often the most difficult stage. The client is revealing and facing the very problems that are causing them so much disturbance. At the same time, they are exploring within themselves for their own inner resources. It is not surprising that stage 2 is called "the dark night of the soul." The intensity of the process means that the client's sympathetic nervous system is usually aroused, which is often accompanied by psychobiological responses such as an increase in sweating, heart rate, and breathing, together with a feeling of heat. Clients have said it feels as if they are literally "burning up." This is highly characteristic of client experiences in stage 2. The client needs to re-learn how to access their natural problem-solving capacities after long periods of resisting, avoiding, or dissociating from their issues. Therapeutic reframing questions that reflect the client's immediate behaviors can be helpful here.

> *Yes, breathing like that often means your mind and body are getting ready to deal with an important issue. Will you allow it to continue for another moment or two until you recognize what it is?*
>
> *Can you actually enjoy how you are … (sweating, shaking, trembling, nervous, confused, uncertain, or whatever) for just a moment or two, as a sign that you are working hard and on your way to dealing with whatever is troubling you?*
>
> *Have you ever let yourself have a good shakeup (or whatever) before, just like this … so you could really reorganize yourself?*

The Therapist

The most important role of the therapist in stage 2 is to encourage and support the client's inner journey where they are likely to encounter negative memories and emotions. In everyday life the client typically retreats, quits, or in some way blocks the natural process of ultradian arousal and their natural learning and problem-solving. It might feel counter-intuitive to encourage arousal in the client. It may seem kind to guide the client to a place of calm and peacefulness in order to *manage* their distress. To *solve* a problem, however, the mind–body needs to arouse itself to do some active work.

When a client accesses past painful states they may experience varying degrees of *emotional catharsis*. The therapist's role is to support this inner accessing so the client does not break it off prematurely before natural problem-solving and symptom resolution has a chance to take place. The following are some more examples of key questions the therapist might ask to facilitate the client's safe sense of control during this phase of arousal.

Can you let yourself continue to experience that for another moment or two in a private manner – but only long enough for you to know what it leads to next?

Good, can you stay with that only long enough to learn what it is all about?

Will it be OK to allow yourself to continue experiencing that privately for a while, difficult though it may be, so you can learn what you need for healing (or problem-solving or whatever)?

And will it be all right to keep most of that a secret that you don't have to share with anyone … unless you choose to share just a word or two?

Each of these questions has the fail-safe facility for the client to choose not to continue, but they also have the control to inform the therapist how the client feels and whether they can continue.

Stage 3: Breakthrough

The Client

How the client manifests the sudden burst of insight or realization that heralds the breakthrough from the struggle of stage 2 into the resolution and creative expansion of stage 3 is very unpredictable. It can come in an energetic burst or it may happen without the therapist noticing because it has been a very private and personal experience for the client. Some clients continue on into stage 3 and 4 under the therapist's facilitation. Others have been known to simply open their eyes, declare the session a wonderful success, and begin to share a little, a lot, or, sometimes, nothing at all. What is obvious, however, is that, at the moment of breakthrough, the struggle and difficulty of stage 2 has passed through a critical phase shift and the client transforms in some way. The task of the therapist is to continue being client-responsive and facilitating the client's journey without interrupting or disrupting.

The Therapist

The therapist can share their awareness of the client's experiences with simple encouragement.

Yes, noticing interesting things there?

Umm, something important to recognize about that?

Sometimes, there seems to be an inward pulling within the eyeball and the client's whole head may even pull backward slightly – occasionally with a slight expression of surprise or a momentary frown. Again, be observant and supportive.

Ahh, something surprising?

Yes! The courage to receive that as well?

Experiencing that, too, can you not?

Sometimes there is a moment of absolute stillness as if the client is receiving something from within with bated breath. There may be a slight smile and the head may slowly nod "yes" with minimal repetitive movement. Support this behavior with these questions.

Mmm – receiving something you like?

Worth receiving?

Yes – and more?

Stage 3: Illumination

The Client

The profoundly significant shift from crisis and catharsis to the moment of insight and then the release of tension as they move into stage 3 is often accompanied by a sense of relief, surprise, and laughter. Clients may softly whisper, "It's strange, weird, odd!" The use of such words means that they are experiencing something new. They may even mention, "Something really new, something I was never aware of before suddenly popped into my mind." Clients can be full of questions about these moments of creative experiencing. The client might seem to be asking questions of the therapist, but it is not uncommon for the client to be talking to themselves as if the new resolved person is telling the old problem riddled person how and why everything is much better. Whether a monologue or dialogue, this process is important to ratify and stabilize the client's new reality.

The Therapist

During this period of inner exploration and emotional release, the client can exhibit many subtle shifts of behavior. There may be sudden increases or reductions in tension. If the client has been working with their eyes closed, there is often periodic or momentary bursts of rapid eyelid vibration or a shifting of the eyeballs from side to side, as if the client is following an inner moving scene. Eye movement is something deliberately enacted during eye movement desensitization reprocessing (EMDR), and there is some research about the relationship of eye movement to healing processes.[29] We also see eyeball movement in REM sleep which indicates dreaming and activity between the limbic area and cortex. Simply observe and be aware that something transformative is probably happening.

---

29 Shapiro, F. (2014). The role of eye movement desensitization and reprocessing (EMDR) therapy in medicine: addressing the psychological and physical symptoms stemming from adverse life experiences. *Permanente Journal*, 18(1), 71–77.

It is not always easy to recognize the transition from the arousal phases of stage 2 to the moments of significant insight in stage 3. Some clients shift uncertainly back and forth between stages 2 and 3 several times before a settling into stage 3. Confirmation that a *unit of the inner work* may be completed can be seen in larger postural adjustments of the head, neck, arms, or legs, as if an opening, loosening, or relaxation is taking place. Previous muscle constrictions and tensions evident in the jaws, hands, and arms seem to "let go" and clients may actually shake themselves out. The client shifts from the metaphorical postures and movements of defensiveness, anger, frustration, sorrow, or depression – so characteristic of stage 2 – to expressions of lifting, lightness, and well-being.

Oddly enough, many clients need help to recognize the value of the spontaneous, creative breakthroughs they are experiencing in stage 3. Some clients can find it hard to accept that it is their creative experience that is the essence of their therapy. It can be difficult to shake loose from the belief that the answer or magic of healing has to come from the therapist or from somewhere outside of themselves. Clients can be all too ready to diminish their critical phase transitions as somehow immature, inadequate, or pathetic. This may be because that is how their creative moments have been put down since childhood, when parents, teachers, or elders did not recognize and support the client's mini-breakthroughs and developing awareness. Creative experience is so often accompanied by what seems to be confusion, rebellion, and emotional chaos.[30] The task of the therapist is to help such clients recognize the value of their own spontaneous therapeutic transitions at this critical moment, and above all help clients to recognize that the locus of creativity and therapy is within themselves.

It is natural for the client to feel very strange and out of their comfort zone. They have moved outward at their growing edge and are best helped with simple, gentle, supportive remarks that are broadly rhetorical. The following questions will help the client to recognize and stabilize their still nascent creative state and emergent insights.

Interesting?

Curious, isn't it?

A little surprise?

Umm – rather unexpected somehow?

Yes, are you experiencing something a little different now?

My goodness, is something really changing now?

30 Rossi, E. L. (1968). The breakout heuristic: a phenomenology of growth therapy with college students. *Journal of Humanistic Psychology*, 8(1), 16–28; Rossi, E. L. (1998a [1972]). *Dreams and the Growth of Personality*, 3rd edn. Los Osos, CA: Palisades Gateway Press.

It is an error, at this crucial time, for the therapist to distract the client by asking for a report or explanation of what has happened. Hold back from efforts to document or interpret the client's process with intrusive questions such as, "Where did the pain go?" "What's happening now?" "Tell me why you feel better now." "What do you understand about yourself now?" Such questions at this stage can interrupt and block the flow of the client's ongoing creative experience. This is the time for the therapist to be patient, to be client-responsive, and stay out of the way.

Stage 4: Verification

The Client

Clients invariably feel good in stage 4, with a sense of relief and well-being. If you utilized some form of symptom scaling in the early part of the session (usually done in stage 1), then stage 4 is the best time to ask them to re-scale their symptoms. If you haven't, then it is just as effective to simply ask the client if there is an improvement. If the client reports that their symptom is less intense, then that helps to validate the therapeutic experience they have just gone through. If the symptom has disappeared completely, this is the time to plan how the client can learn to do this type of inner healing hypnosis for themselves in everyday life. This is a good opportunity to remind clients that they have the best access to this type of inner healing during their ultradian rest periods.

If the symptoms have only eased a small amount, then the client may have achieved only partial success. How can this be built upon in future sessions? To prepare for that further improvement, encourage the client to explore their ultradian healing responses – their natural times of pause, about every two hours – in everyday life. This is an opportunity to invite the client to start a journal of their experiences, if they are so disposed. The journal, if the client chooses to share, can provide hints of the next step that is needed to facilitate further creative phase transitions in healing and problem-solving.

In stage 4, the client is able to develop a conviction of what options are truly possible for them as they facilitate their own development in a practical and realistic way. The exciting thing is when they begin to tell you, the therapist, how they will change their behavior and try to do things differently.

The Therapist

Sometimes clients will spontaneously stretch and open their eyes entirely on their own. When clients do not open their eyes and awaken spontaneously, they may prefer the therapist to facilitate a conclusion to the session. The following basic accessing question style of concluding the session is an excellent way to be sure that the client continues to hold the locus of control within themselves.

> *(1) When (2) something within you knows it can continue this creative healing entirely on its own – at appropriate times throughout the day when it feels natural to take a break and when your*

conscious mind knows it can simply cooperate in helping you to recognize when it is the right time to tune inward – (3) will that give you a feeling, a signal, that it's time for you to stretch, open your eyes, and come fully alert so you can discuss whatever is necessary for now?

It is in this final stage that the client often chooses to engage in some of the talk, analysis, plans, and intentions for future actions. We still recommend maintaining an attitude of restraint, even if the client is keen to talk. The task of the therapist is to continue to facilitate the locus of control within the clients so *they* can interpret, synthesize, and rationalize *their own internal experiences, in their own way.*

The following questions are open ended and undemanding of a response. Clients may choose to remain silent and work on their realizations and resolutions privately or they may begin to spout a fountain of words.

Is there something you would like to share about ...?

Yes ... can you say more about it?

How much of this is new to you?

What is most significant about this for you?

Have you ever understood this before?

What does this lead you to now?

How will this experience help you to make changes in your life?

I wonder if you will you actually do something different in your life this week?

Review

This chapter has explored two important elements, but it has really been about one thing: being engaged with what is natural to life. Therapy is best when it is an expression of the healing capacities of our natural being. The ultradian rhythm and four-stage creative cycle are natural patterns and principles that are ubiquitous not only throughout a wide range of therapeutic theories, techniques, and methods, but also throughout all of life and nature. There are a few more conceptual ideas and principles to discuss in chapters to come, but the foundations for Mirroring Hands have now been presented. We hope you are now comfortable to be shown specific forms of the Mirroring Hands technique. We begin with "What Is and What Can Be."

Chapter 6

What Is and What Can Be

Internal Review

ER: The client is trying to figure out, "Who am I?"

RH: … and the hands … these somatosensory vehicles have been the main contact points for giving and receiving forever …

ER: This is not us trying to be clever. This is the human condition. Now, we are trying to put the locus of the power for transformation inside the client, not inside the therapist …

RH: That can be hard to do …

ER: There are a number of paths, and you must find yours … embracing your uniqueness … that is what you want for you … and the client.

From the Rossi/Hill conversations, June 2016

Mirroring Hands has many variations. Each client creates a new experience. Having said that, we have found, over many years of practice, that a handful of variations have emerged as a reliable group for teaching and for practice. This chapter describes a form of Mirroring Hands that allows the client to first review their story and the history of their problem, and then explore the solutions and other possibilities that have not yet risen to their conscious awareness.

Each form can be differentiated into the four stages. Each stage has a fundamental intention that can be expressed as a basic question. First, we will review the basic questions paired with a sample image. Then, we will explore in more detail how the process flows in practice. This includes the language that can be utilized and the typical responses from clients. Finally, we will share a case study.

Stage 1: Information – Initiation, Sensations

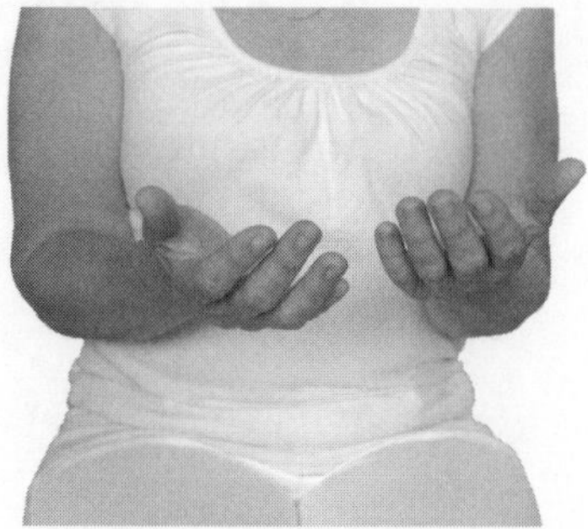

I wonder if you can look at your hands, really look at them as if you have never looked at them before. As you focus deeply into your hands, I wonder if one hand feels different from the other. Is one hand warmer ... heavier ... etc.?

Stage 2: Incubation – Arousal, Feeling

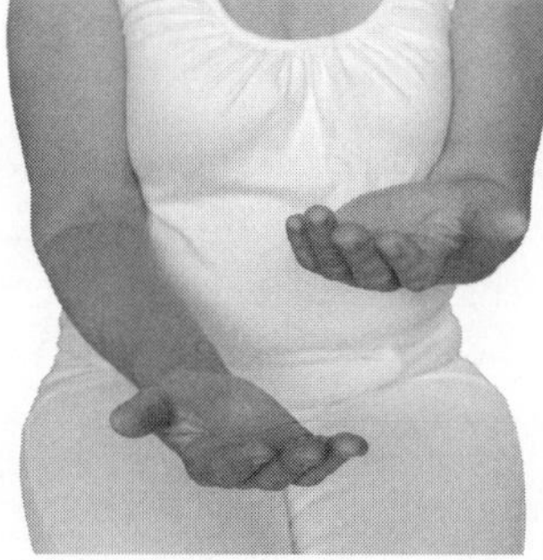

I wonder which hand is able to experience your issue? Will that hand slowly drift to your lap as you gently review the story, the history, and those things you aren't able to say or even remember?

Stage 3: Breakthrough and Illumination – Insight, Intuition

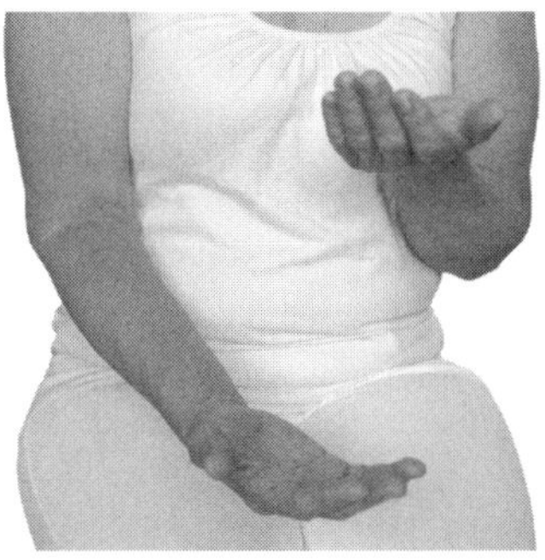

Now ... as we explore the solutions you don't know yet ... will you allow your other hand to drift slowly? ... Will it drift downwards ... or perhaps upwards ... or some other way that happens all by itself ... as you explore new possibilities about how to solve your problem today ... explore all your hopes ... the most interesting and wonderful possibilities of healing and well-being?

Stage 4: Verification – Thinking, Reintegration

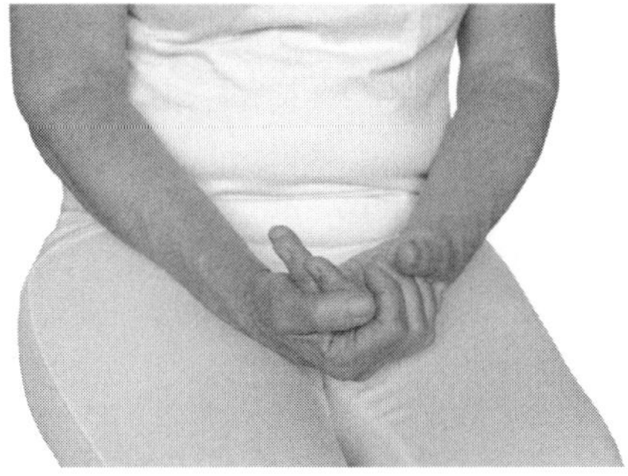

Something interesting you would like to share about that?

What is surprising and unexpected about this that is new to you?

What is most significant and life changing about this for you?

What does this lead you to now?

How will this change your life?

Stage 1: Information – Evoking Observing Consciousness, Curiosity, Focused Awareness, and Positive Expectancy

Begin by guiding the client through the preparation stage (see Chapter 3). It is not vital what sensation differentiates the hands – whether one hand is warmer, or heavier, or a different age, or whatever – allow this to emerge naturally and comfortably. The important thing is that the therapist is responding to the client, gently leading when necessary, but quickly shifting if the client wishes to take some initiative. It is wonderful if the locus of control can move to the client at this early stage, but it is equally good for the client and therapist to proceed together.

It is also assumed that the therapist is confident the client is ready to begin exploratory work. This may come from the therapist's sensitive observation or the client may have told the therapist directly. If the therapist is not feeling comfortable or feels the client is not comfortable, it can be helpful to go through the basic accessing questions first (see Chapter 4), just to be sure that everything, and everyone, is ready before proceeding.

Stage 2: Incubation – Past Problem Review to Activate Positive Motivation and Inner Resources

In stage 2, we ask the client to review the origin and history of their problem. The implicit behavioral response that is commonly suggested is for the hand to drift down slowly to their lap. The client's focus and attention creates an expectancy and curiosity that allows them to safely access the neural networks of their brain that encode their problems, maladaptive behavior, and consciousness, both explicitly and implicitly.[1] Some memories will be familiar and consciously available, others may be hidden, repressed, or forgotten. It is important for the therapist to be closely attentive and responsive to the client as they reveal and face their difficulties. First, we establish which hand is receiving the problem.

> *I wonder which hand might be able to experience your issue (concern, problem, or symptom) and …*

Allow a moment or two for the client to respond to the suggestion.

> *… will that hand be able to make a movement or somehow indicate it's ready to begin …*

---

1 Rossi, E. L. (2002b). *The Psychobiology of Gene Expression: Neuroscience and Neurogenesis in Hypnosis and the Healing Arts*. New York: W.W. Norton; Rossi, E. L. (2004a). *A Discourse with Our Genes: The Psychosocial and Cultural Genomics of Therapeutic Hypnosis and Psychotherapy*. San Lorenzo Maggiore: Editris S.A.S.; Rossi, E. L. (2007). *The Breakout Heuristic: The New Neuroscience of Mirror Neurons, Consciousness and Creativity in Human Relationships. The Selected Papers of Ernest Lawrence Rossi, Vol. 1*. Phoenix, AZ: Milton H. Erickson Foundation Press.

Wait for the response, adding small encouragements as the client may require, and responding with delight and surprise when one hand does, indeed, make a movement.

> *Wonderful … I see that your issue is held in your right (or left) hand … wonderful …*
>
> *I wonder … as you let that hand experience your issue (concern, problem, or symptom), now, will that hand begin to drift down very slowly … all by itself … as your inner mind privately reviews the history, memories, and feelings of your issue (concern, problem, or symptom) … from the beginning and back to the present moment … or perhaps from the present moment all the way back to the beginning …*

This review can take some time, sometimes several minutes and often longer. If the client begins to show negative cathartic reactions (frowning, weeping, etc.) the therapist simply offers emotional support through empathetic supporting and encouraging words (see Chapter 4) or comments such as these:

> *That's right! Do you have the courage … to allow that hand and arm to drift down a bit … with each memory you find yourself reviewing?*
>
> *Yes, not easy … Just allow your inner mind to feel as much of that memory as you need to … and then move on … Allow the next memory … to come up more or less by itself … only as much as you need …*
>
> *That's right … let yourself have the courage to continue … only as long as you need … to experience everything as fully as you need to … privately … and comfortably …*
>
> *That's right … you can really feel this … while another part of you observes wisely … as you learn how to take care of yourself … and expect the best possible outcome …*

A simple, but very effective, way to facilitate a shift in the intensity of the experience for the client is to ask:

> *Would you like to share a word or two about what you are feeling or what is happening right now … or would you like to just continue with your own important work privately … in your own way …?*

This question gives the client an opportunity to share their experience if they wish and vent any excess build-up of anxiety or stress. This question can be utilized at any time during Mirroring Hands, but we recommend you use this sparingly. Sometimes it is just the opportunity that the client is looking for; at other times clients will make it clear that they are in no need of assistance. On one occasion a client put her fingers to her lips to tell the therapist to be quiet. This is an excellent example to show that clients can genuinely enjoy the difficult work because they have a clear sense that their situation is improving.

We have found this therapeutic review of a client's concerns to be "safe." Clients do not undergo a "re-traumatization," even though they are reviewing negative past experiences, because they are in a safe context.[2] First, the negative memories and emotions are not being experienced internally – the review has been externalized by being projected into their hand. If the client begins to internalize, the therapist can remind the client to refocus their attention on to the experience being played out in their hand. As a final "fail-safe," the client can be directed to shift their focus and attention to the other hand.

Assuming all has gone well, the "problem" hand will finally touch down on the client's lap. The therapist can now facilitate the transition to stage 3 of the creative process with:

> *Wonderful … a job well done … and now, I wonder if you will shift your attention to your other hand that is holding the resolution of this issue (concern, problem, or symptom) …*

Stage 3: Breakthrough and Illumination – Facilitating Implicit Problem-Solving and Mind–Body Healing

The emergence of the breakthrough is not easily predictable. Sometimes a breakthrough occurs in the final moments of the "problem" hand arriving on the client's lap. More often, the breakthrough emerges spontaneously during this positive exploration of solutions. The famous a-ha or "eureka" experience of insight is a truly exciting moment whenever it occurs during the Mirroring Hands process, and it is a wonderful moment for the therapist too. *The therapist's main job at this stage is to help the client to recognize and appreciate the value of the new and creative thoughts, feelings, and ideas that emerge spontaneously and unheralded.* Sometimes the client realizes they have thought of these problem-solving options before, but dismissed them due to lack of confidence or lack of support. Here we strongly support them.

> *Now … as we explore the solutions you don't know yet … will you allow your other hand to drift slowly? … Will it drift downwards … or perhaps upwards … or some other way that happens all by itself … as you explore new possibilities about how to solve your problem today? … Will that hand now begin to move slowly as you begin to experience something new? … Yes … moving all by itself … (acknowledge and encourage whichever direction the hands moves) … Explore all your hopes … the most interesting and wonderful possibilities of healing and well-being … Speculate about exciting and fascinating turning points in your life … Create the best of all possible worlds for yourself … Enjoy your best dreams about yourself!*

2 Foa, E., Cohen, J., Keane, T. & Friedman, M. (2008). *Effective Treatments for PTSD: Practice Guidelines from the International Society for Traumatic Stress Studies.* New York: Guilford Press.

The small elements of that dialogue are spoken over whatever timeframe the client needs. Transitioning from the difficulties of stage 2 to the creative possibilities of stage 3 can be fragile and tenuous. Delicate shifts can often be read in the client's facial expressions. Equally, the shifts can emerge in any part of the body. Everything that happens for the client is relevant. Notice carefully the shifts from negativity, stress, sadness, and conflict in stage 2 to the more searching expressions of expectation in stage 3, which are often punctuated with a slight smile or even a short laugh. Sometimes clients will manifest other minimal behavioral cues of their positive attitude and enjoyment of this third stage of their creative experience by spontaneous head-nodding, shaking, rocking, caressing themselves comfortably, or enjoying spontaneous relaxation or a release in other parts of the body. The therapist simply notes these positive shifts with warm and engaged support.

Something pleasantly surprising you can look forward to ...?

Yes, what you really need that is most interesting and important to you ...

Simply receiving and continuing to explore the sources of your strength ... dealing successfully with that issue ...

Yes ... appreciating the value of that as fully as you need ... while taking good care of yourself as that hand finally comes to rest ...

Allow time for the client's hand to come to rest on the lap if the hand drifted down, or on the chest or shoulder if the hand drifted up, or wherever seems settled and comfortable if the hand moved to the side.

Wonderful ... really appreciating yourself for a job well done! ... So much happening and changing ...

Stage 4: Verification – Integration and Reality Testing

It is now likely that the client is ready to return their attention to the general world of the room. Sometimes clients will spontaneously open their eyes and refocus their attention. The following dialogue (from Chapter 4), helps the client to reframe their attention and adds a gentle suggestion regarding continuing their therapeutic work in relation to their ongoing ultradian rhythm at *appropriate times throughout the day* and when it is *the right time to tune in*. As much as possible, continue to facilitate the client as the locus of control:

When ...

A part of you knows it can continue this creative work entirely on its own at appropriate times throughout the day ...

And when your conscious mind knows it can simply cooperate in helping you to recognize when it is the right time to tune in ...

Will that give you a feeling, a signal, that it's time for you to stretch, open your eyes, and come fully alert so you can consider what has happened and share, if you wish, what you might do with what you have learned, in your real everyday life?

The therapist's task in stage 4 is to optimize the benefits that have emerged in stage 3. Depending, of course, on the client's preference to talk about the experience or to remain quiet and private about their discoveries, the therapist can:

- Facilitate a follow-up discussion to validate the client's experiences.
- Help the client to reframe the negative symptoms they brought with them to therapy into an understanding of their strengths and inner resources.
- Explore ways in which the client may incorporate their new realizations into daily life.
- Simply sit quietly in the new healed space, perhaps enjoying just a word or two that emerges relating to their joy, pleasure, strength, or whatever other positive feeling they wish to express.

In stage 4 there is a shift of focus from expanding creativity to incorporating and integrating what has emerged, both explicitly and implicitly. Some clients want to jump back in and do more discovery, others are unsure and untrusting of their own ability to produce such excellent work. It is important to allow time for the ultradian healing response to do its part as the client integrates their new state of being. Biological encoding is self-organized through many processes all the way down to the molecular level of state related gene expression, brain plasticity, and mind–body healing.[3] The following questions can help the client to remain in the space:

Something interesting you would like to share about that?

What is surprising and unexpected about this that is new to you?

What is most significant and life changing about this for you?

How will you remind yourself to do this several times a day?

What does this lead you to now?

How will this change your life?

What will you do in your life that is different now?

---

3 Rossi, E. L. & Rossi, K. L. (2008). *The New Neuroscience of Psychotherapy, Therapeutic Hypnosis and Rehabilitation: A Creative Dialogue with our Genes*. Free ebook available at: www.ernestrossi.com; Cozolino, L. (2017). *The Neuroscience of Psychotherapy: Healing the Social Brain*. New York: W.W. Norton.

If symptom scaling was used prior to the Mirroring Hands process, then this is a good time to check in on how the client feels now. If there has only been a minor change in stress and symptom reduction, perhaps if less than 50% is reported, it may be useful to facilitate another Mirroring Hands process. The client may prefer not to repeat Mirroring Hands, which is just fine, but if you feel the client may benefit, a basic accessing question can be utilized:

> *If your inner nature knows it can do another unit of creative work right now, so you can reach a more satisfactory state, will those eyes close for a few moments so you can fully receive everything you need at this time?*

The client's response will inform you whether they wish to try again or not. If the client is not ready to proceed, or there is just not enough time, it is helpful to remind the client that their mind and body go through a natural cycle of ultradian healing and problem-solving every couple of hours throughout the day and at night, even when they are asleep and dreaming. Assure them that their healing process can continue all by itself, and ask them to notice any changes and improvements that occur over the next few days.

RH's Casebook: Holding Within, Resisting Release

A woman in her late forties presented with a deep sense of upset that had persisted for nearly a year following her divorce. Surprisingly, she appeared to be quite cheery and positive about her future. She had one of those faces that generally looks like she is happy. We spoke about the divorce and some of the difficulties since then, including another relationship that was very unsatisfying. She felt that she had always been able to manage other problems in her life, but just didn't seem to be able to access those resources now. She wanted to find something that seemed hidden from her at this time. We spent most of the first session talking about the past and exploring some of her hopes for the future. She felt confident that another session would help and so we arranged to meet in one week's time.

In the second session, I spoke about the mysteries of our inner world and how I could use a process that could connect her conscious mind to these inner resources. All she had to do was hold her hands out in front of her. She was immediately willing and curious, so I decided to introduce her to Mirroring Hands.

Stage 1

We began with a standard preparation of focus on her hands, exploring her hands like she had never done before. I wondered if one of her hands seemed heavier than the other. It is hard to know why, as the therapist, one sensation is used above another. Perhaps, in this case, it was because her divorce, and the history around it, sounded quite "heavy" and dramatic. Perhaps I was sensitive to her heavy heart. Regardless, her right hand began to bounce within a few moments of asking the question. It was very clear.

Stage 2

> *I wonder which hand might be able to hold this upset ... Will that upsetting energy flow out into that hand ... and will that hand make a movement of some kind to show it is receiving?*

The fingers of her "heavy" hand began to flatten out and then a moment later, curl up.

> *Wonderful ... your heavy hand is taking this feeling, this upset ... yes ... and ... I wonder if you can allow your inner mind to review the story about this upset ... more than the words we have already spoken ... things about this story you have not yet thought about or remembered ... from this moment back to the beginning or perhaps from the beginning back to this moment ... And as these thoughts come to your mind will your hand gently drift down to your lap ...?*

Each ellipsis represents a pause that was entirely client-responsive and interactive. The dialogue took several minutes. Her eyes closed spontaneously midway through the initiating dialogue, and her hand drifted down a tiny distance and stopped. The movement of her hand down to her lap was unlike any I had experienced before. For the next 20 minutes, we continued, mostly in silence. It was clear that a lot was happening for her. Her hand would be still, almost rigidly held, then suddenly drop about an inch (25mm), and stop for another period of internal processing. Tears flowed a number of times, but she showed no interest in wiping the tears away. She was totally engrossed in something of great significance. I would add simple supportive comments when moved to do so:

> *Yes ... wonderful ...*
>
> *Experiencing extraordinary things ...*
>
> *Tears ... yes ...*
>
> *Continuing bravely ... feeling your story ...*

When her hand finally landed on her lap, she gave a big sigh and her head and shoulders fell forward as if exhausted.

Stage 3

Wonderful … what an extraordinary journey! … Will we shift our attention now to your other hand … can we explore the resources and skills and strengths that have been hidden or held back? … Will that hand begin to move in whatever way you wish as you rediscover what you know is within you?

This part of the process was very different. Her hand began to drift upwards, but not in the jerky motion of the "heavy" hand. As her hand drifted up toward her shoulder, her head and shoulders also lifted. Her hand reached her shoulder within a few minutes. I made only two or three supportive comments. In retrospect, it would have been just as well if I had said nothing. When her hand touched her shoulder, she was sitting upright, her eyes remained closed, but her face seemed calm and content. I invited her to return to the space with me.

Stage 4

When … a part of you knows it can continue this creative work entirely on its own at appropriate times throughout the day … and when your conscious mind knows it can simply cooperate in helping you recognize when it is the right time to tune in … will that give you a feeling, a signal, that it's time for you to stretch, open your eyes, and come fully alert so you can consider what has happened and share, if you wish, what you might do with what you have learned, in your real everyday life?

Within a few moments she opened her eyes, while stretching her arms upwards, and giving a large sigh. She was quiet for about a minute and then asked how long we had been going. I asked her how long she thought it was. She felt it was about 10 or 15 minutes. When I told her it was closer to 30 minutes she was startled. Time distortion is a common indicator of deep inward focus and general waking trance.[4] We spoke about her experience, but the most pertinent comment was:

I felt bound, tied down by something. I don't really know what it was … just … bound. But then something happened and it was just all gone. When my hand touched my shoulder I was … no longer bound … I now feel I am able to make all kinds of decisions. I'm not bound anymore …

On follow-up, several years later, she reported:

I really can't tell you what happened. I don't really understand the problem other than I was bound, and I don't know what released it, but I just stopped being bound … and that feeling has

4 Erickson, M. H. (2008 [1964]). The general waking trance: intense mental absorption and response attentiveness. In *The Collected Works of Milton H. Erickson, M.D.* Vol. 3: *Opening the Mind*, ed. E. L. Rossi, R. Erickson-Klein & K. L. Rossi, 271–272. Phoenix, AZ: Milton H. Erickson Foundation Press.

never returned. The divorce was awful, but being bound up by something I couldn't see or touch was so distressing. I guess none of it was in my conscious mind, like you said, and it took something else not in my conscious mind to fix it. Whatever … it worked.

Review

It can seem to be against normal training to imagine that a client can produce effective and successful therapy without being able to verbally describe what occurred. However, we have learned that the messages that emerge from the implicit can be simplistic. The client was only able to describe the problem simply, but the conscious message, *feeling bound*, was enough for her to know that the problem had been detected. That the implicit problem-solving processes emerged as something equally simple, the feeling of *no longer feeling bound*, was also enough for her know there had been a shift and she could begin making positive decisions and planning for her future. All we need is what we need, even if we don't know *exactly* why or how we have arrived at where we need to be.

Chapter 7

Natural, Comfortable, and Sensitive Observation

The Art of Client-Responsive Therapy

RH: … Everything I learn, everything that I come to know, becomes a springboard, not a safe platform.

ER: Yes!

RH: … And from that learning, you springboard into the unknown – beyond the growing edge …

ER: … You are finding comfort in the unknown, the "I don't know" …

RH: Yes, being comfortable that "not knowing" is just an invitation to discover a new springboard.

From the Rossi/Hill conversations, June 2016

Have you wondered about the terms we have been consistently using – *natural, natural problem-solving, comfort,* and *sensitive observation*? In many ways, these words are reasonably well understood, but this chapter will explore them a little more deeply. Although this book is presented as a practitioner's guide to a technique, we expect you may know by now that Mirroring Hands embraces a fresh and sometimes challenging approach to therapy and practice.

Our Journey So Far

We have introduced you to a different approach to thinking that engages with the complexity of life in "Thinking *IN* the Systems of Life" (Chapter 2). Then we took you into non-directive ways of using language with clients as we explored "Unlocking Natural Connections" (Chapter 3) and "Language Principles" (Chapter 4). We have asked you to consider shifting the responsibility for therapeutic change to the client, so the client becomes the locus of control. As an extension to the Rogerian client-centered approach and reflection, we have asked you to consider being a *client-responsive* therapist, who *facilitates* their client's journey through observation and response, without instruction or direction. This approach allows the most effective therapy to *emerge* because the client is the central agent who is connecting to their own natural problem-solving and mind–body healing.

Instead of directing therapy, we ask the therapist to utilize the skills of sensitive observation to *observe, notice,* and *respond* to whatever might emerge into the therapeutic experience. Like a musician performing an improvisation, the therapist intuitively self-organizes their technical knowledge, academic study, and years of practice and experience to spontaneously produce what is needed and what is appropriate in that moment. Erickson often spoke of the uniqueness of every therapeutic experience. The therapy we utilize is best when it is in *response* to the client.[1] Clients *utilize us* – our knowledge, skills, and experience – to find their own natural problem-solving capacities and to generate mind–body healing. We are not healers, after all. We are, however, beautiful, natural, sensitively observing facilitators who help bring resolution and comfort to the lives of others and to our own lives. What a wonderful profession.

Natural

What is natural? Of all the things we might call natural – living things, inanimate things, trees, rivers, rocks, animals, birds, humans, and so much more – the most significant wonder is how all these things interact to produce a natural world. Before human beings developed a brain that could know, understand, and manipulate nature, the development of the natural world occurred without direction, purely from creative interaction.[2] About 13.8 billion years ago, an aggregation of just half a dozen forms of matter, the energy of heat and cooling, density, and time engaged in an interplay that eventually resulted in the emergence of hydrogen and helium atoms.[3] Reactions and interactions continued, constantly feeding emergent changes and creations back into the system, which triggered more change and development. Over billions of years, new properties, qualities, and quantities emerged to become the stars, the galaxies, the planets, and, on at least one planet, living organisms that changed and evolved over time into the many millions of species that live on Earth today.[4] These living species include one that not only knows it is alive, but also knows that it knows – humans are conscious of their consciousness (we are the modern human sub-species

1 Erickson, M. H. (2008). *The Collected Works of Milton H. Erickson, M.D.* Vol. 3: *Opening the Mind*, ed. E. L. Rossi, R. Erickson-Klein & K. L. Rossi. Phoenix, AZ: Milton H. Erickson Foundation Press.

2 Feistel, R. & Eberling, R. (2011). *The Physics of Self-Organization and Evolution*. Weinheim: Wiley-VCH.

3 Bertulani, C. A. (2013). *Nuclei in the Cosmos*. Singapore: World Scientific.

4 Darwin, C. (2008 [1859]). *The Origin of Species*. New York: Bantam Dell.

homo sapiens sapiens – the"ones who know, and know we know").[5] What an extraordinary journey from the existence of matter and energy to the emergence of sentient life. It is hard to imagine that the essential key to this process is such a simple, fundamental quality of complex adaptive systems: self-organization.[6]

Self-Organization is Natural Problem-Solving

Self-organization, as we described in Chapter 2, is one of the most important natural processes. It is how nature solves problems. Our inner implicit world is not dependent on cognitive direction and largely relies on natural self-organizing processes to successfully function.[7] Connecting explicit conscious, cognitive awareness with inner implicit processing is how we actively contribute to our survival and well-being. Before a thought emerges into consciousness numerous implicit processes occur. When the necessary preparation has self-organized there is a rise in emotional intensity that emerges as a conscious self-directing thought, such as *I'm hungry*.[8] Unfortunately, there are many things that interfere with a healthy flow between implicit processes and conscious awareness. Trauma, negative attitudes, pathological injuries, social problems, drugs, violence, and all too many more things interfere with that connection. The barriers, inhibitions, and dysfunctions are all part of the discomfort that motivates clients to seek therapy. Mirroring Hands is able to open that connection, and we know the connection has been opened when the client observes movement and sensations occurring in the hands *as if all by themselves*, independent of conscious thoughts and directions.

The connection that Mirroring Hands opens enables an in the moment, conscious awareness of the sensations that are emerging from internal processes. The client's appreciation of their own awareness usually starts when they become aware that their hands seem to be moving all by themselves. This is an indicator that the connection has been made. Once the connection has been made, it becomes possible to be aware of the ongoing inner processes that are emerging as thoughts, ideas, realizations, and even resolutions. These emergent properties and qualities enter into the client's consciousness in numerous ways. It might be in their felt experience, such as breathing changes, relaxation, or other shifts in energy levels; in emotive perceptions, such as relief, surprise, or happiness; or in beneficial thoughts, such as insight, understanding, or knowing what to do next. These therapeutic insights and realizations are the natural emergent properties and qualities of implicit

5 Siegel, D. J. (2016). *Mind: A Journey to the Heart of Being Human*. New York: W.W. Norton, p. 5.

6 Di Bernardo, M. (2010). Natural selection and self-organization in complex adaptive systems. *Rivista di Biologia*, 103(1), 89–110.

7 Camazine, S., Deneubourg, J-L., Franks, N. R., Sneys, J., Theraulaz, G. & Bonabeau, E. (2001). *Self-Organization in Biological Systems*. Princeton, NJ: Princeton University Press.

8 Scherer, K. R. (2009). Emotions are emergent processes: they require a dynamic computational architecture. *Philosophical Transactions of the Royal Society B: Biological Sciences*, 364(1535), 3459–3474.

problem-solving. The sudden insight into how to resolve the issue was not formed as thoughtful words *internally*, but the internal milieu produced a set of processes and activities in the brain that the conscious mind *translated* into a beneficial thought.

Problem-solving through self-organization occurs within the implicit inner space as a natural function of an adaptive complex system. Many of these processes occur at the molecular level, which is, of course, the domain of molecular and quantum physics. We address the quantum in Chapter 15 and in Appendix B, but bear in mind, as you consider the reasons behind your client's "strange" experience of their hands moving *as if all by themselves*, that this experience is arising from changes in the client's deep biology, including molecular activity in the chromosomes[9] and the interaction of ionically charged molecules in the neurons and synapses.[10] These *fluctuations* shift the balance of possibilities of the system to form probabilities in response to feedback and self-organization. In quantum theory, probabilities fluctuate as a result of changes to the waves of energy that are flowing through the possibility field.[11] Some of these probabilities become actualities and emerge into consciousness in ways that we can both observe and, at the same time, have a subjective feeling about. This subjective feeling is called *qualia*, which is similar to saying a *felt sense*.[12] We will discuss in Chapter 15 the finest subjective sensitivity, which we call our *quantum qualia*, but for now, as you can see, there is still so much for us to understand. We are *at the growing edge*.

It is not essential, however, to understand at a deep level in order to do good therapy, although it is both exciting and important as we move forward in the development and evolution of our understanding of psychotherapy and other healing arts. The following section describes an extraordinary piece of recent research which was a serendipitous opportunity that could not be missed. It gives us insight into the therapeutic advances that are possible when we learn how to tune in to inner processes that function at molecular and quantum levels of energetic activity. In this experiment, physical recordings of activity within the brain were made, which were then able to be translated by the researcher as what the subject was thinking.

---

9 Jorgensen, R. A. (2011). Epigenetics: biology's quantum mechanics. *Frontiers in Plant Science*, 2, 10. https://doi.org/10.3389/fpls.2011.00010.

10 Schwartz, J. M., Stapp, H. S. & Beauregard, M. (2004). Quantum physics in neuroscience and psychology: a neurophysical model of mind–brain interaction. *Philosophical Transactions of the Royal Society B: Biological Sciences*, 360, 1309–1327. doi:10.1098/rstb.2004.1598.

11 Krauss, L. M. (2011). *Quantum Man: Richard Feynman's Life in Science*. New York: W.W. Norton.

12 For a definition see: https://plato.stanford.edu/entries/qualia/.

Researching the Implicit Inner Space

Locked-in syndrome is the terrible situation in which an individual retains conscious mental awareness, while being trapped in a paralyzed and speechless body. In a small number of cases some very minor, almost unnoticeable, controlled movement has been found. In the well-known case of Jean-Dominique Bauby, it was discovered that he was able to control blinking in his left eye. He used that capacity to "dictate" his memoir, *The Diving-Bell and the Butterfly*, which was made into an acclaimed film.[13]

Niels Birbaumer and his team made a major breakthrough in communicating with locked-in patients.[14] In prior research with patients who have no explicit movement, researchers had been exploring implicit brainwave patterns. Unfortunately, none of the brain–computer interfaces used to date, such as EEG, produced a response better than chance. Birbaumer and his team added a measure of the changes in oxygenation in the frontocentral region of the brain using "functional near-infrared spectroscopy (*f*NIRS) and an implicit attentional processing procedure." In essence, oxygen levels increase when brain areas become active. Could this increase produce a distinct pattern for simple thoughts? Four patients were asked simple questions over several weeks to determine the oxygenation and the EEG pattern that persistently represented a "yes" or "no" answer. The researchers produced a greater than chance result of over 70% accuracy. When the patients were asked to respond to the statement, "I love to live" and "I feel happy," to the researchers' and the families' surprise, and relief, the patients answered "yes."

Evidence of the Implicit "Voice" and Mind-to-Body-to-Mind Communication

In summary, the researchers made a non-directive open-ended comment of which the patient was consciously aware but physically unable to answer. In Mirroring Hands, the therapist wonders whether the hand will drift down toward the client's lap without the client consciously directing it to do so. In the research, instead of looking for a conscious cognitive response, the brain–computer interface monitored the patients' implicit responses at the molecular energetic level. In Mirroring Hands, it is the movement of the hand, as if *all by itself*, that is the client's implicit response to inner processes at the molecular energetic level. The research patient's neural mechanisms and energy flow patterns in the brain, which include oxygenation patterns, self-organized into a state that was in concert with their conscious desire to answer "yes" or "no." The researcher was then able to translate

13 Bauby, J-D. (2009). *The Diving-Bell and the Butterfly*. London: Fourth Estate; *The Diving Bell and the Butterfly* (2007). [motion picture]. Dir. J. Schnabel. Paris: Pathé.

14 Chaudhary, U., Xia, B., Silvoni, S., Cohen, L. G. & Birbaumer, N. (2017). Brain–computer interface-based communication in the completely locked-in state. *PLOS Biology* 15(1), e1002593.

this EEG and oxygenation response as an emergent property that represented the word "yes" or "no." In Mirroring Hands, the internal state aligns with whatever is required for the brain to translate the implicit information into a beneficial thought, sensation, or activity that enables the client to create a beneficial change not only in their thinking but also in their quantum qualia and throughout their complex system of self.

This experiment shows mind-to-body-to-mind communication in action. It shows that implicit self-organizing processes occur beneath conscious cognitive awareness; that these properties can emerge as thoughts, ideas, emotions, and motivations; and that they can be utilized by the client to creatively facilitate their own ongoing beneficial change toward health and well-being. The client's inner world, which has been "paralyzed" and is unable to communicate, finds a way into conscious awareness through the Mirroring Hands process. Most therapists can see this unfolding as they observe the client. As tempting as it may be to inform and assist the client with our observations and knowledgeable opinions, the task of the therapist is not to be the one who *knows* about the client, but to facilitate the client's process of *knowing* about themselves.

It might seem surprising but the messages that emerge into consciousness are often quite simplistic and ambiguous. We have already discussed the simple sensation that arises from the complex set of implicit processes concerned with nutritional needs which results in the thought, *I'm hungry*. It seems that evolution has not selected for detailed conscious awareness of implicit processes. Our conscious mind only needs to know enough to stimulate a helpful response. We then respond to messages that emerge into our conscious awareness with actions (behaviors), thoughts (ideas), and emotions (affect).[15]

Our most attention grabbing sensation is pain. Pain is a ubiquitous sensation that urges us to do something to resolve or repair the cause.[16] Other behaviors are triggered by emergent sensations, like "tiredness" which directs us to rest or sleep, and "sickness" which prompts a complex set of behaviors commonly called "sickness behavior," which urges us to get rest, keep infection away from others, and eat chicken broth.[17]

Not all emergent sensations are about difficulties and problems. "Peacefulness" is an indicator of inner calmness and safety, and is one of the sensations during an ultradian healing response period. "Love" is a very simplistic conscious awareness of something that is more complex than can be described in hundreds of volumes. "Happiness," "pleasure," "satisfaction," "joy," and "contentment" are all positive sensations. These positive states invite, and enable, exploration and expansion at the growing edge to promote

---

15 This paper contains hundreds of interesting references regarding conscious and non-conscious processes: Morsella, E. & Poehlman, T. A. (2013). The inevitable contrast: conscious vs. unconscious processes in action control. *Frontiers in Psychology*, 4, 590. http://doi.org/10.3389/fpsyg.2013.00590.

16 Blom, J. H. G. (2017). Pain and attention. Thesis. University of Twente, Netherlands. doi:10.3990/1.9789036542715.

17 Dantzer, R. (2009). Cytokine, sickness behavior, and depression. *Immunology and Allergy Clinics of North America*, 29(2), 247–264. doi:10.1016/j.iac.2009.02.002.

what Barbara Fredrickson described as "broaden and build."[18] Expansion at the growing edge includes the development of new thoughts, ideas, and emotional states. It also includes all the implicit processes that are involved in the generation of those thoughts and ideas of which we are totally unaware.

We now know that positive states, which include the state created by Mirroring Hands, produce changes in gene expression,[19] which give rise to healthy activity of the immune system, promotion of cellular health, and stimulation of the endocrine system to produce the hormones that regulate our biology toward well-being.[20] The research that has discovered these inner processes is fascinating, but the most important message is that a therapist only needs to notice and respond to the natural messages emerging from the client to be confident that mind–body healing has been activated. There may come a time when we are able to monitor gene expression in real time to be sure, objectively, that positive mind–body healing is in progress. In the meantime, we are endowed with natural subjective feelings and sensations – quantum qualia – which guide our therapeutic confidence.

Comfort

Comfort is a very powerful message about what is happening within. However, comfort is a word whose meaning seems to have been hijacked in recent times. Comfort has come to be about life being easy, soft, absolutely no pain or struggle, unchallenging, and almost hedonistic. Nowadays, it seems more important, and even normal, to prefer an easy, "comfortable" life than to engage in the challenge of expanding at the growing edge. In fact, marketing and advertising highlight the "comforts" of a product as the most attractive qualities.[21] We are certainly not saying that comfort should be avoided, but it needs to be better understood. The verb "comfort" comes from the Latin *confortare*

18 Fredrickson, B. L. (2005). The broaden-and-build theory of positive emotions. In F. A. Huppert, N. Baylis & B. Keverne (Eds.), *The Science of Well-Being*, 216–239. Oxford: Oxford University Press. doi:10.1093/acprof:oso/9780198567523.003.0008.

19 Cozzolino, M., Cicatelli, A., Fortino, V., Guarino, F., Tagliaferri, R., Castiglione, S. et al. (2015). The mind–body healing experience (MHE) is associated with gene expression in human leukocytes. *International Journal of Physical and Social Sciences*, 5(5), 1–31. http://www.ijmra.us/2015ijpss_may.php.

20 Atkinson, D., Iannotti, S., Cozzolino, M., Castiglione, S., Cicatelli, A., Vyas, B. et al. (2010). A new bioinformatics paradigm for the theory, research, and practice of therapeutic hypnosis. *American Journal of Clinical Hypnosis*, 53(1), 27–46; Rossi, E. L., Iannotti, S., Cozzolino, M., Castiglione, S., Cicatelli, A., & Rossi, K. L. (2008). A pilot study of positive expectations and focused attention via a new protocol for optimizing therapeutic hypnosis and psychotherapy assessed with DNA microarrays: the creative psychosocial genomic healing experience. *Sleep and Hypnosis*, 10(2), 39–44.

21 Wibowo, J. (2016). Plush Sofas invites dogs onto the couch in new comfort campaign. *Mumbrella* (August 22). https://mumbrella.com.au/french-bulldog-finds-comfort-new-plush-sofas-ad-389603; Chaudhari, D. (2017). The advertising world hates women who are comfortable in their skin. *Feminism in India* (January 2). https://feminisminindia.com/2017/01/02/advertising-hates-women-comfortable-skin/; Samios, Z. (2017). Bonds tells tales of uncomfortable underwear in new Leos campaign for Comfytails. *Mumbrella* (February 6). https://mumbrella.com.au/bonds-tells-tales-of-uncomfy-undies-in-new-leos-campaign-424205.

which means "to strengthen greatly." In that context, to feel comfort is to feel strengthened. Equally, to help someone to strengthen is to give comfort. Comfort is achieved by easing or relieving those things or feelings that make you feel weak or that weaken. Unresolved physical pain, the pain of emotional distress, constraint and restriction, tension, worry, fear, shame, and guilt all cause discomfort. Easing and relieving any or all of these can produce a sensation of comfort, and that comfort enables someone to feel stronger, more capable, and able to find greater enjoyment of life.

When a client comes for therapy with the implicit stereotyped belief that a good life is *only* when things are easy and unchallenging, just as the advertisements tell us, then they are less likely to want to work hard to resolve their difficulties. Mirroring Hands bypasses this limitation by creating a strengthening comfort immediately: first, by being a very simple process and, second, by connecting with the client's strengths – their natural inner processes, cycles, and rhythms. In Mirroring Hands, we look to the sensation of comfort, in both client and therapist, as an important indicator that the difficulties and challenges of the process are being experienced in safety, with natural ease, and with a positive expectation that any struggle is worthwhile.

Comfort as a Message

Comfort has not been extensively researched. In positive psychology, Martin Seligman describes comfort as one of the positive emotions that is involved in the experience of authentic happiness.[22] The "comfort zone" is described by some as a psychological state of feeling at ease and in control of the environment, and experiencing low levels of anxiety.[23] The most detailed research comes from Katherine Kolcaba in the field of nursing.[24] She shows that healing and well-being are enhanced when medical care includes *giving comfort* to patients. If giving comfort enhances a patient's healing experience, then the person experiencing greater comfort must be producing changes in their implicit processes that are enhancing natural healing activity. Comforting actions that are added to the patient's experience feed back into the therapeutic system, triggering implicit activities that enable problem-solving and healing processes. The *feedback loop* of self-organization is how we produce mind-to-body-and-back-again-to-mind healing. The beneficial, problem-solving, and healing changes that occur implicitly through natural self-organization create new conditions within the system that emerge in the client's conscious awareness as the sense of comfort or of being comfortable.

Kolcaba shows that comfort includes physical ease and relief from distress. She found that when a patient's comfort needs are met, the patient is strengthened. This is indicated by reductions in

22 Seligman, M. E. (2013). *Authentic Happiness: Using the New Positive Psychology to Realize Your Potential for Lasting Fulfillment.* New York: Free Press.

23 Stutz, P. and Michels, B. (2012). The comfort zone. *Psychology Today* (May 8). https://www.psychologytoday.com/blog/the-tools/201205/the-comfort-zone.

24 Kolcaba, K. (2003). *Comfort Theory and Practice: A Vision for Holistic Health Care and Research.* New York: Springer.

pain, calming of emotional centers in the brain, and a shift from negative self feelings to feelings of self-efficacy. Clients in psychotherapy often report that when they feel they have more control, they feel more comfortable. Mirroring Hands, as we have shown, places great importance on the strength the client finds being the locus of control.

There are two essential ways in which Mirroring Hands engages the client's comfort:

1 Using encouraging, supportive, and non-directive language that helps the client to feel safe and at ease (see Chapter 4).

2 Using a client-responsive approach which allows the client to remain in touch with a personally oriented "comfort zone." By carefully attending to the client, the therapist can be aware of what is natural for the client, when and where the client feels safe, and provide rapid relief from distress.

As clients begin experiencing positive emotions, or are able to shift their focus away from the negative *toward* the positive, they often report feeling more comfortable. It simply makes sense to orient therapeutic activities to the strengths of the client. One of the most telling comments from a client is when they say something like, *"I'm comfortable with that"* or *"That works for me,"* even when the task is difficult or challenging. The basic accessing question connects with the client's permission and willingness to engage in therapy at the very outset, stepping past resistance and cognitive interference.

Clients describe the comfort they feel with their therapist in a number of ways: the comfort of being eased or relieved of their difficulty; being comfortable with the therapist, which is a natural response to an engaged, client-responsive therapeutic relationship; being comfortable with the therapeutic approach, which can be achieved through negotiation between therapist and client in a client-responsive manner; and their comfort being maintained during the therapeutic experience, which is managed by regularly checking in with the client, observing sensitively, and utilizing non-directive language. All these aspects of comfort are achievable during Mirroring Hands.

There are many more things happening within the client as they experience comfort. It is simply not possible to be consciously aware of those inner implicit processes. During Mirroring Hands there is a promotion of positive broadening and building, natural problem-solving, easing of distress, and changes in the energy and information flow patterns in brain and body. These self-organizing processes involve gene expression, protein synthesis, endocrine production, brain plasticity, and more. The entire system is acting together in a simultaneous cooperation of which the client is largely consciously unaware. Fortunately, the client can be confident that all these things are happening simply by noticing when they are feeling more comfortable.

The Therapist's Comfort

So far we have been addressing the client, but there is another important person who also needs to monitor their comfort – the therapist. Being comfortable during therapy is so important in helping to avoid the distress of therapist burnout, which is far too common. Ideally, therapists should feel comfortable in their work. Noticing feelings of discomfort in yourself, as the therapist, can be an early warning that the therapeutic experience is not going well, but often it can be a sensitivity to the client's proximity to a phase shift when a breakthrough is imminent.

Your discomfort can prepare you for client resistance and avoidance so that you can facilitate their progress toward breakthrough and stage 3. Whether you feel comfortable or uncomfortable, it is always good to regularly review the progress of therapy. Therapists can conduct their own inner review, check in with the client, and, at a later time, seek out a deeper exploration with a supervisor or colleague. Noticing the changing experience of comfort is a valuable indicator to enhance the quality of your facilitation of the client's therapeutic experience and of your own professional performance.

Sensitive Observation

What does *sensitive observation* mean? *Observation* is fairly straightforward – to be aware through careful and directed attention, but *sensitivity* is a word that is used in general language in a number of different ways. Broadly, it is a heightening of reactivity to stimuli, which might include emotions, light, movement, and other sensorial experiences. Jung described "innate sensitiveness" in 1913 as an innate predisposition to be affected by negative childhood experiences.[25] Sensitivity is often used in this context of fragility and negative affect. Sensitive people might be easily offended or feel like emotional sponges who both notice and absorb all the surrounding emotions. If the therapist is fragile and negatively affected by the client, then the therapeutic experience will suffer. It is not necessary to personally experience the client's pain or emotional struggle in order to be sensitive. If sensitivity to the client causes the therapist to feel pain or distress, then this is a clear message to seek out supervision or some other assistance. Unmanaged or unregulated sensitivity is a sure path to burnout, or what some call empathy or compassion fatigue. We suggest that therapeutic sensitivity is the *ability to notice subtle sensations and emotions.*

The operative word is *subtle*, meaning minimal, not obvious, delicate, and not easy to notice. When the two words, *sensitive observation*, are brought back together, the definition becomes the *activity of noticing, within the scope of the therapeutic environment, changes and shifts that might be very subtle*

25 Aron, E. J. (2004). Revisiting Jung's concept of innate sensitiveness. *Journal of Analytical Psychology*, 49(3), 337–367.

and not easy to notice. In Chapter 15 and Appendix B, we update how sensitivity on the quantum level ("the quantum qualia of human experience") can become a new inner resource that functions as a widening and deepening of consciousness. That new consciousness becomes a major asset for facilitating the current and future evolution of all schools of psychotherapy. Our Mirroring Hands protocol is, above all, an easy to learn method of heightening people's most valuable hidden potentials – their natural problem-solving and mind–body healing – for facilitating the quantum qualia of their consciousness and cognition, health, and well-being with the *quantum microscope* of their creative mind.

What We Do

The therapist's sensitive observation notices the emergent properties and qualities which are the indicators that the client is experiencing natural problem-solving and mind–body healing. This will include their overt emotions and thoughts as well as their implicit processes. Both explicit and implicit processes emerge as emotions, thoughts, behaviors, and reactions to the environment. The importance of sensitive observation is to be noticing all these expressions. The correct response becomes apparent at the time. We will show an example in a moment. Remember, there could be many things happening, some quite obvious, and others might be so subtle as to be almost imperceptible. The question then arises, "What if I miss something?" This is a reasonable question, and certainly this can happen, but usually there is enough that is noticed and being responded to for therapy to proceed productively. In our experience, we have never had a client complain about lack of sensitivity.

When teaching a Mirroring Hands workshop, one of the students asked about the recently completed demonstration: "Richard, when you asked the client if they *would like to share a word or two, or perhaps just continue with their private work*, was that because you noticed the volunteer's lips moving, ever so slightly?" To the student's surprise he answered, "No, I have no recollection of her lips moving at all." This prompted a valuable conversation on the nature of explicit and implicit noticing. The therapist also has emergent properties and qualities from implicit processes. A great deal goes on within, or non-consciously, before our conscious mind "catches up." Mirror neurons are just one of the extraordinary mechanisms in the brain that operate prior to conscious awareness.

Implicit, Explicit, and Mirror Neurons

We have known about the mirror neuron system since the mid-1990s. Rizzolatti and his team stumbled on the discovery that certain neurons will fire in the brain when we observe movement *as if we were making that movement ourselves* and that this occurs beneath conscious perception.[26] The mirror neuron response gives someone an implicit sense of the movement capacities, potentials, and intention of the other person (and to some extent of any moving life form). This is an innate system that allows us to make important decisions about safety, withdrawal, or attractiveness (approach) and a variety of perceptions about the other person. In subtle situations that don't require an overt action, like running away, people describe their toward or away "attitude" as being a "gut feeling."

We now understand that this is an emergent property – in this case a thought and attitude – from the complex implicit activity of the mirror neuron system. As we have mentioned before, emergent thoughts are often not very specific, but are helpful, providing the message is enough for us to begin a helpful action. The point of this lengthy example is that sensitive observation is occurring on an implicit level as well. There are other implicit perceptions, including emotional empathy and intuitive perceptions, where we may not notice what literally happens. We rely on our implicit processes to create an emergent property or quality to push into our conscious awareness.

We need to take this one step further: the client may also not be consciously aware of what has emerged, especially when it is a motor action. This includes body movements and facial expressions. It is the same process as when the hands move *all by themselves*. On inquiry, the volunteer in Richard's workshop reported that she was totally unaware that her lips were moving. That movement was an emergent property for her as well. The volunteer was very clear, however, that the timing of her being asked to share a word or two was absolutely perfect. It had allowed her to move forward in the Mirroring Hands experience in a way that very important for her. This is a good example of the difference between facilitating and directing. It is also a good example of how it is possible to trust our sensitive observation at the implicit level. Experience builds the therapist's confidence to follow and work with what arises spontaneously.

RH's Casebook: The Subtlety of Synchrony

Later in the same demonstration, the client began to shed tears and her nose also began to run. Initially, she seemed to be undisturbed by the messy fluids on her face and her eyes remained closed, so I didn't interfere. I had consciously observed her tears and gestured to the class for a tissue. A

26 Fadiga, L., Fogassi, L., Pavesi, G. & Rizzolatti, G. (1995). Motor facilitation during action observation: a magnetic stimulation study. *Journal of Neurophysiology*, 73, 2608–2611; Rizzolatti, G. & Craighero, L. (2004). The mirror neuron system. *Annual Review of Neuroscience*, 27, 169–192.

student put one in my hand. The volunteer continued and I waited patiently, with the tissue in my hand, resisting all temptation to interrupt her process by directly giving her the tissue. She was loudly narrating the memory that was playing out in her head. She was emotional, but very much in control of what she was doing and what she was saying. At some point our hands moved together simultaneously, she took the tissue, wiped her nose, and had a sudden breakthrough. She passed through the phase shift, which had been hanging in the balance for some 15 minutes, and into stage 3. Spontaneously, she opened her eyes and began to speak rapidly and excitedly of the revelation she had just received through the action of wiping her nose. We won't share the details here but it was a profound moment.

The same student asked, "How did you know when to give her the tissue? You held it close by for several minutes." My answer was the same as for the previous question, "Consciously, I can't tell you that I knew at all, although I expect that I was so closely in tune with the volunteer that I moved my hand forward in sensitive response to the movement her hand was making." The volunteer surprised us even more when she explained, "I needed that tissue at that exact moment. I can't remember whether I knew Richard was holding a tissue. In my mind's eye, there was a tissue floating right in front of me. I knew that all I needed to do was take it, wipe my own nose, and release myself from my dependence on ..." She continued to describe what she had released.

There are so many things that can be noticed when working with a client. Sensitive observation begins the moment the client enters your space and continues until they leave. Many things might transpire during the Mirroring Hands practice, but the Mirroring Hands approach encompasses the therapist's entire engagement with the client. An observed awareness and a felt sense of the client begins even before names are shared: how they walk, how they sit, where they sit, their direction of eye gaze, fluctuation in vocal tone, the words they use, how they breathe, when and how they shift position, little body movements, and changes in facial expression. The possibilities are endless. What you, the therapist, do is also vital: where you sit, when you move, how you conduct the initial intake, your first question, and so on. The client is noticing all these things, too, and responding to them in an explicit and implicit way.

The Nine Implicit Voices

In addition to this host of subtle possibilities that may be playing out during a session, there is always more. A list follows, that we will describe briefly, which we call the *nine implicit voices*. These are lifestyle and biological indicators that can add to your insight and awareness of the client. Wellness and movement toward health and well-being is something that occurs everywhere in someone's biology, and so indicators might come from unexpected or unusual places.[27]

27 Hill, R. (2006). *How the "Real World" Is Driving Us Crazy! Solving the Winner/Loser World Problem*. Sydney: Hill & Hill.

1 **Skin**: Pallid skin color is an indicator of poor circulation which can be from affective issues, such as depression, but also fear and especially anxiety/panic. Skin elasticity is an indicator of immune system health. Inelastic skin can indicate high inflammatory chemicals and oxidative stress. Both can be a response to excess cortisol from worry and distress.[28]

2 **Sleep**: Sleep is one of the most important factors in all health but especially mental health. Lack of sleep reduces tolerance to pain and can make life very uncomfortable. Mental disturbance is both caused by and causes poor sleep. The use of electronic devices before bed also negatively affects sleep.[29]

3 **Sun**: Sunlight is necessary for the production of vitamin D. Vitamin D can be ingested in food or supplements, but there is no substitute for the action of the sun. It is called a vitamin but is much more like a hormone (i.e. a messenger for cellular behavior). Vitamin D is transformed in the body to become a transcription factor in gene expression in the brain.[30]

4 **Sugar**: This is broadly about what people eat, but also specifically about how much and what type of sugar they eat. Weight gain is a stress on the body which adds numerous problem chemicals – for example, levels of cortisol and inflammatory chemicals rise. This also stimulates oxidative stress. Reducing dietary sugar is one of the easiest ways to improve mental health and strengthen the whole system.[31]

5 **Sitting**: This is about exercise. The majority of our biological tissue is dedicated to one thing – helping us move. Large areas of our brain are involved in motor activity. It is natural to move about and unnatural not to. Many of the chemicals in the body that are now causing us problems are naturally catabolized during exercise. Increasing movement and activity is another simple way to relieve depression.[32]

6 **Stress**: Stress has so many expressions in the brain and body which change the mindset and the state of consciousness. Short term stress, resolved within an ultradian cycle or two, is not particularly damaging, but ongoing stress becomes a confusion and disorientation. Reducing stress is readily achieved with Mirroring Hands and utilizing the ultradian healing response.[33]

---

28 Fried, R. G. (2013). Nonpharmacologic management of psychodermatologic conditions. *Seminars in Cutaneous Medicine and Surgery*, 32(2), 119–125.

29 Milojevich, H. M. & Lukowski, A. F. (2016). Sleep and mental health in undergraduate students with generally healthy sleep habits. *PLOS ONE*, 11(6), e0156372.

30 Humble, M. B. (2010). Vitamin D, light and mental health. *Journal of Photochemistry and Photobiology B: Biology*, 101(2), 142–149.

31 Devlin, M. J., Yanovski, S. Z. & Wilson, G. T. (2013). Obesity: what mental health professionals need to know. *American Journal of Psychiatry*, 157(6), 854–866.

32 Sharma, A., Madaan, V. & Petty, F. D. (2006). Exercise for mental health. *Primary Care Companion to the Journal of Clinical Psychiatry*, 8(2), 106.

33 Chetty, S., Friedman, A. R., Taravosh-Lahn, K., Kirby, E. D., Mirescu, C., Guo, F. et al. (2014). Stress and glucocorticoids promote oligodendrogenesis in the adult hippocampus. *Molecular Psychiatry*, 19, 1275–1283.

7 **Sex**: Libido can be a readily noticeable indicator of mental and biological health. Illness, stress, affective disorders, PTSD, and harbored trauma all contribute stress based chemicals into the system that negatively affect libido. The client's sexual activity can be a ready indicator of improvement or decline.[34]

8 **Pain**: Pain is the dominant stimulus for someone to act. Pain is felt in both physical and emotional situations. Social rejection registers in the pain centers of the brain and can be a useful indicator in issues of self-esteem and family/social connections.[35]

9 **Face**: The face tells us a million things. Facial expressions often tell us what someone is thinking before they know they are thinking it. The ability to recognize faces and facial expressions is important to mental health, social inclusiveness, and managing in life. Testing can be used, but sensitive observation of how the client responds to facial cues during therapy can give some indication too.[36]

All Too Hard

Being aware of all these myriad behaviors, emotions, thoughts, explicit and implicit responses, and so much more might seem daunting, and the question might even emerge, "Do I really need to know all these things, especially if I can easily follow the manual of a recognized therapy?" That, of course, is something that only the individual can answer, but it might be interesting to recall a conversation between Ernest Rossi and Milton Erickson back in the 1970s. The following exchange, and many more wonderful papers and transcriptions, is published in volume 3 of the 16 volume set, *The Collected Works of Milton H. Erickson*.

Erickson, his friend Dr. Marion Moore and I (ER) had spent some time discussing how to be a good therapist. We discussed the myriad of cues and clues that emerge during the therapeutic experience. Erickson and Moore insisted that everything from minor facial expressions to metaphors to a casual comment can provide a rich resource. They counseled that a good therapist has an open heart, an open mind, subjective and objective awareness, a keen sense of noticing and the ability to see the illumination of the path to enlightenment for both patient and therapist.

34 See: http://www.healthline.com/health/depression/sexual-health#overview1.

35 Gatchel, R. J. (2004). Comorbidity of chronic pain and mental health disorders: the biopsychosocial perspective. *American Psychologist*, 59(8), 795–805.

36 Wolf, K. (2015). Measuring facial expression of emotion. *Dialogues in Clinical Neuroscience*, 17(4), 457–462.

The final words of the conversation capture it, in all its simplicity:

> *Rossi: So we have to find out how to read faces. We have to find out how to read inflection of words, minimal cues that the patient gives about their underlying problem. That's what this is all about.*
>
> *Erickson: Yes.*
>
> *Rossi: That's a lot of work! You don't just sit there and talk and empathize.*
>
> *Erickson: Yes!*[37]

37 Rossi, E. L. & Rossi, K. L. (2008). Novel activity-dependent approaches to therapeutic hypnosis and psychotherapy. In *The Collected Works of Milton H. Erickson, M.D.* Vol. 3: *Opening the Mind*, ed. E. L. Rossi, R. Erickson-Klein & K. L. Rossi. Phoenix, AZ: Milton H. Erickson Foundation Press, p. 278.

Chapter 8

Holding Both Sides of the Mirror

Revealing Potential and Possibility

ER: Then later I would generalize it, "If you have your problem in one hand, what do you have in the opposite hand?" What's the opposite of a problem? Well, obviously, a solution! So, if this is the problem, what is happening in the other hand is the opposite – a cure or a-ha experience of psychological insight or stage 3 of the creative cycle. Then the word "opposite" became very important in my mind, just as it was for Carl Jung.

From the Rossi/Hill conversations, June 2016

In this chapter, we utilize Mirroring Hands to help the client see the other side of their problem. The old expression, "Can't see the wood for the trees," is exactly what happens to most of us when overwhelmed by problems, difficulties, and struggles. If the problem can be pushed to *one side*, allowing for the possibility of something else coming into the *other side*, then the client has a much better chance of finding a solution, rather than being stuck in the problem. To separate or find a distinction between the parts is to *differentiate*. This form of Mirroring Hands can separate, or differentiate, to produce the fundamental essence of both the *problem* and *not the problem*.

When the problem dominates, the client creates a *problem dominated system* which is more likely to allow difficulties, stresses, and emotional disruptions to emerge. It is important to appreciate that self-organization and emergence function regardless of whether they produce a positive or a negative outcome. Self-organization responds to the qualities of the feedback. Differentiating the elements of the system, however, is not reductionism. It is separating the parts so they can be explored independently. The parts are not disconnected, just differentiated.

We can learn why this helps from Ilya Prigogine, the Nobel Laureate who developed the concept of self-organization in complex systems based on his studies of the second law of thermodynamics. He described the benefits of differentiation in this way:

> differentiation between different parts of a system, or between the system and its environment [means that] ... further processes that would be impossible in an undifferentiated medium may be switched on ... to manifest its *potentialities*. [Differentiation is] ... a prerequisite to *information*.[1]

Differentiation releases, or unlocks, the possibilities inherent in the individual part(s). When the parts are entwined/entrained/embedded in the product of the whole system, they lose their

1 Nicolis, G. & Prigogine, I. (1989). *Exploring Complexity: An Introduction*. New York: W.H. Freeman, p. 74 (italics added).

individual states and become part of a new combination, which has its own expression and possibilities. A simple example is when a musician isolates a small section of the music and works with just that part to see what emerges. Once all the richness of that part has been discovered, the newly enriched section is reintegrated into the larger piece. In the same way, an actor will work with just a word, a phrase, or a scene in a script and explore the possibilities within that fragment. Many of the possibilities of that fragment of the play can be lost when embedded in the complete script. Again, we stress that we are not speaking of reductionism. The fragment is never considered to be a complete script. It is only differentiated in order to explore the particular scope of possibilities, then the enriched fragment is linked back into the larger work to become an integrated collective again. The same applies to the client's narrative – that is, their "script of life."

It may seem counter-intuitive to be separating parts of the problem when the client is most likely already suffering from dissociations and disintegration. There is, however, an important difference between dissociation and differentiation. *Dissociation* is about a detachment that makes interaction and integration impossible. The barriers, disruptions, and interferences are maintained in a negative feedback loop by the problem, which might include traumas, pathological problems, and negative attachment. *Differentiation,* in the context we are using it here, is the process of distinguishing and temporarily isolating integrated parts in order to examine their individual qualities.

Even a simple differentiation into two elements can stimulate new information and new perspectives that can turn the whole problem around to make resolution and recovery possible. The form of Mirroring Hands we teach in this chapter allows the client to safely explore any number of differentiated opposites – off/on, isn't/is, can't/can, problem/not problem, failure/not failure, barrier/open, difficult/easy, and so on.

Using Mirroring Hands to reveal polarities can open up possibilities in many difficult therapeutic situations:

- *Pain management* is very often focused on the pain. Mirroring Hands allows the client to place the pain in one hand, creating the reasonable question of what is in the other. The pain can be differentiated with regard to the location, especially non-specific peripheral neuropathy.[2] The pain's intensity can be placed in one hand and a lower intensity into the other. How can the client shift themselves from the high intensity hand to the lower?
- *Addiction* can totally overwhelm all other thoughts. Differentiating *addiction* from *not addiction* can open the client to remember all those things that are not the addiction and are overpowered by the addiction. This is often very effective because it brings up family, being loved, health, and safety. It is also possible to differentiate the elements of the addiction between the hands. It can be possible to explore the pleasant side of the addiction and the

2 See the peripheral neuropathy fact sheet at: https://www.ninds.nih.gov/Disorders/Patient-Caregiver-Education/Fact-Sheets/Peripheral-Neuropathy-Fact-Sheet.

unpleasantness of the side effects. Perhaps the fingers can be used to create a more complex differentiation.

- *Somatic responses* appear spontaneously and can be an indicator of something very important. Examples are a movement in one part of the body, changes in breathing, sudden stiffness, sudden awareness of an odor, and gut reactions. The hands can be used to explore the somatic response, the specific body location, or whatever is expressed. In one hand is the noticed somatic sensation/activity. What is in the other hand?

In describing how to explore the polarities, the opposites, we will, again, first show the basic four question stages, then we will explore more literally how those questions flow in practice. Finally, we will share some case studies.

Hands Polarity: Four Stages of the Creative Process – Converting a Problem into a Resource

Stage 1: Information – Initiating Sensations

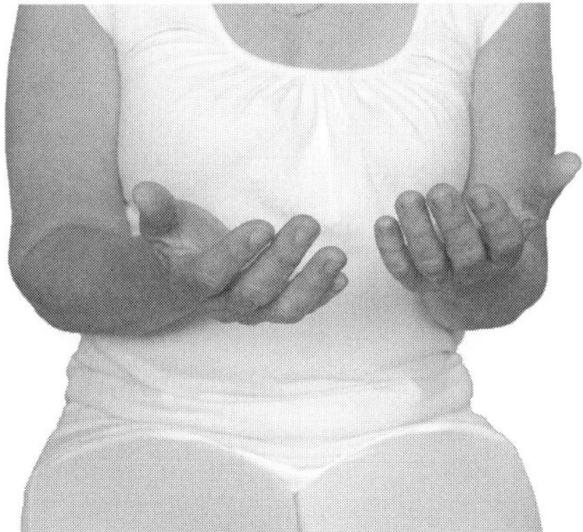

When you are ready to do some important inner work on that problem, will you place your hands with your palms up as if you are ready to receive something?

As you focus on those hands, in a sensitive manner, I wonder if you can begin to know which hand seems to experience or express that fear (or whatever the negative side of the client's conflict may be) more than the other? Will that hand make some kind of movement to show it is the hand that is holding that fear (or whatever)?

Stage 2: Incubation – Arousal, Feeling

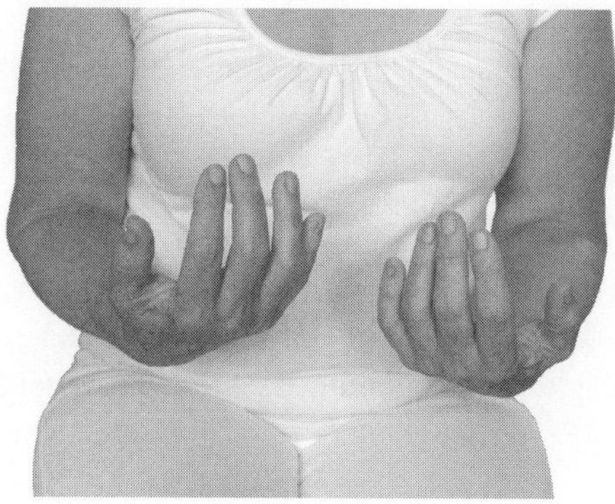

Wonderful … now I wonder what you experience in your other hand by contrast at the same time?

Wonderful … I wonder how you might experience both sides of yourself at the same time! Can you can let yourself continue to experience both sides together and explore what begins to happen between them? I wonder how those hands might interact with each other? Will those hands move toward each other or perhaps away, or in some way that only the two sides of the problem know how to do? … Will it be OK to share a word or two about what begins to happen? Or will you just continue your inner work privately?

Stage 3: Breakthrough and Illumination – Insight, Intuition

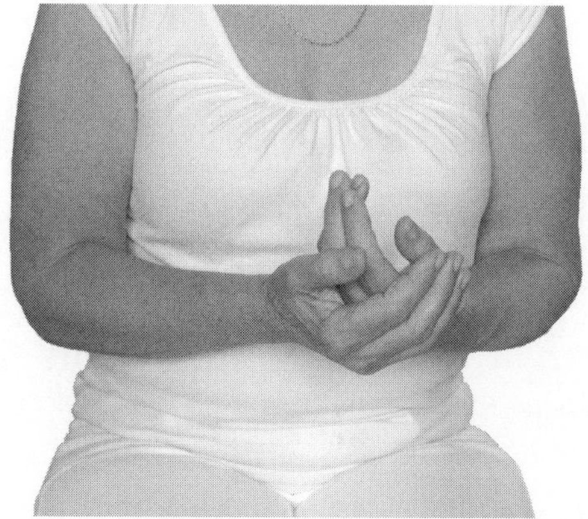

Interesting?

Something changing?

Is it really possible?

Good … now can you let yourself continue to experience both sides of your "self" in those hands at the same time … in this new way … with what you have suddenly realized … becoming aware … Will it be OK to share with me a word or two about what begins to happen between them? Or just continue your wonderful work privately …

Stage 4: Verification – Reintegration, Thinking

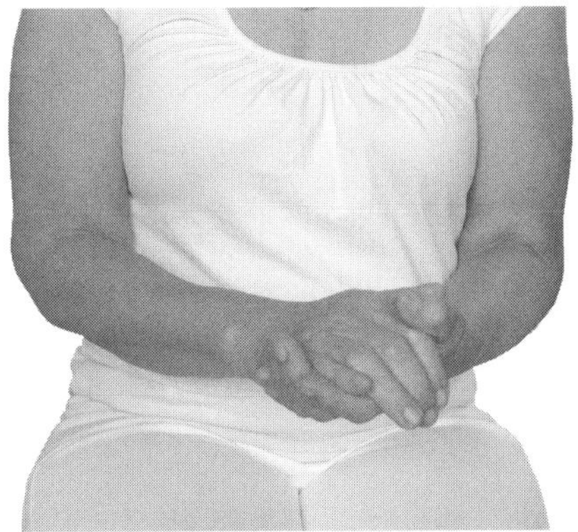

What does all that mean to you?

How will your life be different now?

How will your behavior change now?

What will you do that is different now?

Let us now explore this process more deeply and in more detail.

Stage 1: Information – Voluntary Engagement and Hand Differentiation

This preparation is much shorter than the formal version we described in Chapter 3. It is a way to quickly bring the client into the process and shift the locus of control toward the client. This is a useful method for a few reasons, including that you may feel that the client is not inclined to engage in a lengthy preparation. It is also effective for a client who is familiar with Mirroring Hands and is likely to engage quickly.

When you are ready to do some important inner work on that problem, will you place your hands with your palms up as if you are ready to receive something …

It is always helpful for the therapist to demonstrate along with the client. This helps the client who is unsure and reinforces the action implicitly through mirror neurons. This helps to build rapport and engagement between therapist and client. Also, always be client-responsive. The client may choose to begin the process but not want to put the hands palms up. They may want to go palms down. If the client is agreeing to engage, but also determining some of the process, then that shows they are taking on the locus of control, which is exactly what we want!

As you focus on those hands, in a sensitive manner, I wonder if you can begin to know which hand seems to experience or express that fear (or whatever the negative side of the client's conflict may be) more than the other? Will that hand make some kind of movement to show it is the hand that is holding that fear (or whatever)?

Even if you remain alert and in sensitive observation you may still miss very subtle cues. If the client seems to be ready to move forward or is waiting for you, it is reasonable to simply ask if they are ready to move on. The client will usually respond with a nod or shake of the head.

Stage 2: Incubation – Allowing the Opposites to be Experienced and Interact

As soon as the client acknowledges that one hand seems to express the negative aspect of their conflict, it is a sign that they have made some kind of connection with the previously unconscious or hidden dynamics of their conflict. The client has, in effect, given up their usual outer reality orientation and is now engaging and responding to their inner realities as they might in a dream or fantasy. The therapist continues by evoking a contrasting, opposite, and what is usually more positive side of the conflict. The client is challenging themselves to realize and acknowledge what is "not the problem."

Wonderful … now I wonder what you experience in your other hand by contrast at the same time?

When the client responds by labeling or describing a contrasting experience in the other hand, the therapist then continues to engage the dynamics of the client's conflict:

Wonderful … I wonder how you might experience both sides of yourself at the same time! Now I wonder if you can let yourself continue to experience both sides together and explore what begins to

> *happen between them? I wonder how those hands might interact with each other? Will those hands move toward each other or perhaps away, or in some way that only the two sides of the problem know how to do? … Will it be OK to share a word or two about what begins to happen? Or will you just continue your inner work privately?*

Clients typically respond with a series of uncertain hand movements and may begin to verbalize experiences as their emotions, symptoms, and inner conflicts become engaged. It sometimes seems as if clients are "acting out" their conflicts in a self-directed, mythopoetic adventure within the safe boundaries of the experimental "theater" of Mirroring Hands. Their experience may be symbolic and even unreal and extraordinary. Simply allow the client to pursue whatever is naturally emerging for them. Clearly, we are focusing attention on the hands, but the client might have a response anywhere in the body in any number of ways. Remain observant and sensitive. The therapist's task is to simply observe how the client seems to become *entranced* with their own spontaneous and semi-autonomous experience of *transforming* their inner conflicts into more or less involuntary observable behavior. Clients will often go through a mildly cathartic process during which they may express anguish and pain along with the relevant psychodynamics of their problems. Their head, eyes, hands, arms, and fingers sometimes seem to move in an involuntary manner, characteristic of automatic handwriting or finger signaling, which has been well described by Rossi and Cheek.[3] Continue to respond to the client with supportive and encouraging words as seems appropriate.

Whenever a client is working hard in stage 2 there is the imminent possibility of a breakthrough occurring spontaneously. How that breakthrough manifests is, of course, unpredictable. The important thing is to be right there with the client acknowledging and reinforcing any positive changes.

Stage 3: Breakthrough – Opening Up to Possibilities; and Illumination – Interactive and Positive Exploration

There is often a particular moment when the client shows a radical shift, although it can also be a bit more gradual with a number of small shifts that collectively produce a major shift. Sometimes the client will speak to you, at other times they express this facially and physically. Breakthrough supportive comments recognize that something significant is shifting:

> *Interesting?*
>
> *Something changing?*
>
> *Is it really possible?*

3 Rossi, E. L. & Cheek, D. B. (1988). *Mind–Body Therapy: Ideodynamic Healing in Hypnosis.* New York: W.W. Norton.

Clients usually function on many psychological levels at the same time. On one level they are experiencing and moving in a more or less involuntary manner. On another level they are simultaneously observing themselves and responding to spontaneously generated inner forces and fantasies. On yet another level they are apparently directing their own psychotherapeutic inner work and describing it to the therapist. The exact dialogue you might use will vary depending on the client. We will give some case examples shortly. In principle, you will want to use words that facilitate the client's continuing exploration of this new inner self-organization.

> *Good … now can you let yourself continue to experience both sides of your "self" in those hands at the same time … in this new way … with what you have suddenly realized … becoming aware … Will it be OK to share with me a word or two about what begins to happen between them? Or just continue your wonderful work privately …*

Simply allow the client to continue their private work and respond to whatever they might choose to communicate about their experience. Again, depending on the client, you may feel it is best to help them to return to alertness with the process we have previously described (*When … Some part of you knows that …* etc.) or the client will spontaneously bring themselves back to the room and ready themselves to talk about their experience. If the client chooses to quietly and privately explore their experience, just be with them in whatever way is appropriate.

Stage 4: Verification – Integration and Reality Testing

> *What does all that mean to you?*
>
> *How will your life be different now?*
>
> *How will your behavior change now?*
>
> *What will you do that is different now?*

Allow the client to express themselves in whatever way gives them comfort and a sense of where they are heading and how they might approach life now. Remind the client that their natural ultradian rhythm will give them numerous opportunities, as many as one every two hours or so, to continue their conscious and non-conscious integration of these new discoveries and realizations.

Casebook Examples

ER's Casebook: Fear and Fantasy

Stage 1: Information – Data Collection, Initiation

A scholarly looking young man complained of feeling weak and being a failure. He was directed to the initial palms-up hand position, *Can you tell me which hand feels weaker and more of a failure at this moment?* After a moment of self-reflection he hesitantly acknowledged that his right hand felt a bit weaker. I then asked, *And what do you experience in your other hand by contrast?* He took a slow deep breath and admitted the other side seemed lost in daydreams of heroic adventures.

Stage 2: Incubation – Arousal

Wonderful, how you can experience both sides of yourself at the same time! Now, I wonder if you can let yourself continue to experience both sides together and explore what begins to happen between them? The "weaker" right hand began to tremble and after a few moments I asked, *My goodness is that hand really trembling all by itself?* Blushing somewhat, the young man admitted that the right hand was shaking all by itself because it was so nervous about a fantasy that the left hand was experiencing. I deeply respected his privacy by not asking him to tell me what his fantasy was. Instead, I quietly supported his obvious struggle by asking, *I wonder if you have the courage to allow that to continue privately within yourself for another moment or two so you can experience what takes place next?* His eyes closed at this point and many private emotions crossed his face as his hands slowly approached each other and then retreated just before they touched.

Stage 3: Breakthrough and Illumination – Insight

The hands eventually touched in a seemingly accidental manner and, as they did so, his entire body went through a slight startle response. I quietly questioned, *Quite a surprise?* He merely nodded his head slowly a few times as the hands now touched each other again and again in a tentative, exploratory manner. After a few minutes the left "fantasy" hand covered the fearful and still trembling right hand. After a few moments the trembling stopped and the anxious expression on his face was replaced by calm and perhaps even the slightest of smiles. After a few more moments, when his apparently calm and satisfactory state seemed stabilized, I quietly asked, *And is that now going well?* After about 30 seconds of delay he silently nodded his head yes and asked, *I wonder if that is really possible?*

After a few more minutes of silent inner contemplation he finally opened his eyes, stared at the floor, and slowly stretched and touched himself on the arms, head, sides, and legs, which is very characteristic of people coming out of a hypnotherapeutic state.

To my silent look of inquiry he described how he had been reading recently that humans are essentially "herd animals" who take comfort in each other's presence and touch. In his apparently spontaneous inner work, he explored an inner drama of how it might be possible to touch a young woman he had met recently "without acting like a creep and offending her." He explained how he finally imagined going on a hike with her, and as they moved through more and more difficult terrain their hands might reach out to each other and then finally touch to support each other.

Stage 4: Verification – Reintegration

The final stage of this therapeutic session was to engage the young man in a discussion about the possibility that he could in fact ask his woman friend out for just such a hike in reality. He acknowledged that he could and would. At the same time, his left fantasy hand kept grasping his formerly trembling but now calm right hand. After a few moments of such absent-minded "hand play" he looked up at me sheepishly and said, *Such stuff as dreams are made on.*[4] We both smiled, stretched, looked at the clock, and realized it was time for the session to end.

We spent the next few sessions discussing how his occasional feelings of being weak and lost in fantasy were actually indications that he was going into a creative state of introversion during which he needed to experience and recognize how he needed to take new steps to move forward in his life. His previous "symptoms" of being a weak failure, lost in fantasy, was thereby reframed into a creative resource. Instead of rejecting his fantasies, he treated them as important *messages* from his intuitive self about his strengths and positive planning ideas.

RH's Casebook: Not Knowing

Stage 1: Information – Data Collection, Initiation

A man in his early thirties was struggling with his relationship. He and his partner decided to separate for a short time to see if they could work out if the relationship would survive. We had established a number of important issues through preliminary discovery conversations. He struggled with not knowing what to do, what his partner was really thinking, and whether he really wanted to rekindle the relationship or not. He was so used to making decisions and getting on with

4 Shakespeare, W. (1998). *The Tempest.* Oxford: Oxford University Press, Act IV, Scene 1, lines 1887–1888.

things, but now he felt lost and disempowered, out of control. We kept coming back to the same issue – he doesn't know.

I asked him if he might like to explore what he doesn't know. He nodded. *When you are ready to look into the world of what you don't know, will you lift your hands up in front of you?* He immediately raised his hands. I purposely didn't ask whether he wanted palms up or down as I knew he was already committed to the process and I wanted to minimize my influence. *Which hand do you feel is the hand that holds what you don't know?* He stared intently at his hands and moved the hands up and down as if weighing them up. After about minute of this the right hand stopped bouncing, and he showed he had decided on the left hand as the hand that doesn't know. He didn't look to be totally comfortable and so I asked, *I wonder if you have some feeling in your hand of what you don't know? A color ... a shape ... a texture...?* His fingers wiggled for a moment or two and he said, *Like ... nothing ... smoke ... empty ... inside me, empty ... painful ...* Not wanting him to upset himself, I shifted his focus.

Stage 2: Incubation – Arousal

OK, that's wonderful, you are really feeling what it is to not know ... But if you turn your attention to your other hand, I wonder what you are holding in that hand? After a moment he replied, *What I do know. Ah!* I respond with surprise, *That makes sense. I wonder what it feels like to hold both of those, at the same time ... what your hands have to say to each other?* His hands begin to bounce again, as if weighing each other up in this new context. I asked if he wished to share a word or two, but he quietly and privately continued to weigh up his hands.

Stage 3: Breakthrough and Illumination – Insight

After about 10 minutes his hands suddenly stopped bouncing. I said something simple to assure him that I was noticing, *Yes ... something important ...* His hands remained still, his face showed deep concentration, then he suddenly opened his eyes, in full awareness of me and being in the room, and said, *I know what I know ...* I simply encourage, *Wonderful!* He continued, *What I know is ... that I don't know. That's crazy! I know I really need to know, and what is making me so upset is that I don't know, but that is what I know ... I know I don't know.* I encouraged and facilitated his continuing realizations. *What an amazing revelation ... how incredible ... because you have talked about this quite a bit, but now you bring them together and suddenly it's ...* I left him to complete the sentence. After a moment's pause, he said, *It makes sense. I don't want to be in charge of my partner, but I do that, I know I do that. Can I really be in charge, but in charge of* not knowing? *I just have to wait ... wait ... If I push for facts and details now I'm just going to ruin everything ... I have to be patient. I know that now.*

Stage 4: Verification – Reintegration

We spent another 15–20 minutes talking about how this new realization could be practiced to help his relationship issue. He spontaneously began to talk about how this would help him at work as well. I reminded him that he might continue to process this, especially overnight. I suggested that he record his early morning thoughts for the next few days and we could discuss those and other things that might come up during the next few days at his next visit. We met four more times. We utilized this polarity, using Mirroring Hands, at various times to explore a few more "opposites" – *separating/staying together, being alone/having another relationship, letting his partner decide/making the decision himself*. In the end, his partner decided there was no recovery possible. The last two sessions were spent dealing with that pain, so we explored *pain/not pain*, each process revealing and helping him to repair himself and build his personal strength.

Review

The evolution of psychotherapeutic technique from Freud to Erickson over the past 100 years has been away from direct suggestion and programming toward the facilitation of mind–body communication within the client. The therapeutic innovations of this century increasingly avoid outside influence so the client has an opportunity to explore the *critical phase transitions* of their own evolving personality and consciousness. In Mirroring Hands, as soon as the client acknowledges experiencing two or more sides of their symptom, problem, or personality in different hands or parts of the body, the therapist can assume that the process of inner connection has been successfully engaged. The client's inner dynamics are primed for a self-therapeutic engagement to take place. The therapist then merely wonders aloud what will happen next between the different forces or parts that are being experienced and encourages whatever autonomous psychodynamic process that evolves, more or less, all by itself.

After about 10–20 minutes of inner self-encounter many clients spontaneously remark, with a sense of satisfaction, that the inner process is now over – but sometimes with disappointment. They feel satisfied when they sense they have received an important insight. They can also be wistfully disappointed when they feel they have received something of value, but they feel, intuitively, that there is much more that needs to come. This disappointment is not surprising in the context of people thinking in a linear way – *I solve this one problem and then I no longer have a problem*. This thinking ignores the complexity of the larger system of which the problem is just a part. The beauty, however, is that when we think *in* the system it is so much more exciting. We can be *comfortable* in knowing that there is more to do. In fact, we can assume that all kinds of different things might emerge when even one problem is resolved. For the therapist, it is enough to warmly support the client's reality of the moment.

Some clients solve significant problems. Others make some progress, but they need more time for their inner world to synthesize the new realities of their evolving relationship to themselves. The most important learning for the client is to recognize that there is an ongoing activity that is their inner creative experience. They have done more than just solve a single problem. It is often helpful to remind them of the four stages of the creative process and their ultradian rhythm so the client can appreciate the ongoing evolution that is taking place within themselves.

The benefits that occur from creating a deeper and more comfortable relationship with the self is obvious when we see clients, and ourselves, making connections between the outer and inner worlds. We see this happening physically during Mirroring Hands when the hands seem to move *all by themselves*. This begs the question, why do so many people feel disconnected from themselves and from others? Certainly, personal trauma, insecure attachments, or other individual issues in life can cause this, but personal and social disconnection seems so much more widespread. Is something else happening that creates disconnection? And if there is, what can we do to counteract it? That is what we will explore in the next chapter. Is there an elephant in the room? Yes, there is. Is there a way to get rid of the elephant and turn on an interested and integrating state of being? Yes to that too.

Chapter 9

Curiosity and the Elephant in the Room

What We Miss

ER: … people have problems. Why? Because they don't know how to listen to themselves and their own impulses, their own truth, their own myth. Why don't people all follow their inner passion? Because the outside world overwhelms them …

RH: This is the winner/loser idea of mine …

ER: So, I don't think I ever wrote it, but the basic human problem is that too many people have lost their voice. No one told you to be a poet when you were a child … it's the educational system … reliance on group testing and competition … the competition for who is going to be the dominant voice, rather than who has the most sensitive understanding … who is going to see the world in a new light – like Einstein …

… people have problems not because they have problems, but because nobody taught them how to respect their own genius.

From the Rossi/Hill conversations, June 2016

This chapter explores two important elements of experience: one that interferes with our capacity to engage with and enjoy life – *the winner/loser world* – and another which turns on those capacities and is fundamental to Mirroring Hands – *curiosity*. We first describe the disturbing corruption of winning and losing that pushes people into a protective, defensive, and isolating consciousness. The second part dives deep into the multiple forms of curiosity and how curiosity can shift consciousness from disrupting to therapeutic and then on to the integrating consciousness of well-being. Curiosity supports us as we expand at the growing edge. We will explore the wonders of curiosity in the second part of the chapter, but perhaps we should get the "elephant in the room" out of the way first.

The Winner/Loser World

How often do we see clients who are embarrassed about what they wear because they can't afford the current fashion? Do you see clients who worry about what the neighbors think or whether they have a good enough job? Have you met parents who stress over the future success of their kids? Do you see kids who are buckling under the pressure of all their extra-curricular activities, from summer school to gymnastics to dance classes and more? Do you hear people yearning to know how to get a win in this world, who are frustrated and disappointed with themselves when people call them a loser? Do you know people who live their lives by what they read in magazines or see on television? Something has happened to how people determine their worth and value in the world. The measure has shifted from our personal growth and development as we do our best to face the challenges of life, to whether we are good enough to live up to the expectations and needs of the outside world. Losing has become a sign of failure and winning has become the necessary way to gain approval and acceptance. The locus of control has shifted.

Although many seek therapy for help with personal, traumatic, disturbing, and disrupting events that have become emotional and psychological problems, something else is also happening that seems to affect just about everybody. Regardless of the personal difficulties in someone's past, almost everyone will feel, at times, that they are not good enough or not "measuring up" to what they believe the world expects of them. The outside world – the society and culture in which we live – can be so demanding that it can become overwhelming. For some people this feeling can be just a passing difficulty, but for others, especially for those who already have personal issues, it is a constant pressure that negatively affects their feelings of self-esteem and self-worth, and often leads to even more serious problems. Even more concerning is that these "external" pressures are so common and so pervasive that they have become background assumptions in daily living. Somehow, it has become normal for many people to *only* feel OK about themselves when favorably judged by the standards that other people set or that society demands. We are under pressure to "win." To be judged a failure is to be a "loser." It seems that it is no longer about doing your best but about winning or losing. We call this social environment of externalized expectation and judgmentalism the *winner/loser world*.

Eric Berne discussed the terms winner and loser in the mid-1960s in relation to transactional analysis.[1] It might be that the words have taken on different meanings since then, but there is a fundamental difference in these views. Berne describes winners as those who are able to manage, even when errors are made, whereas losers lack self-efficacy and the mental state to learn and grow. We don't make the distinction between winners and losers, but identify a winner/loser mindset that affects those who struggle to win *for fear of losing* and those who will do whatever they can to escape losing in order to be a winner. The group that Berne called winners are described in the winner/

1 Berne, E. (1996 [1970]). *Games People Play: The Basic Handbook of Transactional Analysis*. New York: Ballantine Books.

loser world theory as those who take on challenges, learn, and grow, regardless of the external evaluation of success or failure.

Most people reading this will have sat for an exam and know that it can be a difficult and stressful time. How much stress and anxiety did you feel about the need to get a high score? If you received a low score, did you think about the people who would be disappointed or who you had let down, and were you afraid of what they might think of you? Was an opportunity withheld, did you feel bad about yourself that you had failed, or that you were you to blame or at fault about what went wrong? Did you feel shame or guilt for not meeting expectations? Did you feel like not trying anymore or even giving up? If you did any of these, then you are among good company, including the authors. You have tasted the unpleasant "pain" of being dominated, and possibly overwhelmed, by the winner/loser world.

The Elephant in the Room

The winner/loser world creates a separation in the relationship with our self, and with others, as we sacrifice who we really are to be the person that the winner/loser world approves of. In essence, this creates a *disrupting consciousness*, making everything else in life more difficult. The resulting negative feedback loop triggers emergent properties of emotional, mental, and behavioral problems. One of the central functions of Mirroring Hands is to assist the client to re-establish their self-relationship which has become disrupted or disorganized. Certainly, there are always individual problems that need to be resolved, but even when these wounds are healed, sending the client back into the "war zone" of the winner/loser world can not only undo the good work but sometimes make things worse.[2]

Revealing and understanding this elephant in the room can, in itself, be enough for some clients to manage and re-engage with their natural problem-solving and mind–body healing. Mirroring Hands is an ideal process for helping clients to differentiate the effects of the winner/loser world. The external fears and expectations can be held in one hand, and the inner capacity to naturally face the challenges of daily life can be held, and realized, in the other. It is very exciting to watch a client "get it" and begin to reclaim ownership of how they assess their value and worth.

2 Corrigan, P. W. & Watson, A. C. (2002). Understanding the impact of stigma on people with mental illness. *World Psychiatry*, 1(1), 16–20.

The "Real World"

Many people use the term "real world," unwittingly, as a colloquial expression for the winner/loser world. People returning from holidays can be heard lamenting that they have had a lot of fun, enjoyed feeling calmer, more relaxed, and, often, revitalizing their relationship, but now they have to get back to the "real world." It is as if there is no choice, and all those enjoyable things have to be put aside. Young people who speak of their future dreams can be told by others that they won't be able to do that in the "real world." It is surprising that this "real world" – a place full of restrictions, limitations, needs, and expectations – is given preference and hierarchical superiority. It is unfortunate, but more and more the winner/loser world standards and expectations are taken for granted and become the "rules" we *should* live by. No wonder people feel they are not good enough. How is it possible to cope with the confusing struggle of trying to be like someone who is not really you? People reframe the way they think and alter the way they behave to meet these externally determined standards and expectations. Some develop affective disorders like anxiety or depression, or one of the many other negative responses that emerge from enduring the winner/loser world experience. The social status aspect of the winner/loser world problem was explored thoughtfully by Alain de Botton in his book, *Status Anxiety*.[3] Can you see the pattern here? Can you relate to the problem? It is just like Cinderella's ugly sisters who tried to force their feet into the glass slipper to win the heart of the prince. They were trying to be something they were not, but they had become so used to the concept of doing whatever the winner/loser world wanted, and would reward them for, that they were prepared to submit to pain and disfigurement to "succeed."

The Winner/Loser World Mindset

The winner/loser world mindset is an emergent state of mind from a system that is persistently receiving negative feedback from a low level, chronic fear of social rejection. Social rejection, disapproval, and exclusion from social rewards is not only a psychological distress,[4] but can also be felt as a physical pain.[5] It is, unfortunately, a maladaptive response. Graffiti on a wall in Romania astutely comments, "Adapting to a sick society is not a sign of mental health."[6] Stress naturally triggers defensive, protective behaviors, but this is to help us survive a real and present danger.[7] When stress is not able to be

3 de Botton, A. (2005). *Status Anxiety.* London: Penguin.

4 Sanders, R. (2014). New evidence that chronic stress predisposes brain to mental illness. *Berkeley News* (February 11). http://news.berkeley.edu/2014/02/11/chronic-stress-predisposes-brain-to-mental-illness/.

5 Eisenberger, N. I. & Lieberman, M. D. (2004). Why it hurts to be left out: the neurocognitive overlap between physical and social pain. *Trends in Cognitive Sciences*, 8, 294–300.

6 Personal communication with Daniel Siegel, March 2017, Santa Monica, CA.

7 Smith, S. M. & Vale, W. W. (2006). The role of the hypothalamic-pituitary-adrenal axis in neuroendocrine responses to stress. *Dialogues in Clinical Neuroscience*, 8(4), 383–395.

managed or resolved, it becomes distress. The winner/loser world is not resolvable. It is both not real – an abstraction, a social attitude – and also real in that it has become part of the social construct, and so is persistent in the background of daily life. This creates an ongoing, chronic stress that shifts people from naturally seeking how to relieve or resolve demand to managing by adapting to the problem, largely by normalizing it. This adaptation creates a *winner/loser world mindset.*

There are a number of tell-tale indicators that someone is in a winner/loser frame of mind, including:

- An increased sense of personal *isolation* and *exclusion.*
- *Events* shift from being valuable learning experiences to being evidence of whether someone is a winner or a loser, which can be used to denigrate or to self-punish and self-sabotage.
- Information, advice, suggestions, or comments that could be mindfully received as useful and helpful are taken as *instructions* and interpreted as a criticism that the "instructor" is better and smarter, which means, by default, that you are less knowledgeable and therefore a loser.
- Everything becomes a *competition* that needs to be won, rather than a personal challenge that is an opportunity to learn.
- An imperative need to be *right,* not at *fault* or to *blame,* promotes the defensive behavior of making sure someone else, or everyone else, is wrong, at fault, or to blame.[8]

In the winner/loser world, you *have to* achieve expectations and satisfy demands in order to be deemed a success and receive the rewards. This pressure can drive some people toward socially and ethically unacceptable behaviors which are justified as "just trying to get ahead." They *need* to win. Behaviors like cheating, bullying and dominating others, road rage, aggression, and even violence become powerful temptations. Substance abuse is often about trying to "get out of it," where the "it" they are trying to "get out of" is often the winner/loser world.

Stereotype Threats

An important part of the foundational research that supports the winner/loser world theory was conducted at Stanford University by Steele and Aronson in 1995.[9] They looked at "stereotype threats." These are pervasive negative social attitudes about certain groups that become assumptions in the background social fabric that negatively and implicitly affect that group. They first looked at the long term negative social attitude in the United States regarding the intelligence of African-Americans. Their research found that they could negatively influence the scores in a

8 Hill, R. (2006). *How the "Real World" Is Driving Us Crazy! Solving the Winner/Loser World Problem.* Sydney: Hill & Hill.

9 Steele, C. M. & Aronson, J. (1995). Stereotype threat and the intellectual test performance of African-Americans. *Journal of Personality and Social Psychology,* 69, 797–811; Steele, C. M. (1997). A threat in the air: how stereotypes shape intellectual identity and performance. *American Psychologist,* 52, 613–629; Steele, C. M. (1998). Stereotyping and its threat are real. *American Psychologist,* 53, 680–681.

questionnaire given to Stanford University students. They told a mixed group of students that the questionnaire was just a set of questions for a research project. The results were in line with the students' general university performance. When they asked another group to do the questionnaire, they were told it was a test that diagnosed intellectual ability and would be counted in the final year's results. On average, the African-American students' results were five points lower. The Caucasian and Hispanic groups showed no significant change in performance. To test the theory further, they told a third group that it was just a general test and then, halfway through, announced that it was an intelligence assessment test and that the marks would be counted. The average results for the African-American group dropped in that second half of the questionnaire. Something happened in the way these research subjects processed the questions.

Many of the students' brain processing (i.e. the pathways of neuronal firing and the information retrieved) changed. The research did not investigate what the students were feeling, but it might be safe to assume that the responses were implicit (i.e. not consciously perceived). For some, the stereotype threat may have triggered implicit self-esteem fears, some may have become nervous and defensive, some may have been more aggressive or agitated. These shifts in mental state include what we describe as changes in the *quantum qualia* of their experience as the energetic flow of charged particles moving in and out of axons and across neurons change their probability outcomes, and therefore the thoughts that emerge from the complex system of the brain.[10] The bottom line is that, outside of the students' conscious control, a negative socially pervasive concept had influenced them on an implicit level and disrupted their normal behavior and state of mind. These negative stereotype threats are *in addition* to specific negative messages that an individual may receive through poor parenting, bullying, and other forms of personal negative criticism.

Other stereotype threats have been researched:

- Women's math performance.[11]
- Whites with regard to appearing racist.[12]
- Students from low socioeconomic backgrounds compared with students from high socioeconomic backgrounds on intellectual tasks.[13]

---

10 Rossi, E. L. & Rossi, K. L. (2014b). Quantum perspectives of consciousness, cognition and creativity: the Dirac equation in a new contour integral model of brain plasticity. *Journal of Applied and Computational Mathematics*, 3(6), 183. http://dx.doi.org/10.4172/2168-9679.1000183.

11 Spencer, S. J., Steele, C. M. & Quinn, D. M. (1999). Stereotype threat and women's math performance. *Journal of Experimental Social Psychology*, 35, 4–28; Walsh, M., Hickey, C. & Duffy, J. (1999). Influence of item content and stereotype situation on gender differences in mathematical problem solving. *Sex Roles*, 41, 219–240.

12 Frantz, C. M., Cuddy, A. J. C., Burnett, M., Ray, H. & Hart, A. (2004). A threat in the computer: the race implicit association test as a stereotype threat experience. *Personality and Social Psychology Bulletin*, 30, 1611–1624.

13 Croizet, J. & Claire, T. (1998). Extending the concept of stereotype threat to social class: the intellectual underperformance of students from low socioeconomic backgrounds. *Personality and Social Psychology Bulletin*, 24, 588–594; Harrison, L. A., Stevens, C. M., Monty, A. N., & Coakley, C. A. (2006). The consequences of stereotype threat on the academic performance of white and non-white lower income college students. *Social Psychology of Education*, 9, 341–357.

- Men compared with women on social sensitivity.[14]
- Whites compared with Asian men in mathematics.[15]
- Whites compared with blacks and Hispanics on tasks assumed to reflect natural sports ability.[16]
- Young girls whose gender has been highlighted.[17]

As a stereotype threat, the winner/loser world has become taken for granted, unquestioned, and is literally embedded in the construct of daily life and our social institutions. We see it in our examination systems in schools; businesses push people by rewarding those who meet expectations and punishing those who don't; advertisers use the winner/loser world to convince you to buy products to make you a "winner." "To the winner go the spoils," "the winner takes it all," "winning at all costs," and "the ends justify the means" are all common phrases that reflect the normalization of externally determined winning and losing. The unnaturalness and discomfort of the winner/loser world is reflected in the counteracting phrases that have emerged: "It's not about winning, it's how you play the game," "It's better to have loved and lost than never to have loved at all," and "You are all that you ever need to be." If the winner/loser world did not exist, we would not have the first group of phrases and we would not need the second.

Review

In the context of complex systems, the winner/loser mindset can be viewed as an emergent property from the feedback response to the constant and pervasive externalized evaluation and expectation, and the associated fear of social rejection and criticism. It just "gets" you, and because it is implicit you have no conscious awareness or control of it. In the positive natural process of personal challenge you sometimes achieve what you want and sometimes not. You can't win all the time, and not winning does not mean you are a loser. Not winning is simply a natural part of the process of learning and improving for the next challenge.

The key to resolving the winner/loser world problem is not to cure the winner/loser mindset, but shift into another one. Finding release from the clutches of the winner/loser world *is* possible. Changing our mindset is about changing the energy and information flow in the brain.[18] That

---

14 Koenig, A. M. & Eagly, A. H. (2005). Stereotype threat in men on a test of social sensitivity. *Sex Roles*, 52, 489–496.

15 Aronson, J., Lustina, M. J., Good, C., Keough, K., Steele, C. M. & Brown, J. (1999). When white men can't do math: necessary and sufficient factors in stereotype threat. *Journal of Experimental Social Psychology*, 35, 29–46.

16 Stone, J. (2002). Battling doubt by avoiding practice: the effect of stereotype threat on self-handicapping in white athletes. *Personality and Social Psychology Bulletin*, 28, 1667–1678.

17 Ambady, N., Shih, M., Kim, A. & Pittinsky, T. L. (2001). Stereotype susceptibility in children: effects of identity activation on quantitative performance. *Psychological Science*, 12, 385–390.

18 Siegel, D. J. (2016). *Mind: A Journey to the Heart of Being Human*. New York: W.W. Norton.

may sound like an oversimplification, but that is exactly what Mirroring Hands can achieve. We have already discussed the importance of shifting from a disrupting consciousness to a therapeutic consciousness. This brings us to a natural quality, fundamental to Mirroring Hands, which has a profound effect on brain state and state of mind. That quality is *curiosity*.

Curiosity

Changing "State"

Being stuck in a way of thinking is an almost impossible "state of mind" in which to resolve problems. Carol Dweck and colleagues at Stanford University showed that people in stuck mindsets are more likely to try to *prove* their state of mind rather than *improve* it.[19] You can't *make* a depressed person cheer up, or *make* an anxious person calm down, or *tell* a traumatized person not to worry about it. This is questioning something that is very true for that person. To move toward beneficial change, the client needs to find the courage and capacity to explore both the damaged parts within and their future possibilities at the growing edge. To be able to do this, the client needs to be *less afraid and fearful*, so they are less likely to suffer further trauma or other personal distress. As if their own personal issues are not enough, the winner/loser world looms like an invisible elephant, so removing that very large and heavy "straw" from someone's back can help to relieve and calm. Clients need to feel the possibility for growth and be encouraged by a pleasing feeling when they make that growth. Curiosity, more than any other state, enables all these requirements.

Curiosity establishes a state of being that shifts the mind, altering the flow of energy and information in the brain,[20] changes the biology all the way down to gene expression and protein synthesis to alter the biochemical milieu,[21] and enables the quantum qualia of a therapeutic consciousness.[22] Recent research shows that curiosity has a positive influence on psychological well-being and emotional

---

19 Dweck, C. S. (1988). A social-cognitive approach to motivation and personality. *Psychological Review*, 95, 256–273.

20 Alcaro, A. & Panksepp, J. (2011). The SEEKING mind: primal neuro-affective substrates for the appetitive incentive states and their pathological dynamics in addictions and depression. *Neuroscience and Biobehavioral Reviews*, 35, 1805–1820; Litman, J. A. (2005). Curiosity and the pleasures of learning: wanting and liking new information. *Cognition and Emotion*, 19(6), 793–814.

21 Rossi, E. L. (2002b). *The Psychobiology of Gene Expression: Neuroscience and Neurogenesis in Therapeutic Hypnosis and the Healing Arts*. New York: W.W. Norton.

22 Rossi, E. L. & Rossi, K. L. (2011). Decoding the Chalmers hard problem of consciousness: qualia of the molecular biology of creativity and thought. *Journal of Cosmology*, 14. http://journalofcosmology.com/Consciousness126.html. Reprinted in: R. Penrose, S. Hameroff & S. Kak (Eds.) (2011). *Consciousness and the Universe: Quantum Physics, Evolution, Brain, and Mind*. Cambridge, MA: Cosmology Science Publishers.

exhaustion,[23] and that curious people are less affected by social rejection,[24] have a broader scope for learning,[25] and enjoy increased arousal and activation of the natural inner reward system.[26] We will show you how to foster curiosity in your clients shortly, but, first, the following case example shows how curiosity can shift a client's state of mind to allow natural problem-solving and mind–body healing to emerge spontaneously.

RH's Casebook: In the Overwhelm of Grieving

I received a phone call from a distressed and grieving client who had recently lost her husband. She was only in her mid-forties and the death was sudden and tragic. She was inconsolable, tearful, exhausted, and desperate. There was nothing that could be said to make the grief less or brighten the starkness of her life. All the things she found unbearable were largely true. She needed to shift her *state*, even though it was not possible to shift her *reality*. Neither sympathy nor even empathy had given her any solace. Being on the phone, it was not conducive to utilize Mirroring Hands, so I utilized a curiosity approach.

I reminded her of something I had said in a recent session, "Your husband hasn't gone. He's just changed the way he stays." I asked her to look around the room and see the places where he used to linger – his favorite chair, the books he liked to read, where she could imagine him staying. She began telling me about the various parts of the room where she could feel his presence. I was utilizing the polarity principle of Mirroring Hands – where he is, where he isn't; where you are standing alone, where you can stand in his presence. I then asked her if she could think of other parts of the house where she could feel him "stay." She paused and mentioned a few. Then I suggested that when we finished the call, she could explore the house and find all those places, those things, and those memories as best she could. We were quiet for a little while, maybe 20 or 30 seconds and she discovered she had stopped crying. She also discovered that she did not feel so desolate. Suddenly she said, "Richard, what did you just do? What did you do to me? I am still sad, but I seem OK now. What did you do?" I told her that I had helped her change the way her brain was working, the way her heart was beating, the way she was breathing, and, most importantly, what she believed was

---

23 Wang, H. & Li, J. (2015). How trait curiosity influences psychological well-being and emotional exhaustion: the mediating role of personal initiative. *Personality and Individual Differences*, *75*, 135–140.

24 Kawamoto, T., Ura, M. & Hiraki, K. (2017). Curious people are less affected by social rejection. *Personality and Individual Differences*, 105, 264–267.

25 Gruber, M. J., Gelman, B. D. & Ranganath, C. (2014). States of curiosity modulate hippocampus-dependent learning via the dopinergic circuit. *Neuron*, 84(2), 486–496.

26 Jempa, M., Verdonschot, R. G., van Steenbergen, H., Rombouts, S. A. R. B. & Nieuwenhuis, S. (2012). Neural mechanisms underlying the induction and relief of perceptual curiosity. *Frontiers in Behavioral Neuroscience*, 6, 5. doi:10.3389/fnbeh.2012.00005.

possible. I saw her again several days later and she told me that she continued to feel OK – at least, she was able to manage. She was very grateful.

This is just one example of the sudden change of *experiential state* that happens when curiosity is ignited. In the preparation phase of Mirroring Hands we begin with the stimulation of curiosity with discovery: "*Look at those hands like you have never seen them before …*" We also use curiosity in a playful and imaginative way: "*I wonder if one of those hands feels different, heavier or warmer …*" Later in the process, we also facilitate the client's curiosity in another and very important way. We ask them to be curious about what their experience might mean, what it teaches, what expands out of the experience: "*I wonder if those hands are able to communicate or inform each other, in some way, about something you haven't yet known or imagined, almost all by themselves …*"

The Three Pillars of Curiosity

The research into curiosity is not as extensive as you might expect about something so fundamental to our well-being, although there have been a few more papers in recent years. Litman and Jimerson conducted interesting work in the early 2000s.[27] They described two aspects of curiosity: curiosity for deficit – those things that are not known and driven by feelings of uncertainty, and curiosity for interest – a pleasurable attraction to novelty regardless of whether any information is acquired. They didn't explore what we suggest is the most valuable aspect of curiosity – curiosity for meaning – but this is certainly discussed in other fields, including philosophy.[28] In our update of these research terminologies, we describe the three pillars of curiosity as:

1 Curiosity for information

2 Curiosity for play

3 Curiosity for possibility/meaning

These facets can be differentiated for description and discussion, which we will do shortly, but just like the facets of a gemstone or the pillars that support the roof of a building, optimal curiosity is a balanced expression of all three. Disproportionate focus on one or other of the pillars can produce an unstable situation. For example, the modern world seems disproportionately inclined toward a curiosity for information but largely as a continuous stimulus. Rather than *being interested*, the focus is more about demanding the outside world provides *relief from boredom*. This can leave people stuck in stage 1 of the creative cycle – craving something new and entertaining, but with little interest in using the information to develop personally.

---

27 Litman, J. A. & Jimerson, T. L. (2004). The measurement of curiosity as a feeling-of-deprivation. *Journal of Personality Assessment*, 82, 147–157; Loewenstein, G. (1994). The psychology of curiosity: a review and reinterpretation. *Psychological Bulletin*, 116(1), 75–98.

28 Frankl, V. (2006 [1958]). *Man's Search for Meaning*. Boston, MA: Beacon Press.

The curiosity approach to stage 1 is to ignite interest, fascination, and wonder – the numinous. The catchphrase is, "*That's interesting!*"

Stage 2 can be a difficult stage, and as we've said before, it is sometimes described as the "dark night of the soul" because this stage involves the effort to discover how the new information is personally relevant, how to make sense of it, and how the information connects to create a solution or beneficial change. Most clients come to us stuck in stage 2 as they become enveloped by their problem and see no way out. Engaging with curiosity in stage 2 stimulates interest and the courage to explore. It also opens the freedom to play with the information to allow for serendipitous emergence. Being open to possibilities not only increases the likelihood of creating a breakthrough, but also opens the door to personal meaning.

The curiosity approach to stage 2 is to search for what lies beneath the surface issue – the emergent property – and discover what this is *really* all about. The catchphrase is, "*What is the message in this problem?*"

Stage 3 is a creative and expansive stage that is full of play, possibility, and creating with the new understanding of how to arrange the information toward positive personal growth. It is very hard, if not impossible, to move into stage 3 if stuck in stage 1 or 2. Mirroring Hands can hold the stuck state in one hand, giving the client the opportunity to hold different possibilities in the other, which can lead to a breakthrough.

The curiosity approach to stage 3 is to creatively explore the new realizations and how they might make it possible to reintegrate both within and without. The catchphrase is, "*What can I create from this?*"

In stage 4, curiosity for possibility and meaning is directed at determining how the creative growth from stage 3 can be encoded, organized, implemented, and then integrated into daily life.

The curiosity approach to stage 4 is to gently explore how the realizations, resolutions, and creative discoveries can be integrated into the *self* for personal growth, health, and ongoing well-being. This is the period of the ultradian healing response. The catchphrase is, "*How do I make this part of my life?*"

The Curiosity Mindset

When a client walks in the room they are usually in a disrupting consciousness. It is reasonable to assume that they might feel uncomfortable, somewhat defensive and protective, probably not all that keen to discuss their issues, and very wary of getting in too deep. They may be feeling some anxiety or be manifesting symptoms of depression or other affective issues. We don't yet know the client's expectations, or their beliefs about the role of the therapist, or their role. This is not the best mindset, or brain state, for engaged therapy. Moving them into a therapeutic consciousness is the first phase of work with the client. What we want the client to feel is positive anticipation of what is to come. It is important to calm the fearful activity of the limbic area, so it helps for the client to shift into a broader focus of clarity and attention. All these qualities have correlations in brain activity and simultaneous adjustments in the neuro-biochemical milieu (see Appendix A).

The brain changes in relation to conditions and so every shift of mood, attention, focus, and intention in response to the environment, including other brains and minds, is dynamically reflected in the neuro-biochemical milieu.[29] The wonderful thing about curiosity is that it positively affects the neuro-biochemical milieu *toward* a therapeutic consciousness. The curiosity mindset stimulates movement and interest toward things; an exploratory, interested, wondering mind; an openness to learning; heightened focus and attention; a sense of pleasure and purposefulness – all perfect mental conditions for a therapeutic consciousness to emerge.[30] Mirroring Hands begins this process by simply asking the client to look at their hands like they have never done before and see things they have never seen before.

Let us unpack the three pillars:

29 Panksepp, J. (2010). Affective neuroscience of the emotional BrainMind: evolutionary perspectives and implications for understanding depression. *Dialogues in Clinical Neuroscience*, 12(4), 533–545; Birren, S. & Marder, E. (2013). Plasticity in the neurotransmitter repertoire. *Science*, 340(6131), 436–437; Dulcis, D., Jimshidi, P., Leutgeb, S. & Spitzer, N. (2013). Neurotransmitter switching in the adult brain regulates behavior. *Science*, 340(6131), 449–453.

30 Rossi, E. L. & Cheek, D. B. (1988). *Mind–Body Therapy: Ideodynamic Healing in Hypnosis*. New York: W.W. Norton; Rossi, E. L. (2004c). Gene expression and brain plasticity in stroke rehabilitation: a personal memoir of mind-body healing dreams. *American Journal of Clinical Hypnosis*, 46(3), 215–227; Hope, A. E. & Sugarman, L. I. (2015). Orienting hypnosis. *American Journal of Clinical Hypnosis*, 57(3), 212–229; Erickson, M. H. (2010). *The Collected Works of Milton H. Erickson, M.D. Vol. 6: Classical Hypnotic Phenomena, Part 2*, ed. E. L. Rossi, R. Erickson-Klein & K. L. Rossi. Phoenix, AZ: Milton H. Erickson Foundation Press; Campbell, J. & Moyers, B. (1991). *The Power of Myth*, ed. B. S. Flowers. New York: Anchor Publishing.

1. *Curiosity for information (CFI)* is the curiosity for what is not known, to fill a lack of knowledge, of understanding, of experience, or of perception. Information can come from the bottom up (i.e. in response to sensory information from the body), and can also be generated from top-down thinking. CFI can be triggered in different ways. It can be a personal question, a stimulation from the environment, or something that comes across the "social synapse" from other people's brains and minds.[31] CFI begins when there is a realization that something is not known, and it continues (assuming the exploration isn't abandoned) until the answer is found. The energetic drive and motivation from CFI wanes once the information is discovered. The moment the answer is discovered there is a pleasurable reward in the form of a puff of endorphins. This explains, in part, the almost addictive nature of inquiry and investigation. It also gives us some insight into the attraction of quiz shows and trivia competitions.

2. *Curiosity for play (CFP)* is a wonder, an interest, or a fascination in *whatever is happening now*. It is in the timeframe of the immediate. Play is pleasurable, and playful curiosity is often seen in children but also in adults when the weight of responsibility is put aside for the pleasure of playful exploration in the moment. CFP is an engagement in unregulated, self-organizing, playful activity which we know is important in developing social awareness and boundaries as well as social bonds.[32] Important information spontaneously emerges from play. People have asked why, when they play a sport, they don't always have a pleasurable experience. This is very important because an organized sport is not curious play. Curious play is when there are no rules, overt regulation, or organization. Interestingly, rules and organization often emerge as the play experience progresses, but that is very different from having the rules imposed. It is the same during therapy. Play is an incredibly important and useful tool in therapy to shift people out of negative states into more receptive, engaged, and integrating states. Mirroring Hands often begins in a playful way and playfulness can be added during the process.

3. *Curiosity for possibility/meaning (CFPM)* is a wonder, an interest, and a fascination in what else is possible and what this might mean. The timeline of CFPM is largely about the future because possibility and meaning are yet to be discovered, and so can only be manifest in a future moment. CFPM, in a unique and strange way, can be present in the moment as a motivation to move into the future to where and when possibility might manifest. It requires the person to step out of "now," and out of the "held past," into a new state of being. CFPM changes the mindset, brain state, and neuro-biochemical milieu of someone who is enduring depression, even if only temporarily. Loss of connection with the future is one of the damaging aspects of depression. Anxiety, on the other hand, is a fear of moving into the future. We propose that CFPM reduces the activity of the fear centers in the brain, which opens the

---

31 Cozolino, L. (2016). *The Neuroscience of Human Relationships: Attachment and the Developing Social Brain*, 2nd edn. New York: W.W. Norton.

32 Ginsberg, K. R. (2007). The importance of play in promoting healthy child development and maintaining strong parent–child bonds. *Pediatrics*, 119(1). http://pediatrics.aappublications.org/content/119/1/182.

> possibility of connecting and engaging with the future as a positive place – even for anxious clients. CFPM utilizes our natural creative capacities and encourages us to explore metaphor and representation, to look for meaning and self-reference, to positively anticipate what else might be, and to be an agent in what might be created. CFPM is the most rewarding and beneficial pillar of curiosity that can be present at all times, even when the other pillars are not active. CFPM can be both a state of mind – a state that exists in the moment, and a state of being – a fundamental state from which all other states emerge from moment to moment. Being timeless, it is possible for CFPM to be a constant undercurrent of our persona.

You might appreciate now how the winner/loser world mindset, as an elephant in the room, limits and restricts our interest in exploration and possibility. Possibility thinking and meaning making are also limited by insecure attachment styles, PTSD, peer pressure, bullying, inflammatory processes affecting the immune system, stress, and overwhelming social demands.[33] All of these things contribute to the effect of putting a lid on our access to the expansive possibilities of life. It is precisely because of all these restrictions and constraints to CFPM that Mirroring Hands can be such a helpful process. We utilize curiosity at the very beginning of Mirroring Hands to facilitate the client's connection with their implicit self-organizing inner world. By facilitating a curiosity mindset in the client, *and* in the therapist, *and* in the therapeutic experience, the transformational processes of change, realization, and healing are better able to emerge.

Stories of Curiosity

There are lots of wonderful stories of people using curiosity to shift mindsets so that problem-solving can occur and lives can transform in response. These stories embrace the inspiration and possibility of curiosity as a state of mind and, even deeper, as a state of being.

Teaching

In the dramatic film production *Freedom Writers*, we experience a situation that is concerned with both learning and therapy.[34] The film begins in the childhood years of a student who witnesses a drive-by shooting. Her voice-over tells us, "and I saw the war for the first time." The story follows the experiences of teacher Erin Gruwell in her struggles to teach at a school which busses in minority students from disadvantaged neighborhoods. In a memorable scene, Gruwell draws a line on the

33 Tugade, M. M. & Fredrickson, B. L. (2004). Resilient individuals use positive emotions to bounce back from negative emotional experiences. *Journal of Personality and Social Psychology*, 86(2), 320–333. http://doi.org/10.1037/0022-3514.86.2.320; Gallagher, M. W. & Lopex, S. J. (2007). Curiosity and well-being. *Journal of Positive Psychology*, 2(4), 236–248.

34 *Freedom Writers* (2007). [motion picture]. Dir. R. LaGravenese. Hollywood, CA: Paramount Pictures.

floor and asks any student who knows someone who has been killed to step over the line. Every student steps across. As Gruwell increases the number of people they know who have been killed, many students stay put. Their pain and discomfort and their total lack of curiosity is obvious. Their lives are about survival, not adventure or exploration. Gruwell tries to reach out to the students and is finally successful when she begins to teach them about the Holocaust and takes them to the Museum of Tolerance. For the first time the students' minds are opened to possibilities they had never contemplated. Gruwell also invites various Holocaust survivors to talk with her class about their experiences. Their curiosity about these people who have suffered beyond their own suffering was the big change. Gruwell asked them to write their own diaries which were eventually published as a book, *The Freedom Writers Diary*. Their stories not only describe the facts of their lives, but also their dreams and wishes. The stories were about their possibilities.

Interrupting Tragedy

Don Ritchie was known as the "Angel of the Gap."[35] The Gap had become a location for suicide in Sydney, Australia. Ritchie lived nearby and began to regularly patrol the cliff edge to see if he could help those who had taken themselves to the edge. He saved many lives with a very simple strategy. He would ask them to share their story over a cup of tea. It seems too simple, but this question opened a possibility in the mind of the person standing on the cliff edge. The difficulty with suicide is that all sense of possibility, other than death, has been lost. The surprise of the question was enough to shift their mindset to include something of the future and the possibility of their continued presence – at least for the timeframe of a cup of tea. There is a literal meaning to the cup of tea and the telling of their story, but it is the other meanings, metaphors, and associations that can open doorways of possibility. These would vary with each person, but you can imagine that the cup of tea could represent a gift, or perhaps something that their mother or aunt would make, or something warm and comforting. The opportunity to talk and tell their story also meant that someone cared, that they mattered to someone. All these things were possibilities that had been disconnected and pushed away. The simple and gentle question reintroduced the possibility of living.

The Voice of Life

An example of curiosity, and all three pillars in action, is found in an extraordinary TED Talk given by Professor Clifford Stoll in Monterey in 2006.[36] To describe him as eccentric might be an understatement, but this wonderful, wide-eyed, unkempt, gray-hair-standing-on-end professor prances

35 Kwek, G. (2012). Death of the Angel of the Gap. *Sydney Morning Herald* (May 14). http://www.smh.com.au/nsw/death-of-the-angel-of-the-gap-the-man-who-saved-the-suicidal-from-themselves-20120514-1ymle.html.

36 Stoll, C. (2006). The call to learn [video]. *TED.com* (February). https://www.ted.com/talks/clifford_stoll_on_everything.

erratically about the stage as he leads us through a number of fascinating, surprising, and curiosity igniting topics. The highlight is the story of when he was at the University of Buffalo in 1971. An anti-Vietnam War protest had turned into a riot on campus, to which he was largely oblivious. Stoll was walking through the campus wondering what was going on when a policeman started to chase him. He says, "I ran into the clock tower in Hayes Hall and I saw the pendulum swinging and thought to myself, 'Wow, the square root of its length is proportional to its period.'" This is a brain in play, which interrupted the stress of being chased by a policeman with a baton. He escapes the police officer by running up the stairs to the top of the bell tower where he looks down to see students below throwing bricks, and being hit by police, and sprayed with tear gas. He wonders, "What am I doing here?" This is, in some part, straightforward CFI, but this question opens the door for the bigger question about what he is doing in his life. He began to wonder about something more important: *What might he discover in this bell tower? What is the meaning of all this craziness?* Suddenly he remembers that a tutor once told him that bells often have an inscription, so he goes over to the bell, wipes off the pigeon droppings and finds a message. The last words are the most extraordinary: "It is the voice of life that calls us to come and learn." For all his eccentricities, Professor Stoll asks us to look beyond the literal experience of learning and see that the real purpose and meaning of learning is to respond to the *voice of life*.

Review

Are we suggesting that curiosity is a voice of life? We humbly suggest, yes. It is not the only voice, and not all voices are pleasant or even desirable, but it is a voice that has the capacity to render so many of the negative and destructive voices silent or, at least, subdue them. It is very hard to be angry while being curious. It is almost impossible to be curious and gripped by fear at the same time. It is contradicting to be curious and depressed. Curiosity can tame anxiety so that the future is no longer such a frightening place. Of all the voices of life, curiosity provides a broad ranging, healthy, and productive foundation. The therapist can achieve so much of their task of facilitating the client's engagement with their own problem-solving and mind–body healing by simply being curious and deeply interested in the client and in the co-created therapeutic experience.

The winner/loser world has emerged as part of our cultural development. It has become so commonplace that it is now embedded in the constructs of modern culture to the point where it is now a negative background influence on our well-being – a stereotype threat. Curiosity, on the other hand, is a wonderful state of mind, and state of being, that enhances our capacity to safely and comfortably follow our symptoms, problems, and distresses to the message that they represent. In the curiosity state of mind, and especially in the curiosity state of being, we can engage with, and enable, our own natural problem-solving and mind–body healing. How wonderful that we can begin to facilitate all this activity, all this inner "magic," simply by inviting someone to look at their hands like they have never seen them before.

Chapter 10

Clearing Out the Negative, Preparing for the Positive

Closing the Door

ER: Our job is to get a sense of where they are, what is occupying them, and get them to work with it … and I want them to see a negative and a positive. Most people are coming to us because they are stuck in the negative, alone, and they don't know how …

RH: … to get out of it, get unstuck?

ER: Get them engaged with themselves …

From the Rossi/Hill conversations, June 2016

Closing the Door is a form of Mirroring Hands that seeks to facilitate a shift in the balance between what is bothering the client, which they would prefer not to have, and what they would like to keep and make stronger. This is especially effective when the client has a sense of what is bothering them, but only in a general way. The client may be experiencing a difficulty in some aspect of daily life, such as not feeling good about school or work, or having difficulty sleeping, or having unwanted feelings such as jealousy or negative self-thoughts. This form is useful for behavior issues that are overwhelming or addictive, such as being unable to stop the chatter in the head, smoking, over- or under-eating, and for calming emotional states such as anxiousness and anger. It is equally effective for underwhelming states, such as depression, disappointment, general sadness, and grief – anything the client wants to have *less* of in their lives.

First, we will review the fundamental questions differentiated into the four creative stages, then we will explore more deeply how the process flows in practice, showing the language that can be utilized and the typical responses from clients, and then conclude with some case examples.

Stage 1: Information – Sensations

Apply the standard preparation to differentiate an energetic sensation in the hands.

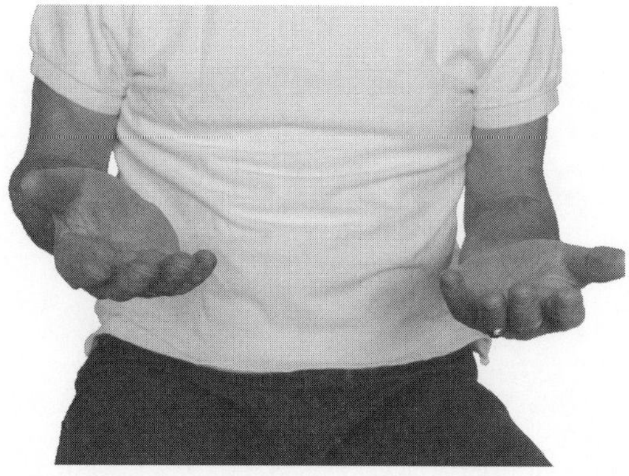

I wonder if you can look at your hands, really look at them as if you have never looked at them before. As you focus deeply into your hands, I wonder if one hand feels different from the other. Perhaps one hand is warmer (or heavier, or older, or whatever the client chooses to respond to) …

If you were to send that problem out to one hand, I wonder which hand that would be … the warm (or cool, heavy, light, or whatever the client has determined) hand … or perhaps … will that hand give some indication that it is ready to receive this problem?

Stage 2: Incubation – Arousal, Feeling

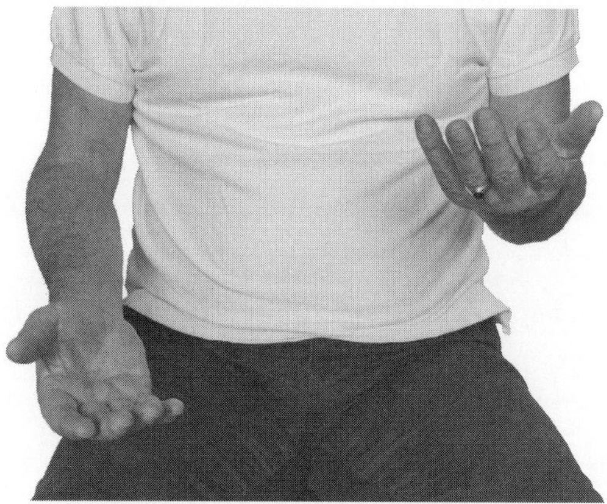

Wonderful … and, now, those things that are bothering you … the energy behind them or whatever it is … that we don't even consciously know exactly what it is … will you be able to send that feeling, that problem, out into your chosen hand? … Can you share a word or two about what you feel, or see, or sense, or smell, or whatever is happening in your hand? … Or will you just continue

with your private process? … And as you feel this flow out into your hand, I wonder if your hand might drift slowly down toward your thigh … finally landing when you have done all you can at this time?

Stage 3: Breakthrough and Illumination – Intuition, Insight

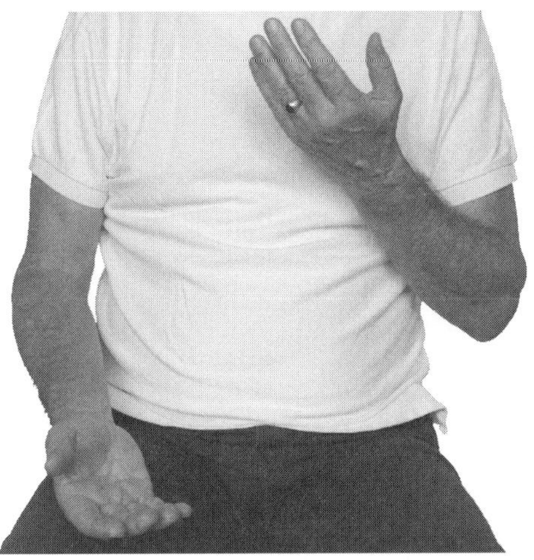

Excellent! … Now … I wonder if you can shift your attention to your other hand that has been waiting so patiently … and will the feeling or sensation that represents all the wonderful things inside you, that make you strong and able to manage this issue and solve this problem, and whatever else this strength within you can do that we don't even realize at this time … will that flow out into that waiting hand? … Can you share a word or two about what you feel, or see, or sense, or smell, or whatever is happening in that hand? … Or will you just continue silently with your private process? … Now, as your hand fills with this wonderful, powerful, healing strength … will that hand drift toward the place on your body that the negative feelings came from just a few minutes ago? … Do you know where that place is? … Will that hand move to that place and close the door, stopping any of that negativity being able to return?

Stage 4: Verification – Reintegration, Thinking

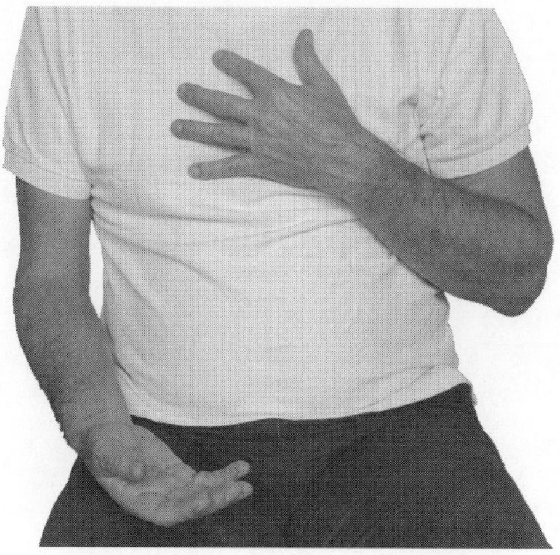

How wonderful … that strong, healing hand … protecting your inner world … I wonder what you might like to do with that negativity, that problem, that you have in the hand on your thigh? … Will you get rid of it somehow … someway … something that satisfies you? … Wonderful … let it go … throw it away … (or whatever the client chooses to do) … And now, return your attention to your strong hand, protecting you and strengthening you … and would you like to share how you are feeling right now … or would you just like to continue concentrating that healing strength?

(At the appropriate time, use the standard recovery to attention: When … a part of you knows that you can, etc.)

Let us now explore the process in more detail.

Stage 1: Information – Externalizing the Negative and Discovering the Positive

It is important to establish a differentiation between the hands, although there is no limitation on how this is achieved, whether using the standard preparation that creates a heavy, warm, or older hand, or whatever method emerges at the time between you and the client. They are then free to choose which hand wishes to receive the "problem" and the "solution." Notice the additional dialogue that might emerge, depending on the needs of the client.

I wonder if you can look at your hands, really look at them as if you have never looked at them before. As you focus deeply into your hands, I wonder if one hand feels different from the other. Perhaps one hand is warmer (or heavier, or older, or whatever the client chooses to respond to) … and will that hand show us in some way that it is the warmer (or heavier, etc.) hand …

It may be that the client's hand makes a distinct movement, but it may also be something very subtle. Facilitate the possibility that the hand is signifying something …

Just a twitch there … just your little finger … I wonder if that is the signal … of what you feel?

Once the client is confident which hand is which, continue with the first phase of differentiating the "problem" from the "not problem" within the client.

If you were to send that problem out to one hand, I wonder which hand that would be … the warm (or cool, heavy, light, or whatever the client has determined) hand … or perhaps … will that hand give some indication that it is ready to receive this problem?

Now they have begun to send the "nature" of their problem out into their hand, the process moves on to stage 2.

Stage 2: Incubation – Actualizing the Ambiguousness of the Problem

In stage 2 we ask the client to allow the energy to emerge from within and represent itself in the hand. Clients are usually fascinated by the forms, shapes, colors, textures, and other imaginations that come to their mind during this stage.

Wonderful … and now, those things that are bothering you … the energy behind them, or whatever it is … that we don't even consciously know exactly what it is … will you be able to send that feeling, that problem, out into your chosen hand?

Sensitively observe the client for spontaneous responses, both macro and micro, in the hands or anywhere else in their body. Add supportive and encouraging comments as seems appropriate. It is good to give the client an opportunity to speak about what is happening to them, but allow them to continue silently and privately if they wish.

Can you share a word or two about what you feel, or see, or sense, or smell, or whatever is happening in your hand? … Or will you just continue with your private process?

Allow a moment or two for the client to respond to the suggestion.

> *And as you feel the flow out into your hand, I wonder if your hand might drift slowly down toward your thigh ... finally landing when you have done all you can at this time?*

The hand may drift down slowly or quite quickly – both responses regularly occur. A fast movement down indicates that the larger percentage of the "problem" emerged at the first request. A slow drift down indicates a client who is enjoying creating a clearer sense of what they have in their hand, even if there are no verbal details and only sensations. Whatever emerges is true for the client, and most report that they feel their inner world "knows" what these sensations are all about. Whenever the hand lands on the thigh or in the lap, the client is declaring that they are ready to move on to the next phase.

Stage 3: Breakthrough and Illumination – Holding the Power of Healing and Strength

Always acknowledge the client's completion of any part of the process, even if they shift rapidly to something new: *Wonderful ... you are able to complete one thing and take yourself where you need to go ... please continue in your own way ...* The key to Mirroring Hands is to always be client-responsive, which means there is little or no resistance and often the therapist has to work hard to keep up.

> *Excellent! ... Now ... I wonder if you can shift your attention to your other hand that has been waiting so patiently ... and will the feeling or sensation that represents all the wonderful things inside you, that make you strong and able to manage this issue and solve this problem, and whatever else this strength within you can do that we don't even realize at this time ... will that flow out into that waiting hand?*

Include as many pauses as you feel are appropriate and helpful for the client. The ellipsis periods included here are only suggestions.

> *Can you share a word or two about what you feel, or see, or sense, or smell, or whatever is happening in that hand? ... Or will you just continue silently with your private process?*

The heightening of the client's sensorial, imaginative, and largely symbolic awareness of their stronger healing capacities enhances the process. This is not so much about forming a rational description as it is forming a broad ranging awareness that there is "something" within them that their logical brain doesn't need to know or understand in order to exist and be effective.

> *Now, as your hand fills with this wonderful, powerful, healing strength and ability … will that hand drift toward the place on your body that the negative feelings came from just a few minutes ago? … Do you know where that place is? … Will that hand move to that place and close the door, stopping any of that negativity being able to return?*

The client may need to be helped to clarify just where the "negative" energy came from. Simply shift attention to that investigation. Sometimes the client's hands will move out of the current position. Simply facilitate the return of the hands to the therapeutic positions when they are ready to proceed. Once the "healing hand" has arrived at its destination, allow time for the client to react and respond to the new position of the hand and however that affects them. The balance of "problem" to "not problem" is now different. We want to confirm and verify that in a stage 4 process.

Stage 4: Verification – Integration, Reality Testing

> *How wonderful … that strong, healing hand … protecting your inner world … I wonder what you might like to do with that negativity, that problem, that you have in the hand on your thigh? … Will you get rid of it somehow … someway … something that satisfies you? … Wonderful … let it go … throw it away … (or whatever the client chooses to do) …*

Clients will perform all kinds of fascinating actions from throwing away what is in their hand, to wiping it on the furniture, to blowing it away. Don't hesitate in offering a tissue or letting them clean their hand on something in the room. This is a grand moment of symbolic, ritualistic release of whatever they have been able to shift out of their inner self. All the while, encourage the client to keep "the door closed" with their strong healing hand while they rid themselves of the negative.

> *… And now, return your attention to your strong hand, protecting you and strengthening you … and would you like to share how you are feeling right now … or would you just like to continue concentrating that healing strength?*

At the appropriate time, if the client has not spontaneously revived themselves to begin discussing their experience, use the standard recovery to attention.

> *When …*
>
> *A part of you knows it can continue this creative work entirely on its own at appropriate times throughout the day …*
>
> *And when your conscious mind knows it can simply cooperate in helping you recognize when it is the right time to tune in …*

Will that give you a feeling, a signal, that it's time for you to stretch, open your eyes, and come fully alert, so you can consider what has happened and share, if you wish, what you might do with what you have learned, in your real, everyday life?

If you have not used the standard recovery, it can be helpful to remind the client that they can do this process again for themselves. It is best to utilize the ultradian healing response period of about 20 minutes to shed a little more of the negative and reinforce the positive healing strength that has always been there.

RH's Casebook: Insecure Attachment

A woman in her mid-thirties presented for help with her extreme shyness and lack of social confidence. Over four sessions of conversation she revealed her difficulties, experienced throughout her childhood, not only with her mother, resulting in insecure attachment issues, but also her difficulties in socializing with her peers in her small village. She felt that she was making some progress in understanding more about herself, but she asked if I could do something to help her with the "horrible" way she felt when in social situations. We discussed some of the *why* and *how* that might be happening, which she felt all made sense, but that "sense" wasn't doing anything for her feelings. I suggested we try Mirroring Hands.

Stage 1

She agreed and so I proceeded with a standard preparation. She felt that her right hand was "heavier" and that it was the hand that was ready to receive the problem – that "horrible" feeling.

Stage 2

I wonder if you can let that horrible feeling come out from inside you and into your heavy, right hand? …

She stared intently at her right hand, but I noticed that her eyelids began to blink slowly.

And I wonder if you might be more comfortable with your eyes closed, to imagine and feel …

Her eyes closed, she let out a long breath, and I noticed that her fingers began to close in a little.

Ah, yes … wonderful … something happening … something in your hand? …

She responded:

> *Yes … I feel … like a weight … cold …*

I simply repeat:

> *Cold … yes … heavy… uh huh … and as that feeling continues to come out of you into that right, heavy hand … will that hand drift down to your lap … just as slowly or quickly as you wish … getting as much of that horrible stuff out as you possibly can … as is possible for you …*

Without prompting, she tells me:

> *It's like metal … hard and cold …*

I support:

> *Hard, cold … yes …*

Again she speaks unprompted:

> *What is it? Why do I have this?*

Even though she is asking a specific question, it is not my task to give my opinion. Instead, I continue to facilitate her experience:

> *I wonder if you don't need to know right now … just feel it … something in you knows what it is … cold, metal, heavy … moving out from within you … outside … your hand getting lower now …*

Over the next four or five minutes her hand drifts slowly down to her knee. I respond:

> *Wonderful … you have done enough for now … so courageous of you … so brave …*

Stage 3

> *And I wonder if there is something else within you that is not that cold metal … something different that is about the best of you … can that feeling come into your left hand, the lighter hand? …*

Her head shifts toward her left hand, although her eyes remain closed. Her facial expression loses some tension and her mouth relaxes for a few moments and then re-tenses.

She says:

> *I don't know … there's nothing good in me …*

It is not surprising that she struggles with finding a positive feeling and believing in her self-worth. I gently encourage:

> *Maybe you don't need to know … I wonder if you can just let this happen for a while … almost all by itself … and see what happens, even though you don't know or even believe … something else … inside …*

We sit quietly for a few minutes. Her little finger seems to twitch, ever so slightly. I respond:

> *Something … yes … wonderful …*

(It can be hard to sit quietly and not try to help, but this will just impose on the client's process. Just be confident in your natural capacity for patience and your ability to be client-responsive.) After another couple of minutes, she declares:

> *Yes! … I feel something … surprising …*

I respond:

> *Surprising … yes … I see …*

She continues:

> *… stronger, but warm, soft … like a jelly ball …*

I support her:

> *So amazing … not nothing … now warm… a jelly ball … wonderful … and as you keep feeling this jelly ball grow, will that hand move toward the place where that cold metal came from and close that door? Can we close that door with that jelly ball, so nothing gets back in?*

Slowly, her hand moves toward her body, eventually landing on her throat area. This relates to her many stories of being told to be quiet as a child and her social shyness which often left her speechless. When her hand lands on her throat, she begins to breathe heavily and tears begin to fall. I stay quiet. After a few minutes she opens her hand and protectively holds her throat.

Stage 4

So, how about we don't let any of that cold metal back in? ... What would you like to do with that metal in your right hand? ... Anything you want ...

She opened her hand and dropped the metal object onto the floor and kicked it away.

We spoke for another 15–20 minutes about her childhood. Although we had discussed these matters before, there was a difference. This time she spoke about where the warm "jelly ball" might have come from. She found some light moments and even some fun times. She was able to identify a few people who had helped her in her childhood. Until now she had forgotten about them. It seems that her inner voice had not.

She continued to improve over her next visits. She accepted her shyness as a natural temperament. The horrible feeling continued, but much less. Over time it continued to diminish.

RH's Casebook: Inner Mental Chatter

The previous case took nearly 85 minutes. This case took only about 15 minutes to satisfy the client's needs. The client was a woman in her mid-eighties who regularly presented to the clinic to another therapist for remedial massage therapy. She had utilized my services three times and we had regular short conversations in the waiting room. Her main concern was about how to manage getting older. Medical problems were mounting and recently she'd had a serious operation to resolve heart issues. I saw her in the waiting room and she didn't look well or happy. She told me that she wasn't sleeping and felt nauseous most of the time. Her head was full of chatter about what will happen in the future and if there will be much future. She just couldn't quieten this chatter. I felt that directly after her massage, she would likely be in a period of ultradian healing response. I asked if she would like to pop into my room after her massage for a quick process. She agreed, with thanks.

Stage 1

We had used Mirroring Hands once before and she was a particularly good subject. I decided to launch straight into the process without preparation, but this may also have been an intuitive response to the way that she was raising her hands as I spoke. By the time I had finished asking the first question, her hands were raised to waist height and she was staring intently at them.

I wonder if you might be able to send that chatter out of your head ... and I wonder if you already know which hand can receive and hold that chatter?

Her eyes shifted rapidly to her left hand.

> *Excellent! ... You already know and that left hand is ready to receive and hold that constant chatter ... I wonder if you are feeling something about what is happening in your hand ... Do you want to share a word or two with me, or do you just want to continue with your own private thoughts?*

Stage 2

She closed her eyes and lifted her head, as if looking through her eyelids out into the distance, and said:

> *It's like ants or bugs, all scrambling about my hand, but I feel like something is coming toward me from the outside, from the distance ...*

I respond:

> *OK, something from within, like bugs, and something coming from a distance ... yes ... I wonder if this ...*

She continued to stare blindly into the distance as her hand started to drift downwards. I continued to support her process:

> *Wonderful ... your hand drifting down ... I wonder if it will go all the way down to your lap ... and still something ... coming ...*

The immediateness of her self-induced "trance" is not surprising as she is such a good subject, but it is difficult for the therapist to remain client-responsive and allow the client to continue their own process without helping or interfering for some explanation. I have some suspicions as to what might be coming from the distance, but it is not my task to know for the client; it is my task to assist the client to know about themselves. I continued to support her:

> *Yes, continuing to allow the chatter to flow into your left hand ... and watching that something that is ...*

She continued for a minute or two and then quietly spoke:

> *I feel it ... in my hand now ... it's the chatter, too ... filling from both directions ...*

The fingers of her left hand seemed to open wider and the hand seemed to tremble or struggle in some way to stay up. Her face tensed and her feet moved a little on the floor. The hand suddenly fell onto her knee and after a few moments slid off her knee and hung limply down beside her, resting on the front of the chair. I continued to support and encourage. She seemed very engaged with whatever she was experiencing. I encouraged and supported her:

> *Wonderful … that hand is full … has done enough … filled from inside and outside … not even holding it anymore … just dangling … I wonder if you can leave that chatter, that outside something, where it is and focus your attention on your right hand that is still raised in front of you?*

Her head, eyes still closed, moved toward her right hand. She said with some surprise:

> *How is this hand still up like this? I can't hold my arm out like this for this long. It's not even tired …*

I replied:

> *How amazing is that? Doing something that isn't even possible! I wonder if you can do something else that might seem impossible … I wonder if you can allow whatever it is within you that is so strong and secure and calm and relaxed to flow out, like an energy, into your right hand? … Are you ready to do that now … and will your hand do something to show us both that something wonderful is happening?*

Almost immediately her hand began to move in a small circle. I continued to facilitate the process:

> *And I wonder if that right hand can know where the bugs came from and move toward that place in your body and close the door … to keep the bugs from getting back in?*

Stage 3

In a flowing motion, her right hand swung over her heart. She shook her limp, left arm and raised that hand to cover her right hand in an X formation. She shook her head, then nodded her head, then shook it again, and then brought her head into the center and opened her eyes, looking over at me. Her hands stayed in position. She was quiet at first and then she began to tell me what she was thinking.

> *My heart is very important. It's much better now, but it's still an old heart. That thing from the outside is death. I know it's coming, but it didn't get me, it just joined the chatter. I'm letting death chatter in my head … that's a bit weird … it's a big waste of my time.*

We explored the concept and the reality of death for her. She described how she found it hard to not feel threatened by being older, but also how much she enjoyed being alive and how she was still a very active woman. The important realization from this session was:

> *By listening to this chatter, I'm letting death in early … Get out of my head … your time will come soon enough!*

Stage 4

I suggested that each time the chatter starts she could do this process again for herself. Whatever it is in her left hand, she can call on that, hold it over her heart and make death wait. In the meantime, she can let life in. She later reported that the negative thoughts still emerged from time to time, but the uncontrollable chatter had stopped and she is sleeping much better. The nausea turned out to be a side effect from a medication she was taking for her heart. This was changed and she seemed to be much better.

Review

It can be very helpful for client and therapist to work through issues and bring them into language, description, and literal understanding. It can also be very helpful to allow the process of inner self-organization to create problem-solving and mind–body healing without ever being able to describe the details. This also taps into the concept of right hemisphere and left hemisphere function, which is well described and discussed elsewhere by people like Allan Shore[1] and Iain McGilchrist.[2] Suffice it to say that our consciousness is not limited to what can be spoken. Equally, we have an inner world that continues to process and engage a multitude of systems that are the basis of the emergent property we call our *conscious awareness*.[3] There is always more to us than meets the eye. It is possible to open connections between the inner and outer world through Mirroring Hands, but it is not always necessary to use the hands to create the connection. In the next chapter, we show there are other ways to apply Mirroring Hands as a therapeutic approach.

---

1 Schore is widely published. These books are seminal texts: Schore, A. N. (1994). *Affect Regulation and the Origin of the Self: The Neurobiology of Emotional Development*. New York: Psychology Press; Schore, A. N. (2003). *Affect Disregulation and Disorders of the Self*. New York: W.W. Norton.

2 McGilchrist, I. (2009). *The Master and his Emissary: The Divided Brain and the Making of the Western World*. London: Yale University Press.

3 Wang, J. (2006). Consciousness as an emergent property. *Disputatio philosophica: International Journal on Philosophy and Religion*, 8(1), 89–119.

Chapter 11

Symptom Scaling for Enlightenment

The Symptom is a Message

ER: What the client is stuck with … and how to get them engaged with their own inner resources … that's another task of the therapist …

RH: … to be sensitive and notice …

ER: … even if they say "I don't want to deal with it!" then go with that and allow them to spend a little time "not dealing" with anything … to enjoy and engage in that feeling …

RH: Client-responsive …

ER: Exactly! They will want to get some work done soon enough …

From the Rossi/Hill conversations, June 2016

Most clients seek therapy because they are experiencing something that is making their lives difficult, be it emotional, behavioral, psychosomatic, or whatever they find debilitating or distressing. Therapists call these subjective feelings *symptoms*. As we have seen, Mirroring Hands can be used to differentiate a client's symptom from what is "not the symptom" – we seek to discover the message that lies behind or beneath the symptom.[1] The protocol of Mirroring Hands shown in this chapter can be used when the client is currently experiencing or manifests their symptom during a therapy session. The process invites the client to assess the *intensity* of the symptom and find the "something more" that the symptom might represent.[2] This creates an opportunity for the client to regain the locus of control, and also to engage with the *critical phase shift* that the symptom may be forecasting. We are seeking to trigger changes in the intensity and experience of the symptom to reveal the deeper message.

Symptoms are rarely the actual problem; they are emergent properties of inner processes which attract our attention in order to stimulate some action to resolve the situation. They are often simplistic, sometimes ambiguous, and even confusing because the symptom can often bear little or no resemblance to what is finally realized. The real purpose of a symptom is to stimulate us to respond

---

1 Rossi, E. L. (1996). *The Symptom Path to Enlightenment: The New Dynamics of Self-Organization in Hypnotherapy. An Advanced Manual for Beginners*, ed. K. L. Rossi. Los Osos, CA: Palisades Gateway Press.

2 See the curiosity approach in Chapter 9.

– just as we find ourselves heading to the refrigerator when we get the "symptom" of *I'm hungry.*[3] Symptoms emerge to lead us somewhere, or shine a light on something, but always to attract attention – our own or someone else's.

Symptom scaling is when the client self-assesses the severity of their symptom, usually on a scale of 1–10 (where 1 is slight, 5 is average, and 10 is the very worst). Symptom scaling is an excellent way for the client and the therapist to gauge changes in the client's condition both during a session and across sessions. The therapist can utilize a symptom scaling of the client's current state to help the client maintain the safety of an objective perspective. The main benefit of symptom scaling is to begin the process of returning the locus of control to the client. It also gives the client an opportunity to both experience the symptom and hold an objective view of their subjective experience.

We begin by simply asking the client to show the intensity with an outstretched arm as a "scaling meter." We will demonstrate the process in case examples, as well as two other variations – one which follows the symptom as it manifests in the body and does not use the hands at all, and another which uses the standard client preparation that establishes a drawing or repelling "energy" between the hands. The focus in this form of Mirroring Hands is not so much on the differentiation, or polarity, created between the hands, but on the qualities and quantities of the symptom itself. We will describe a generalized structure and dialogue first, before presenting the specific case studies.

The Four Stages of Symptom Scaling

Stage 1: Scaling Level of Awareness

When the client complains of a feeling, sensation, distress, disturbance, or other distinct symptom that they are experiencing *in the current moment*, we take it as a mind–body signal that needs attention – that is, a signal to start inner work straight away that may lead to problem-solving and/or healing. We initiate this inner work by asking the client what they feel is the *intensity of the symptom* they are experiencing right now on a *subjective scale of awareness* measured from 1–10, where 1 is little or no problem, 5 is average, and 10 is most intense.

3 See: http://goodnesssuperfoods.com.au/2012/08/why-hunger-is-a-good-thing-dr-jo-explains/; and https://bengreenfield-fitness.com/2012/03/is-being-hungry-bad/.

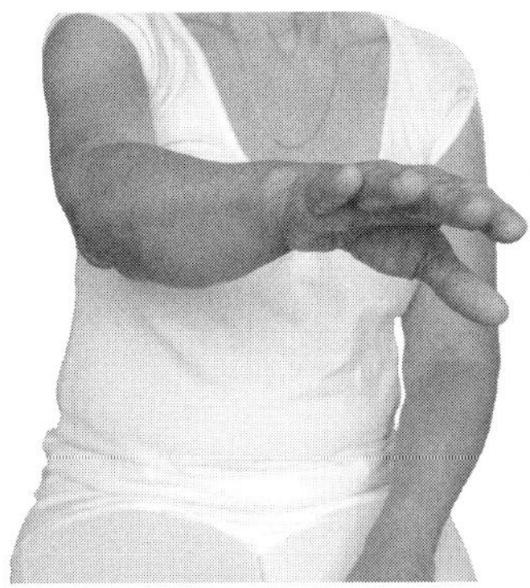

Can you hold your arm out as if it is a lever that can tell us how strongly you are experiencing those feelings? … And will you let me know how bad they are on a scale of 1–10, where 10 is the worst?

The therapist accepts with positive regard whatever subjective scaling the client offers of their level of awareness of symptom intensity and continues with stage 2 as follows.

Stage 2: Initiating Inner Work

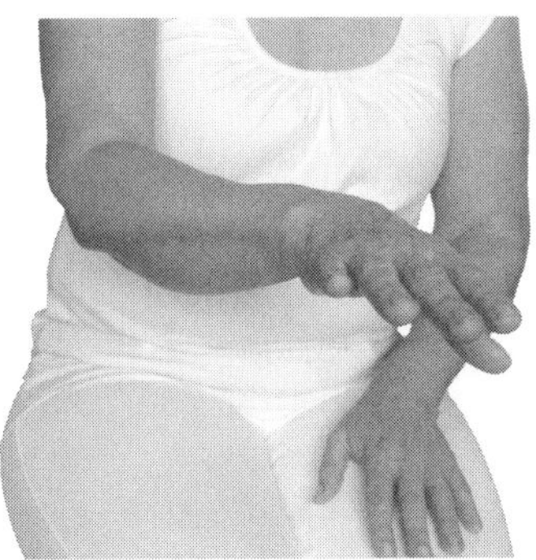

Good! And as you continue sensing your symptoms … how are you experiencing yourself? … Just noticing whether you are becoming more intense or less … or becoming more aroused or relaxed … or becoming … As you continue watching your arm, can you let yourself be so sensitive that your arm goes up if the feelings get worse and your arm goes down when you feel better?

That's right, the courage to allow that to continue all by itself for another moment or two until … you experience a little surprise?

It does not matter what the client's initial state may be. We are only interested in what is *changing*. *Any change may mean that potentially therapeutic dynamics are being engaged!* After about three or four minutes of inner experiencing, the client is again asked to subjectively scale the level of awareness that is being experienced. Of course, the therapist is being attentive to the client's well-being during this time, being mindful that the client does not become overly subjective and internalized, with the possibility of re-traumatization. Reviewing their symptom scaling will refresh their observer state.

> *Yes ... wonderful ... what number are you experiencing at this moment?*

The therapist, of course, accepts whatever the client presents. There are only three possible responses.

Option 1: A higher subjective scaling number

Some clients may become more aroused initially, sometimes with a temporary increased awareness of symptoms, emotionality, catharsis, and so on. That is, the initial movement of their level of awareness shifts upward to what we would call the "high phase" of the ultradian rhythm. The therapist, of course, immediately accepts and facilitates this.

> *Ah, that's interesting ... noticing how you can become more aware of (whatever symptom) for a moment or two as you get in contact with it so the therapeutic process can begin ... What courage to continue experiencing and wondering about the changes taking place, almost all by themselves ...*

If the client continues to move toward the high phase with increasing arousal, maintain their objective distance with scaling questions, but also relate and reflect the courage of the client as they proceed toward their phase shift. Increased arousal is indicating that a critical point is ahead. Remember, the symptom is not the issue, just the messenger. The client's arousal is a combination of moving toward a breakthrough and the client's inner resistance to the message that is seeking to be known. The therapeutic opportunity comes up when the client begins to talk about, or even complain about, other *symptoms* or *negative thoughts* coming into their experience. This is the client's spontaneous experience of *symptom substitution* which is the beginning of opening up to the symptom's meaningful message. The new complaints may also be other "stepping stone" emerging symptoms and the core message is still to be revealed. We call this the "merry symptom chase."

Option 2: A lower subjective scaling number

There may be an immediate or slow drop in the awareness of the symptom – typically with the client moving toward a natural relaxation. That is, the initial movement of their awareness is downward to the "low phase" of the ultradian rhythm. The therapist immediately accepts this and facilitates with the following:

Good, allowing yourself to appreciate your good fortune (wonderful blessing, etc.) in experiencing that natural therapeutic movement … toward greater relaxation and comfort … How amazing that your (whatever symptom or problem) seems to be healing itself … when you allow it … And as you simply allow that healing to continue all by itself … will you tell me occasionally what number you are experiencing? … How wonderful to know you can continue to explore this way of cooperating with your natural healing response …

It is a fortunate situation, indeed, when the client goes into a spontaneous remission or natural healing. We really don't know, of course, whether the good experience will last. Is this a deep healing experience or perhaps a mindful calming to a more comfortable state, or perhaps even a sublimation or denial of the message behind the symptom? Further work will make that more apparent. We can, however, support whatever positive possibility the client may have discovered through the process.

Continuing to deeply appreciate learning how this healing can continue all by itself … And will it be possible for you to let yourself continue learning how to experience this natural ultradian healing response a few times throughout the day when you need to?

Option 3: No change in subjective scaling number

With no change in subjective scaling number after a few minutes (at most five minutes with no subjective or objectively observable behavior change), the therapist accepts that something may not be working. For whatever reason the client's inner dynamics have not become engaged. Certainly, a seed may have been planted for future work but for now a fresh approach is needed. Interpretations by the therapist or any implication that the client is resisting or failing are to be avoided! The client needs support for learning how to do this kind of inner work.

Ummm … it is possible that you are content to just become stable, no worse, no better … If there is something else within, it is not ready to express itself yet … How wonderful for your inner world to know that it is OK to just stay with the status quo … for now … Maybe you would like a little practice … Would you like to continue for another moment or two now … to experience whatever comes up all by itself that you feel you would like to talk about next … or is that enough for now … or is something else coming up within you right now?

Stage 3: A Path to Enlightenment

Clients may gradually shift into the dynamics of stage 3 of the creative process with a cognitive insight or natural ultradian shift in awareness, emotions, and/or symptomatic experience. The therapist's task is to facilitate a recognition of the deeper or hidden messages that "chasing" the symptom path has revealed, and then to help the client engage with whatever meaning or wisdom comes up about themselves.

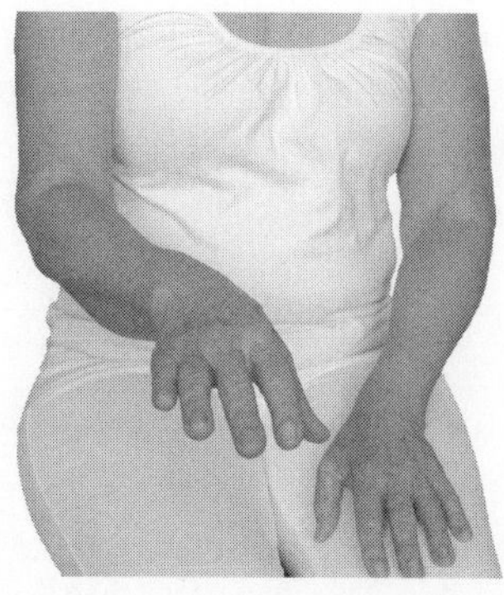

Ummm … rather profound possibilities in what you say … yes, it is well known that an illness (or whatever problem) can sometimes lead to a new level of meaning and wisdom … lessons you can learn … a surprising path to enlightenment … Is this the first time you realized that about yourself? … I wonder what else might come to you about your new understanding … and how will you continue cultivating this new awareness? Learning everything you need? … And what number is it at now?

Stage 4: Verification – Reintegration

Most clients are pleasantly surprised, having gone through an experience that often feels like a valley of shadow and doubt, to find themselves in a better place after a shorter (5 or 10 minutes) or longer period (up to about 90 minutes). They often wonder aloud about what the therapist did to make them feel better. Of course, the therapist did nothing but facilitate their natural ultradian dynamics of problem-solving and healing. The therapist can be frank about their role in the process and introduce the idea that the client can learn to do this on their own with just a little practice.

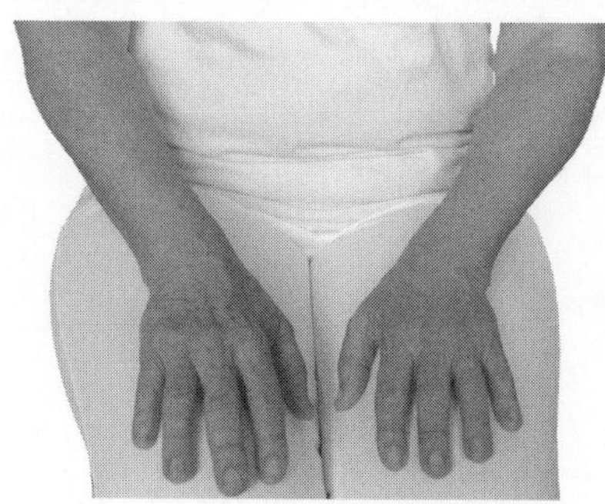

Congratulations on staying with what your inner self really needed you to spend some time with ... Notice how I simply encouraged you to experience the honesty of those feelings ... and how they somehow transformed ... Will you be able to do this for yourself? How can this help you from now on? What changes will you now make? What will you do differently this week?

The client may ask about how to control their symptoms, be they emotions, thoughts, or body sensations. Therapists need to keep out of the way of natural problem-solving and healing, and sometimes the client's rational desire to cognitively control their experience can be as much of an interference. The rise in mindfulness training is a response to this same issue of wanting to find some peace, but we want to do more than just achieve a peacefulness and acceptance. We also want to allow for learning and personal development at the growing edge.

Yes, I know you want to be able to control this healing process ... but you have just had a wonderful experience of symptom relief and also a deeper understanding of meaningful things in your life now and for the future ... all by simply relating to yourself in a sympathetic manner ... You can continue this private inner healing experience by simply learning to recognize when the natural phase of inner healing hypnosis wants to take place all by itself and you let it ... Um-hum, yes, you let it ...

Symptoms: An Emergent Property

Symptoms are an emergent property of inner processes that arise without any conscious direction. It is important to pay attention and respond to symptoms, but we now know that they can be drawing attention to anywhere in the complex system that involves many elements, including implicit memories and feelings, somatic memories, negative schemas, defensive "programming" from past traumas, and other distressing experiences that have created disconnection and disintegrations that need repair. Symptoms manifest to draw our conscious attention to the fact that we have a deeper problem that requires us to do something – make a decision, take some action, or make some change – in order to help resolve the deeper problem. It is also important to be aware of the physical problems that have triggered symptoms. Irritability, volatile temper,[4] anxiety,[5] and depression[6] can

4 Duke University Medical Center (2004). Anger, hostility and depressive symptoms linked to high C-reactive protein levels. *ScienceDaily* (September 23). www.sciencedaily.com/releases/2004/09/040922070643.htm.

5 Salim, S., Chugh, G. & Asghar, M. (2012). Inflammation in anxiety. *Advances in Protein Chemistry and Structural Biology*, 88, 1–25. doi:10.1016/B978-0-12-398314-5.00001-5.

6 Harrison, N. A., Brydon, L., Walker, C., Gray, M. A., Steptoe, A. & Critchley, H. D. (2009). Inflammation causes mood changes through alterations in subgenual cingulate activity and mesolimbic connectivity. *Biological Psychiatry*, 66(5), 407–414.

be symptoms of inflammation in the system which is affecting mood. Symptom scaling with Mirroring Hands can open the client's awareness to the possibility of a physical cause. The key is to pay attention to the comments that emerge when there is change in the client's scaling.

Because symptoms arise from a problem oriented system, they provide negative feedback if left unchecked. This is the process behind re-traumatization and negative memory reconsolidation.[7] Negative feedback also manifests in affective states,[8] psychosomatic complaints,[9] somatoform disorders,[10] inflammatory processes and immune system problems,[11] as well as changes to the gut biota[12] and the subsequent impacts on mental processes and the brain's microglial "immune" system.[13] A dysfunctional system will self-organize in an increasingly dysfunctional way. The system moves further and further away from natural problem-solving and well-being. The expanding complexity that emerges from unresolved emotional and mental health issues can continue for long periods of time, resulting in the need for all kinds of healthcare to treat the plethora of symptoms and subsequent disorders, rather than finding the essential problem and resolving that. People often seek therapy to cure their symptom, but a good therapist knows that the symptom is often not the problem. Symptoms are like a doorway or a pathway to the problem and to the client's problem-solving and mind–body healing capacities – *a pathway to enlightenment.*

The symptom is both an opportunity to take action *and* the starting point to investigate and explore for the deeper triggers. Symptoms arise to agitate for action. When symptoms appear, it is often an indication that the system is ready for a phase shift. This pathway can be lost when we only treat the symptom, whether this is by sublimation, denial, dissociation, medication, or directive therapy. Note: always seek medical attention and advice if the client is physically affected, even if it is possible to assist and relieve symptoms though affective therapy.

When the client is experiencing a symptom in the session, take advantage of the opportunity for healing processes to be enacted in the moment. The following case examples demonstrate three forms of symptom scaling in Mirroring Hands.

---

7 Tronson, N. C. & Taylor, J. R. (2007). Molecular mechanisms of memory reconsolidation. *Nature Reviews Neuroscience*, 8, 262–275. doi:10.1038/nrn2090.

8 Peil, K. T. (2014). Emotion: the self-regulatory sense. *Global Advances in Health and Medicine*, 3(2), 80–108. http://doi.org/10.7453/gahmj.2013.058.

9 Carey, T. A., Mansell, W. & Tai, S. J. (2014). A biopsychosocial model based on negative feedback and control. *Frontiers in Human Neuroscience*, 8, 94. http://doi.org/10.3389/fnhum.2014.00094.

10 Looper, K. J. & Kirmaye, L. J. (2002). Behavioral medicine approaches to somatoform disorders. *Journal of Consulting and Clinical Psychology*, 70(3), 810–827.

11 Mueller, D. L. (2003). Tuning the immune system: competing positive and negative feedback loops. *Nature Immunology*, 4, 210–211. doi:10.1038/ni0303-210.

12 Luzupone, C. A., Stonbaugh, J. I., Gordon, J. I., Jansson, J. K. & Knight, R. (2012). Diversity, stability and resilience of the human gut microbiota. *Nature*, 489, 220–230. doi:10.1038/nature11550.

13 Lull, M. E. & Block, M. L. (2010). Microglial activation and chronic neurodegeneration. *Neurotherapeutics*, 7(4), 354–365. doi:10.1016/j.nurt.2010.05.014.

ER's Casebook: Heroin Addiction

Stage 1: Information – Data Collection, Initiation

A local resident of Needle Park had finally stumbled into a community rehabilitation center and, after a drying out period, is being seen for a private session by an addiction counselor, who is a former addict himself and wise in the ways of withdrawal. The addict complains of withdrawal symptoms: pain, negative emotions, and flashbacks. He feels too sick to talk.

The counselor holds his arm straight out in front of himself (as illustrated in the first symptom scaling photo on p. 169) and says, *Let's work with that right now! Can you hold your arm out as if it is a lever that can tell us how strongly you are experiencing those feelings? … And can you let me know how bad they are on a scale of 1–10 where 10 is the worst?*

The recovering addict holds his arm out, fixes his attention on it, and tentatively says it feels like 6.

Stage 2: Incubation – Arousal

The counselor slowly lowers his own hand while saying in a low voice, *As you continue watching your arm, can you let yourself be so sensitive that your arm goes up if the feelings get worse and your arm goes down when you feel better?*

The counselor notices that his subject's arm quivers a bit, his face flushes, his breathing becomes more shallow, and a fine sheen of sweat makes his forehead and nose slightly shiny. The arm quivers up a bit and the subject begins to frown and grimace in obvious discomfort. The counselor continues, *That's right … the courage to allow that to continue all by itself for another moment or two until …* After a full minute the arm is still going up very slowly and the subject gasps, "Until what, man?!"

Cool as a cucumber the counselor replies, *Until you experience a little surprise … And what number are you experiencing now?*

Stage 3: Illumination – Insight

The arm suddenly bobs downward momentarily about an inch or two and the counselor immediately responds with, *Um-mmm!?*

The subject, in slight surprise, looks at his now drooping hand and says, "Hey, it's getting tired, you know. I got problems, man. I really don't need this." The counselor persists with, *What number is it at now?* The recovering addict with a tight gasp says, "It's up to 8 and getting worse all the time!" After another moment the counselor offers, *And I wonder just how bad it's going to get before …?* The subject's face turns red, his fist clenches and he sputters, "No use even talking to you, you ain't saying nothing!" The counselor persists with, *What number is it at now?* He hears the subject grumble that it's now down to 5.

The counselor, with mock gravity, now wonders aloud whether it will get worse again before it gets better. The arm tentatively makes another effort to bob up a bit, perhaps to a level 6 and then sags rather quickly down to a level 3 or 4. The subject now takes a giant step toward recovery by willfully dropping his arm all the way down to his lap and saying, "Enough of this shit, man. I got problems I got to talk about, you know?" The traditional view might be to regard his impatient breaking off of the arm signaling as resistance. It is only resistance, however, to continuing the arm signaling. The client's impatience to now speak about his problems actually means that the therapist's arm signaling approach has succeeded, since the client is now ready to go on with his therapy by talking about his problems.

Stage 4: Verification – Reintegration

The now obviously relieved subject pours out his story and current concerns with a modicum of insight here and there, to which the counselor responds affirmatively in his best non-directive manner. And so it goes. Toward the end of the session the counselor inquires again about what number describes how the subject feels now. The recovering addict ruefully rubs his arm and grumbles that he is sick and tired of feeling bad and doing this numbers game but says, "I feel a lot better now and I'll let you know when I need another shot in the arm."

What are the dynamics of this therapeutic interaction? Erickson frequently explored experience, although he never used this word to describe it. Erickson called this process a "yo-yoing of consciousness" or a "yo-yoing of symptoms,"[14] which would be experienced as alternately getting worse and better.

The paradox, Erickson believed, is that clients do not realize that as they allow symptoms or pains to get worse for a moment and then better, they are actually gaining control over them. We can speculate that this is not a paradox but rather the best way for clients to engage their own state-dependent memory and learning systems through alternating states of ultradian arousal and relaxation. These alternations are associated with the release of hormones and messenger molecules on all levels of mind–body communication to mediate psychotherapy.[15]

It is now well known that all addictive drugs achieve their effects by mimicking the molecular structure and functions of our natural hormones and messenger molecules (neurotransmitters and

14 Erickson, M. H. & Rossi, E. L. (1981). *Experiencing Consciousness: Therapeutic Approaches to Altered States*. New York: Irvington Publishers, p. 51.

15 Rossi, E. L. (1993 [1986]). *The Psychobiology of Mind–Body Healing: New Concepts of Therapeutic Hypnosis*, 2nd edn. New York: W.W. Norton.

neuromodulators). Many of these are the same messenger molecules that encode stress and traumatic experiences in a state-dependent manner and are responsible for the amnesias, dissociated states, and general symptomatology of the addictions.[16]

ER's Casebook: Vaginal Herpes

Stage 1: Information – Data Collection, Initiation

A client in her thirties who is going through a period of great emotional stress in personal relationships suddenly begins to experience unusual and uncomfortable sensations of heat in her vagina and, upon medical examination, is diagnosed as having an outbreak of vaginal herpes for the first time in her life. She claims she has had no new sexual partners for over three years and her current partner has apparently been faithful. How come herpes now?

I initiated her into a state of inner search by introducing her to symptom scaling: *On a scale of 1–10, where 10 is the worst you have ever experienced that heat and 5 is average, just how strong is the sense of heat in your vagina right now?*

She replied that the heat is 7 right now, and crossed her legs with a facial grimace of distaste. I asked her, *Do you have the courage to really receive honestly just what you are feeling right now, so you can fully experience what it leads to next?*

Stage 2: Incubation – Arousal

She responded with her feeling that the herpes is the source of the heat she is feeling and it seems to be getting worse by the moment as she focuses on it. I slowly and quietly murmured an incomplete sentence: *I wonder if you can stay with it until …* Her eyes closed as she apparently focused inward. Her body tensed and she leant forward slightly over the next few minutes as she hesitantly whispered the following series of apparently spontaneous symptomatic transformations and free associations with many pauses: "Now the heat is shifting around a little to my butt on the left cheek … Now heat is moving through my body everywhere … it's like a burning allergy … my head hurts … feels like an outbreak of psoriasis on my scalp … I feel like I should confess it all to my mother like I did as a kid … my right shoulder aches … Why is my right side trembling? … Why am I starting to cry? … Why do I still try to get approval from my mother even when she never gave it but only punished me instead? … I'm burning up with heat all over!"

16 Rossi, E. L. (1987). From mind to molecule: a state-dependent memory, learning, and behavior theory of mind–body healing. *Advances*, 4(2), 42–60; Rossi, *Psychobiology of Mind–Body Healing*.

Stage 3: Illumination – Insight

For a few tense minutes she continued with, "Burning! Burning! I know … I know I have to leave [her current boyfriend]. I always knew it was only temporary, really, but now I really do have to leave … He punishes me, too, even when he doesn't know it … My left knee is twitching uncontrollably … Can't you make it stop? … Oh, I'm tired of all this … I will leave … I'm getting sleepy … I feel warm … just warm now … I really have to leave [boyfriend]." Her body sagged back and she remained silent for about three or four minutes as her face gradually became calm, smooth, and apparently relaxed.

Stage 4: Verification – Reintegration

I looked at the clock and with a mild sense of concern noticed there were only 10 minutes left to the session. I cleared my throat and murmured, *Yes, and is that still going well?* After a moment she shifted her feet, nodded her head, yes, adjusted her posture to a more normal sitting position, blinked a bit, and finally opened her eyes. I then asked, *And I wonder what number describes what your level of comfort is now?* Somewhat surprised, she acknowledged that she was at 1 or 2 or maybe zero. It's no longer a feeling of heat in her vagina, but rather a feeling of warmth, or is it a slight pressure, or an awareness somehow. I asked her if she now knows what she has to do and she nodded yes. She made a few remarks about how she experienced it as a sense of relief to know that she can make up her own mind. She will leave her boyfriend and later she will tell others about it. By the next session a week later she reported that she had navigated the separation well. The herpes and burning sensations are apparently gone.

RH's Casebook: Anxiety Attack

Stage 1: Information – Data Collection, Initiation

A semi-regular client, who worked nearby, rang for an immediate session – she was in the beginning of an anxiety attack. I told her to come straight over. She arrived within a few minutes. She was very anxious and could have been heading for a panic attack. I immediately sought to externalize her anxiety (we had done several Mirroring Hands processes before and so she needed no explanation of what I was asking): *I wonder if you can hold your hands in front of you and really focus on them like we have done before … and with palms facing … Can you feel an energy between those hands?* She nodded. *And if you can now feel that energy as the energy of your anxiety …* Her gaze was fixed on her hands. I continued to facilitate her process: *Will those hands show us how intense your anxiety is right now, on a scale from 1–10, where 1 is slight and 10 is the very worst?* Her hands began to move apart.

I asked her to tell me the number so that I could appreciate the scale she was creating between her hands. She replied shakily, "That's 7½ …"

Stage 2: Incubation – Arousal

I reacted with a simple acknowledgment of her assessment: *OK … is there something you want to do with that energy, that anxiety between your hands?* She watched her hands intently, almost wide eyed. The hands began to move apart slowly. She said, "No … I want them to slow down … come closer … don't do that …" The hands were moving apart, which she didn't want, but they were moving slowly, which she did want, so I drew her attention to that quality: *Yes, I see you are slowing the hands … how wonderful that you can do that … What number do you feel you are at now?* She took a deep breath, "Nearly 8½ …" Again, I emphasized her control of the situation: *So,* not *8½, maybe* nearly *8½, but slowed down … I wonder how much more you will slow everything down?* After about half a minute her hands seemed to stop. She seemed to have gained control of the rising of her anxiety. I saw this as an expression of a phase shift.

Stage 3: Breakthrough and Illumination – Insight

She sat still, hands unmoving in front of her, for several minutes before suddenly speaking: "Everything in my life is like a 9 …" She was opening up to the extent of her distress. I continued to focus on her controls: *Your life … like a 9 … although here, with me, not much more than 8 … I wonder what number you need to be now so that we can talk about the number 9 things in your life?* She looked away from her hands for the first time and seemed to think about it: "Maybe 5 or 4 …" As she spoke her hands began to move closer. I waited less than a minute till her hands seemed to stop and asked, *And what number is your anxiety now?* I was careful to specify that I was asking about her anxiety and not other areas of her life. "About 6 …"

I continued supporting her achievement: *Ah, that must feel a little better … we're nearly able to talk about those things in your life … As you feel more ready to talk with me, will those hands come a little closer and your anxiety come down a little more?* She was clearly feeling more relaxed: "Yes, I want to talk about it … so unfair… nothing I could do …" Her eyes began to tear up. I took this as a positive discharge of her upset, at least more positive than anxiety: *So brave of you to share with me, and so wonderful that you can bring yourself down to a 5 or a 4 so we can do just that … What number are we at now?* Her hands began to lose their stiffness and she wiggled her fingers a little: "I really do want to tell you … yes, 5, maybe 4 … Let's talk now …" Her tears began to roll down her cheeks, but she was not sobbing and seemed to be comforted by the tears.

She spoke about the relationship issue we had been dealing with previously and about the new problems with her current employment. Although this was a productive stage 3 discharge, I wondered what her realization had been that enabled her to gain control over her anxiety. Eventually, she revealed her breakthrough: "I always put my energy in the wrong place. More than that, I let other people put my energy in the wrong place. I see that now. That's what we've been talking about all this time ..." I assured her that we were working toward what she needed and it looks like she now knows what she needs to know.

Stage 4: Verification – Reintegration

For the first time she talked about what she was going to do to change things, rather than just manage them. This was our fifth and last session, although I saw her again in the street and she reported that she was now able to use her "hands" whenever her energy seemed to be in the wrong place. I was happy to see the locus of control where it should be – within her.

Review

We are not trying to teach how to control symptoms. We are looking to discover where the symptoms will lead us. Learning how to have a healing relationship with yourself is to learn how to cooperate in a natural, comfortable way with the natural cycles and rhythms and to be sensitively aware of the messages that emerge from time to time from the self-organizing processes continuously occurring in the inner implicit world. Ernest Rossi, more than twenty years ago, called this a *symptom path to enlightenment*.

It is precisely when the client, and you, feels fatigued, when the symptoms seem to be getting worse, that we know the natural inner system is calling out for a period of healing hypnosis. We need to work carefully through this process with clients. There are a number of highly popular self-development programs that deliberately push participants toward critical phase shifts. This can be completely liberating for some, but if there is no regulation or individual care when allowing symptoms to intensify, some can be left worse off than when they started. Symptom scaling in Mirroring Hands is all about facilitating the client's safe passage along their symptom path to an enlightenment.

The important thing for therapists and clients to learn is not to be afraid of symptoms. Find a rapport with your symptom as a valuable messenger who only seeks to bring something important to your attention. The intention of our human system is, where possible, for things to get better, for problems to be solved, and for there to be a healing that produces integration and well-being. Find the conversation that the symptom is trying to open – right down into your inner, implicit world. Feel the intensity and ask it where it is taking the therapeutic process. It is only by ignoring or suppressing symptoms that we cause more distress. The greater the intensity, the closer you are to a place of phase shift where it is possible to leap outward at the growing edge.

Chapter 12

Improvising, Drama, and Mirroring Hands

The Flow of Client-Responsive Therapy

RH: I remember how I was trained to respond with minimal cues, but to be client-responsive we need to be responding to minimal cues … involuntary actions, sounds, facial expressions, moods, tiredness, focus, distractedness …

ER: Yes, there's a lot going on …

RH: The crazy thing is, I learned about being client-responsive when I was a professional actor. Really good training for psychotherapy …

ER: I trained with Lee Strasberg …

RH: My goodness, Ernie, that's amazing!

ER: I learned how to be private in public. That's what actors understand …

RH: Yes, indeed …

ER: … and clients, who often have no idea how to talk about what is really troubling them, are genuinely comforted when we let them work privately. It's a big relief. Then they manage to get something out and you respond with how wonderful they are to be able to do that.

RH: We should all do a little acting in our lives.

ER: Yes, to be totally responsive …

RH: … and constantly surprised not only at what the other person does, but also how they inspire your next action.

ER: We should do some acting workshops for therapists … write something about that …

From the Rossi/Hill conversations, June 2016

Improvisation is defined as: to create spontaneously, without preparation, from what is available. In essence, improvisation happens in the moment in response to what is happening in the moment. Although it is not possible to prepare or predetermine a spontaneous reaction, it is founded and enriched by all the ways in which life has prepared the participants up to this moment. When a therapeutic activity emerges into a therapist's mind, it is shaped by what the therapist has learned, their past experiences, and even their future imaginings and expectations.

Improvisation is used very successfully *as* a therapy, most notably in drama therapy. During Mirroring Hands, improvisation is utilized *in* the therapy. It is a fundamental factor of the process. Therapeutic techniques and approaches are commonly taught as if from an instruction manual. It is almost contradictory, however, to be client-responsive *and* follow a practical manual. Having said that, it can be very important and sometimes necessary for therapists to utilize a formalized therapy, administer questionnaires, and assign various tests. These have their place and can be very helpful, but they are not designed as opportunities for a client to explore themselves in a *personal, private,* and *self-directed* way.

Self-exploration

The primary focus of Mirroring Hands is to facilitate the client's self-exploration and for the therapist to be non-directive and client-responsive. This means that every Mirroring Hands experience involves improvisation. Although Mirroring Hands has a structured framework, utilizes language principles, and has distinct forms, much of what happens is an improvisation between the client and therapist. The preparation stage (stage 1) can often begin in a predictable way (although not always), but if a client shows they are not ready to proceed during the preparation phase, it is not unusual to improvise with other therapies, including formal therapies. This is done in a client-responsive way to help the client shift into a more receptive and productive therapeutic consciousness. We remind you again that we believe a therapist needs to have a broad "classical" knowledge base, just as an improvising musician needs to have practiced the scales and played formalized music for many years in preparation for improvisation.

Mirroring Hands is more likely to move in surprising directions in stage 2 as the client confronts their unique problem. In stage 3, the client enters unknown territory as they respond to their breakthrough discovery with an outpouring of creative possibilities. In stage 4, both therapist and client are working at the growing edge as the new "territory" is embraced and implemented into what will become the client's new way of life. The following case examples show how individual sessions of Mirroring Hands can shift in unique directions quite easily. Sometimes the shifts and changes spontaneously emerge as a total surprise, even for the client. The therapist needs to have their wits about them to keep up as the client engages in their extraordinary therapeutic journey.

ER's Casebook: Client Invention

At a conference, I accepted a volunteer from the audience. A woman in her sixties settled into the chair beside me and I began by silently raising one of my hands. She mirrored my action, but instead of looking at her own hand, she was intently looking at mine. In my surprise, I didn't raise my other hand, allowing her to remained fixated on my already raised hand. Fortunately, I was quick witted enough not to try to "correct" her by telling her to look at her own hand. Instead, I waited patiently for what she would do next. Before I was able to say anything, I noticed a slight quiver in a couple of her fingers. The movement was rapid enough to indicate that it was the involuntary type of movement that comes from within, and not consciously driven. Her focus shifted from my hand to her own as her fingers began to move more noticeably. After a few minutes, I said, *And knowing you can share as much or as little of that as you wish ... only what I would need to hear to help you further ...*

She began to speak quietly about what was happening between her fingers. She felt that the fingers were moving as if all by themselves and she felt that they represented people in her life. Her forefinger was herself, her thumb was her husband, and the little finger was one of her children. Then she brought her other hand forward, declaring that the other little finger was another child. She began to describe how her fingers were representing uncles, aunts, grandmothers, brothers, and so on. Her emotional expressions began to shift and her vocalization changed as the fingers were "talking" to each other. She continued to alternate between talking and a silent play between the fingers of both hands.

It seemed clear that she did not need my interference, so as she continued, I looked out into the audience to see how they were reacting to the demonstration. To my surprise, I noticed that quite a number of people in the audience were also engaged in their own private finger play. Because this was a demonstration at a conference, with limited time, I had to find an appropriate moment to bring the process to a close. We were able to spend a few minutes discussing how this had helped and what changes she might make to her daily activities and with her family. I finally reminded her that her learning and healing could continue during the ultradian healing periods that can occur as often as every couple of hours. I had never participated in a Mirroring Hands experience like this before, and only rarely afterwards.

RH's Casebook: Invention in the Moment

My daughter, a journalist, was working in Beirut when I answered a late night phone call from her. It would have been early evening, around 8pm for her. She had recently discovered that she had "something on her brain" which may be a cancerous growth. We had found very good medical support close to where she was living, but this was a stressful time. The following is an edited version of the highlights and relevant elements of the conversation. I am represented by "R" and my daughter by "D."

D: Dad, I'm coming back from the doctor and I'm a bit freaked out.

R: Are you home?

D: No, I'm sitting in a stairwell on the way home. I don't want to go home and upset (my husband) any more than he already is. I'm freaking out. What can I do?

We spoke about what had happened at the hospital. The information from the doctor was detailed and useful, but not very helpful for her emotional state. It was necessary for me to behave more like a therapist than a father. I carefully explained what the technical information might mean and what she might be feeling physically and emotionally. This seemed to be helpful. I began to assess her level of anxiety.

R: What can you see about you?

D: I don't know. Nothing much. The lighting is not good.

R: Are you able to get up now and go home?

D: I don't know what I want to do, Dad. Is there anything you can do to help?

Being in a poorly lit stairwell in Beirut is not comforting and she was not thinking clearly. Her voice was shaky and tense. I determined that she was in a state of anxiety that was affecting both her thinking and her mobility. This also suggested that she might be close to panic. I wanted to draw her attention away from her internal fear and trauma. What could I do over the phone? I spontaneously began a Mirroring Hands process.

R: Darling, can you see your hands?

I realized as I spoke that she was holding her phone, so one hand was not available.

R: I know you can only see one hand. That's OK. What else can you see in front of you?

D: Umm … I don't …

R: I wonder if you can see your knees?

D: Yes, Dad.

R: I wonder … what do they look like? … What are you wearing? … Can you see the color? …

She began to describe the jeans she was wearing. I encouraged her to look for anything interesting about the color, the material, and the way she was holding her knees. Then I asked:

R: And I wonder if one of those knees is a strong knee, maybe stronger than the other?

D: Yeah … I guess my right knee is stronger … you know, because of my back …

R: OK … and right now … as you feel that anxiety within you, causing you all sorts of upset and worry … will you share that struggle with one of those knees … maybe the strong right knee … maybe the other knee …

D: The strong knee is a good idea. I can do that …

Because I was not able to see what was happening, I did not pause for too long. It was important to maintain the connection.

R: Yes, that's wonderful … and can you feel something change for the better?

D: Yes, Dad, a bit better …

R: And I wonder about the other knee … can you shift your attention to that left knee? … I wonder what that knee feels, while your right knee has the strength to share your anxiety?

She began to speak about the things that were difficult and made her feel weak, unable to manage, and afraid for the future. Without the confusion of her anxiety, she was better able to sort out her thoughts and we planned how she could share the information from the doctor with her husband. After some 25–30 minutes on the phone, she had recovered enough to get to her feet and complete the walk home.

This was the first time in my experience that Mirroring Hands had become "Mirroring Knees," but it is a perfect example of including other parts of the body, if and when that is what the client makes available. Utilizing a basic accessing question allowed us both to discover what might be possible, and what was acceptable, to both her explicit and implicit worlds. Most importantly, I was able to connect her to her own problem-solving and mind–body healing because once the phone call ended she would be on her own again. We were both confident, as we said goodbye, that she had regained the locus of control.

(An excellent medical team at the hospital in Beirut was able to operate soon after. The surgeon was able to successfully remove a surface located oligoastrocytoma. She has recovered well and, several years after the event, has had no recurrence.)

Mixing Mirroring Hands in with Other Techniques

We have shown that Mirroring Hands is not a technique that is limited in its use. Mirroring Hands can be utilized at any time. Mirroring Hands is a process that can break through a barrier or resistance, or those times when the client and/or the therapist feel unable to access what needs to be known. Mirroring Hands can be utilized to open a door or reveal something hidden, and then the session can return to the previous protocol. In the very first example presented in this book's introduction, the therapist was in the process of standard rapport building. The client's emphatic hand gestures triggered the therapist's spontaneous shift to Mirroring Hands. That proved to be a very beneficial direction to take.

Regardless of what therapeutic protocol has revealed the restriction, shifting the resistance can be achieved by asking the client to place the dominating position in one hand. Once this has been done, attention can be shifted to what is in the other hand (i.e. what is "not that dominant position"). As we described in Chapter 8, creating a differentiation between the polarities of a situation releases the potentials and possibilities of each element.

RH's Casebook: With Rogerian

A client presented with a non-specific, general discomfort about her life. She had some neurological damage after an early age stroke. Although now in her thirties, she found it hard to sit still. This was quite apparent, but I wondered whether this was partly due to her very quick and highly imaginative mind. The session began in a Rogerian listening and supporting framework. She told a rambling narrative that was hard to follow at times. It was difficult to know which parts of her narrative were important. As the conversation proceeded, I began to notice a somatic behavior – her foot jiggled in an agitated way, but every now and again it would stop for a sentence or two and then become agitated again. After a short while she paused and asked for my reflections. I reflected back those things she had said while her foot was still. Her eyes widened, she sat forward, and wondered incredulously how I had known to choose only the things that really mattered to her.

I asked her if she might like to agitate her foot and notice what thoughts and feelings came to her. She began jiggling her foot and related what was coming to mind. The thoughts were short and jumped from one thing to another. We continued this for about 10 minutes when she began to slow down. I asked her what was happening and she replied, "I'm actually getting bored with myself!"

I then wondered what might come to her mind if her foot was still. Again, I asked her to notice and relate her thoughts and feelings as they emerged. For the first time since entering the room she was quiet and thoughtful. I reassured her that she did not need to share any words with me, only those that she wished to. She began to share a few things, but then quietly enjoyed her own private thoughts for the next 15 minutes or so.

This was an improvised "Mirroring Foot" process that allowed the client to find her *important voice* and distinguish this from her *chatter*. The movement in her foot was the symptom/message that emerged from her implicit world. She now had an indicator of when her mind was producing important and meaningful thoughts. This was an important piece in the puzzle of her reclaiming some control of her mental processes. She declared this to be a very satisfying session.

RH's Casebook: With CBT

A female in her late twenties was mandated by her workplace for cognitive behavioral therapy (CBT). She was having arguments with other staff members. It was apparent that she was not quick witted and her records showed a below average IQ. We were completing one of the standard CBT forms which asks for, among other things, the client's current thought and a possible alternative thought.[1] She was becoming upset as she struggled to find any alternative thoughts. She was having no appreciable problem naming the triggers for her thought, what emotions she was experiencing, and the justifications for her thought. However, when asked what the contradictions to that thought were, and what alternatives might be reasonable, she was very resistant. The more she thought about the justifications for her thought, the more she was convinced that her thought was correct. Filling out the form became distressing. She was worried what the people at work would think about her answers.

I suspected that part of her resistance might also be a winner/loser world issue. She seemed quite fearful of being wrong and failing in her thinking. Somehow, any alternative thought was in competition with her original thought. It suddenly felt natural for me to utilize Mirroring Hands in an attempt to shift her fear of losing and being shamed. After a brief discussion, she agreed that there *might* be another thought in her mind, and that thought *could* be interesting and helpful. I began with a very quick preparation question so as not to lose her attention:

> *We know that you are interested in finding whether there might be another thought in your mind ... If you would like to do that now, will your hands raise up in front of you, so your elbows are at a right angle ...*

1 See, for example: https://psychologytools.com/cbt.html.

She has the option to stop the process right here, but if she raises her hands, then she is making a personal contract with herself to explore this possibility. She did, indeed, raise her hands.

> *Wonderful! Already something extraordinary is happening … maybe there is a very important thought in your mind that you have never thought about before … If we look carefully at those hands … I wonder which hand might be the one that represents that extraordinary thought … but first, which hand is able to hold the thought you have already written down … the thought we have been talking about …*

The client stared at her hands quite intently.

> *And will the hand that can hold the thought you know all about, will that hand somehow give us a sign that it is ready … a movement … almost all by itself…*

The client (represented by "CL") moves her right hand up and down while saying:

> *CL: I think it's this one …*
>
> *RH: It certainly looks that way! How extraordinary that your hand seems to know all by itself that it can hold your thought! Will that thought comfortably go into that hand? … Is there anything we need to do now to help that thought or help that right hand?*
>
> *CL: No … everything seems OK … pretty good …*
>
> *RH: Wonderful! … So can we now shift our attention from your right hand to your left hand … I wonder what extraordinary thought that hand might be holding? … Something else within you that is not the thought you have in your right hand … Something you have never thought before …*
>
> *CL: No … well … maybe … I don't feel like I am in any trouble in my left hand … it feels kinda … not … guilty.*
>
> *RH: Yes, not guilty … not in trouble … yes …*
>
> *CL: This hand doesn't have any thoughts … and it is not getting into trouble … maybe I think too much …*
>
> *RH: Think too much … I haven't heard you say that before … I wonder what that means …*

The client then began to talk about how she becomes confused when she has to think, and sometimes wishes that she was asleep all the time so her thoughts wouldn't give her so many problems. The idea that she might think too much was an important breakthrough. We spoke for a little while and then she became silent. I left her to quieten her brain and her thoughts. Later we returned to the CBT program sheet which she was now able to complete. She discovered something through

Mirroring Hands which was a struggle with the CBT form – that her alternative thought was to not have any thought at all about the issue.

Review

Improvisation is a natural part of Mirroring Hands and is a natural factor in a client-responsive approach. When you think about it, daily living is a constant improvisation. Things continually come along to surprise and generate an unexpected response or reaction. Improvisation does not mean to be flying blind, however. Preparations for a therapeutic session can include various materials and a general session plan, but it is not possible to prepare the *specific* words or *detailed* actions for a *client-responsive* session.

An improvisation is as rich as what the participants bring with them into the improvisational space (i.e. how they have prepared). If an actor enters an "improvisational space" with a piano, sits down, and begins to play Rachmaninoff, then it is reasonable to say that the person has had many years of preparation with piano lessons and performance experience. If they play "Chopsticks," then another level of preparation is being expressed. Similarly, in therapy, the client and the therapist both enter the "therapeutic space" with years of preparation, a plethora of expectations, and a host of disruptors, perturbators, and attractors (factors that affect self-organizing systems – see Chapter 2) that will pull, push, and draw the therapeutic experience in various directions. The therapeutic experience is an unpredictable dance of creativity, curiosity, and possibility that the client cannot ordinarily achieve on their own in their current everyday life.

Mirroring Hands follows the actions and reactions of the client, self-organizing from the client and therapist's collective wellspring of knowledge and experience, in a mutual effort to engage with the natural problem-solving and mind–body healing capacities that lie within us all. The case examples in this chapter show a small selection of the many different and surprising directions in which a Mirroring Hands process can go. Symptoms emerge as indicators, signposts, and cracks in doorways to the deeper truth of the issue and to the natural resolution. But what can the client do in-between sessions when the therapist is not there? Can an individual assist themselves? The next chapter explores this question and shows how it is possible to facilitate a solo Mirroring Hands experience.

Chapter 13

Personal Access to Your Growing Edge

Solo and Personal Use of Mirroring Hands

ER: … the power for transformation is inside the client, not the therapist …

RH: … and the mirroring is not deceitful, as can be in some things. Whenever I do it, with clients or even on my own, I am truly intrigued by my hands.

ER: There is a flow, a wisdom, and a knowing within each person that they have the ability to go toward health, and I believe that everybody really wants to move toward health …

RH: The question is, "How do I do it?"

From the Rossi/Hill conversations, June 2016

Can people utilize Mirroring Hands without the participation of a therapist to facilitate? The simple answer is yes, but the experience will be very different. The therapist's years of practice, and the many other things that a therapist can facilitate beyond the Mirroring Hands process, creates a unique therapeutic relational experience. The purpose of Mirroring Hands, however, is to open a connection within an individual to their own natural problem-solving and mind–body healing. These natural processes are available to us all in one way or another. This chapter will explore:

- How individuals can utilize Mirroring Hands outside of a formal therapy session.
- How Mirroring Hands can assist in sensitive situations with cared for others including partners, family, and children.
- The many ways in which people can benefit from the ultradian healing response.
- A new solo Mirroring Hands process that engages with the ultradian healing response at the growing edge.

Self-Care and Caution

If you are in any doubt or concern that self or solo work is not adequate, or you feel uncomfortable or unsure, or if symptoms persist, seek professional help. At all times in life, if there is loss of consciousness, difficulty in breathing, or serious physical distress, seek medical help immediately.

Messages from Within

Let us first recall some important fundamentals: Mirroring Hands, and the Mirroring Hands approach, is not just a cognitive process, but the opening of a connection, a communication channel, between cognitive consciousness and our inner, implicit self-organizing world. The inner world expresses itself through emergent properties and qualities that are able to be noticed, consciously acted on, and reflected upon. When these messages from within are integrated positively and productively into our daily living, we create *beneficial change*. These messages come in many forms, including thoughts, behaviors, emotions, and sensations. In therapy, these messages are often called symptoms, but they are messages nonetheless.

It is a reasonable and common practice – not only in therapy, but also in schools, businesses, at home, and in relationships – to consider the pros and cons when trying to resolve a problem. Thinking in dichotomies (cause and effect, right and wrong, good and bad, safe and dangerous, etc.) has a basis in nature, but it is a simple, and even simplistic, view of the complexity of life situations. In Mirroring Hands, we are not just simplistically looking at what is in one hand and what is in the other. The key purpose of the act is to differentiate between the two hands to allow the *possibilities* of the elements to emerge. Otherwise, there is only the dominating element.

To put it another way, it is not just about rationally thinking it through, although that is an important part of every process, but having the patience to wait for something to emerge from within. As we have seen, implicit messages can sometimes seem to appear *all by themselves*. It is about allowing the time to "sit with" the process, to sensitively observe, and to notice what emerges. Then it is a matter of responding in a way that moves you toward resolution, health, and well-being. It is the time you take to pause and wait that makes the difference.

We have already described that we have a natural period, called the ultradian healing response, about every couple of hours, when we can benefit from a 10–20 minute pause. The ultradian healing response is consistent with stage 4 of the creative cycle. Equally, we have other natural periods that flow across the ultradian rhythm: a time for exploring (stage 1), for self-examining (stage 2), and for insight and creative release (stage 3). To be engaged with the flow of our ultradian rhythm, all we need to do is pay attention to the messages and signals, and consciously cooperate. We remind you of the script we have suggested for the closing of a Mirroring Hands process:

> *When ... your unconscious knows it can continue that inner healing ... and when ... your conscious mind knows it can cooperate by helping you recognize those periods during the day ... will you find yourself awakening?*

Self-Care

An important part of facilitating Mirroring Hands is to help the client open and then close the process. In solo practice, it is not so difficult to begin, but a natural closing point needs to be put in place. We will look at how two of the facilitated forms, Closing the Door and Holding Both Sides of the Mirror, can be modified to close in a safe and comfortable way.

1. Closing the Door (Chapter 10)

This form is the most suited to solo practice because there is a natural closing point when the "positive" hand touches the body. It is then just a matter of allowing the resulting positive feelings to strengthen and comfort for a minute or two. The intention of this practice is to both reduce and discharge what is disrupting or disturbing, and also to amplify the presence and awareness of hidden strengths, creative problem-solving, and self-comfort. There is usually a natural sense that the process is over – all that needs to be done is complete – and it is safe to return to normal activities.

Stage 1

Selecting which hand will receive the "negative" and which will receive the "positive" only requires a moment or two of focus on the hands to notice which feels different in whatever way makes sense in that moment. Then choose which hand will receive whatever is bothering you. There is no need to raise the hands in front of you unless you wish to. Because this can be practiced anywhere, and at any time, it may not always be convenient to raise the hands. We will demonstrate this in the case examples.

Stage 2

Allow the "energy," the feeling, or inner sensation (which we also call the *quantum qualia*) to flow out into the hand, just as happens in a facilitated session. To control the timeframe, mentally set a point when you will shift attention to the "positive" hand. This might be a feeling, such as a certain weight, or when the energy is a certain size in the hand, or even after a certain time period.

Stage 3

The breakthrough is the intuitive decision that you have expelled as much of the negativity as necessary and you are ready to "close the door" on what has been expelled. Before shifting attention to the other hand, be clear in your mind that the negative property is contained in the hand and not able to flow back into your inner space. Then, allow whatever may be within you that can overcome the negative issue – solve it, resolve it, conquer it, be stronger than it – and whatever else is wonderful and extraordinary about you, to flow out to your "positive" hand. This energy does not need to come entirely out of your body, but form an "energy pillar" between the body and the hand. When you can feel that flow between body and hand, begin to draw the hand toward the part of the body from which the negative energy emerged. When your "positive" hand touches and covers that part of the body you are "closing the door." You may feel as if your "positive" hand has moved *all by itself* or you might consciously move the hand. Either is effective in solo work.

Stage 4

Feel the *positive wonder of you* fill what was once occupied by the negative issues to create a new, safe stronghold within. Let that positive process continue on its own as you return your attention to the "negative" hand. What would you like to do with that energy now? Shake it off? Throw it away? Put it in the rubbish? Seal it in a bag and then throw it away? Do whatever you believe gets rid of that negativity. Once rid of it, your attention can return to the positive interplay occurring under your "positive" hand. Allow that to continue for as long as you need. When you feel it is time, allow your hands to return to normal activity. Remember that you will continue to benefit from this healing process throughout the ensuing day and night, even if only at the implicit level. You can repeat the explicit physical activity of "closing the door" as often as you feel is natural and comfortable (strengthening).

RH's Casebook: Sleeping

"Closing the door" is a very successful way to bring on healthy sleep when the mind is racing, you are not feeling well, or you seem unable to sleep for reasons you don't understand. An anxious client found that she could sometimes name what was keeping her awake, but she could also, just as effectively, focus on the thought, *All those things, whatever they are, that are interfering with my sleep, get out into my right (or left) hand.* Equally, when in stage 3, she would think, *Everything inside me that can help me sleep and can give me peace and calm, please make yourself known in my left (or right) hand.* Being in bed when she began the process, her hands were usually alongside her body. As she discharged the problem into her "negative" hand, she found that her arm would move away from her body. The "positive" hand moved to the wherever it needed to go to "close the door." The first time she did this, she needed to repeat the process three times. The next time she tried, she woke some hours later to find her "positive" hand on her chest. She now finds that she falls asleep during her first attempt.

RH's Casebook: Work Stress

I follow my own advice when I feel stress during work and take a break to go for a walk. The traffic lights nearby have a surprisingly slow cycle. One day, I noticed that my left hand felt cooler in the breeze. Without moving my hands from my side, I wondered if I could send whatever energy, ideas, worries, physical sensations, and muscle aches out into my left hand. Then, I mentally sent the calming things about me and the good feelings I had in my life into my right hand. Nobody at the crossing paid much attention when my right hand lifted up to my shoulder. By the time the lights changed for pedestrians to cross, I was feeling much calmer and more relaxed. This is now a regular three-minute dose of ultradian healing that I enjoy whenever I wait for those traffic lights.

RH's Casebook: Anger Management

A client was troubled by his build-up of anger, largely from his frustration at others. Our sessions were going well and he found that Mirroring Hands was making a big difference in his ability to control the build-up. He was concerned, however, that he still had some difficulty. We rehearsed a solo use of Mirroring Hands. Instead of letting his anger build up, he found he could open the door and let the anger pour out into his hand. He would then "close the door" and discard the anger. He was then able to focus on the positive things he had revealed to himself during therapy.

RH's Casebook: Addiction

A client needed something to help him dissipate the temptation to play poker machines. He had to pass some five hotels with machines on his way to and from work. We compiled a strategy that included changing the route he used to avoid the hotels, but we also used a solo practice of Mirroring Hands to help him find his strengths. The negative hand was usually the hand nearest the hotel and his positive hand was able to draw him – he described it as being dragged away – from the hotel doorway.

These are just a small sample of the ways in which an individual can amplify their strengths and diminish the disruptions that interfere with their enjoyment of life. Solo practice is a way to help someone manage an issue at the time it occurs. We do not consider it safe for individuals to explore unknown psychological territory and unknown areas of their inner world with solo practice. That is best left for facilitated therapy. There is no danger in solo practice that is exploring for strengths. As we have stated before, the problem is being sent *away* from the inner self and the process is always under the user's control.

Holding Both Sides of the Mirror (Chapter 8)

The purpose of this form, as a solo Mirroring Hands, is to help shift a stuck situation or to open the mind to those things that are hidden by something dominating or overwhelming. Again, this is not about cognitive deductions, but creating a pause that allows hidden aspects of the situation to emerge and stimulate some sort of change. Stuck situations are in rigidity and need stimulation, whereas overwhelming situations are chaotic and require some sort of calming and balance. This can be hard to achieve when all you can see and feel is being stuck or overwhelmed.

Stage 1

When you feel you are ready to access something to help you change your current situation, raise your hands in front of you and calm your mind. Focus your attention on your hands and the natural processes of your body. Notice your breath, your heartbeat, what happens when you take a deep breath, what the sounds and smells around you are. Allow yourself to notice the differences between your hands, even just the obvious difference of one being on the right side and one on the left. When you know which hand is more prominent, project the stuckness or the overwhelm out to that hand.

Stage 2

When you have a clear sense that you have isolated the issue to one hand, turn your attention to the other hand. What is in that hand? Is anything in that hand? Is there something within you that wishes to be projected into that hand? Is there something in that hand that wants to help you? Ignite your curiosity about the possibilities that you have been unable to appreciate until now, until the stuckness or the overwhelm has been moved to one side.

Stage 3

Notice all the changes. How are you breathing? What does your beating heart feel like? Is there something new in what you hear and smell? Do you feel any emotions rising? Do you hear a word, a phrase, or a sentence in your mind? Is there something you can feel in your hand? What is the opportunity for change that these things are offering you? What do you know in this moment that was hidden before? Is there any reaction from the hand that is holding the stuckness or overwhelm?

Stage 4

What can you now do with these sensations and new realizations to resolve your situation? Take some time to embrace all these new things and start to develop the strategy or begin the plan to implement these changes. Do you still feel stuck or overwhelmed?

The results of "revealing the opposite" can range in effectiveness. Regardless of the outcome, this solo practice, at the very least, shows that the stuck or overwhelming difficulty can be isolated. The benefits of this process are likely to continue throughout the day and even in your dreams, so it is a good idea to pay close attention to the thoughts and feelings that emerge over the next day or two. It is a good idea to write them down or record them on a mobile phone for later review. It is important to remember that the implicit world continues to self-organize problem-solving and stimulate mind–body healing even though you are not consciously aware that it is happening.

ER's Casebook: Pain

The client suffered from a sharp pain in his shoulder that would wake him up. He was reticent to take too many painkillers, so we had been working on creating changes in the pain experience so that it was more manageable. Mirroring Hands had been helpful at the clinic. His breakthrough was the realization that he had the power to change the shape of his pain. He wondered if he could use the process himself when the pain attacked and so we rehearsed solo practice. The next time he woke in pain, he was able to rapidly choose a "sharp pain" hand and isolate the sharpness to that hand. He was then able to shift his attention to his other hand, which he called the "long pain" hand. He found that when he focused his attention on the long pain hand, the pain would extend and distribute. Although he still had the pain, it was not as intense and he was better able to manage the discomfort. We have attempted other transformations of the pain with varying success, but he was regularly able to convert the sharp pain to a long pain and so minimize his analgesic intake.

RH's Casebook: Creative Block

A writer sought help for what he thought was procrastination. When we discussed the issue, he realized that it was more about being stuck at a point in the writing. The longer he struggled to find what to write next, the more his mind was blank of ideas. He would then leave his computer and do other things, hence his first impression that it was procrastination. He was able to make little breakthroughs at the clinic, but he wanted to be able to do this at his desk. We rehearsed how to do solo practice. At the next session, he reported that when he isolated the "stuckness" to one hand, it felt like a high wall. When he shifted attention to his other hand, he was particularly aware that his breathing changed and his heartbeat seemed to be stronger. His eyes were closed and he could imagine the wall in front of him. To his surprise, he could feel himself, at least in his mind's eye, getting taller. After a short spurt of this "growth" he found that he could look over the wall and "see" the next part of the story. He wasn't sure if it was a literal vision or just the thought rising into his consciousness. Regardless, he was now able to "get over" the barrier to his writing.

Care for Others

Solo practice is helpful for an individual to create a positive shift in a difficult situation, but sometimes a person is too overwhelmed to self-facilitate a Mirroring Hands process. A caring "other" might be able to help. A parent, partner, or close friend usually has the trust and rapport that is needed. It can help the distressed person to move the "negative" elements to one hand, which separates and even isolates the problem. It is then possible to explore the "positive" side. Projecting the overwhelming issue out into the hand can also give the person a sense of having some control over it. Rather than being something that is distressingly overwhelming them or disturbingly within them, they can hold it and perhaps even move it about. This, on its own, can be a very empowering shift.

The carer begins by inviting the person to imagine projecting the problem/issue/upset into their hand. Assure them that this is a way they can "get a grip" of it and even "move it away." When they are ready to shift attention to the other hand, the carer only needs to use simple language to talk about the positive thoughts and feelings that emerge. The purpose is to get the "negative" out of the way so the "positive" can be accessed to help the person feel stronger. It might feel comfortable to end with a "closing the door" process or just a comforting and relieving hug. If the carer is being responsive, then whatever spontaneously emerges will be helpful for the other person.

These are some of the situations in which a "carer practice" has been helpful:

- Parent and child:
  - Helping a child fall asleep in a facilitated version of "closing the door" (described earlier for solo practice).
  - Calming anger and frustration can be facilitated by directing the emotion to one hand and allowing what has triggered the emotion to be expressed in the other hand.

  - Relieving and calming a fearful upset, such as being bullied, can be helped by putting the bullying (or the bully) into one hand and allowing the child to engage with their self-value and self-esteem in the other hand.
  - Managing an upset between friends by isolating the immediate catastrophe in one hand and recalling past positive experiences of the friendship in the other hand.
- Partners:
  - When arguments turn to hyperbole – *always, never, can't* – these extremes can be sent to one hand and the more balanced truth of the matter can be explored in the other hand.
  - A sudden and upsetting disappointment can be eased by sending the upset to one hand and allowing the changes and new possibilities to be present in the other hand.
- Emotional first-aid:
  - When an emotional response is overwhelming the other person, the carer can extend their sensitive empathy to the overwhelmed person and, at the same time, gently direct the emotional activity to one side and eventually into one of the hands. This can help to shift the overwhelming engulfment to an emotion they can hold, and perhaps even begin to observe at a distance from the body.

These examples are not meant as a thorough training program. Competency at utilizing Mirroring Hands as a solo or carer practice might require additional training and experience. This can be gained through workshops, demonstrations, and private tuition. These examples are intended to show the sorts of common issues that can be helped and suggest a few options. You might feel that the life experience and skills you already possess resonate with the Mirroring Hands approach. We hope you can integrate our suggestions to improve your own natural solo and carer practices.

Engaging in the Ultradian Healing Response

Whichever way you are able to utilize solo and carer practices, you can be confident that there is a readily available opportunity for everyone to gain benefit from their natural inner problem-solving and mind–body healing. We are all able to engage with the natural ultradian rhythm and benefit from the ultradian healing response periods throughout the day and night.

As described in Chapter 5, the ultradian healing response is an important period of time in daily life. Energetic activity and arousal levels rise and fall across the 90–120 minute basic rest–activity cycle, which repeats to create the ultradian rhythm. Energy increases through the first part of the cycle reaching a high period of peak performance. High energy peak performance is, of course, unsustainable, and so, in the latter part of the cycle there is a natural falling away of energy and activity.

This fall settles into a period of pause that is the time necessary for recharge, repair, refreshment, and reactivation in preparation for the cycle to begin again. Pushing through these periods of natural pause interferes with more than just energy flow. The 15–20 minute ultradian healing response is a time when important consolidation and integration of the previous cycle(s) takes place.[1] Essential processes at this time include brain plasticity for learning, memory, and problem-solving; immune system responses that enable self-healing; and the integration of newly formed ideas and realizations into daily life.

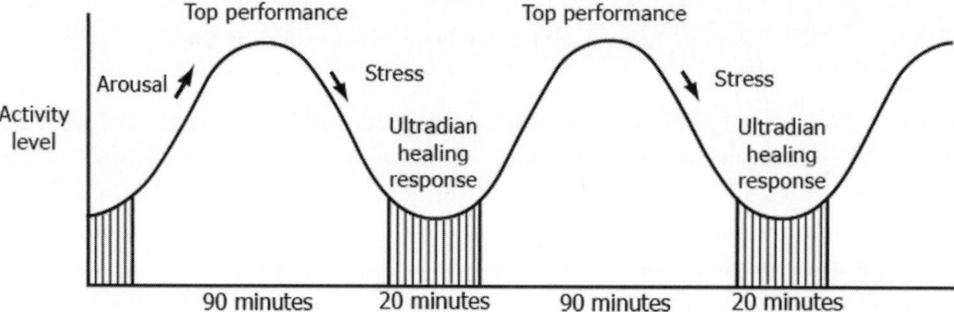

Figure 13.1. The ultradian rhythm

Figure 13.1 (first shown in Chapter 5 where we considered the ultradian healing response) is an idealized representation of the ultradian rhythm. Life is a little less exact, but, in essence, it is natural to pause every two hours or so for about 10–20 minutes. It is no coincidence that it is normal to pause for a meal three times a day and to have a between-meal snack another two or three times a day, and that these pauses are approximately every two hours or so. Increasingly, modern society disregards this natural rhythm as it pushes people to be at peak performance all the time.[2] The answer is not to push harder, but to engage with the ultradian healing response. That is how we can maximize the utilization of our peak performance periods.

The good news is that there are many ways to enjoy the ultradian healing response. One of the most natural is to take a meal or a break with others. An individual will have different preferences for their natural ultradian "pause." The best pause might be to come to a stop, or perhaps be more active to balance a very stationary cycle, or do something fun and playful, or perhaps engage in a quiet, contemplative inward reflection.

1 Rossi, E. L. & Nimmons, D. (1991). *The Twenty-Minute Break: Using the New Science of Ultradian Rhythms*. Los Angeles, CA: Jeremy Tarcher.

2 Schulte, B. (2014). *Overwhelmed: Work, Love, and Play When No One Has the Time*. New York: Sarah Crichton Books.

The following is a selection of common practices, other than enjoying a meal with others, that can be utilized to engage the benefits of the ultradian healing response. We have differentiated the activities into categories, although these are not fixed or instructive. Please utilize these however you find they best fit your needs. We conclude with a special contemplative, mindful Mirroring Hands process – At the Growing Edge.

- **Stop activity**: Sleep, daydream, lie in the sun, spend quiet time with a friend or partner, listen to relaxing music.
- **Change of activity**: Do whatever is the opposite of recent activity – if you were sitting then walk or play a game; if previously active then sit quietly or relax with gentle rhythmic activities like t'ai chi, yoga, or swimming; if working alone then join in a social or family activity.
- **Curious and playful**: Begin or join a spontaneous game, walk in nature, play with your children, sing (preferably with others), play a musical instrument, tell and listen to stories.
- **Contemplative**: There are many deliberate contemplative practices and some that are so natural we have taken them for granted – mindfulness, meditation, painting, dance, preparing a meal, listening to music, knitting, enjoying a sunrise and especially a sunset, contemplating your gratefulness and appreciation of your life.

At the Growing Edge

The following Mirroring Hands experience is a contemplative process that can be practiced solo or can be facilitated by a therapist. Many of the qualities ascribed to the widely popular practice of mindfulness are inherent in this practice. It also stimulates natural problem-solving and mind–body healing, and, as our research has shown, it triggers gene expression, protein synthesis, and brain plasticity, which are the implicit processes at our growing edge.[3] The intention of this exercise is to acknowledge and appreciate the self as it is in this moment *and* engage in our curiosity and wonder about the possibilities of what our life might become. The wonder of life is not in where we are now and what we are in this moment; that is our joy, our reality, our extraordinary achievement. The wonder of life is in the *possibilities* at our growing edge. This is where we are called to adventure and to discover what we might become as we choose to grow.

The following words are our suggestion as a "guiding script" for our special Mirroring Hands mindfulness practice, At the Growing Edge. It can be performed as a solo practice, or with assistance, to

3 Rossi, E. L., Iannotti, S., Cozzolino, M., Castiglione, S., Cicatelli, A. & Rossi, K. L. (2008). A pilot study of positive expectations and focused attention via a new protocol for therapeutic hypnosis assessed with DNA microarrays: the creative psychosocial genomic healing experience. *Sleep and Hypnosis: An International Journal of Sleep, Dream, and Hypnosis*, 10(2), 39–44.

explore the current self and the self that is yet to be. Make a recording of the words, or have someone record them for you, so that you can replay the recording to guide you through the meditation whenever that part within you knows it is the right time to do some creative work and your conscious mind can cooperate, allowing you to take the time to tune in. You can also ask your therapist to facilitate the process with you.

Remember that, at any time, you have the capacity to change or even stop the process. We recommend having a notebook or a voice recording device, such as a mobile phone, nearby in case you wish to record some of the emergent thoughts, feelings, or body sensations. You might do this at the end of the process, but even if you feel the need to record something before the end, you can immediately return to the process. You might choose to leave a voice recorder on for the entire session which you can then review later.

Stage 1: Preparation

Sitting quietly with your hands on your lap, focus your attention on your body as it sits in the chair, your feet on the ground, as you breathe, as the heart beats, and know that your hands are resting patiently in your lap. Close your eyes or leave them open, just as feels natural and comfortable. When you are ready to feel your presence, in the present, who you are, right now, in this moment, will you find one of your hands wanting to rise up in front of you? Allow yourself all the time you need for that hand to rise, as you feel the reality of your own presence in your hand. Nothing right or wrong, nothing good or bad, no fault or blame, no judgment or criticism. Just the truth of who you are, right now … What thoughts or feelings are emerging? What have you learned in order to be where you are now? How have you grown? What have you changed in order to be here, this way, now? … Are you wondering about what you are ready to change? When you are ready for new growth?

Stage 2: Incubation

As you begin to feel the possibilities of change and growth, at what moment will you notice your other hand wanting to rise – as the future of you? What you might be. What you could be. What you are now able to become. Where you are ready to grow … Now, as you hold up the hand of who you can become … that has lifted up beside the hand that holds you as you are … out in front of you … how will those hands share with each other now? … Care for each other now? … Strengthen each other now? … Encourage each other now? … Call out to adventure now?

Stage 3: Breakthrough and Illumination

And as the interplay between your self in the present and your self that is yet to come continues … what thoughts emerge? What visions appear? What feelings arise? Allowing who you are right now to be the launching pad … for what is soon to be … of what might be possible … of knowing something about yourself that you haven't known yet … something more … surprising? … pleasing? … challenging? … exactly what is needed?

Stage 4: Verification

Knowing what you now know … about the next episode of your adventure … which is yet to come … how might you start to grow? … How might you be the change … and bravely explore the you that you don't yet know? Will you soon be able write down or record your inspirations and insights, and those things that you now see as the very best of you, so that you can review these when you feel the time is right and when your conscious mind knows that you can take that time …

The process will naturally come to a close when you begin writing or recording those important thoughts and feeling. You may like to review what you have written or recorded straight away, or you may feel you have done all you can for now and prefer to return to it later. At the Growing Edge is likely to feel suitable when there is a sense of imminent change (i.e. a time of phase shift). It may also be helpful when there is a crisis of self and this process can help to stabilize or revitalize your strengths and your sense of purpose. One client reported in the next session that she was initially a little disappointed immediately after the process because nothing vital or spectacular had occurred. However, she continued to report excitedly that the next day she had had a most extraordinary burst of insight, an a-ha moment, that had enabled her to make a vital decision she had been resisting for some years.

Review

This chapter has a lot of elements, but they are all concerned with ways in which Mirroring Hands can be helpful for someone outside of a formal therapy session. We have also been clear to say that we do not want people to go into unknown, and potentially risky, emotional and implicit territory without someone to assist and to care for their well-being. In that light, Mirroring Hands is a process that can be utilized in many ways, not only in a professional setting but also as a solo and caring practice.

The "difference" between the hands has largely been described as something that is in the mind's eye or is effective even if it is only imagined. Mirroring Hands is a personal and subjective experience where the realizations and transformative changes that result are what is truly important for you. This still leaves us with the curious question as to whether there *really* is a biological energetic difference between the hands. This is an interesting question that warrants investigation. The next chapter shares the data from a set of experiments we conducted using a device that measures electrovolt differences and changes over time. We have correlated these graphs with the phenomenological experience of the experimental subjects, including experiments conducted by the authors.

Chapter 14

Research and Experiments

From Ravitz to Rossi

ER: Every psychotherapy encounter is a field experiment, according to Erickson … I would like to get a wearable bio-recording device … just slip it on, wireless … let the person live their normal life and after a week, get the patterns. We should see the patterns of the 90–120 minute ultradian cycle appear spontaneously …

RH: I guess we're not able to do that yet, but I really felt this Pico apparatus showed me an "energy trail" that mirrored what was happening in my mind. I'm quite convinced it's showing my mental experience, you know, not just sweaty hands but an electrodermal response …

ER: Yes! When you do an EEG, you don't call it a scalp response – it's coming from the neurons, or call an ECG a chest response – you know it is coming from the heart … So a lot is at stake here. Do we just stay at the "skin" level of cognition, or do we find a connection between the cognition and what's really going on in your brain at the quantum level?

RH: Everything we observe is a macro world reflection or expression of deeper quantum activity …

ER: Yes … I think we can assume our Pico research is a physical manifestation, observable to the human eye, of what is going on at this deep, deep level of the quantum. It's a way we can "see" what is happening at the energetic level.

From the Rossi/Hill conversations, June 2016

The experimental results we recount in this chapter are the current version of experiments that originated in the pioneering work of Milton Erickson and Leonard Ravitz about three generations ago.[1] As we detailed in Chapter 1, Ravitz was a pioneer in the measurement of human electrodynamics. In the 1950s, he and Erickson explored these energy changes in subjects during hypnosis. He and Erickson mentored Rossi in the use of the measuring apparatus during the mid-1970s, much of which is documented in Ravitz's book, *Electrodynamic Man*, published in 2002. As far as we know,

1 Erickson, M. H. (2014). *The Collected Works of Milton H. Erickson, M.D.* Vol. 11: *Experiencing Hypnosis: Therapeutic Approaches to Altered States*, ed. E. L. Rossi, R. Erickson-Klein & K. L. Rossi. Phoenix, AZ: Milton H. Erickson Foundation Press.

Ravitz's "Electrometric correlates of the hypnotic state" was the first and only scientific paper on hypnosis ever published in *Science*.[2]

In those days, Ravitz used a Burr–Lane–Nims microvoltmeter, which had "clearly demonstrated that in vertebrates, invertebrates and plants there is a relatively steady, stable voltage gradient of considerable magnitude between any two points – altered only by changes in the fundamental biology of the organism – which exists in well-defined patterns characteristic of the species and to some extent characteristic of the individual."[3] One sensor is attached to the forehead and the other to the palm of either hand (these experiments only tested one side of the body), resulting in a single continuous tracing of the energy fluctuations in the subject's mental experience. Figure 14.1 shows that, during hypnosis, the electromotive force (EMF) tracing becomes more regular and then either gradually increases or decreases in magnitude. At trance termination, there is usually a higher measurement than during the normal waking state. The tracing eventually returns to that of the normal waking state.

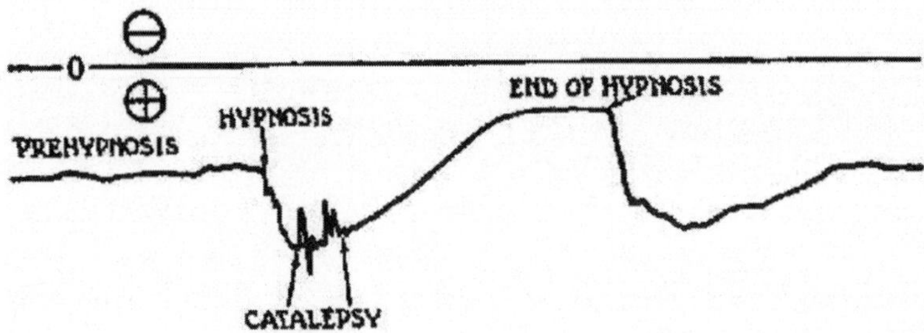

Figure 14.1. Schematic DC (direct current) record of hypnosis as it originally appeared in L. J. Ravitz (1950), Electrometric correlates of the hypnotic state. *Science*, 112, 341–342.

Catalepsy, when used to induce hypnosis, sometimes produced marked EMF changes. Any disturbance of the hypnotic state could be detected immediately by changes in voltage and in the configuration of the tracing. It is thus possible to objectively measure changes in depth of hypnosis. During the mid-1970s, about 25 years after Ravitz's paper was published in *Science*, Erickson, Ravitz, and Rossi used an improved strip-chart recording device (Heath–Schlumberger Model SR-255B[4]), which resulted in a more detailed line recording.

2 Ravitz, L. J. (1950). Electrometric correlates of the hypnotic state. *Science*, 112, 341–342.

3 Ravitz, L. J. (1951). Standing potential correlates of hypnosis and narcosis. *AMA Archives of Neurology and Psychiatry*, 65(4), 413–436. doi:10.1001/archneurpsyc.1951.02320040003001.

4 See patent information at: https://www.google.com/patents/US4715717.

The record of a normal, highly intelligent, 24-year-old female subject during her first hypnotic induction is presented in Figure 14.2.

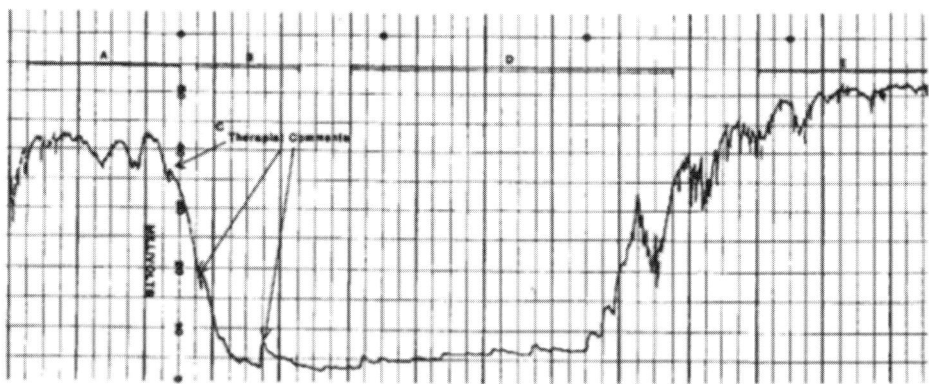

Figure 14.2. Electronic monitoring of DC body potential during catalepsy in millivolts (mV) on vertical axis and time scale of 0.5 inch per minute on horizontal axis: (A) normal awakeness, (B) drop in DC potential during relaxation, (C) momentary response to therapist remarks, (D) characteristically low activity during catalepsy, and (E) typical awakening pattern at higher electronic level than (A).

The erratic, fast activity at the beginning of the record (A) is characteristic of normal waking awareness. Every impulse to activity seems related to an upswing, which then drops out as soon as the impulse is carried through. During simple relaxation, meditation, and hypnosis, the record smooths out and usually drops dramatically as the subject gives up any active effort to direct mind or body. During (B), a few slow upswings are noted during the beginning of the hypnotic induction as the subject apparently tries to attend to the therapist's remarks. During (C), these drop out as trance deepens and the record shows a characteristically flat, low plateau with only low amplitude slow waves. At the beginning of (D), as the trance is deeply experienced, even the low amplitude activity drops out and a smooth line record is obtained. When the subject remains mentally quiescent with an immobile (cataleptic) body, there are no peaks or valleys in the record. When the subject initiates mental activity in the latter part of (D), the four-stage creative cycle of peaks and valleys are frequently recorded, albeit with personal variations. The awakening periods at (E) usually appear at a higher level than the initial basal waking level (A). This higher level is maintained for a few minutes until the record comes back to normal.

It is difficult to say that these records specifically measure "hypnotic trance" because similar measures appear in a subject during relaxation, meditation, or sleep. These states all lower mental activity (lower millivolts) and presumably induce greater relaxation or inward focus of attention. It is not surprising that the body responds with similar energetic patterns when moving through a mentally calming experience of whatever type. This does indicate that the energetic change the line graph depicts is a natural psychobiological process that is occurring *within* the subject. The value of the line graph as a therapeutic tool is in the additional meaning that the subject can decipher as they correlate the line graph with their personal narrative of their experience. Of course, there needs to be more research measuring the validity and reliability of the objective correlations between the amplitude and frequencies of the subject's subjective experiences. It would be interesting to explore how the EMF line graph can be utilized for biofeedback. As the subject witnesses the graphic expression of their energetic activity, how might that alter the subject's therapeutic consciousness and cognition?

The Erickson–Ravitz archival devices are no longer available commercially. The updated technology is a Pico ADC-20/ADC-24 data logger with ± 39 to ± 2,500 mV input.[5] This apparatus is an improvement and allows for both hands to be connected at the same time to show any difference in activity between left and right. The following section documents a selection of experiments that show the relationship between the line graph and the subject's felt experience.

Symmetry and Contrast

Case 1[6]

A 42-year-old woman, who was a well-functioning CEO of a business enterprise, sought assistance in resolving an important and stressful business issue. The line graph in Figure 14.3 records left and right sides concurrently, in symmetry. Interestingly, her left and right side reading was almost identical. The darker line (usually blue in full-color readings) is the right side reading and the lighter line (usually red) is the left side reading. When she was shown this recording she immediately became brightly animated and explained: "Oh! I know what this is all about! Here right in the middle is a high peak when I became excited with a new insight that solved a business problem I've been working on! It was a real a-ha experience! Then I reviewed it several times with these smaller peaks, and when I was sure I would remember it, I opened my eyes."

5 See product information at: https://www.picotech.com/data-logger/adc-20-adc-24/precision-data-acquisition.

6 Rossi, E. L. & Rossi, K. L. (2016b). A quantum field theory of neuropsychotherapy: semantic mind–brain maps and the quantum qualia of consciousness. *International Journal of Neuropsychotherapy*, 4(1), 47–68. doi:10.12744/ijnpt.2016.0047-0068.

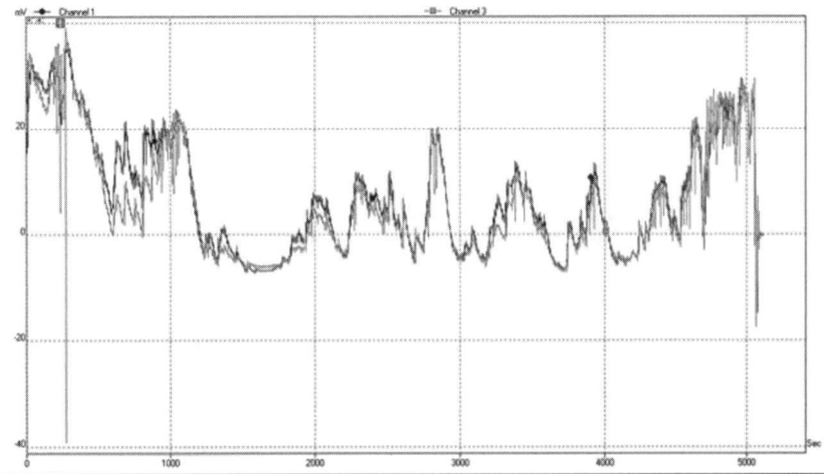

Figure 14.3. Symmetrical bioelectronics of consciousness.[7] Notice the peaking amplitude in the middle of her recording, which apparently recorded an excited a-ha experience (stage 3), followed by three peaks of mental activity as she reviewed and verified the insight (stage 4), after which she opened her eyes and returned to full attention.[8]

These observations suggest how this recording may illustrate the bioelectronic correlates of the four-stage experience of creative consciousness and cognition during neuropsychotherapy. Stage 1 is the normal default state of ordinary consciousness at about 10 minutes. The initial neuro-psychotheraputic drop of more than 20 mV in stage 2 is the typical indication of an inner focusing of attention and expectancy for about 15 minutes. In this particular recording, an ascent with a series of two or three rising peaks for about 10 minutes then culminated with an a-ha peak at stage 3. This was followed by a series of three descending peaks for about 15 minutes when the subject was apparently reinforcing her memory, which culminated in the characteristic stage 4 peak that was slightly higher (at about 25 mV) than her initial default state.

7 Rossi, E. L. (2002b). *The Psychobiology of Gene Expression: Neuroscience and Neurogenesis in Therapeutic Hypnosis and the Healing Arts*. New York: W.W. Norton; Rossi & Rossi, Quantum field theory of neuropsychotherapy; Rossi, E. L. (2007). *The Breakout Heuristic: The New Neuroscience of Mirror Neurons, Consciousness and Creativity in Human Relationships. The Selected Papers of Ernest Lawrence Rossi, Vol. 1*. Phoenix, AZ: Milton H. Erickson Foundation Press.

8 Rossi, E. L. (2012). *Creating Consciousness: How Therapists Can Facilitate Wonder, Wisdom, Truth and Beauty. The Selected Papers of Ernest Lawrence Rossi, Vol. 2*. Phoenix: AZ: Milton H. Erickson Foundation Press.

Case 2

The client was a professional woman who had suffered a hemorrhagic stroke 20 years previously. Her line graph (Figure 14.4) is recorded in a "mirror" form (different from the symmetrical form in Figure 14.3). This subject also experienced an a-ha moment. This mental insight, or what we can also describe as a *moment of phase shift*, is reflected in the bioelectronic activity measured by the Pico apparatus. Notice how the first 1,500 seconds (or about 25 minutes) of the recording begin with the typical downward slope characteristic of hypnotic induction. This was interrupted by a sudden burst of bioelectronic activity at about 1,650 seconds, with a great widening of her quantum electrodynamic field when she apparently "got it," whatever "it" was. This very striking expansion (widening) was followed by a symmetrical narrowing of her quantum electrodynamic field, between 0 mV and -5 mV for another 1,500 seconds or so. Such rapid changes in electromagnetic polarity were regarded by Ravitz as heralding significant shifts in consciousness, cognition, emotions, and behavioral dynamics in normal individuals as well as psychiatric patients.[9]

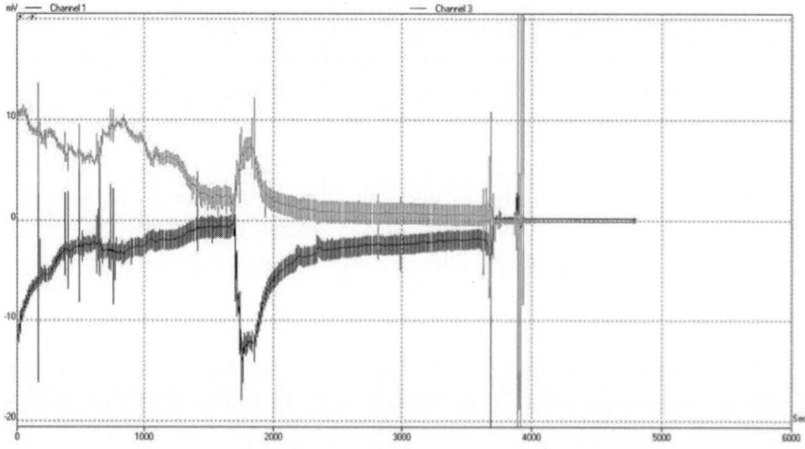

Figure 14.4. Electrodynamic recording of a professional woman who had suffered a hemorrhagic stroke 20 years previously.

9 Ravitz, L. J. (1962). History, measurement and applicability of periodic changes in the electromagnetic field in health and disease. *American Archives of New York Science*, 98, 1144–1201.

The Rossi/Hill Experiments

Figure 14.5. Pico sensors attached to RH.

During the Rossi/Hill conversations of 2016, we conducted several experiments using the Pico apparatus. RH was the subject and ER facilitated the experience utilizing a client-responsive approach. The Pico apparatus was attached – a central sensor to the forehead, with a left and right sensor to the palm of each hand. The Pico apparatus is sensitive to movement, and so it was necessary to remain still during the experience, although this was not found to be difficult. The value of including these experiments is that we have direct access to the thoughts of the subject and the unusual condition in which the facilitator and subject are discussing the experience as equals, avoiding the stereotypical hierarchy effects of therapist/client.

Experiment 1

The following is an edited version of the notes made by RH within an hour of the session. The notes are followed by an edited version of the dialogue between ER and RH immediately after the experience. The Pico graph is shown in Figure 14.6. Figure 14.7 is a zoomed in section to highlight a specific event during the session.

RH's report

The Pico system was attached and organized. I sat quietly and comfortably in the chair with no sense of urgency or impatience. ER gave a simple suggestion:

> *So, what I want to do with this session, I want to rely on your best way of going into self-hypnosis, relaxation, and meditation, what we have been talking about as a positive and beneficial state of therapeutic consciousness and cognition – just do whatever is appropriate for you that leads you to whatever you are seeking in this experience.*

This request was very suitable for me and within a few minutes I felt very relaxed, with my attention focused on the feeling of my outward breath. ER made very few verbal comments throughout the experience, but I was comfortable with his presence and with the freedom to do as I wished. I took particular care to allow things to happen "all by themselves" and to just accept whatever came into my conscious awareness.

At around 1,000 seconds I accidentally dislodged the sensor and caused a large blip on the graph. Shortly after the sensor was reattached, I noticed my little finger twitching. I seemed to have no ability to control it. I remember giving my forearm the mental suggestion that the movement of my little finger was in its control and perhaps it could do something about the twitching. Shortly after the twitching did stop, but I had no sense that I had consciously controlled it. The Pico reading seems to reflect this as a lift in activity of the lighter line at around 1,400 seconds.

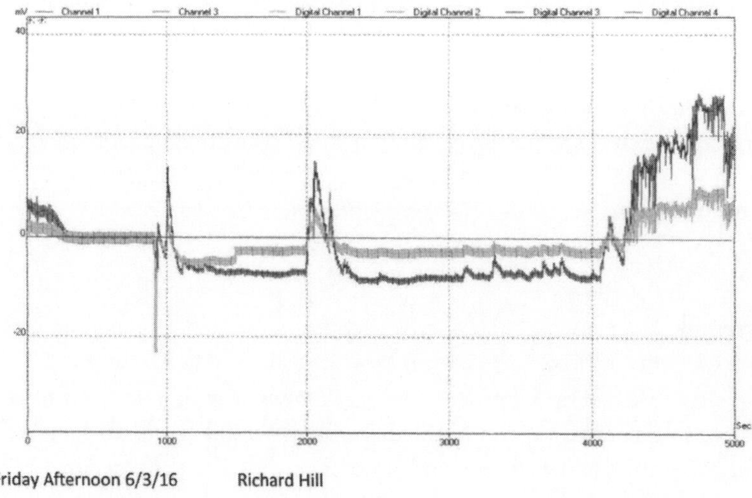

Figure 14.6. The first experiment with Richard Hill as subject and Ernest Rossi as facilitator.

A sudden, unexpected event occurred at around 2,000 seconds (Figure 14.7) that was shocking and disturbing. I remember I was imagining myself in a comfortable scene, something like a cafe or cafeteria. I was sitting at a round table. There were other people in the room. Suddenly there was something like a brightening of the light and then, almost like an atomic bomb blast, "whoosh," everything was destroyed, vaporized. I remember having a physical reaction, most notable a sharp inward breath that made a clacking sound as my tongue and velum rattled with the sudden breath. I felt myself stiffen and my brow furrow, but I also felt no need to open my eyes or change my body position. I found that I was still alive, somehow not annihilated, although I was now in a barren, cloudy, light filled scene. I looked around for the cause of the blast, but soon decided it was pointless to continue investigating. I returned to a relaxed state and, surprisingly quickly, I began to visualize more scenes. The Pico reading shows the rapid increase at the catastrophic event, but also the rapid drop in energy very soon afterwards at around 2,200 seconds when I returned to relaxed visualization. The darker line dropped even lower and this seemed to reflect my feelings that I had gone deeper into my imaginings.

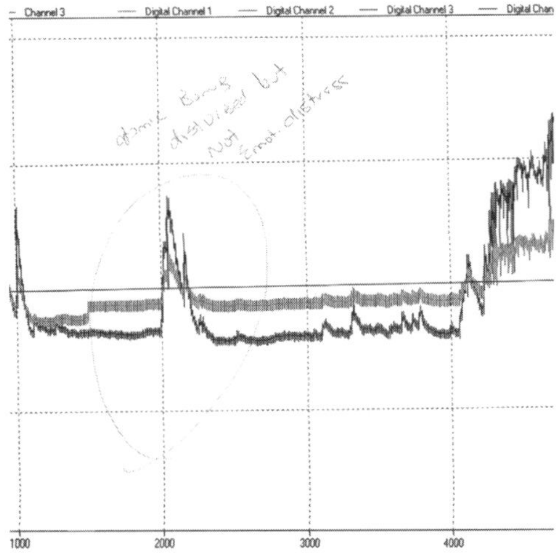

Figure 14.7. Highlight of the catastrophic event in the first experiment.

I went on to experience a number of visual thoughts that had no dialogue. They came in and out like short vignettes. Not all the scenes were relevant, but I seemed to know which ones to give heed to. Several scenes left me feeling "out there on my own," which made me partly sad, while partly accepting that this was just a truth for someone at their growing edge. Two very meaningful scenes, which were set in the future, played out in my mind (which are not being included here), followed by a series of scenes that left me feeling positive and hopeful about the upcoming process of writing the book. I didn't notice how much time had passed, but I eventually noticed some involuntary movement in my foot, which is reflected in the activity at around 4,100 seconds. This expanded to leg twitches and it became clear in my mind that the experience was drawing to a close and I was implicitly telling myself to return to general attention.

I opened my eyes and looked over to ER. He raised his eyebrow lightly in a pleasant "welcome back." ER invited me to speak about my experience, but only if I wished. I did wish to as I was keen to recount the "disaster" event.

Following is an edited transcript of the conversation immediately following my return to general attention (around 4,600 seconds). The Pico recording continued for a while as we spoke.

> RH: It was quite an event! It felt like a catastrophic event that was happening to me ... I was disturbed but, strangely, not distressed.
>
> ER: Just continue with your recollection. Do you see on the graph that you are coming back to your normal state, but you can see that you certainly had quite an event.
>
> RH: But, see how I became quite content again ... I enjoyed a whole series of visual imaginings that seem to show up in the peaks in the darker line from 3,100 to about 3,900. But that event was like an atom bomb. I think I eventually said to myself, "I survived. It hasn't killed me. I'm still here." I want to share with you that my life has been like that. I'm going along well and then, suddenly, a catastrophe. That has happened quite a few times ...
>
> ER: Wow!
>
> RH: This reminds me ... I've never been destroyed ...
>
> ER: Fortunately ...
>
> RH: Yes ... it's good now ... good.
>
> ER: But we caught a mini psychological trauma of some sort?
>
> RH: Yes, but not from within. It came from without.
>
> ER: Out there ... in the environment?
>
> RH: But I didn't take it personally.
>
> ER: Good!
>
> RH: That helps ... it helps ... yeah.

RH's Therapeutic Review

The most prominent issue in my mind is most likely to be the task of writing this book because it is both exciting and filled with risk and difficulty. I feel that I was trying to tell myself that no matter what the world throws at me, I will survive – as I have many times before. Despite the financial catastrophes in my life and the emotional losses, I have always survived. The two main visual imaginings during the session (not included for privacy) demanded that I make a decision or at least choose a direction. It may be that I tend to wait for a catastrophe before I choose a change in direction. The setting for this session is that I am sitting in a room with Kathryn and Ernest Rossi, as we explore not only the book but also what is likely to be a new direction in my life. I feel I am being *informed* by my inner mind that it is not what the world throws at me that is the concern, but that I quickly and comfortably return to what my own mind can create.

Experiment 2

The second solo session was held the next morning. The Pico graph is shown in Figure 14.8. The induction was similar, with ER inviting RH to find his own best therapeutic consciousness and cognition in order to explore whatever might be discovered. This session, however, proved to be a very different experience. About halfway through, RH chose to open his eyes and engage with ER, although remaining in a relaxed, almost somnambulistic state. RH and ER watched the progress of the Pico readout on the monitor and discussed how this related to RH's experience.

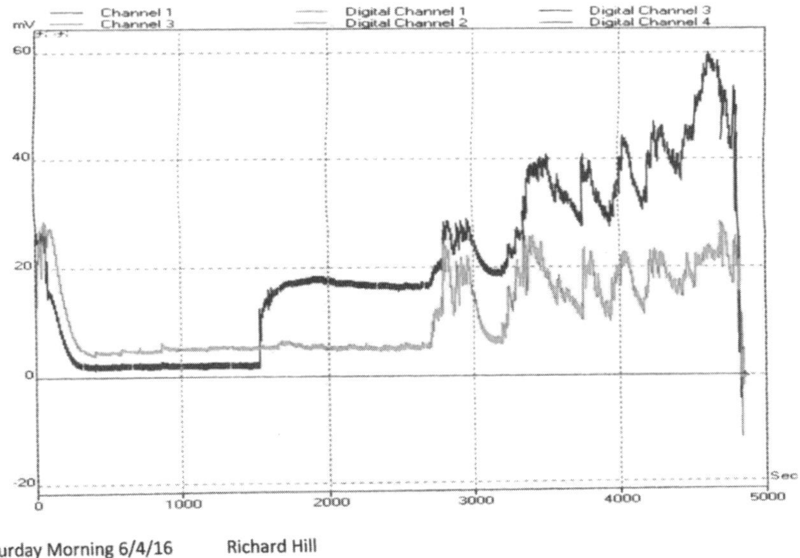

Figure 14.8. The second experiment with Richard Hill as subject and Ernest Rossi as facilitator.

The following are edited sections of the conversation:

> ER: … and this is where you seemed to wake up a little (900 seconds) … and then slip back into trance even as you gazed at the screen … Now you are waking up more (1,800) … you have … the choice … to go back or stay out … It looks as though there is a struggle?
>
> RH: Yeah …
>
> ER: One part of you wants to come out …
>
> RH: I keep telling myself to wake up, but look at the lighter line – it's going "Noooooo. I need a little more …"

RH closes his eyes and relaxes, opening his eyes again at around 2,800 seconds.

> ER: (3,200) OK …
>
> RH: Yeah, ah … my lighter line is … suddenly much more active … but my darker line is going off into the stratosphere …
>
> ER: Holey smoley … some part of you went off … heading toward 40 …
>
> RH: Yeah …
>
> ER: … and what is your intuition as to what the darker is recording and what the lighter is recording?
>
> RH: I feel that the lighter is my comfort … err … the darker feels like an activity … but I'm not sure what that activity is … I can see that a lot is going on, but … I can feel the lighter line more …
>
> ER: Uh huh …
>
> RH: … It's like waking up at 2am … somnambulistic …
>
> ER: … I have imagined the darker line as the observer, constantly monitoring the outside world … look it's going up again …
>
> RH: Oh, my …
>
> ER: The observer going up and the comfort still OK …
>
> RH: I'm listening to you, but mostly I am interested, I'm curious …
>
> ER: Oh, my! … are we recording curiosity?
>
> RH: … it feels like it …
>
> ER: How curious and profound that the lines are still apart, although they are following a similar path … I don't know which is the leader and which the follower.

RH: For me, I can feel the difference and now I can see the difference. The right and left side can be doing something different, but still be connected and working toward something that helps the whole of me … Look, I am going up again (4,400) … these are big thoughts … but comfortable is good with it all, still 25 or so …

ER: So this is, I believe, where the cognitive is matching what is within us … somehow reflecting in the macro conscious level, reflecting something …

RH: … that everything is made of the same conceptual stuff …

ER: Protons, and electrons, positrons and gluons, the fundamental particles.

RH: That's the nature of the particles, but even they are fundamentally inherent of a concept …

ER: Yeah …

RH: … and that concept pervades … and it's expressed in everything else …

ER: Yes …

RH: … so an activity of the biology is reflected in the psychology …

ER: … and as you are expressing yourself, your blue line is taking off, while the red line is staying comfortable. It's like your intellectual functions are manifest in your wonder, your curiosity, an intellectual adventure … You feel confident, no threat to your integrity, like an oboe player going on a riff … while the inner you feels confident that you could create an original bit … This graph looks so different from yesterday's.

RH: Yes … and phenomenologically my visual experiences were different from yesterday …

ER: The shock was yesterday …

RH: … but today is more interesting, maybe because of yesterday … that darker line has been …

ER: Yes, this is your curiosity, being at your growing edge …

RH: Yet, I'm comfortable …

ER: Exactly!

Therapeutic Review

The benefit of this experience is well captured in the conversation. It was not only in the deep inner reflection of RH, but in thinking about these reflections in connection with the activity recorded in the Pico graph. Even though we have not yet done the science to show exactly why the left and right energy measurements are different and how these different levels coexist to produce a single conscious experience, there is no denying that the differences were evident and that RH could translate the technical data into a positive personal perception. Is this the same as the translation of a technological measure as shown in the locked-in patient experiments in Chapter 7? Arguably, yes. This is another interesting question for future research and investigation. The deep realizations of RH, that ER described as a creative "riff," are a major breakthrough of this experience. These thoughts emerged into consciousness from the creative interaction between *both* RH's implicit natural problem-solving processes *and* the conscious translation of the information in the Pico graph.

Review

All of the subjects were able to remember important moments of emergent insight and then recognize the corresponding spikes in the Pico graph. This was very clear to the business woman in Case 1, and the stroke victim in Case 2. RH was also able to relate conscious experiences with movements in the line record on the Pico graph. What was equally fascinating, and somewhat surprising, was when RH reported conscious perceptions that did *not* correspond to the movement of one or other of the graphic lines. Because it was possible for RH to watch the Pico graph emerging, we could witness the real-time *incongruence* between conscious perception and the implicit state that the Pico graph was recording. In fact, the lighter line of the Pico graph was translated by RH, at one point, to be implicitly telling him that it was more beneficial for him to quieten conscious cognitive activity and return to inner reflection. If the therapist is sensitive to both the cognitive responses of the client *and* the implicit quantum qualia that the client may be feeling in various non-conscious ways, then the therapist's client-responsive improvisations will be deeply in tune with the client. Even though it may feel as though this is happening *all by itself* (i.e. without conscious direction), these improvisations enable the client to tune in to their own natural problem-solving and mind–body healing.

The experiments with the Pico apparatus in this chapter show:

- That it is possible to have distinct differences between the left and right fields of the body.
- That this can be measured energetically in the hands.
- That these measurements can be correlated with the phenomenological experience of the subject.

There is, of course, much more research required and more questions to be posited as we seek to better understand the mechanisms of Mirroring Hands. One of the most interesting but demanding fields of inquiry is to explore what is happening at the micro scale of energetic activity. To explore what is happening to produce variations in electrodynamic activity, we must explore the quantum world, which is very different from the "classical," or macro, world we know. Although physicists are yet to understand exactly how the two worlds coexist, there is no doubt that what happens in our observable world is a manifestation of things that also occur in the quantum field. The next chapter takes us into that extraordinary world and we share our investigations of how, among other things, our natural rhythms and cycles are the felt experience of something very small and very extraordinary.

Chapter 15

Down the Rabbit Hole

Quantum and the Yet-To-Be-Known

ER: … it's even deeper than being a facilitator … throughout history wise people have written lines of poetry about light … modern concepts of consciousness are tied to the amplitude, or intensity, of when you get enough … The human eye can, supposedly, make out one photon, although others say five or six. How many photons do you need to get an idea from the unconscious – the quantum – up to the threshold of intuitive awareness? Then curiosity carries you through …

RH: … so … it's not just science, it's a feeling … Can we really feel the quantum? I think I did … well, something … during our Pico experiments … quantum – what an exciting mystery!

From the Rossi/Hill conversations, June 2016

What does it *mean* to understand quantum field theory? What do we need to know about it, and why? What does it do for us? For most people, understanding quantum field theory is in stage 2 of the creative cycle: it is difficult and testing, can seem distant, and even unnecessary for daily living. This is natural for stage 2, however, as we progress toward the breakthrough that releases the emergent creative changes and growth. While so many of us are in stage 2, it is not surprising that the mere mention of quantum theory can be enough to make some eyes glaze and some brains shut down.

Stage 1, the information stage, has been progressing for more than 100 years. There have been many people involved in the development of quantum theory. Contributors include, in the early stages, Max Planck,[1] who was challenged by Albert Einstein,[2] who was then challenged by Niels Bohr.[3] The French physicist Louis de Broglie[4] expanded on special relativity theory's concept that particles can exhibit wave characteristics.[5] Modern quantum mechanics was established by 1925 through

1 Planck, M. (1909). On the law of distribution of energy in the normal spectrum. *Annalen der Physik*, 4, 553.

2 Pais, A. (1979). Einstein and the quantum theory. *Reviews in Modern Physics*, 51(4), 863–914; Fine, A. (1993). Einstein's interpretations of the quantum theory. *Science in Context*, 6(1), 257–273. doi:10.1017/S026988970000137X.

3 Bohr, N. (1913). On the constitution of atoms and molecules. *Philosophical Magazine*, 26(6), 1–25. http://hermes.ffn.ub.es/luisnavarro/nuevo_maletin/Bohr_1913.pdf.

4 de Broglie, L. (1970). The reinterpretation of wave mechanics. *Foundations of Physics*, 1(1), 5–15; Hanle, P. A. (1977). Erwin Schrödinger's reaction to Louis de Broglie's thesis on the quantum theory. *Isis*, 68(4), 606–609. doi:10.1086/351880.

5 Hendry, J. (1980). The development of attitudes to the wave-particle duality of light and quantum theory, 1900–1920. *Annals of Science*, 37(1), 59–79.

the work of German physicists Werner Heisenberg,[6] Max Born,[7] and Pascual Jordan[8] and the Austrian physicist Erwin Schrödinger.[9] Heisenberg formulated his uncertainty principle in 1927,[10] and he and Niels Bohr developed the Copenhagen Interpretation around that time.[11] Also around that time, Paul Dirac began the process of unifying quantum mechanics with special relativity by proposing the Dirac equation for the electron.[12] The Dirac equation achieves the relativistic description of the wave function of an electron that Schrödinger failed to obtain. We explore Dirac and his important equations in Appendix B (An Integrated Quantum Field Theory of Physics, Math, Biology, and Psychology).

So, you can see that quantum field theory is not new, and has developed out of the greatest minds in physics. We are only now beginning to get some insight into what personal relevance and value the quantum world might have for our daily living. We are beginning to *feel* that the quantum world might be helpful for us. The struggle to make it so has produced a number of popular interpretations that range from oversimplification to quite wrong, but maybe this is all just part of the natural struggle of stage 2. Some, perhaps, are just finding a quick way into people's wallets, but let us leave that aside as we explore the possibilities of the quantum world for meaning and purpose in our day-to-day living, the practice of psychotherapy, and all the healing arts. Research is revealing that quantum processes are not so distant or irrelevant for some very familiar processes. These include photosynthesis in plants and, possibly, our sense of smell. But we will begin with another story of birds.

---

6 Enz, C. P. (1983). Heisenberg's applications of quantum mechanics (1926–33) or the settling of the new land. *Helvetica Physica Acta*, 56(5), 993–1001.

7 Pais, A. (1982). Max Born's statistical interpretation of quantum mechanics. *Science*, 218(4578), 1193–1198.

8 Schroer, B. (2010). Pascual Jordan's legacy and the ongoing research in quantum field theory. *European Physical Journal H. Historical Perspectives on Contemporary Physics*, 35, 377–434.

9 Rohrlich, F. (1987). Schrödinger and the interpretation of quantum mechanics. *Foundations of Physics*, 17(12), 1205–1220.

10 Roth, W-M. (1993). Heisenberg's uncertainty principle and interpretive research in science education. *Journal of Research in Science Teaching*, 30(7), 669–680. doi:10.1002/tea.3660300706.

11 Hanson, N. R. (1959). Copenhagen Interpretation of quantum theory. *American Journal of Physics*, 27(1). http://dx.doi.org/10.1119/1.1934739.

12 Breit, G. (1932). Dirac's equation and the spin-spin interactions of two electrons. *American Physical Society*, 39(4), 616–624; Rossi, E. L. & Rossi, K. L. (2014b). Quantum perspectives of consciousness, cognition and creativity: the Dirac equation in a new contour integral model of brain plasticity. *Journal of Applied and Computational Mathematics*, 3(6), 183. http://dx.doi.org/10.4172/2168-9679.1000183.

The European Robin

There is no doubt that the quantum world is a very different place. It is described as spooky and weird, but this is because it is a world where particles can exist in two or more places at once, spread themselves out like ghostly waves, tunnel through impenetrable barriers, and even possess instantaneous connections that stretch across vast distances.[13] We hope that you explore these mysteries of the quantum world beyond the pages of this book, but it isn't absolutely necessary for you to know the fine detail of these quantum behaviors. In this chapter, we are going to ask you to accept that these weird qualities *do* exist. We live in the "classical" world, largely based around Newtonian physics, which is also called the "macro" world.[14] We live within a set of natural "rules" that apply even to quite small objects that we can only see with a microscope. The quantum world is even smaller and exists in subatomic space where the rules can be very different.

How do the activities of these subatomic particles help the tiny European robin fly large distances without a compass, or even its ability to recognize landmarks, and still arrive exactly where it needs to go? Quantum theory suggests a possible answer and an example of how quantum behavior contributes directly to classical world functions. Studies of the European robin suggest that it utilizes the quantum concept called *entanglement,*[15] which Einstein called a "spooky action at a distance."

Entanglement is the quantum phenomenon where two particles are locked in a correlation, literally a co-relationship, where their quantum "spin" will always be dependent on, and relational to, each other, regardless of the distance between them. In atoms with more than one electron, it is possible to have paired electrons in a state of *quantum entanglement*, which, if split, will be disengaged from a stable state within the atom. This is complicated a little because the electrons in an atom are not particles orbiting the nucleus like planets, but exist as waves of probability in orbital planes around the nucleus. This is just one of the weird and spooky things in quantum mechanics that we just need to accept for the moment. So, the electrons can return to their stable state only when they return to their correct and correlated alignment because of what is called the Pauli exclusion principle.[16] This means the electrons cannot recombine with the nucleus until their states are aligned, one up and the other down. Studies show that electrons that have been separated are affected by a magnetic field.[17]

---

13 Starr, M. (2015). Physicists prove Einstein's 'spooky' quantum entanglement. *CNET* (November 20). https://www.cnet.com/au/news/physicists-prove-einsteins-spooky-quantum-entanglement/; Grant, A. (2015). Confirmed: quantum mechanics is weird. *Science News* (October 21). https://www.sciencenews.org/blog/science-ticker/confirmed-quantum-mechanics-weird.

14 See: https://www.britannica.com/science/classical-mechanics.

15 Fickler, R., Krenn, M., Lapkiewicz, R., Ramelow, S. & Zeilinger, A. (2013). Real-time imaging of quantum entanglement. *Scientific Reports* 3, Article: 1914; Science Alert (2014). The best explanation of quantum entanglement so far (September 9). https://www.sciencealert.com/watch-the-best-explanation-of-quantum-entanglement-so-far.

16 See: https://www.aps.org/publications/apsnews/200701/history.cfm.

17 Hamish, G., Hiscock, H. G., Worster, S., Kattnig, D. R., Steers, C., Jin, Y., Manolopoulos, D. E., Mouritsen, H. & Hore, P. J. (2016). The quantum needle of the avian magnetic compass. *Proceedings of the National Academy of Sciences of the United States of America,* 113(17), 4634–4639.

In the retina of the European robin, and perhaps in other species, a photon of light entering the eye will strike the atomic particle, separating an entangled pair of electrons of an atom.[18] The energy of the photon is absorbed by the collision and so it does not continue to the optic nerve to contribute to visual perception. Remember, we are only talking about a very small percentage of photons striking atoms. Most continue to the optic nerve for normal vision. These separated but entangled electrons begin to wobble in relation to the magnetic field, something they did not do while in a stable, entrained state. When the robin flies in the right direction, the electrons are oriented by the magnetic field into the proper alignment and the electrons recombine. When the electrons recombine, they release the energy they absorbed from the photon, which is received by the optic nerve. This is perceived by the robin in such a way that it can "see" which way it needs to fly.

It is not that the robin has a conscious thought about electrons being in correct alignment. The robin, most likely, simply has a *sensation* that flying in that particular direction is beneficial. This is a subjective experience of what it is like to be flying in the right direction. In humans, this type of subjective sensation or feeling is called *qualia*.[19] We don't know whether the European robin has the sense of qualia, but if it did, we suggest that the sensation is better described as *quantum qualia*.[20] We will describe how humans might have quantum qualia in our experience of smell shortly, but next we explore how a process that is fundamental to our survival is made possible through quantum activity.

Photosynthesis

Photosynthesis is the process by which the chlorophyll molecules in plants capture energy from sunlight, but this works with high efficiency because of the process of *quantum coherence*.[21] In simple terms, when a photon hits a chlorophyll molecule it energizes one of the electrons, which is converted into what is called an *exciton*. This exciton passes through the cell as an energy packet to enable the conversion of carbon dioxide. It has long been puzzling to botanists that the energy of the exciton, despite being transported through the cell, is preserved at close to 100%. Classical physics suggests that it should take some time to bounce around inside the photosynthetic machinery in

18 Morello, A. (2014). The quantum world around you [video] (August 26). https://www.youtube.com/watch?v=tnfur3fqklc&list=PLqSkUknJX0S9olTYuJ5SOl1D6pbzaPuWx.

19 See: https://plato.stanford.edu/entries/qualia/.

20 Rossi, E. L. & Rossi, K. L. (2016b). A quantum field theory of neuropsychotherapy: semantic mind–brain maps and the quantum qualia of consciousness. *International Journal of Neuropsychotherapy*, 4(1), 47–68. doi:10.12744/ijnpt.2016.0047-0068.

21 Romero, E., Augulis, R., Novoderezhkin, V. I., Ferretti, M., Thieme, J., Zigmantas, D. & van Grondelle, R. (2014). Quantum coherence in photosynthesis for efficient solar-energy conversion. *Nature Physics*, 10, 676–682. doi:10.1038/nphys3017.

the cell, and lose considerable amounts of energy, before emerging on the other side. An experiment, first carried out in 2007 in Berkeley, California, showed how the energy packet achieved the extraordinary feat of choosing the perfect pathway each time.[22] It did this not by acting like a particle but like a quantum wave. In the quantum state, the energy packet is able to be in what is called *quantum superposition*, or to be in all positions at once, like a spread out wave. The best possible pathway is then actualized, and the energy packet arrives both quickly and with a minimal loss of energy. This can only happen in the quantum world at the subatomic level of energetic particles. The quantum process in photosynthesis is directly responsible for the efficiency of plant growth and, possibly, the subsequent survival of life on Earth.

Our Sense of Smell

Smell is a very important sense in humans and can stimulate vivid memories and emotional responses. It is now theorized that our sensitivity to smells is directly facilitated by quantum behaviors. The early theory was that our nostrils are able distinguish different odors through molecular receptors in the nasal cavity. The challenge to this theory is that some molecules are very different yet have very similar smells, but others are very similar yet have very different smells. The molecular difference between vanilla and eugenol, for example, is very small, but eugenol smells like cloves. Luca Turin, a chemist at the BSRC Alexander Fleming Institute in Greece, suggested that the key was not the shape of molecules but the quantum properties of their chemical bonds.[23] When the molecule of an odor attaches to a receptor in the nose, it is reacting at the quantum level of energetic bonds. As a result, an electron is energized in a particular way and is able to do what is called *quantum tunneling*.

In quantum tunneling, an electron can jump from point A to point B without actually having to travel through the space between. Weird, we know, but just accept this for now. When the electron leaps to the other side of the receptor, it is thought to trigger a signal to the brain that the receptor has come into contact with that particular molecule. Turin confirmed his hypothesis by testing two odor molecules that have very similar chemical bonds. He knew that sodium sulfide smells like rotten eggs. He then tested borane and it did, indeed, smell very much like rotten eggs.

22 Engel, G. S., Calhoun, T. R., Read, E. L., Ahn, T-K., Mančal, T., Cheng, Y-C., Blankenship, R. E. & Fleming, G. R. (2007). Evidence for wavelike energy transfer through quantum coherence in photosynthetic systems. *Nature*, 446, 782–786. doi:10.1038/nature05678.

23 Gane, S., Georganakis, D., Maniati, K., Vamvakias, M., Ragoussis, N., Skoulakis, E. M. C. et al. (2013). Molecular vibration-sensing component in human olfaction. *PLOS ONE*, 8(1), e55780. https://doi.org/10.1371/journal.pone.0055780.

The qualia of smells, therefore, is more than a subjective sense of a classical world observation. It fits with the concept of quantum qualia. How much of our subjective experience, our *felt sense,* has a direct relationship to our sensitivity to quantum qualia is not known because we are only at the beginning of discovering how the quantum world is experienced in the classical world. We urge you to discover more about our explorations into the knowledge of quantum field theory, and how it can inform us about psychotherapy and Mirroring Hands, in Appendix B, but first, let us prepare our minds a little more.

Can We Be Quantum? Let There Be Light!

If we are made up of all these atoms and subatomic particles, then why can't we be in two places at once, pass through walls, and communicate instantly across distances? The promise that this is somehow possible is misguided and perhaps even deliberately deceptive. The link between the quantum world and the classical world is still, certainly, one of the big questions of physics and has perplexed greater minds than ours. It may be that once particles become plentiful enough to create complexity that this disrupts quantum phenomena. We just don't know, but we are a body of trillions of cells and quantum weirdness seems to shift at some point. It *is* possible to have objects of the classical world behave in quantum ways, but they need to be frozen to near absolute zero and be in a vacuum, which is not much like the classical world. Quantum skeptics like to cite this misconception – that the quantum cannot be associated with life because life could not exist near absolute zero. ER tells this story:

> ER: Recent research finally convinced me of the reality of the human ability to sense, perceive, and respond to the quantum level. It proves that the quantum underpins sensation and perception which is, of course, the basis of consciousness, cognition, and behavior. A generation ago when scientists first tried to measure how many photons … you know that photons are the smallest particle or unit of light and are quantum particles … the split-screen experiments?[24]
>
> RH: Yes, Ernie, both particles and waves …
>
> ER: Right … Anyway, the scientists wanted to know how many photons were necessary to hit the retina before we could see light. At first they found varying answers from hundreds to thousands or millions of photons, depending on how sensitive their measuring devices were. As their measuring devices improved over the years the number of photons needed to see light gradually became smaller and smaller. Finally, it was confirmed that a single photon was all that

24 Strnad, J. (1986). Photons in introductory quantum physics. *American Journal of Physics*, 54(7), 650. http://dx.doi.org/10.1119/1.14526; Merali, Z. (2015). Quantum physics: what is really real? *Nature News*, 521(7552), 278–280. http://www.nature.com/news/quantum-physics-what-is-really-real-1.17585.

was necessary.[25] Clear evidence that we are quantum creatures – and at room temperature! The implications of this sensitivity to the quantum qualia is at the core of human experience. This is profound!

From the Rossi/Hill conversations, June 2016

Erwin Schrödinger, who was so important in the development of our understanding of the quantum world, mused philosophically in his book, *What Is Life?*[26] He suggests that the quantum world might provide the *order* to maintain life in the classical world which, according to the laws of thermodynamics, moves toward increasing disorder. Schrödinger suggested that the inheritability of DNA, which is achieved with molecules made of very few particles, does not seem to fit with the thermodynamic rules of order moving to increasing disorder and increasing complexity. Paradoxically, living organisms are very orderly. Is Schrödinger right when he suggests that the order of living organisms is based on an as yet unknown connection between the *order* of the quantum world and the *disorder* of the classical world? We wonder if this has any bearing on the way our hands seem to move all by themselves and the implicit capacity for problem-solving and mind–body healing. Are these expressions of quantum qualia? Is our quantum qualia sensitive to the energetic states of the quantum world, and how might this relate to the energetic states of the classical world? We just don't know, yet.

ER believes that the next step in advancing the evolution of psychotherapy is to answer these questions, and more, about these classical/quantum transitions in everyday life, which must also underlie psychotherapy. Appendix B explores some of the more profound implications of this search:

> The major practical implication for our integrated quantum field theory of physics, math, biology, and psychology for the current evolution of psychotherapy is to help people learn to value and tune in appropriately to the most highly sensitive and ineffable quantum qualia of their observer-operator to help them navigate the perils of everyday acute and chronic stress that generate the most common forms of psychopathology and the addictions. We need to do away with the common disparagement of "merely subjective experience of intuition and imagination" that favors the pursuit of the so-called "virtues of objective thinking and rational," which can so easily become corrupted by narcissism, ego power, advertising, avarice, and war in cultures that over-value competition … whatever the cost. We need to transcend the rather stale reductive ideologies and manipulative models of psychotherapy … by returning to the living, experiencing, and primacy of the vivid novelty-numinosum-neurogenesis-effect to realize our best creative selves and … [focus on] how the quantum qualia of the human observer-operator during subjective experience can be a causal agent in facilitating health and problem-solving on the objective molecular/genomic level …

25 Tinsley, J. N., Molodtsov, M. I., Prevedel, R., Wartmann, D., Espigulé-Pons, J., Lauwers, M. & Vaziri, A. (2016). Direct detection of a single photon by humans. *Nature Communications*, 19(7), 12172. doi:10.1038/ncomms12172.

26 Schrödinger, E. (2012 [1967]) *What Is Life?* Cambridge: Cambridge University Press.

What About Energy?

We have discussed this topic at length. It can be difficult and contentious to use the word "energy." At the quantum level, energy is fundamental.[27] There is, however, a degree of abuse by pseudoscientific practitioners that creates confusion in the meaning and usage of the term "energy." Some would have you think that it is a power that can be accessed to raise you up above others or give you some advantage. Energy isn't magic, nor is it the mystical panacea that will cure all problems, nor is it the source of power that gives you the advantage over others, over nature, and over the balance of possibilities in the universe. That may be more to do with the winner/loser world than good science. Even when we do talk diligently about energy, it is important to bear in mind that there are different conceptions of energy. Energy can be expressed in various forms, including kinetic, electrical, chemical, heat, light, sound, and vibrational. Energy is also a *potential* that is inherent in an element, but that energy is not expressed, or experienced, until there is an external disruption, like being struck by a photon, or an interaction with a point of difference, such as a difference in electrical charge or polarity. Energetic processes are occurring at fundamental particle levels during therapy, which are experienced as subjective sensations such as cathartic shifts, a-ha moments of insight, and phase shifts through the four stages of the creative cycle.

It is an energetic process that drives the molecular activity of brain neurons that underpins consciousness and cognition. The ionic charge across the membrane of an axon in the brain changes to create a difference in the ionic (electrical) charge.[28] That triggers a process where positively charged sodium ions enter the axon which then causes slightly differently positively charged potassium ions to leave the axon, creating an energetic flow along the axon to the synapse. If there is enough activity energized at the synapse, then particles are released into and across the synaptic cleft to the next neuron. If the energetic activity continues to flow from neuron to neuron, then there is an ongoing *action potential* that produces a neuronal pattern or system of neurons.[29] This pattern of neuronal firing produces an information set that is translated into a thought that emerges into our conscious awareness.[30] We still do not know how the energetic activity of a set of neurons becomes a conscious thought (i.e. Chalmers' "hard problem"[31]), but it does. The activity of the brain is all about flows of

27 Strassler, M. (2013). Quantum fluctuations and their energy (August 29). https://profmattstrassler.com/articles-and-posts/particle-physics-basics/quantum-fluctuations-and-their-energy/.

28 Debanne, D. (2004). Information processing in the axon. *Nature Reviews Neuroscience*, 5, 304–316. doi:10.1038/nrn1397.

29 Kress, G. J. & Mennerick, S. (2009). Action potential initiation and propagation: upstream influences on neurotransmission. *Neuroscience*, 158(1), 211–222. http://doi.org/10.1016/j.neuroscience.2008.03.021.

30 Segev, A., Curtis, D., Jung, S. & Chae, S. (2016). Invisible brain: knowledge in research works and neuron activity. *PLOS ONE*, 11(7), e0158590. https://doi.org/10.1371/journal.pone.0158590.

31 Adolphs, R. (2015). The unsolved problems of neuroscience. *Trends in Cognitive Sciences*, 19(4), 173–175. http://doi.org/10.1016/j.tics.2015.01.007.

energy and the information that the energy flows represent.[32] That process occurs *all by itself* and we only become aware of it when it is translated into something we can consciously experience. Quantum mechanics is fundamental to parts of that process. We don't know exactly how that works either, but as we have described previously, our task, at the very least, as a facilitating therapist, is to be sensitive to the emergent properties, to observe and respond, in the relational improvisation that is the therapeutic experience with your client.

The Quantum Qualia of Health and Well-Being

Our attunement and engagement, through sensitive observation and intuitive awareness, guides us to know when we are experiencing the most beneficial neural patterns, the most beneficial somatic states, and triggering the most beneficial neuro-psycho-biological state of being in which to function, survive, reproduce, and thrive. We may be as naive to deeper energetic activity as the European robin is to entangled particles. Philosophers, artists, and poets have been speculating on how to recognize these ideal states for millennia. Positivity, kindness, compassion, love, goodness, strength, comfort, peace, and well-being are all suggested as indicators that we are in the best state of being.[33] These are, potentially, the quantum qualia of energetic attunement to the ideal state of being human. ER published a paper over ten years ago titled, "Art, beauty, and truth" in the *Annals of the American Psychotherapy Association*, which introduced the concept of engaging in and utilizing the qualia of the therapeutic experience.[34] Murray Gell-Mann, the astrophysicist, knew that one of his equations was correct, even in the face of opposition, because it was too beautiful to be wrong.[35] What on earth is a "beautiful equation"? We might equally ask, how does a bird know that it is flying in alignment to the magnetic field that will take it home? How do we know that we are connected to our inner self when our hands move all by themselves? We suggest that there is a connection through our quantum qualia, our subjective sensation of the quantum world.

---

32 Siegel, D. J. (2015). *The Developing Mind: How Relationships and the Brain Interact to Shape Who We Are*, 2nd edn. New York: Guilford Press.

33 Chapman, H. M. (2011). Love: a biological, psychological and philosophical study. Paper 254. Senior Honors Projects, University of Rhode Island. http://digitalcommons.uri.edu/srhonorsprog/254; Tiberius, V. (2006). Well-being: psychological research for philosophers. *Philosophy Compass*, 1, 493–505. doi:10.1111/j.1747-9991.2006.00038.x; Shakespeare, W. (2004). *Shakespeare's Sonnets and Poems* (Folger Shakespeare Library), ed. B. A. Mowat & P. Werstine. New York: Washington Square Press.

34 Rossi, E. L. (2004a). Art, beauty, and truth: the psychosocial genomics of consciousness, dreams, and brain growth in psychotherapy and mind-body healing. *Annals of the American Psychotherapy Association*, 7 (3), 10–17.

35 Gell-Mann, M. (2007). Beauty, truth, and ... physics? [video]. *TED.com* (March). https://www.ted.com/talks/murray_gell_mann_on_beauty_and_truth_in_physics.

Is this why it is so beneficial to be sensitive to the four-stage creative cycle, the ultradian rhythm, and the ultradian healing response? Is this how we know we are in love? Is this how we know when we are OK, and when we are not? Is the purpose of psychotherapy to facilitate the client's sensitivity to their quantum qualia and open the ideal flow of energy and information at the molecular level to produce problem-solving and mind–body healing? Can we be sensitive to the very small movements and shifts in the quantum space that point the way and give us the subjective awareness that we are "flying in the right direction"? Finally, does understanding quantum field theory help you to achieve this sensitivity?

These are the questions we leave you to ponder, just as we continue to do. Perhaps it is not necessary to know all this. Perhaps it is enough to trust the feeling of what is best, without needing to know the details behind it. We leave you with a last word from our conversations:

> RH: It is interesting, though, every time I learn something about life and the world around me, it's like a springboard at my growing edge. Understanding something new seems to create a shift inside me that stimulates an attraction or a repulsion … my state of being is energized to flow in some way, some direction. I believe that understanding gives me something wonderful, inspiring, and strengthening … it's different for each of us I expect. It must be strange, Ernie, to hear me going on like this after all your years of amazing thought and exploration … you have created so much that has inspired me …
>
> ER: We should write a book about that …

Closing Words

The purpose of your training is not to learn every technique, but to expose yourself to every opportunity to draw close those things that have a natural rhythm, resonance, and profundity with you. These may change over time, as new things emerge into your field and alter the way you work, but not change what you are working toward: enabling the client, through your sensitive participation and relationship, rather than your expert manipulation and direction.

Appendix A

The *Nuntius Nuclei*: A New Neuroscience for Curiosity

Richard Hill, M.A., M.Ed., M.B.M.Sc., D.P.C.

Abstract

This paper proposes that the various nuclei that produce and distribute neurotransmitters throughout the brain are the basis of what has been described as the "chemical balance" of the brain. These nuclei, as an integrated system, are named as the *nuntius nuclei*. Depression is often described as a chemical imbalance, but the biochemistry can also be seen as perfectly "balanced" to produce depression. The feeling of depression may be better interpreted as a biomarker of something else that requires attention. If changing the chemical balance changes affect, then it will be valuable to know how to change the chemical balance in the most favorable way, in the fastest way. It is argued that "curiosity" activates all the *nuntius nuclei* and produces the most beneficial brain state for therapeutic change and learning. This brain state contributes to a curious state of mind that is beneficial for health and well-being.

Keywords: Brain, neurotransmitters, affective states, chemical imbalance, biochemical milieu, *nuntius nuclei*, curiosity, well-being, psychotherapy, neuropsychotherapy

> Basically, I have been compelled by curiosity.
>
> **Mary Leakey, paleoanthropologist (1913–1996)**

Therapists and teachers know that interested, curious clients and students pay attention and learn more (Berlyne, 1954; Engel, 2013). Stimulating their curiosity makes the job of therapy and the task of being a client so much more successful and enjoyable (Borenstein, 2002). New research is establishing some of the neural mechanisms that explain the connection between curiosity and learning. Gruber and colleagues (2014) show that when the brain is in a state of curiosity, learning is enhanced. They noted that curiosity activated the dopaminergic regions of the substantia nigra, ventral tegmental area, and the nucleus accumbens, which then showed a functional connectivity with the hippocampus. They also found that learning is enhanced not just for the target learning, but also for peripheral and non-related learning. The implication is that curiosity creates a brain state that is primed for learning. From an educational and a therapeutic perspective, producing a state of curiosity is going to be very beneficial for the client's learning experience.

To facilitate successful therapy, we need the client to be in a receptive and responsive state of brain and mind. This is beneficial for the therapist as well. This, of course, is one of the reasons why therapy is difficult. Someone with depression or anxiety, or in the throes of painful trauma, has a brain and mind that is more often closed, defensive, resistant, avoidant, and insecure. An important part of building rapport is to establish trust and safety and a sense of positive regard to allow them to move toward beneficial change (Herman, 1998). Whatever change might be made, it will be something that happens at some point in the future. The difficulties are that people get stuck in the past, they can fear or be fearful of the future, and they can be overwhelmed by the present. This is a fracture in their natural flow of life and can be described as a *disrupting consciousness*. Changing this state of mind, this state of being, is often not an easy task.

As therapists, we want to enable people to move forward into the future with a curious interest to explore possibilities and determine new frameworks for living. Curiosity will facilitate an exploratory mindset (Berlyne, 1950; Dember & Earl, 1957). This needs to occur not only in their conscious cognitive state, but also in their non-conscious inner world. To shift into a new state of being throughout the whole complex system that is our biology, there needs to be more than just a cognitive rationale, but a reorganization all the way down to cellular and molecular activity. We are beginning to understand how new experiences are encoded in cellular and microbiological structures in various ways, including in the DNA as epigenetics (Jaenisch & Bird, 2003) or the immune system as acquired or adaptive immunity (Holtmeier & Kabelitz, 2005). Learning is a very important component of change.

There is an increasing pressure for science to provide an "evidence base" to validate therapy, which has, unfortunately, led to an emphasis on reductionist, linear, causal perspectives (De Simone, 2006). Research is, very often, limited to single events or single elements of inquiry. There are good reasons for this, but the process of integration back to the whole person can be neglected or considered too speculative. Specific information certainly has its place and is vital to differentiating the elements, but our biology, from limbs to neurons to genes, is a dynamic, complex, integrated system that operates in an interplay of activity. Considering the whole being often takes a back seat in the pursuit of single pieces of information that provide evidence for a single response – to find the "magic pill."

It is, without doubt, vital to know the specific processes of what happens when neurotransmitters are present in the brain and their specific functions in the neuron and the synapse. This information will inform this paper in many ways. It is interesting, however, how these specific functions engage in a collective, dynamic process that emerges as an emotion or behavior. The "wholism" I speak of is like a concert performance where it is not just the individual players, or that they are working together, but the emergent symphony from all the members of the orchestra that creates a "state of being" and the qualia of the experience.

Is there a neurobiological system that is at the heart of producing beneficial shifts in mental state? By drawing together a broad selection of single domain research, I propose that there is a set of brain regions that act collectively to create the "brain state" of curiosity. They inform other areas of the brain, especially the midbrain and cortex, through the regulation of neurotransmitter production and distribution, to create emergent mental states. It is not unusual for brain areas to be considered to act as collective systems: the limbic area, the basal ganglia, and the hypothalamic–pituitary–adrenal (HPA) axis to name a few. On a broader scale, each cortical lobe – frontal, temporal, parietal, and occipital – is described as having a different collective function. On a broader level again are the left and right hemispheres.

> Curiosity will conquer fear even more than bravery will.
>
> **James Stephens, Irish novelist (1880–1950)**

These brain areas act together in a dynamic interplay that is essential in creating the neuro-biochemical milieu that is experienced as a mental state. Within any dynamic interplay there are always linear, causal, and specific functions, but if we can suspend linear, left hemisphere thinking for a moment, perhaps we can allow ourselves to consider a system where the *state of being* we call *curiosity* emerges from the activity of these brain regions as an integrated, self-organizing, complex system.

A curious mental state (Kidd & Hayden, 2015) is when there is:

- Positive anticipation.
- Increased focus and attention.
- Increased arousal.
- Engaged, "towards" sense of exploration.
- Reduction in negative affect and fearfulness.
- A shift from feeling isolated toward interpersonal relationship.
- A satisfying, euphoric reward at points of resolution, insight, or realization.
- Broader learning and memory capacities.

The neurobiology of these states is known to be created by:

- Dopamine: positive anticipation; movement toward; heightens attention in the pre-frontal cortex (PFC).

- Serotonin: modulates depression, fear, and anxiety; regulates aggression; enables positive mood; promotes other neurotransmitter release.
- Norepinephrine (noradrenaline): stimulates arousal and alertness; enhances memory formation and retrieval.
- Acetylcholine: stimulates arousal, attention, and vigilance.
- Endomorphins: stimulate pleasure, pain reduction, and euphoria.
- Oxytocin: promotes positive social interaction; builds trust; modulates inflammation; increases empathy; modulates fear and anxiety; increases calmness.

These neurotransmitters and neuro-peptides originate in specific sub-cortical regions. Neurons extend out into other sub-cortical and cortical locations as delivery systems. This creates the neuro-biochemical milieu that collectively modulates and regulates the neural activity that produces our experiential self.

- Dopamine:
  - Ventral tegmental area
  - Nucleus accumbens
  - Substantia nigra
- Serotonin:
  - Raphe nuclei
- Norepinephrine (noradrenaline):
  - Locus coeruleus
- Acetylcholine:
  - Nucleus basalis
  - Cholinergic mesopontine tegmentum
- Endomorphins:
  - Periaqueductal gray
- Oxytocin:
  - Paraventricular nucleus

The research relating to these regions, the neurotransmitters they produce, and the effect on our state of being has addressed:

- Positive anticipation: dopaminergic activity from the substantia nigra/ventral tegmental area and nucleus accumbens (Knutson et al., 2001; Gruber et al., 2014).

- Focus and attention on issues that are interesting: norepinephrine from the locus coeruleus (Ashton-Jones & Cohen, 2005) and acetylcholine from the nucleus basalis (Buzsaki & Gage, 1989).
- Calming of stress and hypersensitivity: serotonergic activity from the raphe nuclei (Hornung, 2003).
- Shifting from feeling isolated toward trust and social engagement through increased receptivity in oxytocin receptors in the paraventricular nucleus (Yee et al., 2016).
- Pleasure and satisfaction: endogenous endomorphin and enkephalin rewards from the periaqueductal gray (Blood & Zatorre, 2001).

Neurons project out into the midbrain and cortex to deliver the necessary neurotransmitters. Most research looks for the brain regions that neurotransmitters stimulate. Gruber et al. (2014) have shown the connection between the dopaminergic regions and the hippocampus; the amygdala is known to be calmed by GABAergic neurons that are stimulated by serotonin; norepinephrine and acetylcholine stimulate focus, arousal, and attention in areas such as the PFC and the cingulate; and endomorphins and enkephalins stimulate pleasurable reward in the caudate, striatum, and PFC. These brain regions, found in the upper brainstem and lower midbrain are, collectively, the functional structures of curiosity. Their close proximity can be seen in Figure AA.1.

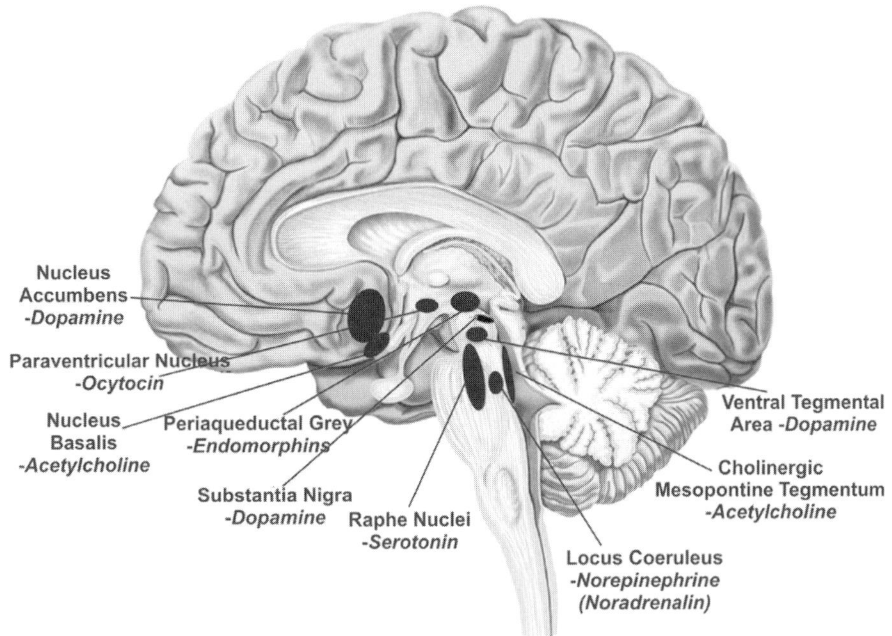

Figure AA.1. The nuntius nuclei

In determining a name, I was attracted by the word *nuntius* which is Latin for "messenger" or "announcer." The collective name is therefore the *nuntius nuclei*. This seems fitting for the nuclei and brain regions that produce neurotransmitters that are the messengers that regulate and modulate the biochemical milieu. The biochemical milieu is a fundamental contributing factor in how various areas of the brain function at any given time, not just in curiosity, so the *nuntius nuclei* will be relevant when considering a number of mental states where the biochemical milieu is involved. In the context of curiosity, the *nuntius nuclei* produce what I propose is the most advantageous biochemical milieu for beneficial therapeutic change, for learning, and for transformational growth.

We have heard the term "chemical imbalance" used extensively in relation to negative mental states (Deacon & Baird, 2009). It is certainly true that any mental state will have a neuro-biochemical milieu and that some mental states are not preferred or desired. It is logical to try to change the biochemical milieu in order to change mental state. It is important to remember, however, that it may be argued that the biochemical milieu for depression is the perfectly balanced milieu to produce depression. It has been shown that depression leads to (or causes), among other things, low levels of dopamine, serotonin, and norepinephrine (Moret & Briley, 2011). Even though these conditions are not what most people would consider a "good" chemical balance, the first thing to investigate is what message is being conveyed by the *nuntius nuclei* in relation to the whole biological system.

What is this state of "depression" telling us about what is happening within the deeper psycho-neuro-biology of this person? That is our first question as a therapist. We also seek to change that mental state, and to do so we utilize various interventions ranging from psychopharmacology, to cognitive therapy, to mindfulness, to yoga, to embodied relational presence, and so many more. The difficulty of therapy is that it is very difficult to change a negative mental state from within that negative mental state. In many ways, that is the intention of psychopharmacology – to change the mental state by shifting the biochemical milieu. Curiosity can change the biochemical milieu rapidly and consistently, and I propose that it does so by directly altering the activities of the *nuntius nuclei* as a mind-to-body effect.

In the light of that, it seems clear that when someone is curious there will be expressions of that state throughout their system. Their neuro-biochemical milieu will be of a certain "balance" which is a shift from their presenting milieu. Barbara Fredrickson (2004) opened the move toward understanding the benefits of positive emotions with her "broaden-and-build" theory. Her work shows that positive emotions are linked with thinking that is unusual, flexible, integrative, creative, open to information, and efficient, which facilitates approach behaviors and broadens a person's sense of possibility in the future. These effects were linked with increases in dopamine levels and positive affect enhancement of attention and arousal, which is linked to norepinephrine and acetylcholine. Negative affect does exactly the opposite by closing down broader attention and focusing on the cause or experience of the negative affect. In her paper, Fredrickson describes the effects of a variety of positive emotions:

> Joy, for instance, creates the urge to play, push the limits and be creative; urges evident not only in social and physical behavior, but also in intellectual and artistic behavior. Interest, a phenomenologically distinct positive emotion, creates the urge to explore, take in new information and experiences, and expand the self in the process. (Fredrickson, 2004, p. 1369)

Fredrickson considered positive emotions, whereas Jaak Panksepp has been developing detailed work on our fundamental emotions over several decades. He has determined seven fundamental emotions: four "toward" emotions – seeking, play, care, and lust; and three "away" emotions – fear, rage, and panic/grief. His work sheds more light on the neurotransmitters that regulate and modulate these emotional states. He recognized the "interaction of multiple neural circuits localized in extended brain regions, from the lower brainstem to the forebrain" (Alcaro & Panksepp, 2011, p. 1806). He also considers that "SEEKING energizes activity, and, with the aid of norepinephrine, may increase concentration and effort to achieve one's goals" (p. 1808). He suggests that anhedonia and helplessness rise when there is a deficiency of the SEEKING emotional disposition and that depression is a "state of reduced engagement with all aspects of the world, due to an endogenous hypo-functionality of the SEEKING network" (p. 1812).

This makes sense to me as a therapist, but the question is: How do we reinvigorate SEEKING in a person who has no sense of need to find anything? The answer is not to promote an emotional response – that is counterproductive for someone with depression or who is overwhelmed by anxiety – but to shift their state of consciousness to being curious *about* their emotional state. Curiosity, as I describe it, has a broad scope that embraces not only the "toward" emotions that Panksepp describes, but also the positive emotions like interest and play that Fredrickson describes. Eliciting the three facets of curiosity in the client will allow positive emotions and the fundamental emotions to emerge in a way that is therapeutically beneficial. Emotions are qualities that emerge from the activity of an investigation, and/or an interest in finding an alternative meaning, all with the intention of revealing possibilities. The changes created by these qualitative outcomes are quantitatively supported by a favorable biochemical milieu. In the state of curiosity, the client is experiencing whatever emerges in the framework of possibility that leads to beneficial change. In curiosity, everything that emerges is utilized in an objectively positive, creative way. That is why the curiosity approach is both productive and safe.

Conclusion

In conclusion, I suggest that curiosity is a state of mind *and* a state of the brain. Curiosity creates a unique mental state where exploration and discovery are desirable, even when the exploration might be of difficulties and traumas in life. I further suggest that curiosity emboldens a person to look both within and to their growing edge for meaning and purpose. Such speculation requires research and verification, but I believe there is enough evidence available now, albeit disparate, to make these conceptual propositions. If we prime our mental state with a sense of interest and wonder, seek out something that is beneath the obvious and superficially apparent, and finally look to create something new, meaningful, and self-relevant from this, we can have a positive effect on not only learning, but also personal growth and all the subsidiary growth that occurs on an interpersonal and inter-environmental level.

Appendix B

An Integrated Quantum Field Theory of Physics, Math, Biology, and Psychology

Ernest L. Rossi, Ph.D.

Abstract

We use the new quantum magnetic resonance microscope to review and update the foundations of the evolution of psychotherapy with an integrated quantum field theory of physics, math, biology, and psychology. We review the top-down psychosocial genomic and cultural perspectives that integrate consciousness, cognition, and the four-stage creative cycle with its molecular-genomic RNA-DNA building blocks. Heisenberg's uncertainty principle is used to re-conceptualize activity-dependent gene expression, brain plasticity, consciousness, cognition, and dreaming as the new foundation for an integrated quantum field theory of the evolution of psychotherapy. We update Dirac's transformational equation set, integrating early quantum dynamics with the new ZX-calculus that is more appropriate for visualizing and computing the cycles characteristic of life, consciousness, and cognition. Because the ZX-calculus is so important for visualizing many novel insights into the modern quantum dynamics of fundamental life processes, we shall frequently refer to it as the ZX-quantum calculus in this presentation to distinguish it from the traditional historical calculus of Newton and Leibnitz. This new ZX-quantum calculus generalizes the observer-operators of current quantum physics to the molecular biology of the four-stage 90–120 minute basic rest–activity cycle and its corresponding four-stage creative cycle of therapeutic problem solving in psychology. We report clinical case studies illustrating how the quantum qualia of these observer-operators are evident in everyday human consciousness and cognition during a wide range of experiences from negative stress and psychopathology to positive life transformations. We propose innovative quantum field theory research to document how the observer-operator in subjective experience can be a causal agent in facilitating health and problem-solving on the objective molecular/genomic level in everyday life as well as psychotherapy with the ZX-quantum calculus.

Keywords: Biology, bra–ket notation, conflict, cognition, consciousness, creative, Dirac, expectancy, experimental, mathematics, neuroscience, observer-operators, physics, psychology, QBism, quantum field theory, quantum microscope, quantum qualia, uncertainty, ZX-calculus

Part 1: A 100 Year Perspective of the Evolution of Psychotherapy

Introduction

We propose an integrated quantum field theory of physics, math, biology, and psychology for optimizing human health and wellness in the current evolution of psychotherapy. Our integrated quantum field theory brings together a variety of interdisciplinary fields ranging from stress reduction, psychosomatics, psychoneuroimmunology, meditation, and mind/body medicine to the psychobiology of optimizing human performance, problem-solving, and creativity. We update Paul Dirac's transformational equation set of early quantum dynamics with the new ZX-calculus as an experimental mathematical bridge between physics, math, biology, and psychology. In Box AB.1 we illustrate how the quantum qualia of human experience during activity-dependent gene expression, brain plasticity, and the creation of new consciousness and cognition may be conceptualized. Students of psychotherapy will learn how the new ZX-calculus can facilitate their practical daily work in bridging the mysteries of Descartes' mind/body gap at quantum level visually in all the figures of this chapter together with many clinical case examples.

Box AB.1. Dirac's transformational equation set from quantum to classical calculus: the quantum qualia of brain plasticity, behavior, consciousness, and cognition

We carefully follow Dirac's own concise mathematical reasoning (Dirac, 1978, pp. 40–41) in this review. Dirac begins with the idea of Schrödinger's wave function in three-dimensional space. The wave function is designated as ψ, a function of the three coordinates x_1, x_2, x_3 that can vary with time:

$$\psi\,(x_1, x_2, x_3; t) \qquad (1)$$

Dirac notes that the usual interpretation of this wave function when normalized is that the square of its modulus $|\psi|^2$ provides the probability of the particle being localized in a particular place. This wave function ψ is a complex number so it can be multiplied by its phase factor $e^{i\gamma}$, where γ is a real number and $e^{i\gamma}$ has a modulus of unity. Dirac then multiplies ψ by $e^{i\gamma}$ to get another wave function designated as Ψ:

$$e^{i\gamma}\,\psi = \Psi \qquad (2)$$

Which now has its modulus squared just as ψ:

$$|\Psi|^2 = |\psi|^2 \qquad (3)$$

This allows Ψ and ψ to have the same probability distribution.

Dirac then notes that γ in equation (2) could be a function of position as well as time, so that the new Ψ has the same probability distribution as ψ in equation (4):

$$\Psi\,(x_1, x_2, x_3;\, t) = e^{i\gamma\,(x_1, x_2, x_3;\, t)}\,\psi(x_1, x_2, x_3;\, t) \qquad (4)$$

However, the new Ψ and the original ψ do not satisfy the same wave equation! This becomes evident when Dirac forms $\partial\Psi/\partial x_r$ with r taking on the values of 1, 2, or 3 so that he obtains equation (5):

$$\partial\Psi/\partial x_r = e^{i\gamma}\,(\partial/\partial x_r + iK_r)\,\psi \qquad (5)$$

Where K_r is a function of position in equation (6):

$$K_r \equiv \partial_\gamma/\partial x_r \qquad (6)$$

Dirac then states: "We would have to consider K_r as something more general, something such that when we take $K_r dx_r$ and integrate around a closed loop, the result need not be zero:

$$\oint K_r\, dx_r \text{ need } \textit{not be equal to } 0 \qquad (7)$$

Dirac then concludes: "If we do that, we get a physical theory which is definitely more general than what we had before" (p. 41). We now interpret Dirac's comment – that the contour integration of equation (7) "*need not be equal to* 0" – as having profoundly new implications for integrating the current day scientific perspectives of physicists, biologists, neuroscientists, and psychologists. This integration illustrates how new awareness could arise from a cycle of activity-dependent gene expression, brain plasticity, and emergent quantum qualia of consciousness and cognition (Rossi & Rossi, 2011, 2013, 2014a, 2014b, 2015).

Integrating the Subjective Quantum Qualia of Mind with Objective Molecular/Genomic Dynamics

This new application of Dirac's (1930) original quantum formulations (Rossi & Rossi, 2011, 2013, 2014a, 2014b) is consistent with Penrose (2004), Wilczek (2002, 2015), and Carroll's (2016, p. 437) insights into "The essence of the Core Theory – the laws of physics underlying everyday life." We show how the highly sensitive quantum qualia of problematic dissociations during stage 2 of the four-stage creative basic rest–activity cycle (BRAC) are the source of quantum level cognitions and conflicts that can lead to war, discord, corruption, hate crimes, terrorism, and other stress related psychosocial pathologies that can be resolved in stages 3 and 4 of the creative cycle. We propose how Quantum Bayesianism (or QBism) concepts of the novel observer-operator have insightful applications in counseling, psychotherapy, translational medicine, and virtually all the mind/body therapies. We conclude with clinical case illustrations of how innovative applications of the ZX-quantum calculus, updating Dirac's bra–ket notation, could conceptualize adaptation and problem-solving on the objective molecular/genomic level to facilitate the evolution of psychotherapy (Heunen et al., 2013; Coecke & Kissinger, 2017).

Why have many cultures developed practices of rest, relaxation, and the inner focusing of attention typical of therapeutic meditation and hypnosis to facilitate health and well-being? Recent research on sleep has uncovered a surprising, yet sensible answer to this question. Sleep clears the mind by permitting 60% more cerebral spinal fluid to wash through the brain to remove the toxic by-products of normal molecular metabolism (Xie et al., 2013). This unexpected finding integrates what we now believe we know about associations between the quantum qualia of the subjective experiences of mind and the objective molecular/genomic dynamics of consciousness and cognition, as well as their utilization in the holistic healing arts such as meditation, mindfulness, and therapeutic hypnosis. Controversial concepts originally formulated in quantum physics (Dirac, 1930; Greene, 2011; Susskind & Friedman, 2014), biology (McFadden, 2000; Baggott, 2011; McFadden & Al-Khalili, 2014) and psychology (Rossi, 2000 [1972], 2007, 2012; Rossi & Rossi, 2014a, 2014b, 2015) over the last century are reviewed and utilized for developing a new mind/body concept of the observer-operator to optimize self-care and health via psychosocial and epigenomic RNA/DNA molecular mechanisms. We propose and illustrate a new quantum Bayesian mathematical notation for conceptualizing a causal role for consciousness and cognition in the theory, research, and practice of psychotherapy on many levels from mind to genes.

Bayesian probability, named after 18th century English clergyman Thomas Bayes, deals with *subjective probability – the degree of belief that an event will occur*. This is in striking contrast with the statistics most of us are taught today, which are about *objective probability – based on counting how frequently something occurs in the outside world*. It is now striking to realize how Bayesian or *subjective probability – the degree of belief that an event will occur* – is very similar to the emerging concepts of psychosocial genomics and *expectancy in therapeutic consciousness (meditation, counseling, psychotherapy expectancy theory in therapeutic hypnosis) which is also concerned with subjective belief.*

In a clear and concise paper, the physicist Hans von Baeyer (2013) outlined a new Bayesian interpretation of quantum information, which we now apply to brain research on consciousness, cognition (Dehaene, 2014), and behavior (Rossi, 2002b, 2007, 2012):

> A new version of quantum theory sweeps away the bizarre paradoxes of the microscopic world. The cost? *Quantum information exists only in your imagination.* In 2001 a team of researchers began to develop a model that either eliminates the quantum paradoxes or puts them in a less troubling form.

> The model, known as Quantum Bayesianism, or QBism for short, re-imagines the entity that lies at the heart of quantum weirdness – the wave function.
>
> In the conventional view of quantum theory, an object such as an electron is represented by its wave function, a mathematical expression that describes the object's properties. If you want to predict how the electron will behave, you calculate how its wave function evolves in time. The result of the calculation gives you the probability that the electron will have a certain property (like being in one place and not another). But problems arise when physicists assume that a wave function is real.
>
> QBism, which combines quantum theory with probability theory, maintains that the wave function has no objective reality. Instead QBism portrays the wave function as a user's manual, a mathematical tool that an observer uses to make wiser decisions about the surrounding world – the quantum world. Specifically, the observer employs the wave function to assign his or her personal belief that a quantum system will have a specific property, realizing that the individual's own choices and actions affect the system in an inherently uncertain way.
>
> Another observer, using a wave function that describes the world as the person sees it, may come to a completely different conclusion about the same quantum system. *One system – one event – can have as many different wave functions as there are observers.* After observers have communicated with one another and modified their private wave functions to account for the newly acquired knowledge, a coherent worldview emerges. *By interpreting the wave function as a subjective belief and subject to revision by the rules of Bayesian statistics, the mysterious paradoxes of quantum mechanics vanish.* (von Baeyer, 2013, pp. 47–48; italics added)

These realizations motivate us to propose and illustrate how quantum field theory could optimize the quantum Bayesian dynamics of expectancy in most schools of therapeutic consciousness and psychotherapy (Rossi, 1988a, 1988b, 1988c, 1988d). We begin by outlining a new quantum Bayesian version of the RNA/DNA field theory of life and consciousness (Rossi, 2002b, 2004c, 2007, 2012; Rossi & Rossi, 2011, 2013, 2014a, 2014b).

An Integrated Quantum Field Theory of the RNA/DNA Dynamics of Life and Consciousness

Our proposal for a very broad functional definition of the role of genes in the *complex adaptive systems* of life (Gell-Mann, 1994; Holland, 2012) is now applied to the integrated quantum field theory of therapeutic consciousness, cognition, behavior, psychology, and health in general in Figure AB.1.

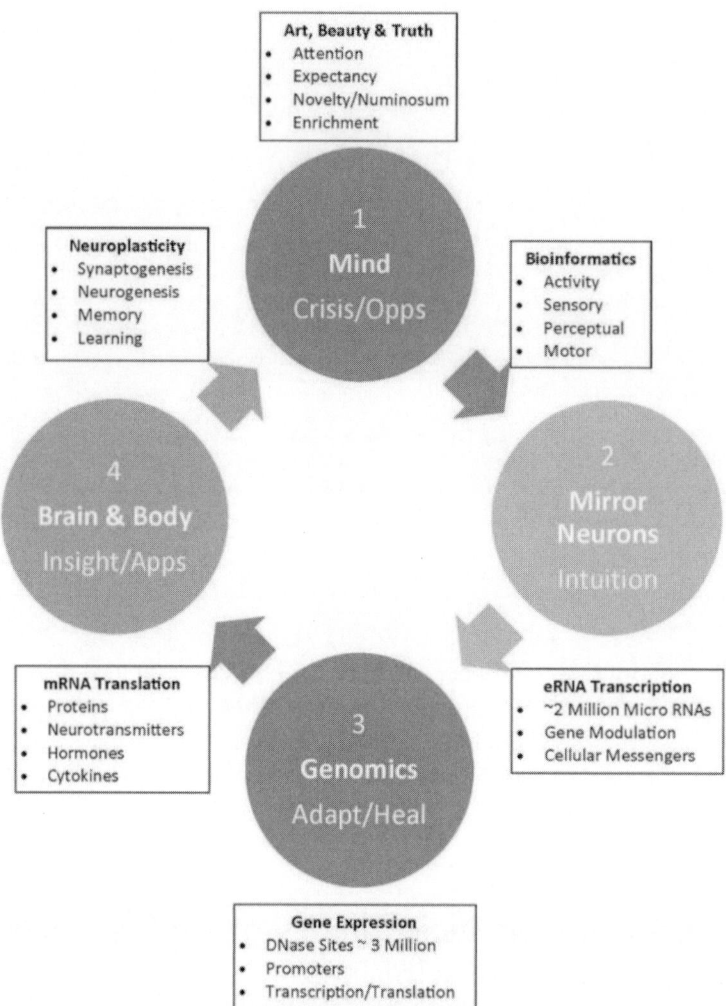

Figure AB.1. An integrated quantum field theory of the observer-operator and the novelty-numinosum-neurogenesis-effect in the RNA/DNA dynamics of psychosocial genomics and psychotherapy.

We have documented how the fundamental systems of life and consciousness are characterized by the wave nature of circadian (daily) and ultradian (hourly) rhythms on all levels from the mind to genes (Lloyd & Rossi, 1992, 2008). We now outline how neuroscience research illustrated in Figure AB.1 underpins a general quantum field theory of consciousness, cognition, and creativity (Rossi, 1993 [1986], 2002b; Rossi & Rossi, 2011, 2013, 2014a).

The Classical Mind/Gene Cycle of Molecular Biology, Consciousness, and Cognition

The top circle of Figure AB.1 updates the classical research on just-noticeable differences (JNDs) that was the original foundation of the psychophysics of sensations and perceptions that defined experimental psychology in the 1890s (Boring, 1950) with the most recent consciousness studies of art, beauty, and truth in the coming age of quantum biology and psychology (McFadden, 2000; Al-Khalili, 2014; McFadden & Al-Khalili, 2014). We now propose how research on the qualia of novelty-numinosum-neurogenesis-effect (NNNE) operates on the quantum level of molecules that makes life possible (Rossi, 2002b, 2005, 2007, 2012). The subjective experience of *novelty* evokes highly motivating experiences of the *numinosum (fascination, mysteriousness, and tremendousness)* (Otto, 1950 [1923]), which turns on gene expression and the growth of the brain that gives rise to new levels of consciousness and cognition (Rossi, 1993 to 2012). Research by the ENCODE project integrated activity- and experience-dependent gene expression and brain plasticity. Key research is now exploring complex adaptive systems of information transduction in the *transcription process* arising from ~2 million eRNAs carrying signals from the physical environment and psychosocial milieus (termed "epigenomics") to genes bearing ~3 million docking sites recently summarized by the ENCODE Project Consortium (2012).

Current research documents the use of DNA microarray technology to measure the expression levels of many thousands of genes simultaneously (Bar-Joseph et al., 2012). This evidence based research in molecular biology has become a new standard for validating personalized medicine. We now propose that this DNA microarray research can also be used to assess the psychosocial genomic validity and reliability of many diverse cultural, historical, and holistic traditions of mind/body healing.

The primary research literature of psychosocial genomics today brings together a variety of top-down psychotherapeutic processes. They include the *relaxation response* (Dusek et al., 2008); *therapeutic hypnosis* (Lichtenberg et al., 2000, 2004; Rossi et al., 2008; Rossi, 2012; Rossi & Rossi, 2013; Cozzolino et al., 2014); *meditation* (Creswell et al., 2012); the *therapeutic placebo* (Sliwinski & Elkins, 2013); *social psychology* (Cole et al., 2005, 2007, 2010, 2011; Cole, 2009); and *yoga* (Lavretsky et al., 2013). The motivation of all psychosocial genomic research is to facilitate the resolution of *stress related psychosocial dysfunctions* (Unternaehrer et al., 2012; Yount & Rachlin, 2014). We mentored the use of DNA microarrays to explore, among other things, the hypothesis that the activation of gene expression, in response to top-down therapeutic protocols, epitomized by the Creative Psychosocial Genomic Healing Experience (CPGHE) and the Mind–Body Transformations Therapy (MBT-T), could provide a scientific foundation for a more general theory of mind/body communication and healing with therapeutic hypnosis (Cozzolino et al., 2014). A full description of the administration, scoring, and clinical application of the top-down creative protocol for facilitating therapeutic cognition is freely available (Rossi, 2012).

Some of the most recent research that has reached the popular press concerns how mindful meditation can modulate gene expression in cancer patients, which has been reported as follows:

> Lead investigator Dr. Linda E. Carlson (2015) and her colleagues found that in breast cancer patients, support group involvement and mindfulness meditation – an adapted form of Buddhist meditation in which practitioners focus on present thoughts and actions in a non-judgmental way, ignoring past grudges and future concerns – are associated with preserved telomere length. Telomeres are stretches of DNA that cap our chromosomes and help prevent chromosomal deterioration – biology professors often liken them to the plastic tips on shoelaces. Shortened telomeres aren't known to cause a specific disease per se, but they do whither with age and are shorter in people with cancer, diabetes, heart disease and high stress levels. We want our telomeres intact.
>
> In Carlson's study, distressed breast cancer survivors were divided into three groups. The first group was randomly assigned to an 8-week cancer recovery program consisting of mindfulness meditation and yoga; the second to 12 weeks of group therapy in which they shared difficult emotions and fostered social support; and the third was a control group, receiving just a 6-hour stress management course. A total of 88 women completed the study and had their blood analyzed for telomere length before and after the interventions. Telomeres were maintained in both treatment groups but shortened in controls.
>
> Previous work hinted at this association. A study led by diet and lifestyle guru Dr. Dean Ornish from 2008 reported that the combination of a vegan diet, stress management, aerobic exercise and participation in a support group for 3 months resulted in increased telomerase activity in men with prostate cancer, telomerase being the enzyme that maintains telomeres by adding DNA to the ends of our chromosomes. (Stetka, 2014)

We now propose that further research with these protocols could replicate these findings in a more standardized form to update the mind/molecular/genomic efficacy of translational medicine recommended as a standard of clinical excellence by Thomas Insel (2009, 2010, 2012), the former director of the National Institute of Mental Health.

The Classical to Quantum Transition of Observer-Operators via Mirror Neurons

The original research on mirror neurons initiated by Rizzolatti and Sinigaglia (2008), Iacoboni (2007, 2008) and others (Grodzinsky & Nelken, 2014) has been greatly expanded in current neuroscience to include epigenomic processes (the integration of nature and nurture) that modulate mind–gene communication. Research on birdsong courtship dynamics, for example, documented how eRNAs ("enhancer RNAs," which enhance gene expression) respond to thought by modulating the transcription/translation cycle of activity- and experience-dependent epigenomic expression.

Clayton, a specialist in songbird neurogenomics, made the salient comment, "This is the first time a microRNA has been shown to respond to a particular thought process" (Saey, 2010; Warren et al., 2010; Gunaratne et al., 2011; Drnevich et al., 2012; Clayton, 2013: p. 62). How could this be possible? Presumably the wave nature of the sound spectra of the birdsong is encoded by the wave nature of molecular eRNA resonance in mirror neurons. We now propose that an analogous cycle of informational transformation occurs in human consciousness and cognition as illustrated in Figure AB.2. *This is the fundamental insight that integrates the top-down paths of mind, consciousness, and the expectancies of so-called "free will" with the bottom-up molecular-genomic paths of communication. We now propose that this is a manifestation of the quantum Bayesian observer-operator, bridging the so-called "Cartesian gap" between mind and body in psychosocial genomics, meditation, and therapeutic hypnosis.*

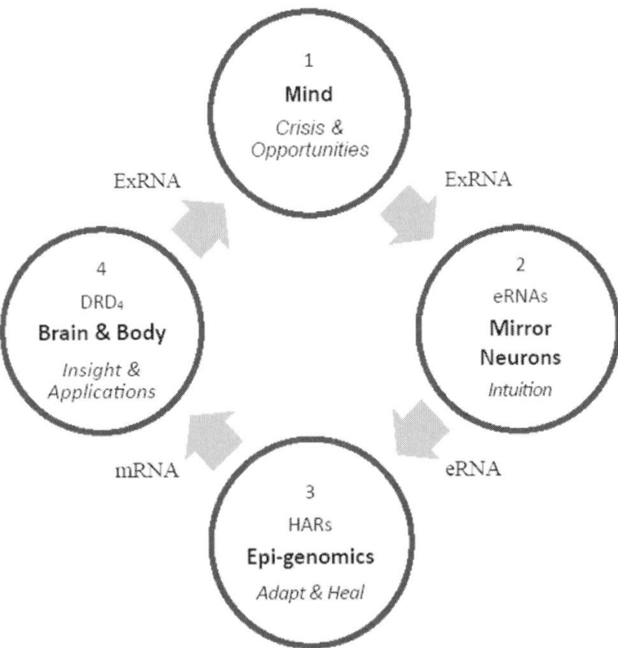

Figure AB.2. Conscious thoughts dialogue with our genes via the bioinformatic epigenomic loop of communication between nature and nurture. Cognitions are converted into eRNAs (enhancer RNAs) to enhance DNA (gene expression), which codes for mRNAs (messenger RNAs), which generate the proteins (hormones, neurotransmitters, cytokines, etc.) and brain plasticity that generates mind/body communication and problem-solving with therapeutic cognition (Rossi, 2002b, 2004c, 2007, 2012; Vedral, 2012). In this context, we propose that Ebstein's (1997) saga of the adventure gene, novelty seeking, and substance abuse associated with the dopamine DRD4 receptor gene could be one example of the psychosocial genomic basis of what we call the novelty-numinosum-neurogenesis-effect in the quantum observer-operator. A multimodal mathematical model of the therapeutic quantum observer-operator in the healing arts has been outlined (Rossi, 2002b, pp. 203–251; Leslie, 2013).

More recent research on the social communication of bats confirms and extends this earlier research on birdsong. Since bats are mammals their calls provide greater detail about their appropriateness as a model of human cognition. A recent issue of *Science* (Morell, 2014) details how the FOXP2 gene, which is associated with cognition and vocal learning in humans, birds, and bats, may be a closer model for human speech. The trills, chirps, and buzzes of bats, for example, can communicate a series of expectancies such as announcing, (1) I am species *P. nathusii*, (2) a male, and (3) specifically I am the only male with this song (4) so land here next to me. (5) We share a common social identity and communication pool. (6) The soft tones of the males lure females, while (7) the harsh tones compete with other males and warn them away. Although these songs typically last only ~1.6 seconds they may contain ~20 syllables combined in specific ways, with individual rhythmic patterns of communication that are appropriate for current life conditions.

Such research on birdsong and bat call syntax and semantics illustrates how behavior encoded in the RNA/DNA transcription/translation cycle could mediate the vastly more complex cycle of information transduction that occurs in human consciousness, cognition, expectancy, and health illustrated in Figures AB.1, 2, and 3 (Gell-Mann, 1994; Sczepanski & Joyce, 2014; Shelka & Piccirilli, 2014). *We propose that this is the fundamental insight of bioinformatics which integrates the top-down path of consciousness, cognition, and expectancy in quantum field theory with the bottom-up molecular-genomic paths of communication within and between individuals.*

Free public databases are being updated daily by the National Institute of General Medical Sciences, which offers information on these advances of the new genetics led by Francis Collins, director of the National Institutes of Health (NIH). The NIH Common Fund provides research grants to catalogue all types of exRNA that flow between mind and body "in blood, tears, saliva and every other body fluid" (Leslie, 2013) to provide a baseline that can be compared with exRNA profiles associated with Alzheimer's, ageing, autism, development, diabetes, obesity, psychiatry, Parkinson's, stress, trauma, etc.

Figure AB.2 gives precise bioinformatic meaning to the commonly used terms of the four-stage creative cycle such as crisis/opportunity (stage 1), intuition (stage 2), adaption/healing (stage 3), and insight/applications (stage 4). The integration of such psychological terms with brain–body research is the psychogenomic foundation in the RNA/DNA transcription/translation cycle of coding for mRNAs, proteins at the molecular-genomic level of therapeutic hypnosis. Key research explores how these proteins, often called "mother molecules," are cleaved into the neurotransmitters, hormones, and cytokines of the complex adaptive system of psychoneuroimmunology (Irwin & Vedhara, 2005), which integrate cells of the mind, brain, and body that ultimately facilitate the dynamics of memory, learning, behavior, and the qualia of consciousness itself in therapeutic cognition (Rossi & Rossi, 2013). *The research illustrated in Figure AB.2 leads us to propose how the quantum field theory of exRNA signaling between nature and nurture is the molecular/genomic underpinning of the complex adaptive dynamics of normal everyday life as well as meditation psychotherapy and other therapeutic approaches to psychosocial and cultural health* (Gell-Mann, 1994; Holland, 2012).

Brain/Mind Plasticity and the Classical/Quantum Transitions

Psychosocial genomic transitions between classical-to-quantum dynamics of stage 2 and quantum-to-classical dynamics of stage 4 are experienced psychologically as illustrated in Figure AB.3. Genomics research via the ENCODE project, which includes qualia and experience-dependent gene expression, is currently manifesting a profound breakout on the epigenomic level. As was stated earlier, key research is now exploring complex adaptive systems of information transduction in the transcription process arising from ~2 million eRNAs carrying signals from the physical environment and psychosocial milieus to genes bearing ~3 million docking sites, recently summarized by the ENCODE Project Consortium (2012). Pollard (et al., 2006; Pollard, 2012) has recently pioneered research into the human accelerated regions (HARs) that are now recognized as groups of genes that are undergoing very rapid adaptation distinctively different from our nearest primate relatives.

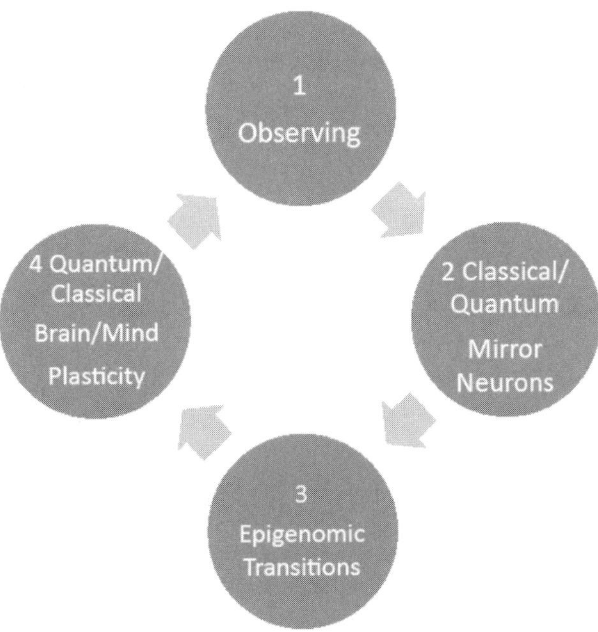

Figure AB.3. The communication cycle of the psychosocial information flow between (1) observing consciousness, (2) the classical to quantum transitions of mirror neurons, (3) the RNA to DNA epigenomic transitions, and (4) the quantum to classical transitions on "the road to reality" (Penrose, 2004) in therapeutic consciousness and health (Rossi, 1993 [1986], 2002b, 2012).

Brain/Mind Plasticity and the Quantum to Classical Transition

Figure AB.3 illustrates how the transitions between classical-to-quantum dynamics in stage 2 and quantum-to-classical dynamics in stage 4 are experienced in the non-linear dynamics of therapeutic consciousness and cognition (Chiarucci et al., 2014). It is interesting to ask, for example, whether the *intuitions of stage* 2 are psychologically sensed, or felt, to be the same or different in comparison with the experience of *insights during stage 4*. This is important because stage 4 of the creative cycle is the quantum-to-classical transition that purportedly takes place in the Penrose/Hameroff "Orch-OR" (orchestrated objective reduction) model of consciousness entangled with microtubules within the cells of brain (Hameroff & Penrose, 1996). Jeong et al. (2014) recently investigated the classical/quantum and quantum/classical transitions in a manner that we believe are consistent with the deep psychosocial genomic dynamics of therapeutic consciousness and cognition. In two pioneering books, the highly esteemed neurobiologist Loewenstein (1999, 2013) presents detailed overviews of how quantum level dynamics underpin the molecular biology of the body, brain, and mind. The research supports some little known but startling work at Carleton University, in Canada, that implies how the quantum Bayesian dynamics are manifest in the wave nature of sleep, dreams, and therapeutic quantum observer-operators (Rossi, 2000 [1972]).

The Quantum Wave Nature of Mindfulness: Consciousness, Cognition, Sleep, and Dreams – The Four-Stage Creative Cycle and the Psychosocial Genomics of Therapeutic Hypnosis

The wave nature of psychosocial genomics, meditation, mindfulness, and, indeed, all holistic forms of mind/body psychotherapy is mapped onto the biological 90–120 minute basic rest–activity cycle (Lloyd & Rossi, 1992, 2008), and the psychological four-stage creative cycle (Rossi, 1967, 2007, 2012) illustrated in the upper curve of Figure AB.4 (see p. 253). The proteomics (protein) profile in the middle curve depicts the energy landscape for protein folding within neurons of the brain into the correct structures needed for adaptive brain plasticity (Cheung et al., 2004). This proteomic profile arises from the functional concordance of co-expressed genes illustrated by the genomics profile below it (Levsky et al., 2002). This psychosocial genomic curve represents the actual gene expression profiles of the immediate-early gene c-Fos, and 10 other genes (alleles), over the typical basic rest–activity cycle of 90–120 minutes. The lower diagram of Figure AB.4 illustrates how the quantum qualia of consciousness, cognition, and behavior are typically experienced within the normal circadian cycle of waking, as well as REM dreams while sleeping (Rossi & Nimmons, 1991; Rossi, 2002a, 2004).

Our most recent addition to Figure AB.4 is to map the quantum equations of Heisenberg's (1927) uncertainty principle and Dirac's (1978) quantum notation (introduced in Box AB.1) onto the biological four-stage basic rest–activity cycle and the psychological four-stage creative cycle, illustrated in the top part of Figure AB.4. In a remarkable book, *The Great Equations*, Robert Crease, chairman of the philosophy department at Stony Brook University, tells the engaging story of Heisenberg's emotional journey as he experienced the ups and downs of the four-stage creative cycle during his discovery of the uncertainty principle and the equations that formulated it. In the following quotes from Crease, we intersperse in [square brackets] our comments on the four-stage creative cycle that Heisenberg is apparently experiencing when he writes his epoch-making uncertainty paper.

> The paper showed how to *compile tables of amplitudes and frequencies associated with transitions between states – he called such tables "quantum-theoretical quantities"* – and how the tables could be related by a new kind of calculus, which he called "quantum-mechanical relations." [This is stage 1 of the four-stage creative cycle integrating *quantum quantities and relations* – this may ring a bell for students of psychotherapy who may have struggled to understand the what, why, and how of Dirac's integration of math and relationships in Box AB.1.] …
>
> Heisenberg then hit a snag. [Snag means stuck, which is the defining characteristic of stage 2 of the four-stage creative cycle.] The tables and the multiplication rule he invented for them obeyed a new kind of algebra that mathematicians had discovered long before, but was unfamiliar to most physicists, himself included. Most strikingly, the rule did not follow the "commutative law," the mathematical principle according to which the order in which one multiplies two numbers does not affect the result: $ab = ba$. When Heisenberg used his new calculus to multiply one quantum-theoretical table (let's call it A) by another (B), the result depended on the order: $AB \neq BA$. The feature "was very disagreeable to me," he said later, and try as he might he could not rid his theory of it. "I felt this was the only point of difficulty in the whole scheme, otherwise I would be perfectly happy." Heisenberg then did what many people do when a nuisance threatens to spoil an invention: he swept it under the rug … Heisenberg concluded his paper with a disclaimer of the sort that is often seen in early papers in a field … The answer, he declared, would have to await *"a more penetrating mathematical investigation."* (Crease, 2010, p. 243; italics added)

Heisenberg, still a very young student, wisely recognized that he was stuck at this point and gave his paper to his academic supervisor, Max Born, to determine if it was worth publishing. In due time, Born recognized that "Heisenberg's funny quantum-mechanical relations were actually the most natural way that mathematicians had discovered to 'multiply' matrices."

> Born was overjoyed. [Overjoyed is characteristic of stage 3 – the a-ha of the four-stage creative cycle.] … He knew that matrices can be noncommutative – the order in which one multiplied them mattered. This explained Heisenberg's embarrassing difficulty that, for instance, the matrix p associated with momentum and q with position did not commute; the matrix pq was not the same as qp (by convention, physicists often indicate matrices with bold symbols). But there was more. This pair of variables – known as canonically conjugate variables – was not commutative, but in a special way. Though Born could not prove it, the difference between pq and qp seemed to be a specific matrix proportional to Planck's constant: $pq - qp = Ih / 2\pi i$, where I is the unit matrix – "ones" along the diagonal entries and zeros everywhere else … Its central feature is what they called the "fundamental quantum-mechanical relation," the strange equation $pq - qp = Ih / 2\pi i$. The paper is a landmark in the history of physics, for it is the first map of the quantum domain. (Crease, 2010, p. 245)

In QBism, the subjective inner world of personal experience, the so-called mysterious and weird physical paradoxes of the objective outer world in quantum mechanics vanish (von Baeyer, 2013). This motivates us to propose that the physicist's problem of paradoxical quantum observations (measurements) over the past century may be transformed into an opportunity for the psychologist today in our integrated quantum field theory of physics, math, biology, and psychology: we call this the "**observer-operator (O_b/O_p)**" and illustrate where this takes place at the peak of the four-stage creative cycle in Figure AB.4. The quantum wave nature of the observer-operator is often experienced psychologically as the novelty-numinosum-neurogenesis-effect – whereby the wondrous, novel, and numinous **observations (O_b)** experienced during "peak experiences" (Maslow, 1968) in the arts, humanities, sciences, and in positive empathic psychosocial relationships automatically **operate (O_p)** to turn on adaptive activity-dependent epigenetic gene expression and brain plasticity to underpin the new quantum qualia of creative consciousness, cognition, and behavior (Rossi, 2002a, 2002b, 2007, 2012). Our new quantum microscope of the creative mind reveals that the ultimate microdynamics of Freud's so-called "unconscious" could now be expressed in the "fundamental quantum-mechanical relations" of the strange equation $\mathbf{pq} - qp = \mathbf{I}h / 2\pi i$ of Heisenberg, Born, Jordan, and others. Fedak and Prentis (2009) describe the profound implications of this quantum equation as the commutation law:

> Indeed, the commutation law is one of the most fundamental relations in quantum mechanics. This equation introduces Planck's constant and the imaginary number "I" into the theory in the most basic way possible. It is the golden rule of quantum algebra and makes quantum calculations unique. The way in which all dynamical properties of a system depend on "h" can be traced back to the simple way in which pq–qp depend on h. In short, the commutation law stores information on the discontinuity, the non-commutativity, the uncertainty, and the complexity of the quantum world. (Fedak & Prentis, 2009, p. 133)

Figure AB.4 illustrates stage 1 of the four-stage creative cycle, which is often described as data collection in science, or the initial recognition of a problem or issue that needs to be resolved in everyday life. Stage 2 is often accompanied by experiences of turning inward, incubation and/or conflict, cognitive dissonance (Festinger, 1957), emotional negativity (Bilalić & McLeod, 2014), stress, emotional regression, and/or uncertainty as one searches for a solution (Rossi, 2007, 2012). In poetry, myth, and saga, stage 2 is often called "the storm before the light," "the dark night of the soul," or some other such metaphor. Stage 3 is the a-ha or eureka flash experience of a new insight or solution to the problem. In neuroscience and psychosocial genomics, we cite research documenting how experience-dependent gene expression, brain plasticity, and new consciousness develop during stage 3. Stage 4 completes the cycle with the growth integrated into new networks of cognitions for formulating a more adaptive reality and self-identity.

In Figure AB.4 we underpin these four stage cycles of biology and psychology with the quantum mathematical formulation of Heisenberg's (1983 [1927]) uncertainty principle: $\Delta\, \mathbf{x}\, \Delta\, \mathbf{p} \geq \hbar/2$, Born & Jordan's (1925) fundamental quantum-mechanical relation: $\mathbf{pq} - \mathbf{qp} = \mathbf{I}h / 2\pi i$, and Dirac's

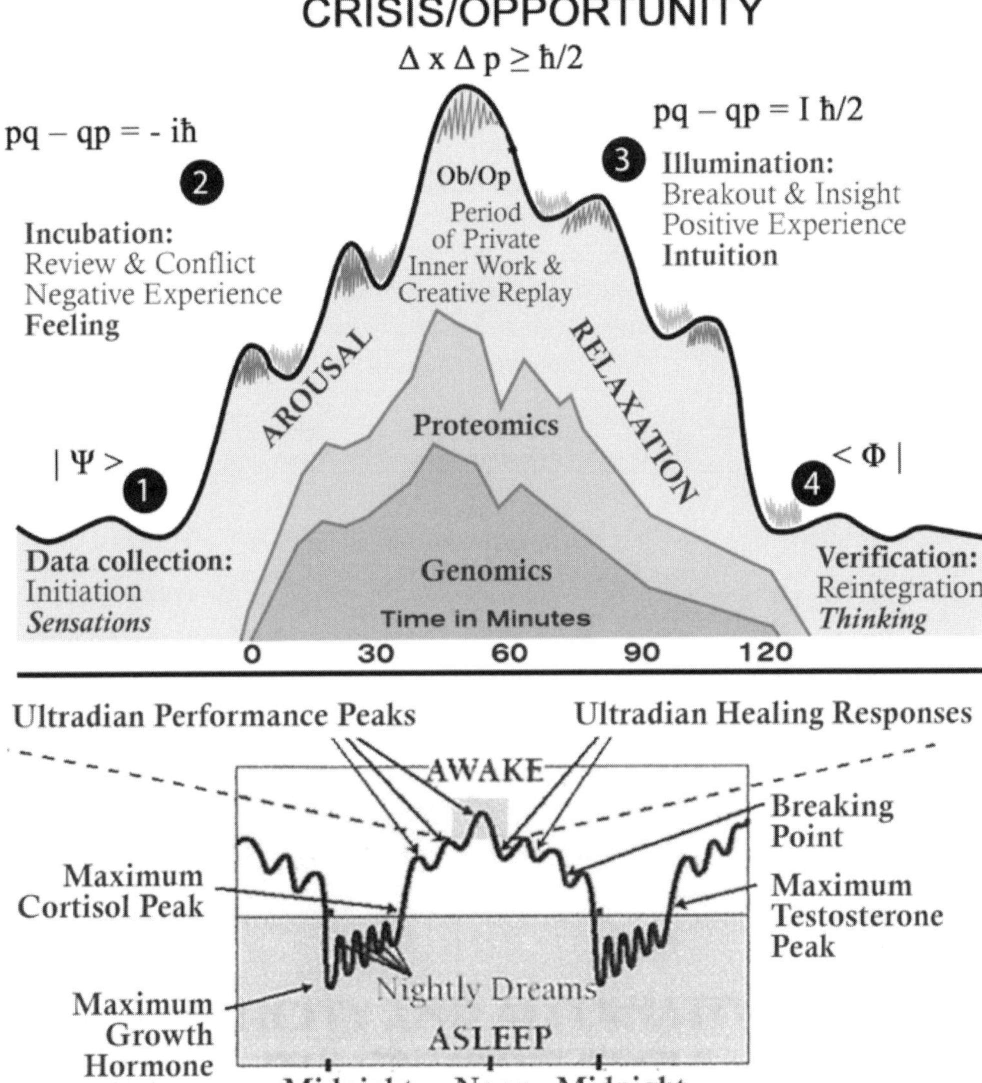

Figure AB.4. The quantum wave nature of the observer-operator (O_b/O_p in the top tip of the crisis/opportunity at the peak of uncertainty) in our integrated quantum field theory of physics, math, biology, and psychology maps psychosocial genomics, consciousness, and therapeutic cognition onto the biological profile of the 90–120 minute basic rest–activity cycle (Lloyd & Rossi, 1992, 2008) and the psychological four-stage creative cycle (Rossi, 1967, 2007, 2012).

(1928) quantum notation: **Bra** $< \Psi_+ |$ **Ket** $|\Psi_- >$, which will be illustrated with clinical case studies later.

Pioneering electronic monitoring of catalepsy during hypnosis by Milton H. Erickson and his early student Leonard Ravitz (1950, 1962) motivated the formulation of a new two-factor theory of therapeutic hypnosis by Ernest Rossi. These compiled graphs and tables of amplitudes and frequencies associated with transitions between states – which Heisenberg called "quantum-theoretical quantities" (Erickson & Rossi, 2014 [1981]; Rossi et al., 2008–2015) – are now being investigated with more advanced EEG methods (Chiarucci et al., 2014; Jamieson & Burgess, 2014). Such research documents how the overall domain of hypnotherapeutic work is a wave function of high and low phase hypnosis in chaotobiological time of mathematical chaos theory, illustrated in Figure AB.5 (Rossi, 2002a, 2002b), which is consistent with the recent calls for reorienting the education, theory, and practice of therapeutic hypnosis (Hope & Sugarman, 2015; Alter & Sugarman, 2017).

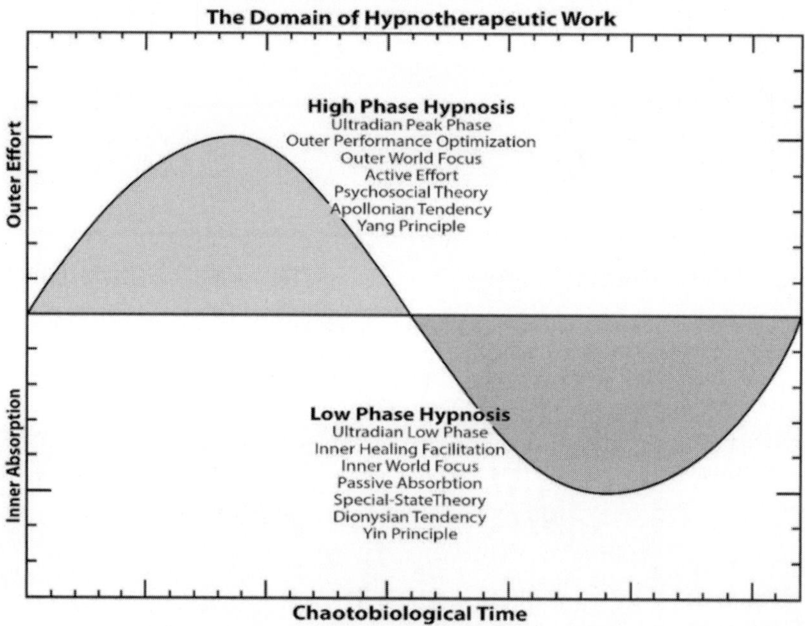

Figure AB.5. The wave nature of the observer-operator quantum qualia of subjective experiencing during the high and low phases of therapeutic hypnosis is conceptualized as the four-stage creative cycle mapped onto the 90–120 minute basic rest–activity cycle of everyday life (Lloyd & Rossi, 1992, 2008; Rossi, 1982,1997a, 1997b, 1998b, 1999, 2002a, 2002b, 2002c, 2005; Rossi et al., 2008–2015; Wagstaff, 2010; Pekala et al., 2010; Mazzoni et al., 2013).

The high performance phases of activity are indicated in the dark shading in the top part of Figure AB.6. These high performance peaks alternate with low phases of healing and recovery during the 90–120 minute basic rest–activity cycle, shown in the lighter shading. The bottom part of Figure AB.6 illustrates the recent research of Xie et al. (2013) documenting the cleaning up of the toxic metabolic waste products of daily conscious work during sleep and dreaming.

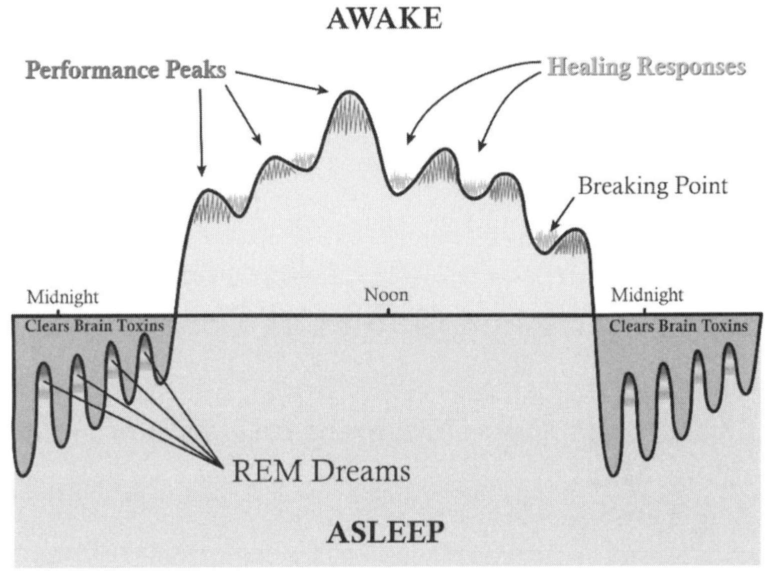

Figure AB.6. Top: A two-dimensional pyramid profile of the quantum wave nature of the four-stage creative process as a basic paradigm of the epigenomic RNA/DNA quantum field theory in the mind/body healing of stress and PTSD during the 90–120 minute basic rest–activity cycle in everyday life, sleep, and dreams, as well as meditation and therapeutic hypnosis. Bottom: Notice the shaded band periods (usually about 20 minutes) of symmetry between waking consciousness (top part) and dreaming (bottom part) which implies how Noether's theorem covers all types of conserved transformations in the integrated quantum field theory of physics, math, biology, and psychology (Lancaster & Blundell, 2014; Klauber, 2015) and to all applications of the therapeutic psychology of consciousness, cognition, and behavior (Rossi & Rossi, 2014a).

The small shaded areas marked "REM dreams" in the lower half of Figure AB.6, and the shaded areas on the right hand side of the lower area, imply how many such alternating phases of RNA/DNA activity during REM dreaming, as well as waking consciousness, which clean up the toxic waste products of brain/mind metabolism during sleep, could be the molecular/genomic foundation of many therapeutic practices that emphasize rest and relaxation (therapeutic hypnosis, prayer, meditation, yoga, etc.) developed independently over the ages by many cultures.

In Part 2 we will outline how recent developments in the ZX-quantum calculus could become the new scientific picture language for documenting our integrated quantum field theory of the creative mind. We illustrate how the quantum dynamics Figures AB.7a through 7e and the ZX-quantum calculus in Box AB.2 are apparently isomorphic, with the gentle curves of the changing states and phases of the basic rest–activity cycle and four-stage creativity cycle in Figures AB.4, 5, and 6. These isomorphisms (similar structures) imply how the classical psychobiological dynamics of Part 1 are underpinned by the quantum dynamics of Part 2. In Part 2 we will learn that the classical calculus with numbers and equations invented three centuries ago by Newton and Leibniz is only a special case of the more general and easier to learn ZX-quantum calculus, which makes an integration of the arts, humanities, and sciences that bridges the so-called "mind/body gap" of Descartes possible.

Part 2: The Quantum Magnetic Resonance Microscope and the Quantum Qualia of Consciousness

How the ZX-Calculus May Document a Quantum Field Theory of the Creative Mind

The alternating wave phases of consciousness, cognition, and creativity, as well as rest, sleep, and therapeutic hypnosis in Figures AB.4, 5, and 6, derived from research on the *classical level of our usual perspectives of everyday life*, are like the *independently derived images on the quantum level produced by the wave equations in various perspectives* in Figures AB.7a, 7b, and 7c. More recent research with the innovative quantum magnetic resonance microscope is illustrated in Figures AB.7d and 7e (Simpson et al., 2017). What could these apparently isomorphic correspondences between the classical and quantum levels mean? Could they all be:

1 A simple coincidence?

2 An artifact explained by QBism and the subjective nature of all human sensation, perception, and cognition, as measured by the early psychophysics of just-noticeable differences?

3 The quantum reality of nature on the ultra-small scale of Planck's constant ($\sim h = 6.626 \times 10^{-34}$ J·s), revealed by images from the quantum magnetic resonance microscope?

If you believe in either or both (1) and (2), you are implying your understanding of Descartes' mind/body philosophical gap and the hard problem of consciousness research remains controversial and unresolved (Chalmers, 1996; Rossi, 2007, 2012; Rossi & Rossi, 2015). If you believe in (3), the convincing reality of the quantum magnetic resonance microscope, then you join those researchers in physics, biology, and psychology who believe that the second creation of quantum reality (Crease & Mann, 1996) is, indeed, as real as all the modern quantum level technology that makes your iPhone, GPS, and smart TV possible. You may now be ready to explore the enlightening possibilities of the quantum qualia of your own personal experience, as well as the therapeutic possibilities of modern mind/body psychology, medicine, and the ZX-calculus that may become the wave of the future. In Figures AB.7a–7e, we present a series of images of the fundamentally wave nature of the quantum domain in *physics*. We hypothesize that they are consistent with the fundamental wave nature of all the molecular genomic cycles of *biology* and *psychology* documented in Figures AB.1–6 (Rossi, 1967, 2007, 2012; Lloyd & Rossi, 1992, 2008).

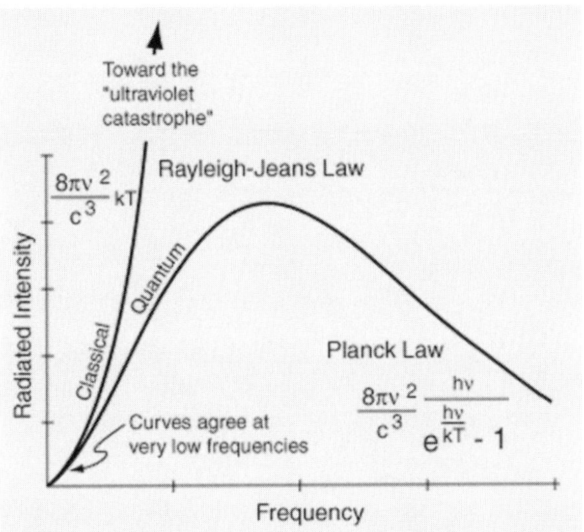

Figure AB.7a. A quantum fingerprint that helps to visualize the difference between Newton's classical dynamics that fails in its Rayleigh–Jeans Law (which implies an impossible infinity called the "ultraviolet catastrophe") versus the quantum curved signature of Planck's Law (Nave, 2016). We now propose that this gently curved quantum signature of Planck's equations and law is consistent with the cyclic wave–nature patterns of life, consciousness, and cognition on most levels from mind to molecules (Rossi, 2012; Rossi & Lippincott, 1992; Rossi & Rossi, 2008, 2013, 2014a, 2014b).

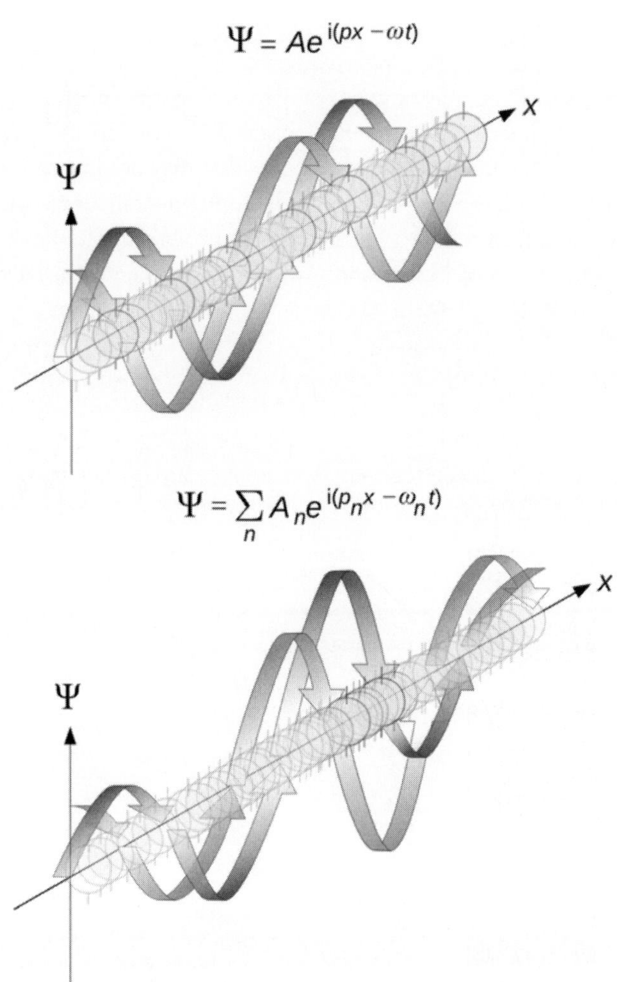

$\Psi = Ae^{i(px - \omega t)}$
Ψ
x
$\Psi = \sum_n A_n e^{i(p_n x - \omega_n t)}$
Ψ
x

Figure AB.7b. De Broglie matter waves and their accompanying quantum wave equations that now await "a more penetrating mathematical investigation" for the unification of our integrated quantum field theory of physics, math, biology, and psychology (Creative Commons: Propagation of a de Broglie wave by Maschen).

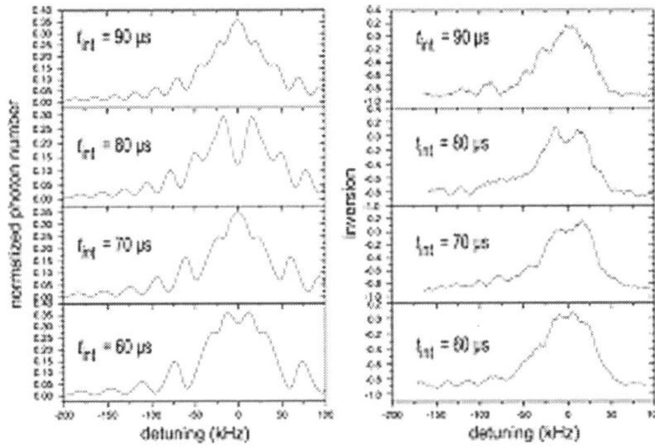

Figure AB.7c. The wave nature of the normalized quantum photon numbers of light often found in the fundamental experiments of quantum physics are strikingly similar to those found in biology and psychology (see Figures AB.1–6 in Part 1).

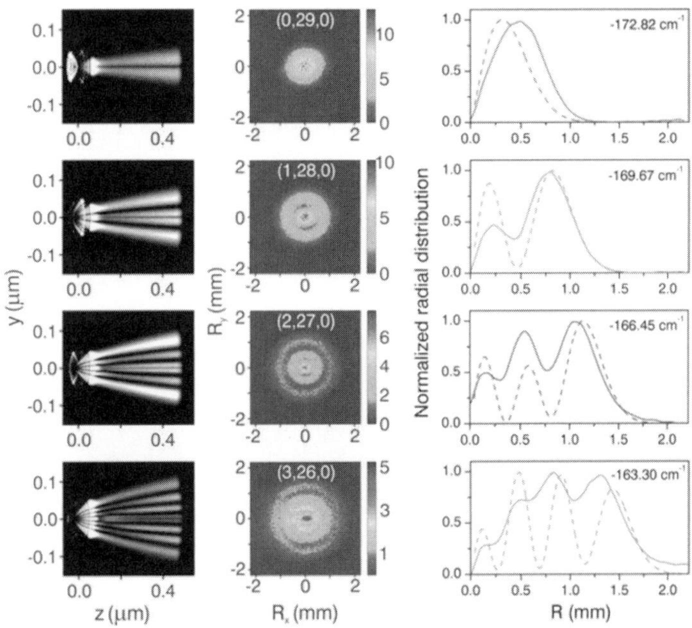

Figure AB.7d. The first direct observation of the orbital structure of an excited hydrogen atom has been made with the quantum microscope by an international team of researchers. The observation was made using a newly developed quantum microscope which uses photoionization microscopy to visualize the structure directly. The team's demonstration proves that "photoionization microscopy," which was first proposed more than 30 years ago, can be experimentally realized and can serve as a tool to explore the subtleties of quantum mechanics (Stodolna et al., 2013).

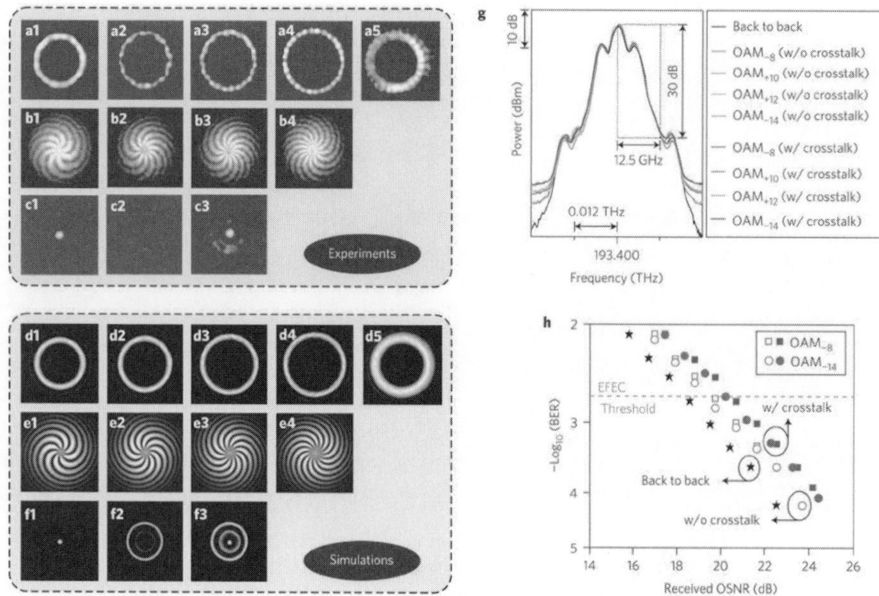

Figure AB.7e. Experimental and theoretical results of measuring the wave function of angular momentum beams of the quantum microscope (Wang et al., 2012). The wave function is a central tenet of information flow in our integrated quantum field theory of physics, math, biology, and the psychology of consciousness and cognition. Mathematically the wave function is the solution to the Schrödinger equation. Notice the similarity between the pyramidal profile in the upper right of this quantum level construction and the pyramidal profiles of biology and psychology in Figures AB.4 and 6.

The apparent isomorphism between data on the classical Newtonian macroscopic level (Figures AB.4, 5, and 6) and microscopic data from the new quantum microscope (Figures AB.7a and 7b) leads us to propose how the basic quantum Bayesian wave nature of many natural epigenomic processes could enhance psychotherapy and all schools of therapeutic consciousness. We now need to assess how such wave patterns are consistent with a more general quantum RNA/DNA psychosocial genomic theory of consciousness, cognition, creativity, and positive expectancy. To do this we introduce some fundamentals about quantum Bayesian dynamics, which are consistent with the ZX-calculus as a fundamental language for an integrated quantum field theory of physics, math, biology, and psychology as well as the arts, humanities, and therapeutic consciousness, cognition, and creativity in general.

Quantum Bayesian Notation 101 for the ZX-Calculus of Therapeutic Consciousness and Cognition

The original publication that began the current quantum Bayesian revolution emphasized how the extreme accuracy of the calculations of *quantum physics probability replaces the determinism of classical Newtonian physics* (Caves et al., 2001). What could Bayesian dynamics really mean for the quantum field theory of mindfulness, psychotherapy, and therapeutic consciousness?

The first fundamental insight for physics, biology, and psychology is that the quantum qualia of subjective experience are probabilistic in the normal consciousness and behavior of everyday life (Crease & Mann, 1996; Rossi, 2000 [1972], 2012; Rossi & Rossi 2014a, 2014b, 2015).

The second fundamental insight is that the highly sensitive quantum qualia of subjective experience are discrete; this means they are quantized into tiny, separate, natural Planck units of sensation, and/or perception (Fuchs, 2001, 2010; Schiller, 2015). The qualia of the redness of red and the blueness of blue, for example, can be experienced as continuous blends in the rainbow, but we can also distinguish about seven separate or discrete colors depending on how we humans choose to interpret them. Mathematicians have formulated an *axiom of choice* in logical systems (Doxiadis & Mazur, 2012) and physicists have had a century of struggle formulating the mathematical notation of light itself having a *dual nature as either discrete particles or smooth continuous waves* depending on how experimental situations are arranged to observe photons (Baggott, 2011, 2015). We now note that letters, words, emotions, and states of consciousness, as well as cognition, mathematics, music, and the four-stage creative cycle, also have a dual nature depending on how we choose to arrange our observations of them. The observer-operator qualia of humans' highly sensitive subjective experience manifests an infinite axiom of choice in creating and organizing its own world. The vast possibilities of human choice can be confusing and stressful in the transitions between stage 2 (incubation/conflict) and stage 3 (illumination/insight) of the four-stage creative cycle (Rossi, 2002b, 2004a, 2004b, 2007; Rossi & Rossi, 2013).

The third fundamental insight is that quantum Bayesian dynamics are manifest (observable) on all levels from mind to genes in living systems (Fuchs, 2011, 2012). Although quantum physics began with the need to resolve the paradoxes that emerged from atomic and subatomic levels, early theorists like Bohr, Dirac, Heisenberg, and Schrödinger realized that the quantum level underpinned the entire universe as well as the molecular chemistry of life and consciousness (Wilber, 1993; Baggott, 2011, 2015; von Baeyer, 2013; Susskind & Friedman, 2014).

The fourth fundamental insight is the central role of quantum Bayesian expectancy in an uncertain world (Fuchs et al., 2013; Fuchs & Schack, 2013). Heisenberg's fundamental uncertainty relationships are the basis for understanding the broad scope of how modern quantum field theory (Lancaster & Blundell, 2014; Klauber, 2015) is challenging our conceptions about creating new consciousness, cognition, and our sense of free will and reality itself (Rossi & Rossi, 2014a, 2014b, 2015). In

Figures AB.7a–e we illustrated how the core concepts and equations of the Born, Heisenberg, and Jordan matrix mechanics and uncertainty (Crease & Mann, 1996) play a fundamental role in the basic rest–activity cycle of biology, which is isomorphic with the four-stage creative cycle of new consciousness and cognition.

Dirac Notation Illustrating the Psychosocial and Cultural Genomics of the Quantum Observer-Operator in Consciousness, Dreaming, and Psychotherapy

In classical psychology, *episodic memory*, originally discovered and defined by Endel Tulving (2002, 2005) can now be assessed by neuroscience imaging of the mind/brain (Kellogg, 2013). Memory and its transformations during learning, REM dreaming, and cognition (Rossi & Rossi, 2015; Rossi, 2000 [1972]) can be easily evaluated with our new quantum Bayesian notation. We illustrate this with the dream and therapeutic intervention in a 78-year-old male patient still recovering from a childhood PTSD perpetuated by his abusive father.

> My father is a young man as he was when he used to beat me badly that I would scream so loudly that our neighbors would knock on our windows yelling, "Stop beating that child!" Anyway, in my dream he is now a nice guy who is building a new home and I am a little boy helping him! The house is now almost finished but there is still fresh dirt piled up roughly around in piles. This dirt is clean but it needs nutrients. So, we scatter organic fertilizer on it so that green grass and flowers and trees will grow real pretty in our new yard.
>
> I can hardly believe I'm now having such a nice dream about my long ago terrible father who abused me sexually! All my life I have hated him and struggled to get away from my family, vowing never to forgive any of them! I left home as a young man and never went back! But, somehow, I now seem to actually like my father and we are doing nice things together in my dream. Can this really be happening to me, doctor? Is this what you call "brain plasticity"?

Brain plasticity, indeed! We summarize the therapeutic reframing of this life story with the observer-operator [**O**] in positively transformative bra–ket notation like this.

$$\langle \psi_{+\mathrm{FUTURE}} | \mathbf{O}_{\mathrm{Psy+}} | \psi_{-\mathrm{PAST}} \rangle$$

Consciousness can function as a Janus-faced positive *quantum operator/observer* $|\mathbf{O}|$ in the intense focus of the dreamwork; to *observe is to operate simultaneously on the past as well as the future!* The patient still has an urgent question. He needs help from the psychotherapist [$\mathbf{O}_{\mathrm{Psy+}}$] to convert the *quantum probability amplitude* of a possible therapeutic reframing of his life story with his father into *the qualia of new quantum Bayesian psychological reality in Hilbert space* (math notation for infinite possibilities). The patient urgently needs the therapist to witness and validate his own newly created and nascent reality by answering, "Yes, this is the result of gene expression and brain plasticity operating successfully within you!" Suppose the psychotherapist had responded with the common but cynical, destructive, and false public opinion: "Too bad it was only a dream."

A young woman dreams:

> I am an apprentice to a baker making a sandwich several yards long! An inspector comes by and asks the baker if he is responsible for making the sandwich. But with a cynical attitude the baker ignores the inspector. I am puzzled in the dream about why the baker is ignoring the nice inspector.

Upon awakening, the young woman's first sleepy early morning thoughts spontaneously replay her dream: she would have told the nice inspector the truth about how the baker was indeed responsible for making the huge sandwich. She intuits the inspector needed this information so someone could be *rewarded* for such excellent work.

In this dream the observer-operator [$\mathbf{O}_{\pm \mathrm{BAKER}}$] was her ambivalent identification the baker. In bra–ket notation there was no complete positive transformation in her dream. She is still stuck in an ambivalent and puzzled stage 2 at the end of her dream.

$$\langle \psi_{\pm PUZZLED} | \mathbf{O}_{\pm \mathrm{BAKER}} | \psi_{\mathrm{-CYNICAL}} \rangle$$

Fortunately, this young woman has the wit to utilize the *axiom of choice* in her early morning thoughts to give her identity a wonderful makeover that generated a positive transformation to stage 4 of the creative cycle. This is expressed in bra–ket notation:

$$\langle \psi_{\mathrm{+REWARDED}} | \mathbf{O}_{\mathrm{+CHOICE}} | \psi_{\mathrm{-CYNICAL}} \rangle$$

During her nighttime sleep her brain was cleared of metabolic toxins (she had been stressfully overworked lately). This meant she could more objectively reconsider the cynical side of her personality that requires therapeutic reframing to empower her to tell the world (the inspector in the dream) the truth about her growing abilities (symbolized by making fantastic sandwiches), so she can be appropriately recognized and *rewarded*.

A depressed middle aged man reports a spontaneous daydream during psychotherapy:

> I am down deep in a bomb shelter with a small group of cowering fearful people. A strong muscular fellow is guarding the exit door so we cannot run out in panic when the bombs start to fall. This guard has a long pole with a soft cushion on the end so he can safely push people back in if they foolishly try to exit when the bombs begin exploding above.

In quantum Bayesian bra–ket notation:

$$\langle \psi_{\mathrm{+INCUBATION}} | \mathbf{O}_{\mathrm{+GUARD}} | \psi_{\mathrm{-WAR}} \rangle$$

Together, the depressed man and the therapist intuited a helpful and hopeful therapeutic interpretation of this dream. The man's depressing dream is a stage 2 expression of the four-stage creative cycle wherein he needs to recognize the realities of his currently dangerous but temporary life situation. The guard is an emergent manifestation of the positive observer-operator in his dream, protecting him and others so they can safely incubate about their condition. There is a need to incubate in stage 2 until appropriate *quantum Bayesian probability amplitudes* of the adaptive RNA/DNA transition/translation dynamics of experience-dependent gene expression and brain plasticity evolve new stage 3 therapeutic possibilities. This hopeful *expectancy* will optimize his ability to recognize the fruits of a good night's sleep in clearing his brain to facilitate gene expression and brain plasticity for creating new quantum qualia of consciousness.

We propose that these clinical vignettes of Dirac's brief bra–ket notation document how an initially dysfunctional quantum qualia of consciousness and cognition have a state, identified with a negative subscript such as ket $|\psi_-\rangle$, that could be a medical or psychological symptom, which is then therapeutically transformed by the observer-operator into a positive final state identified with a positive subscript such as a bra $\langle\psi_+|$. This concise Dirac notation characterizes the typical human condition as problematic – needing a four-stage creative, 90–120 minute basic rest–activity cycle on all levels from mind to activity-dependent gene expression and brain plasticity 12 times a day to evolve life, consciousness, and cognition in an optimal manner.

But why all this negativity in the first place? Why, after 4.5 billion years of Darwinian evolution, has life and mind not achieved a state of permanent positive bliss and nirvana? Our psychologically oriented quantum field theory of cosmos and consciousness suggests an obvious hypothesis about these questions, as suggested by the following statement about "That little minus sign [that] makes a huge difference" between real and quantum numbers:

> We map ordinary dimensions onto ordinary, so-called "real" numbers. We pick a reference point, usually called the origin, and label any point by a (real) number that describes how far you must go to get there from the origin. Real numbers, in a word, are suitable for measuring distances, and labeling continua. They satisfy the multiplication rule,
>
> $$xy = yx$$
>
> Quantum dimensions use a different kind of number, called Grassmann numbers. They satisfy a different multiplication law,
>
> $$xy = -yx$$
>
> *That little minus sign makes a huge difference!* Notably, if we put $x = x$ we get $x^2 = -x^2$, and so we conclude $x^2 = 0$. That strange rule encodes, in the physical interpretation of quantum dimensions, Pauli's exclusion principle: you can't put two things in the same (quantum) place.

> After those preparations, we're ready to meet SUSY. Supersymmetry is the claim that our world has quantum dimensions, and that transformations exist which interchange ordinary with quantum dimension (change), without changing the laws of physics (without change).
>
> Supersymmetry, if correct, will be a profound new embodiment of beauty in the world. Because the transformations of supersymmetry turn substance particles into force particles, and vice versa, supersymmetry can explain, based on symmetry, why neither of those things can exist without the other: Both are the same thing, seen from different perspectives. Supersymmetry reconciles apparent opposites, in the spirit of yin–yang. (Wilczek, 2015, p. 311; italics added)

It will require a great deal of further research on our psychologically oriented quantum field theory to confirm "That little minus sign makes a huge difference" in the therapeutic transitions from negative stress to positive states of creativity. As we have seen, that little minus sign makes a huge difference because it is the sign of *non-commutation* in "fundamental quantum-mechanical relations," evident in that strange equation $\mathbf{pq} - \mathbf{qp} = \mathbf{I}h / 2\pi i$, which is a landmark in the history of physics. It is the first map of the quantum domain that underpins all life, biology, psychology, and the profoundly sensitive quantum qualia of human experience. Consciousness, cognition, and creativity, as we experience them in daily life, as well as meditation and therapeutic consciousness, could not exist without it.

The ZX-Calculus Integrates the Quantum Field Theory of Math, Physics, Biology, and Psychology

In this appendix, we have introduced the new concept of the observer-operator (O_b/O_p) as a pair of mind/body conjugate variables to replace the pq – qp in the non-commutation relation in the fundamental quantum-mechanical equation so that it becomes: $O_bO_p - O_pO_b = Ih / 2\pi i$. At present however, this remains an open problem requiring proofs for our proposed integrated quantum field theory. The major speculation of this appendix is that the new ZX-calculus that has been developed over the past decade will prove to be a fertile field for investigating the quantum foundations of an integrated quantum field theory of all the sciences, humanities, and healing arts. Coecke and Kissinger (2017), two leaders in current quantum theory, outline their introduction to the ZX-calculus in this way:

> The unique features of the quantum world are explained in this book through the language of diagrams, setting out an innovative visual method for presenting complex theories. Requiring only basic mathematical literacy this book employs a unique formalism that builds an intuitive understanding of quantum features while eliminating the need for complex calculations. This entirely diagrammatic presentation of quantum theory represents the culmination of 10 years of research, uniting classical techniques in linear algebra and Hilbert spaces with cutting-edge developments in quantum computation and foundations.

> Written in an entertaining and user-friendly style and including more than 100 exercises, *this book is an ideal first course in quantum theory, foundations, and computation for students from undergraduate to Ph.D. level, as well as an opportunity for researchers from a broad range of fields, from physics to biology, linguistics, and cognitive science to discover a new set of tools for studying processes and interactions.*
>
> *Quantum picturalism* refers to the use of diagrams to capture and reason about the essential features of interacting quantum processes, in a manner that these diagrammatic equations become the very foundation of quantum theory. (Coecke & Kissinger, 2017, pp. 2–7; italics added)

Box AB.2 introduces a few of the axioms, theorems, and dynamics of the kindergarten picture approach to the ZX-calculus (Coecke, 2005, 2010; Coecke & Duncan, 2011; Backus, 2015; Coecke & Kissinger, 2017), which we propose as a new language for expressing concepts, dynamics, and relationships that are consistent with our integrated quantum field theory of physics, math, biology, and psychology.

Box AB.2: A Few Axioms and Proposed Psychodynamics of the ZX-Calculus

The primitive data of our formalism consists of (1) boxes with an input and an output which we call "operation" or "channel", (2) triangles with only an output which we call "state" or "preparation procedure" or "ket", (3) triangles with only an output which we call "co-state" or "measurement branch" or "bra", (4) diamonds without inputs or outputs which we call "values" or "probabilities" or "weights", (5) lines which might carry a symbol which we refer to as the "type" or the "kind of system", and the *A*-labeled line itself which can be conceived as "doing nothing to a system of type *A*" or the "identity on *A*" (Coecke, 2005).

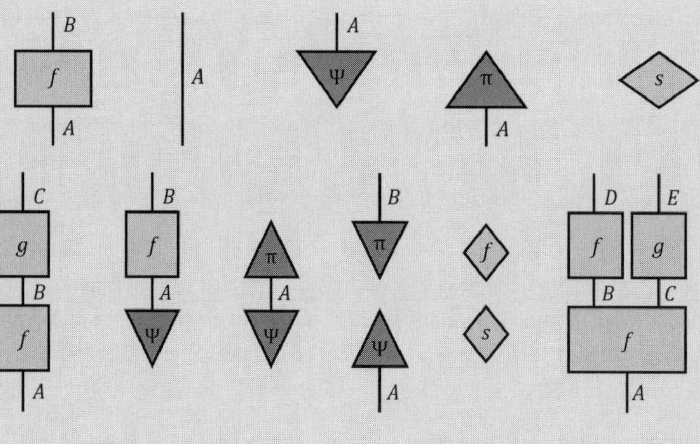

The caps and cups of quantum communication, which we propose as the transference in psychotherapy.

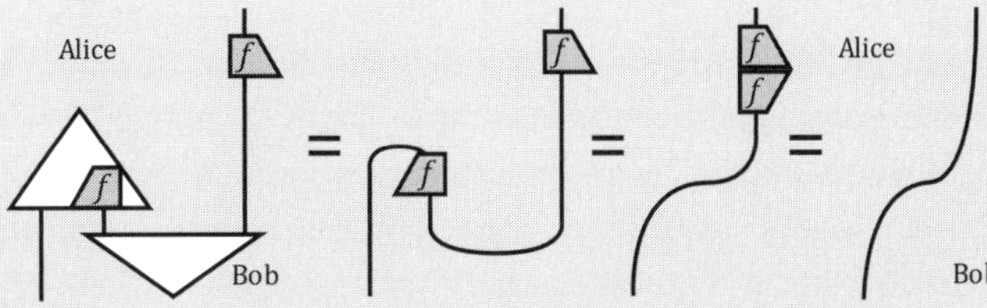

Alice f f f f f Alice = = = Bob Bob

A basic cups and caps picture of the four-stage basic rest–activity cycle of cognition and creativity.

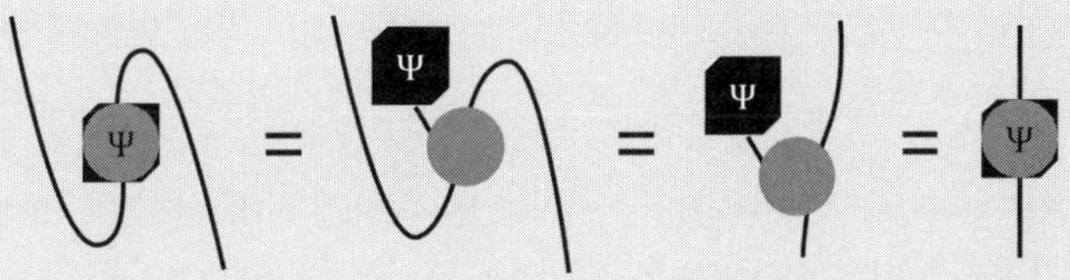

Ψ = Ψ = Ψ = Ψ

An initial effort to picture the ultradian cups and caps of addictions (dark) and recovery (light).

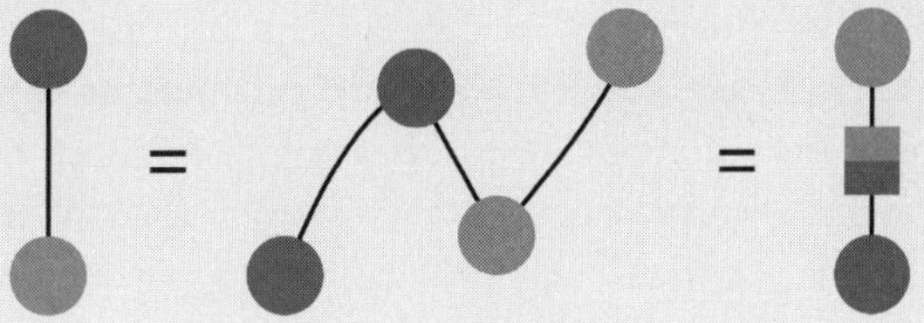

= =

The major practical implication for our integrated quantum field theory of physics, math, biology, and psychology for the current evolution of psychotherapy is to help people learn to value and tune in appropriately to the most highly sensitive and ineffable quantum qualia of their observer-operator to help them navigate the perils of everyday acute and chronic stress that generate the most common forms of psychopathology and the addictions. We need to do away with the common disparagement of "merely subjective experience of intuition and imagination" that favors the pursuit of the so-called "virtues of objective thinking and rationality," which can so easily become corrupted by narcissism, ego power, advertising, avarice, and war in cultures that over-value competition and personal excellence, whatever the cost. We need to transcend the rather stale reductive ideologies and manipulative models of psychotherapy as stimulus/response conditioning, gaming, programming, suggestion, and rather dry cognitive-behavioral transactions by returning to the living, experiencing, and primacy of the vivid NNNE to realize our best creative selves in the quantum evolution of psychotherapy.

Summary

The integrated quantum field theory of physics, math, biology, and the psychology of consciousness, cognition, creativity, and health is proposed for a new conception of the quantum evolution of psychotherapy that is made possible with the innovative quantum magnetic resonance microscope. Research in the integrated quantum field theory is updated with an adaptive RNA/DNA theory of the quantum Bayesian transformations of consciousness, creative cognition, meditation, and therapeutic hypnosis. Alternating classical-to-quantum and quantum-to-classical transitions on all levels from mind to genes, the natural 90–120 minute basic rest–activity cycle of biology and the four-stage creative cycle of psychology are integrated with the wave nature of the ZX-calculus of quantum physics. Surprising tendencies toward cognitive dissonance, conflict, negativity, and psychological regression during stage 2 (incubation/conflict) of the four-stage creative cycle were uncovered during dreams when parsed with Dirac's bra–ket quantum notation. We propose how the highly sensitive quantum qualia of problematic dissociations during stage 2 of the four-stage creative cycle have their source at quantum level uncertainty. We also propose that such psycho-social conflicts have their source in non-commutation pathologies, which could be resolved in stages 3 and 4 of therapeutic consciousness and cognition. Quantum Bayesian concepts of the novel observer-operator are documented with insightful applications for counseling, psychotherapy, medicine, and all the mind/body therapies. Freud's concept of the so-called "unconscious" is no longer entirely unconscious; it can be updated with new explorations of the basic quantum non-commutation equation $pq - qp = Ih / 2\pi i$ and the new ZX-calculus. Integrated quantum field theory research on how *the quantum qualia of the human observer-operator during subjective experience* can be a causal agent in facilitating health and problem-solving *on the objective molecular/genomic level* now needs to be replicated for facilitating the living experience of the quantum evolution of psychotherapy, health, and well-being.

References

Abramsky, S. & Coecke, B. (2017). *Picturing Quantum Processes: A First Course in Quantum Theory and Diagrammatic Reasoning* [Kindle edn]. New York: Cambridge University Press.

Adolphs, R. (2015). The unsolved problems of neuroscience. *Trends in Cognitive Sciences*, 19(4), 173–175. http://doi.org/10.1016/j.tics.2015.01.007.

Al-Khalili, J. (2014). *The Secrets of Quantum Physics* [two-part documentary], BBC Four.

Alcaro, A. & Panksepp, J. (2011). The SEEKING mind: primal neuro-affective substrates for appetitive incentive states and their pathological dynamics in addictions and depression. *Neuroscience and Biobehavioral Reviews*, 35(9), 1805–1820.

Alter, D. S. & Sugarman, L. I. (2017). Reorienting hypnosis education. *American Journal of Clinical Hypnosis*, 59, 235–259.

Ambady, N., Shih, M., Kim, A. & Pittinsky, T. L. (2001). Stereotype susceptibility in children: effects of identity activation on quantitative performance. *Psychological Science*, 12, 385–390.

American Psychiatric Association (2013). *Diagnostic and Statistical Manual of Mental Disorders, Fifth Edition* (DSM-5). Washington, DC: APA.

American Psychological Association Presidential Task Force on Evidence-Based Practice (2006). Evidence-based practice in psychology. *American Psychology*, 61(4), 271–285.

Andersen, M. L. & Tufik, S. (2015). Sleep and the modern society. *Journal of Sleep Disorders and Therapy*, 4: e131. doi:10.4172/2167-0277.1000e131.

Ardito, R. B. & Rabellino, D. (2011). Therapeutic alliance and outcome of psychotherapy: historical excursus, measurements, and prospects for research. *Frontiers in Psychology*, 2, 270.

Aron, E. J. (2004). Revisiting Jung's concept of innate sensitiveness. *Journal of Analytical Psychology*, 49(3), 337–367.

Aronson, J., Lustina, M. J., Good, C., Keough, K., Steele, C. M. & Brown, J. (1999). When white men can't do math: necessary and sufficient factors in stereotype threat. *Journal of Experimental Social Psychology*, 35, 29–46.

Ashton-Jones, G. & Cohen, J. D. (2005). An integrative theory of locus coeruleus-norepinephrine function: adaptive gain and optimal performance. *Annual Review of Neuroscience*, 28, 403–450.

Atkinson, D., Iannotti, S., Cozzolino, M., Castiglione, S., Cicatelli, A., Vyas, B. et al. (2010). A new bioinformatics paradigm for the theory, research, and practice of therapeutic hypnosis. *American Journal of Clinical Hypnosis*, 53(1), 27–46.

Backus, M. (2015). Completeness and the ZX-calculus. Ph.D. thesis. Oxford University.

Baggott, J. (2011). *The Quantum Story: A History in 40 Moments*. New York: Oxford University Press.

Baggott, J. (2015). *Origins: The Scientific Story of Creation*. New York: Oxford University Press.

Bandura, A. (1977). Self-efficacy: toward a unifying theory of behavioral change. *Psychological Review*, 84(2), 191–215.

Bar-Joseph, Z., Gitter, A. & Itamar, S. (2012). Studying and modeling dynamic biological processes using time-series gene expression data. *Nature Reviews Genetics*, 13, 552–564.

Bateson, G., Jackson, D. D., Haley, J. & Weakland, J. (1956). Towards a theory of schizophrenia. *Behavioral Science*, 1(4), 251–264.

Bauby, J-D. (2009). *The Diving-Bell and the Butterfly*. London: Fourth Estate.

Bell, E. (2012). *Winning in Baseball and Business: Transforming Little League Into Major League Profits for Your Company*. Lake Placid, NY: Aviva Publishing.

Berlyne, D. E. (1950). Novelty and curiosity as determinants of exploratory behaviour. *British Journal of Psychology*, 41, 68–80.

Berlyne, D. E. (1954). A theory of human curiosity. *British Journal of Psychology*, 45, 180–191.

Berne, E. (1996 [1970]). *Games People Play: The Basic Handbook of Transactional Analysis*. New York: Ballantine Books.

Berrondo, M. & Sandoval, M. (2016). Defining emergence: learning from flock behavior. *Complexity*, 21(S1), 69–78.

Bertulani, C. A. (2013). *Nuclei in the Cosmos*. Singapore: World Scientific.

Bilalić, M. & McLeod, P. (2014). Why good thoughts block better ones. *Scientific American*, 310(3), 74–79.

Birren, S. & Marder, E. (2013). Plasticity in the neurotransmitter repertoire. *Science*, 340(6131), 436–437.

Blood, A. J. & Zatorre, R. J. (2001). Intensely pleasurable responses to music correlate with activity in brain regions implicated in reward and emotion. *Proceedings of the National Academy of Sciences of the United States of America*, 98(20), 11818–11823.

Blom, J. H. G. (2017). Pain and attention. Thesis. University of Twente, Netherlands. doi:10.3990/1.9789036542715.

Boeing, G. (2016). Visual analysis of nonlinear dynamical systems: chaos, fractals, self-similarity and the limits of prediction. *Systems*, 4(4), 37.

Bohr, N. (1913). On the constitution of atoms and molecules. *Philosophical Magazine*, 26(6), 1–25. http://hermes.ffn.ub.es/luisnavarro/nuevo_maletin/Bohr_1913.pdf.

Borenstein, L. (2002). The impact of the therapist's curiosity on the treatment process of children and adolescents. *Child and Adolescent Social Work Journal*, 19(5), 337. doi:10.1023/A:1020218413598.

Born, M. & Jordan, P. (1925). Zur Quantenmechanik [On quantum mechanics – English translation]. *Zeitschrift für Physik*, 34, 858–888.

Boring, E. (1950). *A History of Experimental Psychology*. New York: Appleton-Century-Crofts.

Boyatzis, R. E. (2006). An overview of intentional change from a complexity perspective. *Journal of Management Development*, 25(7), 607–623.

Breit, G. (1932). Dirac's equation and the spin-spin interactions of two electrons. *American Physical Society*, 39(4), 616–624.

Buzsaki, G. & Gage, F. H. (1989). The cholinergic nucleus basalis: a key structure in neocortical arousal. *Experientia Supplementum*, 57, 159–171.

Calcagno, J. and Fuentes, F. (2012). What makes us human? Answers from evolutionary anthropology. *Evolutionary Anthropology*, 21(5), 184–194. doi:10.1002/evan.21328.

Camazine, S., Deneubourg, J-L., Franks, N. R., Sneys, J., Theraulaz, G. & Bonabeau, E. (2001). *Self-Organization in Biological Systems*. Princeton, NJ: Princeton University Press.

Campbell, J. (2014 [1990]). *The Hero's Journey: Joseph Campbell on His Life and Work*, ed. P. Cousineau. Novato, CA: New World Library.

Campbell, J. & Moyers, B. (1991). *The Power of Myth*, ed. B. S. Flowers. New York: Anchor Publishing.

Carey, T. A., Mansell, W. & Tai, S. J. (2014). A biopsychosocial model based on negative feedback and control. *Frontiers in Human Neuroscience*, 8, 94. http://doi.org/10.3389/fnhum.2014.00094.

Carlson, L., Beattie, T. L., Giese-Davis, J., Faris, P., Tamagawa, R., Fick, L. J. et al. (2015). Mindfulness-based cancer recovery and supportive-expressive therapy maintain telomere length relative to controls in distressed breast cancer survivors. *Cancer*, 121(3), 476–484.

Carroll, S. (2016). *The Big Picture: On the Origins of Life, Meaning, and the Universe Itself*. New York: Dutton.

Caves, C., Fuchs, C. & Schack, R. (2001). Quantum probabilities as Bayesian probabilities. arXiv:quant-ph/0106133v2.pdf.

Chalmers, D. (1996). Facing up to the problem of consciousness. In S. Hameroff, A. Kaszniak and A. Scott (Eds.), *Toward a Science of Consciousness: The First Tucson Discussions and Debates*, 7–28. Cambridge, MA: MIT Press.

Chan, S. (2001). Complex adaptive systems. www.web.mit.edu/esd.83/www/notebook/Complex%20Adaptive%20Systems.pdf.

Chapman, H. M. (2011). Love: a biological, psychological and philosophical study. Paper 254. Senior Honors Projects, University of Rhode Island. http://digitalcommons.uri.edu/srhonorsprog/254.

Chaudhari, D. (2017). The advertising world hates women who are comfortable in their skin. *Feminism in India* (January 2). https://feminisminindia.com/2017/01/02/advertising-hates-women-comfortable-skin/.

Chaudhary, U., Xia, B., Silvoni, S., Cohen, L. G. & Birbaumer, N. (2017). Brain–computer interface-based communication in the completely locked-in state. *PLOS Biology*, 15(1), e1002593.

Chetty, S., Friedman, A. R., Taravosh-Lahn, K., Kirby, E. D., Mirescu, C., Guo, F. et al. (2014). Stress and glucocorticoids promote oligodendrogenesis in the adult hippocampus. *Molecular Psychiatry*, 19, 1275–1283.

Chiarucci, R., Madeo, D., Loffredo, M., Castellani, E., Santarcangelo, E. L. & Mocenni, C. (2014). Cross evidence for hypnotic susceptibility through nonlinear measures on EEGs of non-hypnotized subjects. *Scientific Reports*, 4, 5610, doi:10.1038/srep05610.

Cheek, D. B. (1994). *Hypnosis: The Application of Ideomotor Techniques*. Boston, MA: Allyn & Bacon.

Cheung, M., Chavez, L. & Onuchic, J. (2004). The energy landscape for protein folding and possible connections to function. *Polymer*, 45, 547–555.

Clayton, D. (2013). Genomics of memory and learning in songbirds. *Annual Review of Genomics and Human Genetics*, 14, 45–65.

Coecke, B. (2005). Kindergarten quantum mechanics: lecture notes. arXiv:quant-ph/0510032v1.

Coecke, B. (2010). Quantum picturalism. *Contemporary Physics*, 51, 59–83. arXiv:0908.1787v1 [quant-ph].

Coecke, B. & Duncan, R. (2011). Interacting quantum observables: categorical algebra and diagrammatics. *New Journal of Physics*, 13(4). doi:10.1088/1367-2630/13/4/043016.

Coecke, B. & Kissinger, A. (2017). *Picturing Quantum Processes: A First Course in Quantum Theory and Diagrammatic Reasoning* [Kindle edn]. New York: Cambridge University Press.

Cohen, I., Whitman, A. & Budenz, J. (1999). *Isaac Newton: The Principia. Mathematical Principles of Natural Philosophy*. Berkeley, CA: University of California Press. http://www.jstor.org/stable/10.1525/j.ctt9qh28z.

Cole, S. (2009). Social regulation of human gene expression. *Current Directions in Psychological Science*, 18, 132–137.

Cole, S., Arevalo, J., Takahashi, R., Sloan, E. K., Lutgendorf, S., Sood, A., Sheridan, J. & Seeman, T. (2010). Computational identification of gene–social environment interaction at the human IL6 locus. *Proceedings of the National Academy of Sciences of the United States of America*, 107, 5681–5686.

Cole, S., Hawkley, L., Arevalo, J. & Cacioppo, J. (2011). Transcript origin analysis identifies antigen-presenting cells as primary targets of socially regulated gene expression in leukocytes. *Proceedings of the National Academy of Sciences of the United States of America*, 108, 3080–3085.

Cole, S., Hawkley, L., Arevalo, J., Sung, C., Rose R. & Cacioppo, J. (2007). Social regulation of gene expression in human leukocytes. *Genome Biology*, 8, R189–R189.

Cole, S., Yan, W., Galic, Z., Arevalo, J. & Zack, J. (2005). Expression-based monitoring of transcription factor activity: the TELiS database. *Bioinformatics*, 21, 803–810.

Commissariat, T. (2013). 'Quantum microscope' peers into the hydrogen atom. *Physics World* (May 23). http://physicsworld.com/cws/article/news/2013/may/23/quantum-microscope-peers-into-the-hydrogen-atom.

Conger, C. (2008). How food cravings work. *HowStuffWorks.com* (August 18). http://science.howstuffworks.com/innovation/edible-innovations/food-craving.htm.

Connolly Gibbons, M. B., Mack, R., Lee, J., Gallop, R., Thompson, D., Burock, D. & Crits-Christoph, P. (2014). Comparative effectiveness of cognitive and dynamic therapies for major depressive disorder in a community mental health setting: study protocol for a randomized non-inferiority trial. *BMC Psychology*, 2(1), 47.

Corrigan, P. W. & Watson, A. C. (2002). Understanding the impact of stigma on people with mental illness. *World Psychiatry*, 1(1), 16–20.

Cozolino, L. (2016). *The Neuroscience of Human Relationships: Attachment and the Developing Social Brain*, 2nd edn. New York: W.W. Norton.

Cozolino, L. (2017). *The Neuroscience of Psychotherapy: Healing the Social Brain*. New York: W.W. Norton.

Cozzolino, M., Cicatelli, A., Fortino, V., Guarino, F., Tagliaferri, R., Castiglione, S. et al. (2015). The mind–body healing experience (MHE) is associated with gene expression in human leukocytes. *International Journal of Physical and Social Sciences*, 5(5), 1–31. http://www.ijmra.us/2015ijpss_may.php.

Cozzolino, M., Tagliaferri, R., Castiglione, S., Fortino, V., Cicatelli, A., De Luca, P. et al. (2014). The creative psychosocial and cultural genomic healing experience: a new top-down epigenomic psychotherapeutic protocol. *International Journal of Psychosocial Genomics: Consciousness and Health Research*, 1(1), 18–25.

Crease, R. (2010). *The Great Equations: Breakthroughs in Science from Pythagoras to Heisenberg*. New York: W.W. Norton.

Crease, R. and Mann, C. (1996). *The Second Creation*. New Brunswick, NJ: Rutgers University Press.

Croizet, J. & Claire, T. (1998). Extending the concept of stereotype threat to social class: the intellectual underperformance of students from low socioeconomic backgrounds. *Personality and Social Psychology Bulletin*, 24, 588–594.

Creswell, J., Irwin, M., Burklund, L., Lieberman, M., Arevalo, J., Ma, J., Breen, E. & Cole, S. (2012). Mindfulness-based stress reduction training reduces loneliness and pro-inflammatory gene expression in older adults: a small randomized controlled trial. *Brain, Behavior, and Immunity*, 26(7),1095–1101. doi:10.1016/j.bbi.2012.07.006.

Dantzer, R. (2009). Cytokine, sickness behavior, and depression. *Immunology and Allergy Clinics of North America*, 29(2), 247–264. doi:10.1016/j.iac.2009.02.002.

Darwin, C. (2008 [1859]). *The Origin of Species*. New York: Bantam Dell.

Davis, D. M. & Hayes, J. A. (2011). What are the benefits of mindfulness? A practice review of psychotherapy-related research. *Psychotherapy*, 48(2), 198–208.

de Botton, A. (2005). *Status Anxiety*. London: Penguin.

de Broglie, L. (1970). The reinterpretation of wave mechanics. *Foundations of Physics*, 1(1), 5–15.

de Langhe, B., Puntoni, S. & Larrick, R. (2017). Linear thinking in a nonlinear world, *Harvard Business Review* (May–June). https://hbr.org/2017/05/linear-thinking-in-a-nonlinear-world.

De Simone, J. (2006). Reductionist interference-based medicine, i.e. EBM. *Journal of Evaluation in Clinical Practice*, 12(4), 445–449.

Deacon, B. J. & Baird, G. L. (2009). The chemical imbalance explanation of depression: reducing blame at what cost? *Journal of Social and Clinical Psychology*, 28(4), 415–435.

Debanne, D. (2004). Information processing in the axon. *Nature Reviews Neuroscience*, 5, 304–316. doi:10.1038/nrn1397.

Dehaene, S. (2014). *Consciousness and the Brain: How the Brain Codes Our Thoughts*. New York: Viking.

Dember, W. N. & Earl, R. W. (1957). Analysis of exploratory, manipulatory, and curiosity behaviors. *Psychological Review*, 64, 91–96.

Devlin, M. J., Yanovski, S. Z. & Wilson, G. T. (2013). Obesity: what mental health professionals need to know. *American Journal of Psychiatry*, 157(6), 854–866.

Di Bernardo, M. (2010). Natural selection and self-organization in complex adaptive systems. *Rivista di Biologia*, 103(1), 89–110.

Dirac, P. (1928). *The Quantum Theory of the Electron*. London: Harrison. doi:10.1098/rspa.1928.0023.

Dirac, P. (1930). *The Principles of Quantum Mechanics*. Oxford: Clarendon Press.

Dirac, P. (1978). *Directions in Physics*. New York: Wiley.

Doxiadis, A. & Mazur, B. (2012). *Circles Disturbed: The Interplay of Mathematics and Narrative*. Princeton, NJ: Princeton University Press.

Drnevich, J., Replogle, K., Lovell, P., Hahn, T., Johnson, F., Mast, T. et al. (2012). The impact of experience-dependent and independent factors on gene expression in songbird brain. *Proceedings of the National Academy of Sciences of the United States of America*, 109, 17245–17252.

Duke University Medical Center (2004). Anger, hostility and depressive symptoms linked to high C-reactive protein levels. *ScienceDaily* (September 23). www.sciencedaily.com/releases/2004/09/040922070643.htm.

Dulcis, D., Jimshidi, P., Leutgeb, S. & Spitzer, N. (2013). Neurotransmitter switching in the adult brain regulates behavior. *Science*, 340(6131), 449–453.

Dusek, J., Otu, H., Wohlhueter, A., Bhasin, M., Zerbini, L., Joseph, M., Benson, H. & Libermann, T. (2008). Genomic counter-stress changes induced by the relaxation response. *PLOS ONE*, 3(7): e2576. doi:10.1371/journal.pone.0002576.

Dweck, C. S. (1988). A social-cognitive approach to motivation and personality. *Psychological Review*, 95, 256–273.

Ebstein, R. (1997). Saga of an adventure gene: novelty seeking, substance abuse and the dopamine D4 receptor exon III repeat polymorphism. *Molecular Psychiatry*, 2, 381–384.

Eisenberger, N. I. & Lieberman, M. D. (2004). Why it hurts to be left out: the neurocognitive overlap between physical and social pain. *Trends in Cognitive Sciences*, 8, 294–300.

ENCODE Project Consortium (2012). An integrated encyclopedia of DNA elements in the human genome. *Nature*, 489, 57–74.

Engel, G. S., Calhoun, T. R., Read, E. L., Ahn, T-K., Mančal, T., Cheng, Y-C., Blankenship, R. E. & Fleming, G. R. (2007). Evidence for wavelike energy transfer through quantum coherence in photosynthetic systems. *Nature*, 446, 782–786. doi:10.1038/nature05678.

Engel, S. (2013). The case for curiosity. *Educational Leadership, Creativity Now*, 70(5), 36–40.

Enz, C. P. (1983). Heisenberg's applications of quantum mechanics (1926–33) or the settling of the new land. *Helvetica Physica Acta*, 56(5), 993–1001.

Erickson, M. H. (1964). The burden of responsibility in effective psychotherapy. *American Journal of Clinical Hypnosis*, 6(3), 269–271.

Erickson, M. H. (2008–2015). *The Collected Works of Milton H. Erickson, M.D.*, ed. E. L. Rossi, R. Erickson-Klein & K. L. Rossi, 16 vols. Phoenix, AZ: Milton H. Erickson Foundation Press.

Erickson, M. H. & Rossi, E. L. (1979). *Hypnotherapy: An Exploratory Casebook*. New York: Irvington Publishers.

Erickson, M. H. & Rossi, E. L. (1981). *Experiencing Consciousness: Therapeutic Approaches to Altered States*. New York: Irvington Publishers.

Erickson, M. H. & Rossi, E. L. (2006). *The Complete Works of Milton H. Erickson, M.D. on Therapeutic Hypnosis, Psychotherapy and Rehabilitation. The Neuroscience Edition*, ed. E. L. Rossi, R. Erickson-Klein & K. L. Rossi, 8 vols. Phoenix, AZ: Milton H. Erickson Foundation Press.

Erickson, M. H. & Rossi, E. L. (2014 [1981]). Electronic monitoring of catalepsy: a two-factor theory of hypnotic experience. In: M. H. Erickson, *The Collected Works of Milton H. Erickson*. Volume 12: *Experiencing Hypnosis: Therapeutic Approaches to Altered States*, ed. E. L. Rossi, R. Erickson-Klein & K.

L. Rossi, 63–65. Phoenix, AZ: Milton H. Erickson Foundation Press.

Fadiga, L., Fogassi, L., Pavesi, G. & Rizzolatti, G. (1995). Motor facilitation during action observation: a magnetic stimulation study. *Journal of Neurophysiology*, 73, 2608–2611.

Fedak, W. & Prentis, J. (2009). The 1925 Born and Jordan paper "On quantum mechanics." *American Journal of Physics*, 77(2), 128–139.

Feistel, R. & Eberling, R. (2011). *The Physics of Self-Organization and Evolution*. Weinheim: Wiley-VCH.

Festinger, L. (1957). *A Theory of Cognitive Dissonance*. New York: Basic Books.

Fickler, R., Krenn, M., Lapkiewicz, R., Ramelow, S. & Zeilinger, A. (2013). Real-time imaging of quantum entanglement. *Scientific Reports*, 3, Article 1914.

Fine, A. (1993). Einstein's interpretations of the quantum theory. *Science in Context*, 6(1), 257–273. doi:10.1017/S026988970000137X.

Foa, E., Cohen, J., Keane, T. & Friedman, M. (2008). *Effective Treatments for PTSD: Practice Guidelines from the International Society for Traumatic Stress Studies*. New York: Guilford Press.

Frankl, V. (2006 [1958]). *Man's Search for Meaning*. Boston, MA: Beacon Press.

Frantz, C. M., Cuddy, A. J. C., Burnett, M., Ray, H. & Hart, A. (2004). A threat in the computer: the race implicit association test as a stereotype threat experience. *Personality and Social Psychology Bulletin*, 30, 1611–1624.

Fredrickson, B. (2001). The role of positive emotions in positive psychology: the broaden-and-build theory of positive emotions. *American Psychologist*, 56(3), 218–226.

Fredrickson, B. (2004). The broaden-and-build theory of positive emotions. *Philosophical Transactions of the Royal Society B: Biological Sciences*, 359, 1367–1377.

Fredrickson, B. (2005). The broaden-and-build theory of positive emotions. In F. A. Huppert, N. Baylis & B. Keverne (Eds.), *The Science of Well-Being*, 216–239. Oxford: Oxford University Press. doi:10.1093/acprof:oso/9780198567523.003.0008.

Fried, R. G. (2013). Nonpharmacologic management of psychodermatologic conditions. *Seminars in Cutaneous Medicine and Surgery*, 32(2), 119–125.

Fuchs, C. (2001). Quantum foundations in the light of quantum information. arXiv:quant-ph/0106166.

Fuchs, C. (2010). QBism, the perimeter of quantum Bayesianism. arXiv:1003.5209 [quant-ph].

Fuchs, C. (2011). *Coming of Age with Quantum Information: Notes on a Paulian Idea*. Cambridge: Cambridge University Press.

Fuchs, C. (2012). Interview with a Quantum Bayesian. arXiv:1207.2141 [quant-ph].

Fuchs, C., Mermin, N. & Schack, R. (2013). An Introduction to QBism with an application to the locality of quantum mechanics. arXiv:1311.525v1 [quant-ph].

Fuchs, C. & Schack, J. (2013). Quantum-Bayesian coherence: the no-nonsense version. arXiv:1301.3274 [quant-ph].

Galea, S., Riddle, M. & Kaplan, G. A. (2010). Causal thinking and complex system approaches in epidemiology. *International Journal of Epidemiology*, 39(1), 97–106.

Gallagher, M. W. & Lopex, S. J. (2007). Curiosity and well-being. *Journal of Positive Psychology*, 2(4), 236–248.

Gane, S., Georganakis, D., Maniati, K., Vamvakias, M., Ragoussis, N., Skoulakis, E. M. C. et al. (2013). Molecular vibration-sensing component in human olfaction. *PLOS ONE*, 8(1), e55780. https://doi.org/10.1371/journal.pone.0055780.

Gatchel, R. J. (2004). Comorbidity of chronic pain and mental health disorders: the biopsychosocial perspective. *American Psychologist*, 59(8), 795–805.

Gell-Mann, M. (1994). *The Quark and the Jaguar: Adventures in the Simple and Complex*. New York: Freeman.

Gell-Mann, M. (2007). Beauty, truth and ... physics [video]. *TED.com* (March). https://www.ted.com/talks/murray_gell_mann_on_beauty_and_truth_in_physics.

Gide, A. (1990 [1925]). *Les faux-monnayeurs* [The Counterfeiters]. Harmondsworth: Penguin.

Ginsberg, K. R. (2007). The importance of play in promoting healthy child development and maintaining strong parent–child bonds. *Pediatrics*, 119(1). http://pediatrics.aappublications.org/content/119/1/182.

Greene, B. (2011). *NOVA: The Fabric of the Cosmos* [four-part documentary], PBS.

Grant, A. (2015). Confirmed: quantum mechanics is weird. *Science News* (October 21). https://www.sciencenews.org/blog/science-ticker/confirmed-quantum-mechanics-weird.

Grens, K. (2013a). Feeding time, *The Scientist* (February 1). http://www.the-scientist.com/?articles.view/articleNo/34153/title/Feeding-Time.

Grens, K. (2013b). Out of sync, *The Scientist* (September 1). http://www.the-scientist.com/?articles.view/articleNo/37269/title/Out-of-Sync.

Grodzinsky, Y. & Nelken, I. (2014). The neural code that makes us human. *Science*, 343, 978–979.

Gruber, M. J., Gelman, B. D. & Ranganath, C. (2014). States of curiosity modulate hippocampus-dependent learning via the dopaminergic circuit. *Neuron*, 84(2), 486–496.

Gunaratne, P., Lin, Y., Bemham, A., Drnevich, J., Coarfa, C., Tennakoon, J., Creighton, C. J. et al. (2011). Song exposure alters the profile of microRNAs in the zebra finch auditory forebrain. *BMC Genomics*, 12, 277.

Hameroff, S. & Penrose, R. (1996). Orchestrated reduction of quantum coherence in brain microtubules: a model for consciousness. In S. Hameroff, A. Kaszniak & A. Scott (Eds.), *Toward a Science of Consciousness: The First Tucson Discussions and Debates*, 507–540. Cambridge, MA: MIT Press.

Hamish, G., Hiscock, H. G., Worster, S., Kattnig, D. R., Steers, C., Jin, Y., Manolopoulos, D. E., Mouritsen, H. & Hore, P. J. (2016). The quantum needle of the avian magnetic compass. *Proceedings of the National Academy of Sciences of the United States of America*, 113(17), 4634–4639.

Hanle, P. A. (1977). Erwin Schrödinger's reaction to Louis de Broglie's thesis on the quantum theory. *Isis*, 68(4), 606–609. doi:10.1086/351880.

Hanson, N. R. (1959). Copenhagen Interpretation of quantum theory. *American Journal of Physics*, 27(1). http://dx.doi.org/10.1119/1.1934739.

Hardesty, L. (2010). Explained: linear and nonlinear systems. *MIT News* (February 26). http://news.mit.edu/2010/explained-linear-0226.

Harrison, L. A., Stevens, C. M., Monty, A. N. & Coakley, C. A. (2006). The consequences of stereotype threat on the academic performance of white and non-white lower income college students. *Social Psychology of Education*, 9, 341–357.

Harrison, N. A., Brydon, L., Walker, C., Gray, M. A., Steptoe, A. & Critchley, H. D. (2009). Inflammation causes mood changes through alterations in subgenual cingulate activity and mesolimbic connectivity. *Biological Psychiatry*, 66(5), 407–414.

Hatcher, R. L. (2015). Interpersonal competencies: responsiveness, technique, and training in psychotherapy. *American Psychologist*, 70(8), 747–757.

Heisenberg, W. (1983 [1927]). The physical content of quantum kinematic and mechanics: principle of indeterminism. In J. Wheeler and W. Zurek (Eds.), *Quantum Theory and Measurement*, 62–84. Princeton, NJ: Princeton University Press.

Helmholtz, H. von (1896). *Vorträge und Reden*. Brunswick: Friedrich Viewig und Sohn.

Hendry, J. (1980). The development of attitudes to the wave-particle duality of light and quantum theory, 1900–1920. *Annals of Science*, 37(1), 59–79.

Herman, S. M. (1998). The relationship between therapist–client modality similarity and psychotherapy outcome. *Journal of Psychotherapy Practice and Research*, 7(1), 56–64.

Heunen, C., Sadrzadeh, M. & Grefenstette, E. (2013). *Quantum Physics and Linguistics: A Compositional, Diagrammatic Discourse*. New York: Oxford University Press.

Hill, R. (2006). *How the "Real World" is Driving Us Crazy! Solving the Winner/Loser World Problem.* Sydney: Hill & Hill.

Holland, J. (2012). *Signals and Boundaries: Building Blocks for Complex Adaptive Systems.* Cambridge, MA: MIT Press.

Holtmeier, W. & Kabelitz, D. (2005). Gamma delta T cells link innate and adaptive immune responses. *Chemical Immunology and Allergy*, 86, 151–183.

Hope, A. E. & Sugarman, L. I. (2015). Orienting hypnosis. *American Journal of Clinical Hypnosis*, 57(3), 212–229.

Hopps, J. G., Pinderhughes, E. & Shankar, R. (1995). *The Power to Care: Clinical Practice Effectiveness with Overwhelmed Clients.* New York: Free Press.

Hornung, J. P. (2003). The human raphe nuclei and the serotonergic system. *Journal of Chemical Neuroanatomy*, 26(4), 331–343.

Hoyt, M. F. & Talmon, M. (Eds.) (2014). *Capturing the Moment: Single Session Therapy and Walk-In Services.* Carmarthen: Crown House Publishing.

Humble, M. B. (2010). Vitamin D, light and mental health. *Journal of Photochemistry and Photobiology B: Biology*, 101(2), 142–149.

Huth, A. G., de Heer, W. A., Griffiths, T. L., Theunissen, F. E. & Gallant, J. L. (2016). Natural speech reveals the semantic maps that tile the human cerebral cortex. *Nature*, 532, 453–458.

Iacoboni, M. (2007). Face to face: the neural basis of social mirroring and empathy. *Psychiatric Annals*, 37(4), 236–241.

Iacoboni, M. (2008). *Mirroring People: The Science of Empathy and How We Connect with Others.* New York: Farrar, Straus and Giroux.

Insel, T. (2009). Disruptive insights in psychiatry: transforming a clinical discipline. *Journal of Clinical Investigation*, 119(4), 700–705.

Insel, T. (2010). Faulty circuits. *Scientific American*, 302(4), 44–51.

Insel, T. (2012). Next-generation treatments for mental disorders. *Science Translational Medicine*, 4(155). doi:10.1126/scitranslmed.3004873.

Irwin, M. & Vedhara, K. (2005). *Human Psychoneuroimmunology*. New York: Oxford University Press.

Jaenisch, R. & Bird, A. (2003). Epigenetic regulation of gene expression: how the genome integrates intrinsic and environmental signals. *Nature Genetics Review*, 33, 245–254.

Jamieson, G. & Burgess, A. (2014). Hypnotic induction is followed by state-like changes in the organization of EEG functional connectivity in the theta and beta frequency bands in high-hypnotically susceptible individuals. *Frontiers in Human Neuroscience*, 8, 528. doi:10.3389/fnhum.2014.00528.

Jempa, M., Verdonschot, R. G., van Steenbergen, H., Rombouts, S. A. R. B. & Nieuwenhuis, S. (2012). Neural mechanisms underlying the induction and relief of perceptual curiosity. *Frontiers in Behavioral Neuroscience*, 6, 5. doi:10.3389/fnbeh.2012.00005.

Jeong, H., Lim, Y. & Kim, M. (2014). Coarsening measurement references and the quantum-to-classical transition. *Physical Review Letters*, 112. doi:10.1103/PhysRevLett.112.010402.

Jorgensen, R. A. (2011). Epigenetics: biology's quantum mechanics. *Frontiers in Plant Science*, 2, 10. https://doi.org/10.3389/fpls.2011.00010.

Kang, M. J., Hsu, M., Krajbich, I. M., Loewenstein, G., McClure, S. M., Wang, J. T. & Camerer, C. F. (2008). The hunger for knowledge: neural correlates of curiosity. *Semantic Scholar*. https://www.semanticscholar.org/paper/The-Hunger-for-Knowledge-Neural-Correlates-of-Kang-Hsu/43b06df4bcef7435a12e22dc8bbfb9891e3e3bf7.

Kawamoto, T., Ura, M. & Hiraki, K. (2017). Curious people are less affected by social rejection. *Personality and Individual Differences*, 105, 264–267.

Kellogg, R. (2013). *The Making of the Mind: The Neuroscience of Human Nature.* New York: Prometheus Books.

Kidd, C. & Hayden, B. Y. (2015). The psychology and neuroscience of curiosity. *Neuron*, 88(3), 449–460. http://doi.org/10.1016/j.neuron.2015.09.010.

Kirsch, I. (2001). The response set theory of hypnosis: expectancy and physiology. *American Journal of Clinical Hypnosis*, 44(1), 69–73.

Klauber, R. (2015). *Student Friendly Quantum Field Theory: Basic Principles and Quantum Electrodynamics*, 2nd edn. Fairfield, IA: Sandtrove Press.

Kleitman, N. (1957). Sleep, wakefulness, and consciousness. *Psychological Bulletin*, 54, 354–359.

Kleitman, N. (1982). Basic rest–activity cycle – 22 years later. *Journal of Sleep Research & Sleep Medicine*, 5(4), 311–317.

Knutson, B., Adams, C. M., Fong, G. W. & Hommer, D. (2001). Anticipation of increasing monetary reward selectively recruits nucleus accumbens. *Journal of Neuroscience*, 21(RC159), 1–5.

Koenig, A. M. & Eagly, A. H. (2005). Stereotype threat in men on a test of social sensitivity. *Sex Roles*, 52, 489–496.

Kolb, D. A., Boyatzis, R. E. & Mainemelis, C. (2000). Experiential learning theory: previous research and new directions. In R. J. Sternberg and L. F. Zhang (Eds.), *Perspectives on Cognitive, Learning, and Thinking Styles*, 227–248. Mahwah, NJ: Lawrence Erlbaum.

Kolcaba, K. (2003). *Comfort Theory and Practice: A Vision for Holistic Health Care and Research.* New York: Springer.

Koopmans, M. (2014). Change, self-organization and the search for causality in educational research and practice. *Complicity: An International Journal of Complexity and Education*, 11(1), 20–39.

Krauss, L. M. (2011). *Quantum Man: Richard Feynman's Life in Science.* New York: W.W. Norton.

Kress, G. J. & Mennerick, S. (2009). Action potential initiation and propagation: upstream influences on neurotransmission. *Neuroscience*, 158(1), 211–222. http://doi.org/10.1016/j.neuroscience.2008.03.021.

Kwek, G. (2012). Death of the Angel of the Gap. *Sydney Morning Herald* (May 14). http://www.smh.com.au/nsw/death-of-the-angel-of-the-gap-the-man-who-saved-the-suicidal-from-themselves-20120514-1ymle.html.

Lambert, M. J. & Barley, D. E. (2001). Research summary on the therapeutic relationship and psychotherapy outcome. *Psychotherapy: Theory, Research, Practice, Training*, 38(4), 357–361.

Lancaster, T. & Blundell, S. (2014). *Quantum Field Theory for the Gifted Amateur*. New York: Oxford University Press.

Leslie, M. (2013). NIH effort gambles on mysterious extracellular RNAs. *Science*, 341, 947.

Lavretsky, H., Epel, E. S., Siddarth, P., Nazarian, N., Cyr, N. S., Khalsa, D. S., Lin, J., Blackburn, E. & Irwin, M. R. (2013). A pilot study of yogic meditation for family dementia caregivers with depressive symptoms: effects on mental health, cognition, and telomerase activity. *International Journal of Geriatric Psychiatry*, 28(1), 57–65.

Levsky, J., Shenoy, S., Pezo, C. & Singer, R. (2002). Single-cell gene expression profiling. *Science*, 27, 836–840.

Lichtenberg, P., Bachner-Melman, R., Gritsenko, I. & Ebstein, R. (2000). Exploratory association study between catechol-o-methyltransferase (COMT) high/low enzyme activity polymorphism and hypnotizability. *American Journal of Medical Genetics*, 96, 771–774.

Lichtenberg, P., Bachner-Melman, R., Ebstein, R. & Crawford, H. (2004). Hypnotic susceptibility: multidimensional relationships with Cloninger's Tridimensional Personality Questionnaire, COMT polymorphisms, absorption, and attentional characteristics. *International Journal of Clinical and Experimental Hypnosis*, 52, 47–72.

Lifshitz, M. & Raz, A. (2012). Hypnosis and meditation: vehicles for attention and suggestion. *Journal of Mind–Body Regulation*, 2(1), 3–11.

Litman, J. A. (2005). Curiosity and the pleasures of learning: wanting and liking new information. *Cognition and Emotion*, 19(6), 793–814.

Litman, J. A. & Jimerson, T. L. (2004). The measurement of curiosity as a feeling-of-deprivation. *Journal of Personality Assessment*, 82, 147–157.

Lloyd, D. & Rossi, E. L. (Eds.) (1992). *Ultradian Rhythms in Life Processes: An Inquiry into Fundamental*

Principles of Chronobiology and Psychobiology. New York: Springer-Verlag.

Lloyd, D. & Rossi, E. L. (Eds.) (2008). *Ultradian Rhythms from Molecules to Mind: A New Vision of Life.* New York: Springer.

Loewenstein, G. (1994). The psychology of curiosity: a review and reinterpretation. *Psychological Bulletin,* 116(1), 75–98.

Loewenstein, W. (1999). *The Touchstone of Life: Molecular Information, Cell Communication, and the Foundations of Life*. New York: Oxford University Press.

Loewenstein, W. (2013). *Physics in Mind: A Quantum View of the Brain*. New York: Basic Books.

Looper, K. J. & Kirmaye, L. J. (2002). Behavioral medicine approaches to somatoform disorders. *Journal of Consulting and Clinical Psychology*, 70(3), 810–827.

Lull, M. E. & Block, M. L. (2010). Microglial activation and chronic neurodegeneration. *Neurotherapeutics*, 7(4), 354–365. doi:10.1016/j.nurt.2010.05.014.

Luzupone, C. A., Stonbaugh, J. I., Gordon, J. I., Jansson, J. K. & Knight, R. (2012). Diversity, stability and resilience of the human gut microbiota. *Nature,* 489, 220–230. doi:10.1038/nature11550.

Marks-Tarlow, T. (2008). *Psyche's Veil: Psychotherapy, Fractals and Complexity*. Abingdon & New York: Routledge.

Maslow, A. (1968). *Toward a Psychology of Being*. New York: Van Nostrand Reinhold.

Mazzoni, G., Venneri, A., McGeown, W. & Kirsch, I. (2013). Neuroimaging resolution of the altered state hypothesis. *Cortex*, 49(2), 400–410.

McFadden, J. (2000). *Quantum Evolution. How Physics' Weirdest Theory Explains Life's Biggest Mystery*. New York: W.W. Norton.

McFadden, J. & Al-Khalili, J. (2014). *Life on the Edge: The Coming of Age of Quantum Biology*. New York: Crown.

McGilchrist, I. (2009). *The Master and his Emissary: The Divided Brain and the Making of the Western World.* London: Yale University Press.

Mednick, S. & Erhman, M. (2006). *Take a Nap! Change Your Life*. New York: Workman Publishing.

Merali, Z. (2015). Quantum physics: what is really real? *Nature News*, 521(7552), 278–280. http://www.nature.com/news/quantum-physics-what-is-really-real-1.17585.

Miller, S. D., Duncan, B. L., Brown, J., Sorrell, R. & Chalk, M. B. (2006). Using formal client feedback to improve retention and outcome: making ongoing, real-time assessment feasible. *Journal of Brief Therapy*, 5(1), 5–22.

Miller, S. D., Hubble, M. A., Chow, D. L. & Seidel, J. A. (2013). The outcome of psychotherapy: yesterday, today, and tomorrow. *Psychotherapy*, 50(1), 88–97.

Milojevich, H. M. & Lukowski, A. F. (2016). Sleep and mental health in undergraduate students with generally healthy sleep habits. *PLOS ONE*, 11(6), e0156372.

Morell, V. (2014). When the bat sings. *Science*, 344, 1334–1337.

Morello, A. (2014). The quantum world around you [video] (August 26). https://www.youtube.com/watch?v=tnfur3fqklc&list=PLqSkUknJX0S9olTYuJ5SOl1D6pbzaPuWx.

Moret, C. & Briley, M. (2011). The importance of norepinephrine in depression. *Neuropsychiatric Disease and Treatment*, 7(Suppl. 1), 9–13. http://doi.org/10.2147/NDT.S19619.

Morsella, E. & Poehlman, T. A. (2013). The inevitable contrast: conscious vs. unconscious processes in action control. *Frontiers in Psychology*, 4, 590. http://doi.org/10.3389/fpsyg.2013.00590.

Mueller, D. L. (2003). Tuning the immune system: competing positive and negative feedback loops. *Nature Immunology*, 4, 210–211. doi:10.1038/ni0303-210.

Nave, R. (2016). HyperPhysics. http://hyperphysics.phy-astr.gsu.edu/hbase/hframe.html [website]. Department of Physics and Astronomy, Georgia State University, Atlanta.

Nicolis, G. & Prigogine, I. (1989). *Exploring Complexity: An Introduction*. New York: W.H. Freeman.

Olander, D. (2007). *General Thermodynamics*. Boca Raton, FL: CRC Press.

Ornish, D., Lin, J., Daubenmier, J. et al. (2008). Increased telomerase activity and comprehensive lifestyle changes: a pilot study. *The Lancet Oncology*, 9(11), 1048–1057. doi:10.1016/S1470-2045(08)70234-1.

Ornish, D., Lin, J., Daubenmier. J., Weidner, G., Epel, E., Kemp, C. et al. (2013). Effect of comprehensive lifestyle changes on telomerase activity and telomere length in men with biopsy-proven low-risk prostate cancer: 5-year follow-up of a descriptive pilot study. *Lancet Oncology*, 14(11), 1112–11120. doi:http://dx.doi.org/10.1016/S1470-2045 (13)70366-8.

Otto, R. (1950 [1923]). *The Idea of the Holy: An Inquiry into the Non-Rational Factor in the Idea of the Divine and its Relation to the Rational*, tr. J. W. Harvey. New York: Oxford University Press.

Pais, A. (1979). Einstein and the quantum theory. *Reviews in Modern Physics*, 51(4), 863–914.

Pais, A. (1982). Max Born's statistical interpretation of quantum mechanics. *Science*, 218(4578), 1193–1198.

Panksepp, J. (2010). Affective neuroscience of the emotional BrainMind: evolutionary perspectives and implications for understanding depression. *Dialogues in Clinical Neuroscience*, 12(4), 533–545.

Pascale, R. T., Millemann, M. & Gioja, L. (2001). *Surfing the Edge of Chaos: The Laws of Nature and the New Laws of Business*. New York: Three Rivers Press.

Peil, K. T. (2014). Emotion: the self-regulatory sense. *Global Advances in Health and Medicine*, 3(2), 80–108. http://doi.org/10.7453/gahmj.2013.058.

Pekala, R., Kumar, V., Maurer, R., Elliott-Carter, N., Moon, E. & Mullen, K. (2010). Suggestibility, expectancy, trance state effects, and hypnotic depth. I: Implications for understanding hypnotism. *American Journal of Clinical Hypnosis*, 52(4), 275–290.

Penrose, R. (2004). *The Road to Reality: A Complete Guide to the Laws of the Universe*. New York: Knopf.

Planck, M. (1909). On the law of distribution of energy in the normal spectrum. *Annalen der Physik*, 4, 553.

Plato (1968). *The Republic of Plato*, tr. A. Bloom. New York: Basic Books

Poincaré, H. (2000 [1908]). Mathematical creation [reprinted from *Science et méthode*]. *Resonance*, 5(2), 85–94.

Pollard, K., Salama, S., Lambert, N., Lambot, M. A., Coppens, S., Pedersen, J. S. et al. (2006). An RNA gene expressed during cortical development evolved rapidly in humans. *Nature*, 443 (7108), 167–172.

Pollard, K. (2012). The genetics of humanness. *Evolutionary Anthropology*, 21(5), 184.

Ravitz, L. J. (1950). Electrometric correlates of the hypnotic state. *Science*, 112, 341–342.

Ravitz, L. J. (1951). Standing potential correlates of hypnosis and narcosis. *AMA Archives of Neurology and Psychiatry*, 65(4), 413–436. doi:10.1001/archneurpsyc.1951.02320040003001.

Ravitz, L. J. (1962). History, measurement and applicability of periodic changes in the electromagnetic field in health and disease. *American Archives of New York Science*, 98, 1144–1201.

Ravitz, L. J. (2002). *Electrodynamic Man: Electromagnetic Field Measurements in Biology, Medicine, Hypnosis and Psychiatry*. Danbury, CT: Rutledge.

Reese, E. (2013). Fathers and storytelling – a natural fit. *Psychology Today* (June 15). https://www.psychologytoday.com/blog/tell-me-story/201306/fathers-and-family-storytelling-natural-fit.

Rizzolatti, G. & Craighero, L. (2004). The mirror neuron system. *Annual Review of Neuroscience*, 27, 169–192.

Rizzolatti, G. & Sinigaglia, C. (2008). *Mirrors in the Brain: How our Minds Share Actions and Emotions*. New York: Oxford University Press.

Rogers, C. R. (1957a). A note on the "nature of man." *Journal of Counseling Psychology*, 4(3), 199–203.

Rogers, C. R. (1957b). The necessary and sufficient conditions of therapeutic personality change. *Journal of Consulting Psychology*, 21(2), 95–103.

Rogers, C. R. (2007). The necessary and sufficient conditions of therapeutic personality change.

Psychotherapy: Theory, Research, Practice, Training, 44(3), 240–248.

Rohrlich, F. (1987). Schrödinger and the interpretation of quantum mechanics. *Foundations of Physics,* 17(12), 1205–1220.

Romero, E., Augulis, R., Novoderezhkin, V. I., Ferretti, M., Thieme, J., Zigmantas, D. & van Grondelle, R. (2014). Quantum coherence in photosynthesis for efficient solar-energy conversion. *Nature Physics,* 10, 676–682. doi:10.1038/nphys3017.

Rosen, J. (2004). *Encyclopedia of Physics.* New York: Facts on File.

Rosenberg, T., Gal-Ben-Ari, S., Dieterich, D. C., Kreutz, M. R., Ziv, N. E., Gundelfinger, E. D. & Rosenblum, K. (2014). The roles of protein expression in synaptic plasticity and memory consolidation. *Frontiers in Molecular Neuroscience,* 7, 86. http://doi.org/10.3389/fnmol.2014.00086.

Rosenfeld, B. D. (1992). Court ordered treatment of spouse abuse. *Clinical Psychology Review,* 12(2), 205–226.

Rossi, E. L. (1967). Game and growth: two dimensions of our psychotherapeutic zeitgeist. *Journal of Humanistic Psychology,* 7(2), 139–154.

Rossi, E. L. (1968). The breakout heuristic: a phenomenology of growth therapy with college students. *Journal of Humanistic Psychology,* 8(1), 16–28.

Rossi, E. L. (1982). Hypnosis and ultradian cycles: a new state(s) theory of hypnosis? *American Journal of Clinical Hypnosis,* 25, 21–32.

Rossi, E. L. (1987). From mind to molecule: a state-dependent memory, learning, and behavior theory of mind–body healing. *Advances,* 4(2), 42–60.

Rossi, E. L. (1988a). Perspectives: consciousness and the new quantum psychologies. *Psychological Perspectives,* 19(1), 4–13.

Rossi, E. L. (1988b). Beyond relativity and quantum theory: an interview with David Bohm. *Psychological Perspectives,* 19(1), 25–43.

Rossi, E. L. (1988c). Perspectives: a mind-gene connection: *Psychological Perspectives,* 19(2), 212–221.

Rossi, E. L. (1988d). Non-locality in physics and psychology: an interview with John Stewart Bell. *Psychological Perspectives,* 19(2), 294–319.

Rossi, E. L. (1992). The wave nature of consciousness. In J. K. Zeig (Ed.), *The Evolution of Psychotherapy: The Second Conference,* 216–238. New York: Routledge.

Rossi, E. L. (1993 [1986]). *The Psychobiology of Mind–Body Healing: New Concepts of Therapeutic Hypnosis,* 2nd edn. New York: W.W. Norton.

Rossi, E. L. (1996). *The Symptom Path to Enlightenment: The New Dynamics of Self-Organization in Hypnotherapy. An Advanced Manual for Beginners,* ed. K. L. Rossi. Los Osos, CA: Palisades Gateway Press.

Rossi, E. L. (1997a). The Feigenbaum Scenario in a unified science of life and mind. *World Futures,* 50, 633–645.

Rossi, E. L. (1997b). The symptom path to enlightenment: the psychobiology of Jung's constructive method. *Psychological Perspectives,* 36, 68–84.

Rossi, E. L. (1998a [1972]). *Dreams and the Growth of Personality,* 3rd edn. Los Osos, CA: Palisades Gateway Press.

Rossi, E. L. (1998b). The Feigenbaum Scenario as a model of conscious information processing. *Biosystems,* 40, 1–10.

Rossi, E. L. (1999). The co-creative dynamics of dreams, consciousness and choice. *Psychological Perspectives,* 38, 116–127.

Rossi, E. L. (2000 [1972]). *Dreams, Consciousness, Spirit: The Quantum Experience of Self-Reflection and Co-Creation.* New York: Zeig, Tucker, Theisen.

Rossi, E. L. (2002a). A conceptual review of the psychosocial genomics of expectancy and surprise: neuroscience perspectives about the deep psychobiology of therapeutic hypnosis. *American Journal of Clinical Hypnosis,* 45(2), 103–118.

Rossi, E. L. (2002b). *The Psychobiology of Gene Expression: Neuroscience and Neurogenesis in Hypnosis and the Healing Arts.* New York: W.W. Norton.

Rossi, E. L. (2002c). Psychosocial genomics: gene expression, neurogenesis, and human experience in mind–body medicine. *Advances in Mind Body Medicine*, 18(2), 22–30.

Rossi, E. L. (2004a). Art, beauty, and truth: the psychosocial genomics of consciousness, dreams, and brain growth in psychotherapy and mind–body healing. *Annals of the American Psychotherapy Association*, 7(3), 10–17.

Rossi, E. L. (2004b). *A Discourse with Our Genes: The Psychosocial and Cultural Genomics of Therapeutic Hypnosis and Psychotherapy*. San Lorenzo Maggiore: Editris S.A.S.; Phoenix, AZ: Zeig, Tucker and Theisen.

Rossi, E. L. (2004c). Gene expression and brain plasticity in stroke rehabilitation: a personal memoir of mind–body healing dreams. *American Journal of Clinical Hypnosis*, 46(3), 215–227.

Rossi, E. L. (2005). Einstein's eternal mystery of epistemology explained: the four-stage creative process in art, science, myth, and psychotherapy. *Annals of the American Psychotherapy Association*, 8, 4–11. Reprinted in: E. L. Rossi (2007). *The Breakout Heuristic: The New Neuroscience of Mirror Neurons, Consciousness and Creativity in Human Relationships. The Selected Papers of Ernest Lawrence Rossi, Vol. 1*. Phoenix, AZ: Milton H. Erickson Foundation Press.

Rossi, E. L. (2007). *The Breakout Heuristic: The New Neuroscience of Mirror Neurons, Consciousness and Creativity in Human Relationships. The Selected Papers of Ernest Lawrence Rossi, Vol. 1*. Phoenix, AZ: Milton H. Erickson Foundation Press.

Rossi, E. L. (2012). *Creating Consciousness: How Therapists Can Facilitate Wonder, Wisdom, Truth and Beauty. The Selected Papers of Ernest Lawrence Rossi, Vol. 2*. Phoenix, AZ: Milton H. Erickson Foundation Press.

Rossi, E. L. & Cheek, D. B. (1988). *Mind–Body Therapy: Methods of Ideodynamic Healing in Hypnosis*. New York: W.W. Norton.

Rossi, E. L., Iannotti, S., Cozzolino, M., Castiglione, S., Cicatelli, A. & Rossi, K. L. (2008). A pilot study of positive expectations and focused attention via a new protocol for therapeutic hypnosis assessed with DNA microarrays: the creative psychosocial genomic healing experience. *Sleep and Hypnosis: An International Journal of Sleep, Dream, and Hypnosis*, 10(2), 39–44.

Rossi, E. L. & Lippincott, B. (1992). The wave nature of being: ultradian rhythms and mind–body communication. In D. Lloyd & E. L. Rossi (Eds.), *Ultradian Rhythms in Life Processes: A Fundamental Inquiry into Chronobiology and Psychobiology*, 371–402. New York: Springer-Verlag.

Rossi, E. L. & Nimmons, D. (1991). *The Twenty-Minute Break: The Ultradian Healing Response*. Los Angeles, CA: Jeremy Tarcher.

Rossi, E. L. & Rossi, K. L. (2008). *The New Neuroscience of Psychotherapy, Therapeutic Hypnosis and Rehabilitation: A Creative Dialogue with Our Genes*. Free ebook available at www.ernestrossi.com.

Rossi, E. L. & Rossi, K. L. (2011). Decoding the Chalmers hard problem of consciousness: qualia of the molecular biology of creativity and thought. *Journal of Cosmology*, 14. http://journalofcosmology.com/Consciousness126.html. Reprinted in: R. Penrose, S. Hameroff & S. Kak (Eds.) (2011). *Consciousness and the Universe: Quantum Physics, Evolution, Brain, and Mind*, 210–227. Cambridge, MA: Cosmology Science Publishers.

Rossi, E. L. & Rossi, K. L. (2013). *Creating New Consciousness in Everyday Life: The Psychosocial Genomics of Self-Creation* [video ebook].

Rossi, E. L. & Rossi, K. L. (2014a). An evolutionary RNA/DNA psychogenomic theory of the transformations of consciousness: the quest for therapeutic mind/gene search algorithms. *International Journal for Transformations of Consciousness*, 1, 1–20.

Rossi, E. L. & Rossi, K. L. (2014b) Quantum perspectives of consciousness, cognition and creativity: the Dirac equation in a new contour integral model of brain plasticity. *Journal of Applied & Computational Mathematics*, 3(6), 183. http://dx.doi.org/10.4172/2168-9679.1000183.

Rossi, E. L. & Rossi, K. L. (2015). Optimizing the human condition with psychosocial genomic star maps: implicit processing heuristics in the 4-stage creative cycle. *International Journal of Psychosocial Genomics: Consciousness and Health Research*, 1(2), 5–17.

Rossi, E. L. & Rossi, K. L. (2016a). How quantum field theory optimizes neuropsychotherapy. *The Neuropsychotherapist*, 4(4), 14–25.

Rossi, E. L. & Rossi, K. L. (2016b). A quantum field theory of neuropsychotherapy: semantic mind–brain maps and the quantum qualia of consciousness. *International Journal of Neuropsychotherapy*, 4(1), 47–68. doi:10.12744/ijnpt.2016.0047-0068.

Roth, W-M. (1993). Heisenberg's uncertainty principle and interpretive research in science education. *Journal of Research in Science Teaching*, 30(7), 669–680. doi:10.1002/tea.3660300706.

Saey, T. (2010). First songbird genome arrives. *Science News*, 177(9), 16.

Salim, S., Chugh, G. & Asghar, M. (2012). Inflammation in anxiety. *Advances in Protein Chemistry and Structural Biology*, 88, 1–25. doi:10.1016/B978-0-12-398314-5.00001-5.

Samios, Z. (2017). Bonds tells tales of uncomfortable underwear in new Leos campaign for Comfytails. *Mumbrella* (February 6). https://mumbrella.com.au/bonds-tells-tales-of-uncomfy-undies-in-new-leos-campaign-424205.

Sanders, R. (2014). New evidence that chronic stress predisposes brain to mental illness. *Berkeley News* (February 11). http://news.berkeley.edu/2014/02/11/chronic-stress-predisposes-brain-to-mental-illness/.

Scharmer, C. O. (2016). *Theory U: Leading from the Future As It Emerges*. Oakland, CA: Berret-Koehler.

Scheel, M. J., Davis, C. K. & Henderson, J. D. (2013). Therapist use of client strengths: a qualitative study of positive processes. *Counseling Psychologist*, 41(3), 392–427.

Scherer, K. R. (2009). Emotions are emergent processes: they require a dynamic computational architecture. *Philosophical Transactions of the Royal Society B: Biological Sciences*, 364(1535), 3459–3474.

Schiller, C. (2015). *Motion Mountain: The Free Physics Textbook*. Available at: http://motionmountain.net.

Schore, A. N. (1994). *Affect Regulation and the Origin of the Self: The Neurobiology of Emotional Development*. New York: Psychology Press.

Schore, A. N. (2003). *Affect Disregulation and Disorders of the Self*. New York: W.W. Norton.

Schore, A. N. (2012). *The Science of the Art of Psychotherapy*. New York: W.W. Norton.

Schrödinger, E. (2012 [1967]). *What Is Life?* Cambridge: Cambridge University Press.

Schroer, B. (2010). Pascual Jordan's legacy and the ongoing research in quantum field theory. *European Physical Journal H. Historical Perspectives on Contemporary Physics*, 35, 377–434.

Schulte, B. (2014). *Overwhelmed: Work, Love, and Play When No One Has the Time*. New York: Sarah Crichton Books.

Schwartz, J. M., Stapp, H. S. & Beauregard, M. (2004). Quantum physics in neuroscience and psychology: a neurophysical model of mind–brain interaction. *Philosophical Transactions of the Royal Society B: Biological Sciences*, 360, 1309–1327. doi:10.1098/rstb.2004.1598.

Science Alert (2014). The best explanation of quantum entanglement so far (September 9). https://www.sciencealert.com/watch-the-best-explanation-of-quantum-entanglement-so-far.

Sczepanski, J. & Joyce, G. (2014). A cross-chiral RNA polymerase ribozyme. *Nature*, 515, 440–442.

Segev, A., Curtis, D., Jung, S. & Chae, S. (2016). Invisible brain: knowledge in research works and neuron activity. *PLOS ONE*, 11(7), e0158590. https://doi.org/10.1371/journal.pone.0158590.

Seligman, M. E. (2013). *Authentic Happiness: Using the New Positive Psychology to Realize Your Potential for Lasting Fulfillment*. New York: Free Press.

Shakespeare, W. (1998). *The Tempest*. Oxford: Oxford University Press.

Shakespeare, W. (2004). *Shakespeare's Sonnets and Poems* (Folger Shakespeare Library,) ed. B. A. Mowat & P. Werstine. New York: Washington Square Press.

Sharma, A., Madaan, V. & Petty, F. D. (2006). Exercise for mental health. *Primary Care Companion to the Journal of Clinical Psychiatry*, 8(2), 106.

Shapiro, F. (2014). The role of eye movement desensitization and reprocessing (EMDR) therapy in medicine: addressing the psychological and physical symptoms stemming from adverse life experiences. *Permanente Journal*, 18(1), 71–77.

Shelka, S. & Piccirilli, J. (2014). RNA made in its own mirror image. *Nature*, 515, 347–348.

Siegel, D. J. (2007). *The Mindful Brain: Reflection and Attunement in the Cultivation of Well-Being*. New York: W.W. Norton.

Siegel, D. J. (2015). *The Developing Mind: How Relationships and the Brain Interact to Shape Who We Are*, 2nd edn. New York: Guilford Press.

Siegel, D. J. (2016). *Mind: A Journey to the Heart of Being Human*. New York: W.W. Norton.

Simpkins, C. A. & Simpkins, A. M. (2010). *Neuro-Hypnosis: Using Self-Hypnosis to Activate the Brain for Change*. New York: W.W. Norton.

Simpson, D., Ryan, R., Hall, L., Panchenko, E., Drew, S. C., Petrou, S., Donnelly, P. S., Mulvaney, P. & Hollenberg, L. C. L. (2017). Quantum magnetic resonance microscopy. arXiv:1702.04418 [physics.bio-ph].

Sliwinski, J. & Elkins, G. (2013). Enhancing placebo effects: insights from social psychology. *American Journal of Clinical Hypnosis*, 55, 236–248.

Smith, S. M. & Vale, W. W. (2006). The role of the hypothalamic-pituitary-adrenal axis in neuroendocrine responses to stress. *Dialogues in Clinical Neuroscience*, 8(4), 383–395.

Spencer, S. J., Steele, C. M. & Quinn, D. M. (1999). Stereotype threat and women's math performance. *Journal of Experimental Social Psychology*, 35, 4–28

Spielberger, C. D. & Reheiser, E. C. (2009). Assessment of emotions: anxiety, anger, depression, and curiosity. *Applied Psychology: Health and Well-Being*, 1(3), 271–302.

Starr, M. (2015). Physicists prove Einstein's 'spooky' quantum entanglement. *CNET* (November 20). https://www.cnet.com/au/news/physicists-prove-einsteins-spooky-quantum-entanglement.

Steele, C. M. (1997). A threat in the air: how stereotypes shape intellectual identity and performance. *American Psychologist*, 52, 613–629.

Steele, C. M. (1998). Stereotyping and its threat are real. *American Psychologist*, 53, 680–681.

Steele, C. M. & Aronson, J. (1995). Stereotype threat and the intellectual test performance of African-Americans. *Journal of Personality and Social Psychology*, 69, 797–811.

Stone, J. (2002). Battling doubt by avoiding practice: the effect of stereotype threat on self-handicapping in white athletes. *Personality and Social Psychology Bulletin*, 28, 1667–1678.

Stetka, B. (2014). Changing our DNA through mind control? *Scientific American* (16 December). https://www.scientificamerican.com/article/changing-our-dna-through-mind-control/.

Stiles, W. B., Honos-Webb, L. & Surko, M. (1998). Responsiveness in psychotherapy. *Clinical Psychology: Science and Practice*, 5, 439–458.

Stodolna, A. S., Rouzée, A., Lépine, F., Cohen, S., Robicheaux, F., Gijsbertsen, A. et al. (2013). Hydrogen atoms under magnification: direct observation of the nodal structure of stark states. *Physical Review Letters*, 110(21), 213001. https://doi.org/10.1103/PhysRevLett.110.213001.

Stoll, C. (2006). The call to learn [video]. *TED.com* (February). https://www.ted.com/talks/clifford_stoll_on_everything.

Storr, A. & Holmes, J. (2012). *The Art of Psychotherapy*, 3rd rev. edn. London: Taylor & Francis.

Strassler, M. (2013). Quantum fluctuations and their energy (August 29). https://profmattstrassler.com/articles-and-posts/particle-physics-basics/quantum-fluctuations-and-their-energy.

Strnad, J. (1986). Photons in introductory quantum physics. *American Journal of Physics*, 54(7), 650. http://dx.doi.org/10.1119/1.14526.

Stutz, P. & Michels, B. (2012). The comfort zone. *Psychology Today* (May 8). https://www.psychologytoday.com/blog/the-tools/201205/the-comfort-zone.

Susskind, L. & Friedman, A. (2014). *Quantum Mechanics: The Theoretical Minimum*. New York: Basic Books.

Tiberius, V. (2006). Well-being: psychological research for philosophers. *Philosophy Compass*, 1, 493–505. doi:10.1111/j.1747-9991.2006.00038.x.

Tinsley, J. N., Molodtsov, M. I., Prevedel, R., Wartmann, D., Espigulé-Pons, J., Lauwers, M. & Vaziri, A. (2016). Direct detection of a single photon by humans. *Nature Communications*, 19(7), 12172. doi:10.1038/ncomms12172.

Tronson, N. C. & Taylor, J. R. (2007). Molecular mechanisms of memory reconsolidation. *Nature Reviews Neuroscience*, 8, 262–275. doi:10.1038/nrn2090.

Tuckey, I. (2017). In good time: why are football matches 90 minutes long? Here's everything we know. *The Sun* (January 4). https://www.thesun.co.uk/sport/football/2526687/why-are-football-matches-90-minutes-long-heres-everything-we-know.

Tugade, M. M. & Fredrickson, B. L. (2004). Resilient individuals use positive emotions to bounce back from negative emotional experiences. *Journal of Personality and Social Psychology*, 86(2), 320–333. http://doi.org/10.1037/0022-3514.86.2.320.

Tulving, E. (2002). Episodic memory: from mind to the brain. *Annual Review of Psychology*, 53, 1–26.

Tulving, E. (2005). Episodic memory and autonoesis: uniquely human? In H. S. Terrance & J. Metcalfe (Eds.), *The Missing Link in Cognition*, 3–56. Oxford: Oxford University Press.

Unternaehrer, E., Luers, P., Mill, J., Dempster, E., Meyer, A. H., Staehli, S., Lieb, R., Hellhammer, D. H. & Meinlschmidt, G. (2012). Dynamic changes in DNA methylation of stress-associated genes (OXTR, BDNF) after acute psychosocial stress. *Translational Psychiatry*, 2, e150, doi:10.1038/tp.2012.77.

van den Dungen, W. (2016). *Ancient Egyptian Readings*. Brasschaart: Taurus Press.

Vedral, V. (2012). *Decoding Reality: The Universe as Quantum Information*. New York: Oxford University Press.

von Baeyer, H. (2013). Quantum weirdness? It's all in your mind. *Scientific American*, 308(6), 46–51.

Wagstaff, G. (2010). Hypnosis and the relationship between trance, suggestion, expectancy and depth: some semantic and conceptual issues. *American Journal of Clinical Hypnosis*, 53(1), 47–59.

Wallas, G. (1926). *The Art of Thought*. New York: Harcourt, Brace, and World.

Walsh, M., Hickey, C. & Duffy, J. (1999). Influence of item content and stereotype situation on gender differences in mathematical problem solving. *Sex Roles*, 41, 219–240.

Wampold, B., Flückiger, C., Del Re, A., Yulish, N., Frost, N., Pace, B. et al. (2016). In pursuit of truth: a critical examination of meta-analyses of cognitive behavior therapy. *Psychotherapy Research*, 27(1), 14–32.

Wang, H. & Li, J. (2015). How trait curiosity influences psychological well-being and emotional exhaustion: the mediating role of personal initiative. *Personality and Individual Differences*, 75, 135–140.

Wang, J. (2006). Consciousness as an emergent property. *Disputatio philosophica: International Journal on Philosophy and Religion*, 8(1), 89–119.

Wang, J., Jeng-Yuan, Y., Fazal, I. M., Ahmed, N., Yan, Y. et al. (2012). Terabit free-space data transmission employing orbital angular momentum multiplexing. *Nature Photonics*, 6, 488–496.

Warren, W., Clayton, D., Ellegren, H., Arnold, A. P., Hillier, L. W., Künstner, A. et al. (2010). The genome of a songbird. *Nature*, 464, 757–762.

Weir, K. (2016). The science of naps. *Monitor on Psychology*, 47(7), 48.

Wibowo, J. (2016). Plush Sofas invites dogs onto the couch in new comfort campaign. *Mumbrella* (August 22). https://mumbrella.com.au/french-bulldog-finds-comfort-new-plush-sofas-ad-389603.

Wilber, K. (1993). *The Spectrum of Consciousness*. Wheaton: Quest Books.

Wilczek, F. (2002). A piece of magic: the Dirac equation. In G. Farmelo (Ed.), *It Must Be Beautiful: Great Equations in Modern Science*, 102–130. New York: Granta Books.

Wilczek, F. (2015). *A Beautiful Question: Finding Nature's Deep Design*. New York: Penguin.

Wolf, K. (2015). Measuring facial expression of emotion. *Dialogues in Clinical Neuroscience*, 17(4), 457–462.

Xie, L., Kang, H., Xu, Q., Chen, M. J., Liao, Y., Thiyagarajan, M. et al. (2013). Sleep drives metabolite clearance from the adult brain. *Science*, 342, 373–377.

Yee, J. R., Kenkel, W. M., Frijling, J. L., Dodhia, S., Onishi, K. G., Tovar, S. et al. (2016). Oxytocin promotes functional coupling between paraventricular nucleus and both sympathetic and parasympathetic cardioregulatory nuclei. *Hormones and Behavior*, 80, 82–91. doi:10.1016/j.yhbeh.2016.01.010.

Yount, G. & Rachlin, K. (2014). A novel mouthwash protocol for noninvasive genomic analyses. *International Journal of Psychosocial Genomics: Consciousness and Health Research*, 1(1), 12–17.

Zeig, J. K. (Ed.) (1992). *The Evolution of Psychotherapy: The Second Conference*. New York: Routledge.

Index

Contents key

The birds in this book fall into 27 broad family groupings, each of which is identified by a typical silhouette at the top of the page. Birds are highly mobile and versatile creatures, and occasionally their anatomical adaptations to a particular way of life may outweigh family similarities. For example, swallows and swifts, so similar in appearance, are unrelated, and cranes (which look like herons) are actually related to the crakes and rails. In such cases, for ease of use the page heading silhouette is that which makes identification easiest for the birdwatcher.

Divers *(Gaviiformes)* *(pp. 18–19)* **and Grebes *(Podicipediformes)*** *(pp. 20–21)* are specialist diving birds of both fresh and salt waters, hunting fish and other small aquatic animals. Divers are slim and short-necked, grebes plumper: both have feet with lobed toes set back near a stumpy tail. Their wings are small, beat rapidly, and they fly relatively infrequently.

Fulmars and Shearwaters *(Procellariiformes)* *(pp. 22–23)* are oceanic seabirds with beaks showing clear signs of segmentation and with conspicuous paired tubular nostrils on the ridge. They are masters of energy-efficient gliding, and come ashore only to breed. They feed on fish and plankton caught near the surface.

Gannets and Cormorants *(Pelecaniformes)* *(pp 24–26)* are large fish-eating waterbirds, characterised by powerful beaks. Gannets are maritime, spend most time in the air and dive spectacularly; cormorants spend more time on the water (fresh or salt), dive from the surface, and pursue prey underwater propelled by their large feet with all four toes joined by webbing.

Herons and allies *(Ciconiiformes)* *(pp. 27–32)* **and Crane *(Gruiformes)*** *(p. 82)* are notably long-legged, long-necked wetland birds feeding on various small animals. Most are large, some huge. They have long, dagger-like beaks and stab at their prey. Some have adapted to drier habitats.

Swans, Geese and Ducks *(Anseriformes)* *(pp. 33–58)* form a uniform family, generally aquatic (fresh and salt waters), some carnivorous, others vegetarian. Many dabble for food, while others dive. All are characterised by 'duck-like' beaks and by their triangular webbed feet.

Birds of Prey *(Accipitriformes and Falconiformes)* *(pp. 59–72)* are often called 'raptors', and are characterised by relatively large effective eyes, markedly hooked beaks for tearing flesh (all are carnivorous or scavengers) and by long, usually bare lower legs ending in sharply hooked talons. Females are often substantially larger than males.

Game Birds (***Galliformes)*** *(pp. 73–79)* and **Rails *(Gruiformes)*** *(pp. 81–84)* are generally omnivorous and characterised by bulky bodies and comparatively small heads. Short rounded wings lift them rapidly into flight. Game birds are terrestrial, with upright stance, running powerfully. Rails are marshland birds, with long legs and large feet. Some swim well, some dive.

Waders *(Charadriiformes)* *(pp. 85–116)* are shoreline or marshland birds, feeding on a variety of small invertebrate animals. Most are relatively long-legged, with long toes. Most important identification features to observe (beside plumage colour) are beak length and shape, wing and tail flight patterns and leg colour.

Skuas, Gulls and Terns *(Charadriiformes)* *(pp. 117–130)* are long-winged web-footed seabirds. Skuas are oceanic or coastal, piratical or predatory, but can fish for themselves. Gulls are more omnivorous, larger species predatory, ancestrally coastal but now often occur inland. Terns are smaller, slimmer, shorter-legged, with longer slimmer wings, and dive from the air for small fish prey. Gulls often, skuas and terns rarely, rest on the water.

Auks *(Charadriiformes)* *(pp. 131–133)* are robustly dumpy, short-necked seabirds with short narrow wings and whirring flight. They feed on fish caught by diving from the surface and pursue their prey underwater, propelled by their wings.

Pigeons *(Columbiformes)* *(pp. 135–138)* are heavy-bodied, small-headed vegetarian (largely seed-eating) birds with fast direct flight. There is no distinction between pigeons and doves.

Cuckoo *(Cuculiformes)* *(p. 134)* and **Nightjar *(Caprimulgiformes)*** *(p. 146)* are long-tailed birds with short pointed wings. Both are short-legged and have small beaks, feeding on insects, which are caught in flight by nightjars.

Owls *(Strigiformes)* *(pp. 139–145)* are characteristically stocky, with short tails and an upright stance. Large heads and big eyes surrounded by a prominent facial disc indicate largely nocturnal life-styles. Small animal prey is captured in powerful sharp talons.

Kingfisher, Bee-eater, Hoopoe *(Coraciiformes)* *(pp. 152–154)* form a group with little in common anatomically, but all sufficiently brightly coloured to be readily identified. All are carnivorous, their prey ranging from insects to lizards and fish.

Woodpeckers *(Piciformes)* *(pp. 155–159)* form a close-knit group, featuring a strong straight dagger-like beak, long, strong central tail feathers used as a prop when perched on trunks, and powerful feet with toes distinctively arranged two pointing forward, two back. Their flight is undulating, their calls strident, their drumming far-carrying.

Larks, Pipits and Wagtails *(Passeriformes: Alaudidae, Motacillidae)* *(pp. 160–169)* are largely terrestrial, swift running birds of open habitats. Larks and pipits are heavily streaked and well camouflaged, with a long hind claw; wagtails are more colourful, with long incessantly wagged tails. All eat insects and small soil invertebrates, larks also eat vegetable matter.

Swallows and Martins *(Passeriformes: Hirundinidae)* *(pp. 149–151)* and **Swifts *(Apodiformes)*** *(pp. 147–148)* have short legs, small beaks, streamlined bodies and slim curved wings. Much time is spent on the wing, including catching insect prey and drinking. Swallows and swifts are taxonomically unrelated, but evolution has shaped the outward anatomy of both groups to suit a common life style.

Wren, Dipper, Dunnock *(Passeriformes: Troglodytidae, Cinclidae, Prunellidae)*
(pp. 171–1732) a grouping of convenience, rather than indicating close relationship. All, though, are predominantly brown in plumage, largely terrestrial in habit, (the dipper aquatic) and feed on small invertebrate animals, the wren using a finely pointed beak, the others more robust. The sexes are broadly similar.

Thrushes and Chats *(Passeriformes: Turdidae)*
(pp. 174–189) form an obviously coherent grouping with two major types. Thrushes are larger, stouter-legged and rather longer-tailed, often with a horizontal body posture. Chats are smaller, rounder in the body, with longer, slimmer legs and characteristically flick wings and tail. All share a medium-length pointed beak, stronger in some than others, and have a mixed diet of invertebrate animals augmented by berries.

Warblers and Crests *(Passeriformes: Sylviidae)*
(pp. 190–209) also form a coherent grouping of small birds, mostly migrants, dividing into distinctive sub-groups, the tiny generally greenish, active canopy-feeding leaf warblers and crests; the brown, sometimes streaked, reedbed Acrocephalus warblers and their allies; and the more robust and colourful Sylvia warblers, where the sexes differ in plumage. All have

shortish insectivorous beaks, and depend heavily on insect food, though turning readily to fruit to augment their diet in autumn.

Flycatchers *(Passeriformes: Muscicapidae)* *(pp. 210–211)*. Small, migrant, and rather warbler-like, flycatchers share the habit of catching insect prey in flight. They are short-legged, giving an elongated, horizontal perching posture. Their beaks though short and pointed are broad, with bristles round the gape to increase their catching area, and often close with an audible snap.

Tits and Allies *(Passeriformes: Paridae, Aegithalidae, Timaliidae)* *(pp. 212–219)*. True tits are small, active and agile woodland birds with relatively strong legs and a stubby but powerful beak well suited to an omnivorous diet. They nest in holes which they may either excavate or modify. Long-tailed and bearded tits are not closely related, but possess tit-like beaks and agility. These build complex nests in vegetation.

Nuthatch and Treecreeper *(Passeriformes: Sittidae and Certhiidae)* *(pp. 220–221)*. Short-legged and with strong feet, these spend much time clinging to trunks and branches. Nuthatches are woodpecker-like in beak and habits (but lack strong central tail feathers). Treecreepers have large eyes and longish, finely pointed beaks to extract insect prey from crevices in the bark.

Shrikes *(Passeriformes: Laniidae)* *(pp. 224–225)*. A close-knit group of relatively long-tailed, thrush-sized birds, with falcon-like hooked and notched beaks for grasping and tearing small animal and insect prey, which they sometimes impale on thorns for later consumption. Usually favour exposed perches.

Crows *(Passeriformes: Corvidae)* *(pp. 223, 226–232).* Large among the Passeriformes, crows are usually gregarious in habit and omnivorous in diet. All have powerful beaks, and are opportunist predators as well as scavengers. The true crows are black or blackish, related genera are more strikingly coloured (eg magpies, jays).

Oriole, Starlings, Waxwing *(Passeriformes: Oriolidae, Sturnidae, Bombycillidae)* *(pp. 222, 233, 170)* are similar in size and shape, flying fast and straight on triangular wings. Short-medium length straight beaks suit a mixed diet of fruit and invertebrate animals. Plumage and calls are best distinctive features.

Sparrows, Buntings and Finches *(Passeriformes: Passeridae, Emberizidae, Fringillidae)* *(pp. 234–253)* are small, stocky, rather short-legged, predominantly seed-eating birds, often gregarious. Their beaks are stout and roughly wedge-shaped. Upper mandible ridge is convex in sparrows; lower mandible distinctively larger than upper in buntings. In finches the precise size and shape of the generally triangular beak is a guide to diet and often useful in identification.

Please note the colours in the maps indicate the following: dark grey, resident; mid-grey, winter visitor; light grey, summer visitor.

Introduction

This book gives easily-used identification details linked to full colour photographs, plus information on habitat, food, song and behaviour, for over 230 European birds, covering the species that most birdwatchers could expect to see in a lifetime. This introduction provides advice on how birds use the various habitats in our countryside, on the equipment needed for birdwatching, and on how to get the best out of your birdwatching by developing all-important fieldcraft skills.

PARTS OF A BIRD

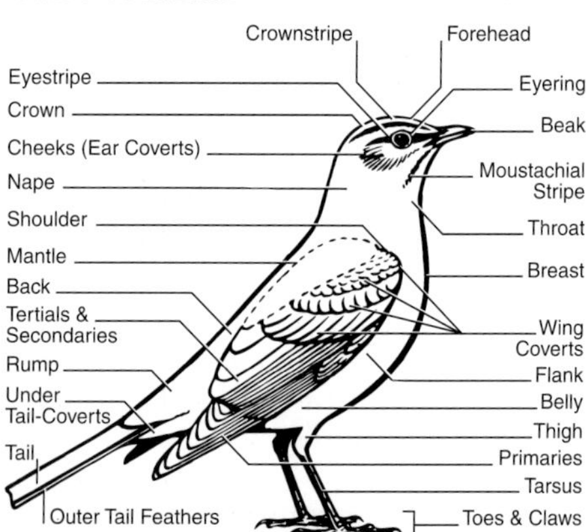

HABITATS AND MIGRATION

Unpredictability is very much a feature of bird life. The most distinctive character of birds (apart from their unique covering of feathers) is their ability to fly. Birds migrate to take advantage of opportunities in one part of the world which last only for part of the year – for example food being plentiful in one area in summer and another in winter. This explains the kaleidoscopic seasonal changes to be seen as migrants depart or arrive. Migration may be over huge distances, from the Arctic Circle to southern Africa or beyond, or be comparatively short-haul. Although this Gem guide covers the birds of the whole of Europe, many birds which do not breed or overwinter in your area will be seen as they come through on passage in spring and autumn. The ability to migrate (occasionally getting blown off course), coupled in many birds with an opportunistic approach to feeding, means that most birds do not necessarily conform to land boundaries laid down by geographers. Migration adds a great deal to the richness of birdwatching.

Nor do birds always stay neatly in the habitat categories that ecologists have attempted to draw for them. Although most of the ducks are associated with the sea or freshwater, kingfishers and dippers with rivers and streams, many birds are not so tidy. Kestrels may be seen over towns, coasts, moorland and motorway, and the gulls are as much at home on farmland and rubbish tip as at sea. Even Blue Tits, traditionally year-round woodland birds, may in midwinter be found in an oakwood, or (equally likely) feeding on an exotic food like peanuts in gardens (or opening milk bottles on town doorsteps to remove the cream), or feeding on insects hibernating in the shelter of the reed stems in a huge, tree-less marsh! In this guide, for each bird we identify the main habitats frequented.

PLUMAGE

Even the plumage of birds changes with time. Feathers are the most obvious external feature of birds, and in many cases are brightly coloured and patterned. Though to us attractive, this patterning serves practical purposes such as attracting a mate, defending a territory, or helping with camouflage. For birdwatchers, plumage is often one of the best identification aids, but there are reasons for caution: as a general rule, males tend to be brighter, and females and immatures duller, as for them camouflage is more important than display. But in many species, the males in winter may also be drab, their bright colours only appearing as the feathers gradually wear down early in the spring.

In most birds, particularly the smaller ones, wear and tear during the year is balanced each autumn by the process called moult, when old feathers gradually fall out and are replaced by new ones. Young birds, two or three months out of the nest, lose their juvenile, often speckled plumage and grow the coloured feathers of the adult for the first time. As this happens, their plumage is a confusing patchwork of old and new. In larger birds like some gulls and birds of prey, the change from juvenile to adult plumage is gradual over three or four years, giving a series of immature plumages making identification quite a problem.

BIRDWATCHING EQUIPMENT

Perhaps the one essential piece of equipment is a pair of binoculars: with these, distant black dots take on an identifiable shape and colour, or the beautiful feather detail of a Great Tit feeding on a garden peanut-holder can be revealed. Binoculars range from cheap to expensive, so a choice over cost and which magnification you will need must be made. There are a few simple guidelines: the binoculars are for you, so they should be comfortable in the hand, easy to use and comfortable hanging round your neck — so do test them outdoors before purchasing. Optical quality tends to increase with price, so with cheaper binoculars (many of which are perfectly satisfactory), check that there are no colour fringes to the images you see, and that telephone poles are not 'bent' by poor lens design. If you wear spectacles, check that you can use the binoculars without removing (or scratching) them. As to magnification, generally avoid more than x10 as they are sensitive to shaking, and let in rather little light. For garden, field and woodland watching, x7 or x8 should be right, if possible with a 'wide angle' field of view. For those who birdwatch mostly on moorland, the coast, estuaries or large reservoirs, x10 is probably the ideal, although these binoculars will be heavier.

A notebook in which you can jot down notes of numbers of species and plumage details and make sketches (particularly of birds new to you) is also a necessity. Take notes immediately you see a new bird: these could turn frustration into satisfaction as the identification problem is later resolved. A pocket fieldguide such as this Gem should always be with you - in your pocket.

As to clothing, common sense is the best guide, but there are points to remember. Avoid bright colours and noisy rustling fabrics. Remember that in exposed habitats, the weather can change (usually for the worse) with surprising speed, so it is always worth having ample warm, wind and waterproof gear. A heavy sweater and a lightweight nylon kagoul or anorak covers most circumstances. On the feet, trainers or baseball boots may be adequate, but on rougher terrain, walking boots may be desirable, and wellingtons are obviously a necessity in wetland habitats. And always take a supply of energy-rich food and drink on longer walks.

FIELDCRAFT

In fieldcraft, the aim is to see birds well without being seen yourself. Experienced birdwatchers rely very much on their ears to give early warning of what is about. Knowledge of bird calls and songs is an invaluable aid to identification: experience is the best teacher, but listening to commercially available recordings is an excellent foundation. Birds also use their ears — the less chatter, laughter and cracking of twigs, the closer you will get. Pause often to listen and look, preferably in a sheltered spot with a good view. Try to merge into the background, using natural features like banks, hedges and sea walls to avoid standing above the skyline. On the coast or in estuaries, check the tide times when planning your visit: often at low tide, the birds will be far out of sight on the mud, at high tide they may have flown off to roost. Remember it is tide times, not night or day, that govern the movements of birds in these habitats. Plan to visit on a rising (preferably) or falling tide for best views, or locate high-tide roosts by watching the flight-lines of waders heading for them — then you could get excellent views. In inland habitats like woodland, again a knowledge of behaviour can help. Birds tend to be active soon after dawn and before dusk, and in summer these are good times to see the singers, and most usefully, become familiar with their songs. In winter, many birds will gather just before dusk to go to roost. In contrast, the middle hours of the day can often be relatively quiet, with few birds moving, especially in a hot summer.

The hides which are a feature of many nature reserves often give excellent views and help you to become familiar with the birds of a particular habitat, and to gain an insight into their daily lives. It is easy to forget that a car, strategically parked, can provide similarly good views; or that our homes offer a privileged view of the birds nearby, especially if the garden has some drinking water and plenty of food both on the bird table and in the form of berried shrubs and other food plants. An amazing range of birds can visit even the average suburban garden.

Although fieldcraft is all about getting close to birds without causing disturbance, always remember to put the birds' interests first. Nesting birds not only demand special consideration, but are mostly protected by law, not just from egg collectors but from any disturbance. By all means watch and enjoy garden birds' nests or follow the progress of tit families using nestboxes. A bicycle mirror fixed to a stick allows you a good view of the nest and contents without leaving a tell-tale track through the surrounding vegetation. If the parent is sitting, pass quietly by and come back later. The Birdwatchers' Code also requires that special consideration is given to newly arrived migrants, tired after a long journey, and to all birds during severe winter weather. In both cases it is vital that they can feed uninterrupted, so remember their needs and do not be over-anxious for a good view. And of course, obey the Country Code, leaving gates shut, keeping to footpaths, controlling dogs, causing no fires and leaving no litter. In essence, respect and protect the whole countryside as a valuable asset.

Red-throated Diver

Gavia stellata

ADULT Large (55 cm), slender-bodied diving waterbird, well streamlined for swimming. Watch for slim, pale, upturned beak. Looks hump-backed in flight, with rapid deep wingbeats. Throat often looks blackish. In winter grey, flecked white above, white below. Sexes similar.

JUVENILE As winter adult.

HABITAT Breeds on N European coasts and moorland lakes, winters on coastal seas, also on fresh waters.

NEST Always close to water.

VOICE Cackling calls, breeding season only.

adult winter

GENERAL Widespread in habitat, never numerous. Black-throated Diver *(G. arctica):* straighter dark beak; Great Northern Diver *(G. immer):* heavy angular head, massive beak.

Great Northern Diver

Gavia immer

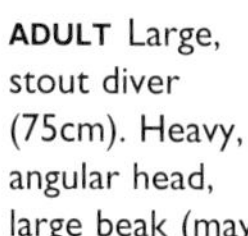

ADULT Large, stout diver (75cm). Heavy, angular head, large beak (may have a bump on the forehead). Long wings and feet, latter project beyond the tail in flight. Shallow wing beats. Black head and neck with check upperpart in summer; dark grey, with barring in wint Pale eye ring.

adult winter

JUVENILE As winter adult with scaly pattern on upperparts.

HABITAT Winters on Atlantic coasts.

NEST Mound of waterside vegetation.

VOICE Loud wailing calls in breeding season.

GENERAL Does not breed in Britain. Black-throated Diver *(G. arctica)* has grey head in summer, and no eyering in winter.

Great Crested Grebe

Podiceps cristatus

adult winter

ADULT Medium (45 cm), slim, slender-necked diving waterbird. Chestnut and black ruff and crest reduced to black crown in winter. Hump-backed in flight, showing white wing patches. In winter, pale grey back, with black, not yellow, dagger-like beak. Sexes similar.

JUVENILE Chick grey with black stripes; later as winter adult.

HABITAT Widespread except in far N; breeds and winters on large fresh waters; also winters on sea.

NEST Raft of waterweed moored to reeds.

VOICE Guttural croaks and honks in summer.

GENERAL Rarer Red-necked Grebe *(P. grisegena)*: smaller, with rufous neck and white cheeks in summer, grey with whitish cheeks in winter.

Little Grebe

Tachybaptus ruficollis

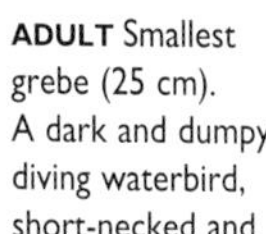

ADULT Smallest grebe (25 cm). A dark and dumpy diving waterbird, short-necked and tail-less in appearance. Chestnut throat often appears blackish. Watch for short dark beak, pale-tipped in summer. In winter, dull brown above, paler below. Rarely flies far except at night, escapes threats by submerging. Sexes similar.

adult winter

JUVENILE Chick grey with black stripes; later as winter adult.

HABITAT Widespread except far N; breeds and winters on fresh well-vegetated waters; some winter on sheltered coastal seas.

NEST Raft of waterweed, moored to reeds.

VOICE Far-carrying whinnying, usually when breeding.

GENERAL Commonest and most widespread grebe.

Manx Shearwater

Puffinus puffinus

ADULT Medium-sized (35cm). Uniformly black above and white below, No capped effect and no white at the base of the tail. Flies over water tilting from side-to-side. alternating long glides on stiffly-held wings, with shallow flaps.

JUVENILE As adult.

HABITAT Breeds in colonies on islands and cliffs facing the Atlantic. Range extends west and north outside breeding season.

NEST In burrows.

VOICE Loud wails, and cackles.

GENERAL Great Shearwater *(Puffinus gravis)* is larger, and has a black cap and a white patch at the base of the tail.

adult

Fulmar

Fulmarus glacialis

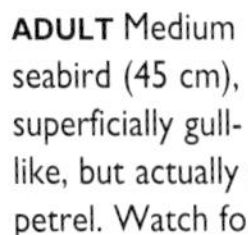

ADULT Medium seabird (45 cm), superficially gull-like, but actually a petrel. Watch for dumpy but well-streamlined body, dark eyes, and stubby yellow beak with tubular nostrils. Distinctive flight on short, straight all-pale wings, often held slightly downcurved. Glides often, with only occasional wingbeats except near cliffs. Sexes similar.

JUVENILE As adult.

HABITAT Breeds colonially on N and W coasts, usually on cliffs; winters in coastal and oceanic seas.

NEST Single large egg laid on bare ground.

VOICE Cackles and croons on breeding ledges.

GENERAL Widespread, locally common; a successful bird, spreads and colonizes new areas, even on buildings.

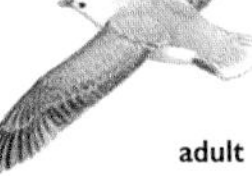

adult

Gannet

24 *Sula bassana*

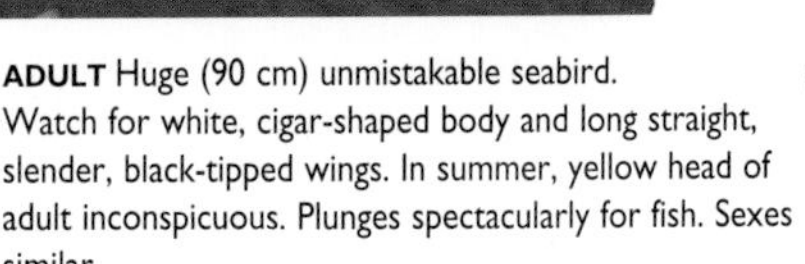

juvenile

ADULT Huge (90 cm) unmistakable seabird. Watch for white, cigar-shaped body and long straight, slender, black-tipped wings. In summer, yellow head of adult inconspicuous. Plunges spectacularly for fish. Sexes similar.

JUVENILE Grey-brown, flecked white becoming whiter, reaches adult plumage after three years.

HABITAT Breeds colonially on cliffs on N and W coasts, dispersing to winter at sea.

NEST Mound of seaweed on bare rocky ledge.

VOICE Harsh honks and grating calls at colony.

GENERAL Widespread, but breeding colonies few though sometimes enormous.

Cormorant

Phalacrocorax carbo

ADULT Huge (90 cm), dark, broad-winged seabird. Watch for thick-necked, heavy-beaked appearance; whitish face of breeding adult. Swims well, diving frequently, emerging to dry wings in heraldic stance. Flies straight, often in groups in V formation. Sexes similar.

JUVENILE Dark brown above with paler underside.

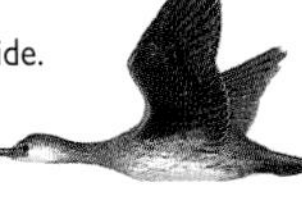

immature

HABITAT Breeds colonially on most rocky coasts, occasionally in trees beside large fresh waters. Winters on coastal seas and larger inland waters.

NEST Untidy mound of seaweed and flotsam on rocks.

VOICE Deep grunts at colony.

GENERAL Widespread in most coastal waters, including shallow muddy bays and estuaries avoided by Shags.

Shag

Phalacrocorax aristotelis

ADULT Large (75 cm), dark, slim-bodied seabird often with greenish sheen. Watch for slender neck and comparatively slim but hooked beak. Has tufted crest in spring. Lacks white patches of Cormorant (p.22), but has yellow gape. Swims well, diving frequently. Sexes similar.

JUVENILE Dark brown above, unlike Cormorant only slightly paler on underparts.

HABITAT Breeds colonially on rocky coasts. Winters on coastal seas, rarely on inland fresh waters.

NEST Bulky and untidy mound of seaweed, often under rocky overhang.

VOICE Harsh grunts at colony.

immature

GENERAL Widespread, but usually less numerous than Cormorant, favouring deeper and clearer sea.

Bittern

Botaurus stellaris

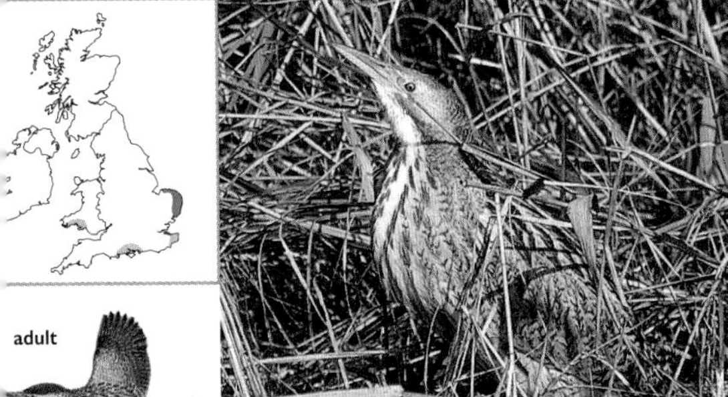

adult

ADULT Large (75 cm), extremely well-camouflaged, brown heron. Finely streaked and mottled plumage strikingly beautiful at close range. Watch for short, dagger-shaped beak and hunched posture. Despite its size, slips imperceptibly and silently between reed stems: if disturbed, freezes in upright posture. Sexes similar.

JUVENILE As adult, but duller.

HABITAT Year-round resident much of central Europe, summer visitor further N. Favours large freshwater reedbeds.

NEST Reed platform among the reeds.

VOICE Distinctive 'foghorn' booming in breeding season.

GENERAL Inconspicuous, more often heard than seen. Declining in numbers in N and W of range.

Little Egret

28 *Egretta garzetta*

ADULT Large (55 cm), slim, all-white heron. Watch for black dagger-like beak, black legs with yellow feet distinctive in flight. Breeding adult has fine filamentous summer plumes on throat and back. Sexes similar.

JUVENILE Duller white, lacking plumes.

HABITAT Summer visitor, breeding colonially in S European wetlands, sometimes resident year-round.

adult

NEST Bulky, in trees overhanging water.

VOICE Honks and shrieks in breeding season.

GENERAL Locally quite common. Rare Great White Egret *(E. alba)*: larger, with heavy yellow beak. Scarce Cattle Egret *(Bubulcus ibis)*: dumpy, with yellow beak and legs. Squacco Heron *(Ardeola ralloides)*: brown-streaked crown and buff back contrasting with white wings. All largely restricted to S Europe.

Grey Heron

Ardea cinerea 29

ADULT Huge (90 cm), long-legged, long-necked heron. Broad, heavily fingered wings and ponderous flight, legs outstretched but neck folded back between shoulders. Paces slowly through shallow water, stabbing fish and other prey. Yellow dagger-like beak may be orange in summer, when plumes on neck and back conspicuous. Sexes similar.

JUVENILE As adult, but drabber, no crest or plumes.

HABITAT Year-round resident or migrant over much of Europe, summer visitor to N and E. Favours lakes or marshland; in winter also coasts and garden ponds.

NEST Bulky, in trees or reedbeds.

VOICE Amazing cacophony of honks and shrieks at nest, elsewhere typically frank if disturbed.

GENERAL Widespread throughout Europe.

adult

White Stork

30 *Ciconia ciconia*

DISTRIBUTION Summer visitor to SW and central/NE Europe.

ADULT Huge (100 cm) and superficially heron-like with long neck and legs and powerful dagger-like beak, but storks fly neck outstretched on broad, heavily fingered wings. Black and dirty-white plumage: breeding adult has shaggy throat feathers in summer. Sexes similar.

adult

JUVENILE As drab adult, brown beak and legs.

HABITAT Feeds fields, marshland, nests in trees or buildings.

NEST Conspicuously bulky.

VOICE Rarely vocal: grunts and hisses at nest.

GENERAL Beak clattering displays between pairs at nest more than compensate for lack of true vocalization. Migrates in flocks over long-established routes. Regular in breeding areas, scarce elsewhere.

Spoonbill

Platalea leucorodia 31

ISTRIBUTION
ummer visitor to videly separated najor wetlands in W, north-central, nd SE Europe.

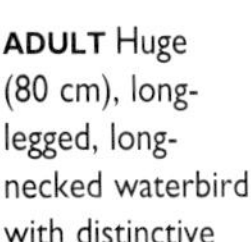

ADULT Huge (80 cm), long-legged, long-necked waterbird with distinctive beak and feeding technique as it sifts through mud and shallows in search of molluscs. All-white plumage, legs and beak black. Usually flies in groups, necks outstretched, in V-formation. Sexes similar.

JUVENILE As drab adult, but with black wingtips conspicuous in flight.

HABITAT Feeds in fresh, brackish or saline waters.

NEST Breeds colonially, usually on reed platforms in extensive reedbeds.

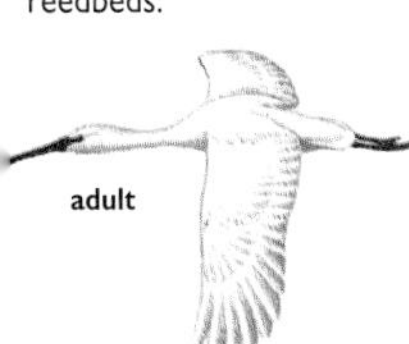

VOICE Rarely vocal: grunts at nest.

GENERAL Regular at breeding sites; vagrant elsewhere.

Greater Flamingo

32 *Phoenicopterus ruber*

DISTRIBUTION Year-round resident or short-haul migrant to breeding areas in S Spain and France.

ADULT Huge (125 cm), unmistakable waterbird, with very long pink legs and long neck, held outstretched in flight when rich pink wings show to best effect. Usually in flocks, flies in loose V-formation. Distinctive banana-shaped beak is held upside down under water, filtering out food.

JUVENILE Greyer, pink after a year or two.

HABITAT Favours extensive, usually shallow, saline or brackish lagoons with mudflats.

adult

NEST Like miniature volcano, built of mud.

VOICE Goose-like honks and cackles.

GENERAL Locally common near breeding sites, vagrant elsewhere. Other flamingo species regularly escape from waterfowl collections, and may turn up anywhere.

Mute Swan

Cygnus olor 33

ADULT Huge (150 cm) and familiar. Watch for S-curved neck and orange-red beak with black knob more prominent in male. Arches wings like sails in defence of territory or young. In flight, broad all-white wings produce distinctive creaking sound. Long pattering take-off run. Sexes broadly similar.

JUVENILE As adult, but grey-buff.

adult

HABITAT Widespread across N and W Europe, summer visitor in N, year-round resident elsewhere. Favours fresh waters of most types, including urban areas. Occasional only on sheltered seas.

NEST Bulky mound of reeds etc beside water.

VOICE Often silent, hisses, grunts in breeding territory.

GENERAL Widespread, only locally numerous. Numbers currently recovering after decline due to lead poisoning.

Whooper Swan

34 *Cygnus cygnus*

Whooper swan – adult

Bewick's swan – adult

ADULT Huge (150 cm) all-white swan. Watch for long, straight neck and wedge-shaped head profile. Beak characteristically black and yellow. Wings quiet in flight, but family parties are wonderfully vociferous. Sexes similar.

JUVENILE As adult, but pale grey-buff.

HABITAT Summer visitor breeding on Arctic tundra, migrant or winter visitor to NW Europe, primarily Britain and Ireland. Favours marshland, estuaries and larger fresh waters.

NEST Bulky mound of vegetation near water.

VOICE Vocal; bugle-like whooping calls.

GENERAL Scarce, but locally regular. Bewick's swan *(C. bewickii)*: much smaller (120 cm), with short, straight neck and shorter black and yellow beak, musical goose-like honking calls.

Pink-footed Goose

Anser brachyrhynchus

ADULT Large (65 cm), neatly-built grey goose. Watch for distinctive dark brown head and short neck, stubby dark beak with pink marking. Legs pink. In flight, grey back and forewings contrast with dark flight feathers. Sexes similar.

JUVENILE Similar to adult.

HABITAT Breeds on tundra, usually on rocky outcrops. Winters across NW Europe on fresh and salt marshland, open farmland, often roosting on large lakes.

NEST Down-lined cup on ground.

VOICE Vocal; distinctive ***wink-wink-wink***.

GENERAL Locally numerous. Scarcer Bean Goose *(A. fabalis)*: similar, but larger (75 cm), longer necked, with large, dark, wedge-shaped beak with yellow markings, legs orange.

adult

White-fronted Goose

Anser albifrons

ADULT Large (70 cm), grey goose. Watch for adult's white forehead and blackish barring on breast. Beak pink (Russian race) or orange-yellow (Greenland race). In flight shows uniformly grey-brown wings with darker flight feathers. Sexes similar.

adult

JUVENILE Lacks white face and black barring.

HABITAT Breeds on high Arctic tundra, winters on NW and extreme SE European coastal and sometimes inland marshes and open farmland.

NEST Down-lined cup on ground.

VOICE Vocal; high-pitched, musical yelping.

GENERAL Fairly widespread, usually in flocks and locally numerous. Rare Lesser White-fronted Goose *(A. erythropus)*: smaller, with more white on head and yellow eye-ring.

Greylag Goose

Anser anser

adult

ADULT Largest (80 cm) and heaviest-built of the grey geese. Watch for thick neck and dark brown head, pink legs and heavy pink (eastern race) or orange (western) beak. In flight shows pale grey forewing patches. Sexes similar.

JUVENILE As dull adult with brown beak and legs.

HABITAT Summer visitor, year-round resident or winter visitor in NW Europe, winter visitor in S. Breeds on moorland and tundra, winters on farmland and coastal marshes. May roost on freshwater lakes.

NEST Bulky, down-lined cup on ground.

VOICE Vocal; cackling and gabbling calls indicate its ancestry of the farmyard goose.

GENERAL Fairly widespread, frequently introduced by man. Locally numerous.

Canada Goose

Branta canadensis

ADULT Largest (75 cm) black goose. Watch for long black neck and head with white chin patch. In flight, uniformly scaly brown wings contrast with black and white rump and tail. Sexes similar.

JUVENILE Resembles dull adult.

HABITAT Occasional vagrants from N America winter with grey geese on marshland. Most European birds (NW and W areas) derive from stock introduced by waterfowl enthusiasts and are year-round residents on larger fresh waters and adjacent grassland.

NEST Bulky down-lined cup, usually near water.

VOICE Strident ***aah-honk***.

GENERAL Though restricted to a handful of NW European countries, is increasing in numbers and spreading.

adult

Brent Goose

Branta bernicla

ADULT Large (60 cm), very dark goose. Looks short necked, with stubby beak. Adult has white collar mark. Breast grey in extreme W birds, blackish elsewhere. Watch for all-black neck and wings contrasting with white rump in flight. Sexes similar.

adult

JUVENILE As adult, white bars on back and wings.

HABITAT Breeds on high Arctic tundra, winte on W estuaries, sheltered bays and nearby fiel

NEST Down-lined cup on ground near sea.

VOICE Vocal; grumbling ***rrruk***.

GENERAL Local, but often numerous winter visitor. Barnacle Goose (*B. leucopsis*): similar size, scaly grey back, white belly and white face contrast with black neck. Winter visitor, favours coastal grassland.

Shelduck

40 *Tadorna tadorna*

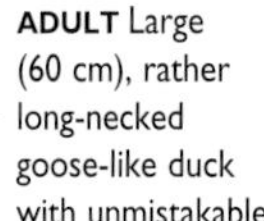

ADULT Large (60 cm), rather long-necked goose-like duck with unmistakable black, white and chestnut plumage. Looks pied at a distance and in flight, when chestnut areas are less conspicuous. Sexes similar, but drake has knob on red beak, duck may have white face patch in summer.

JUVENILE Duckling striped black-and-white, immature greyish above, white below.

adult

HABITAT Summer visitor to S Scandinavia, year-round resident in W, winter visitor further S. Favours estuaries and sheltered sandy or muddy bays, occasional inland.

NEST Usually concealed in burrow, deserted building or dense vegetation; down-lined.

VOICE Whistles and barking ***ack-ack***.

GENERAL Widespread coastally, often numerous.

Wigeon

Anas penelope 41

adult female

adult male

ADULT Medium (45 cm), surface-feeding duck. Drake handsome, duck subdued in camouflage plumage of distinctive cinnamon browns. In flight, both sexes show green speculum; duck shows distinctive white belly, drake bold white patches on inner half of wing.

JUVENILE Resembles female, as does eclipse male.

HABITAT Summer visitor to N, breeding beside tundra pools. Winter visitor to much of central and S Europe, occurring on lakes, marshes, estuaries and coastal seas.

NEST Well-concealed, down-lined grass cup on ground.

VOICE Drake has characteristic piercing whistle; duck a soft, low purr.

GENERAL Widespread and often common in winter.

Gadwall

42 *Anas strepera*

adult femal

adult male

ADULT Large (50 cm), surface-feeding duck, apparently drab except at close range, when beautiful detail is apparent. Drake appears overall dull grey, duck well-camouflaged in browns. Watch for black undertail (drake) and distinctive black and white speculum in both sexes in flight.

JUVENILE Resembles female, as does eclipse male.

HABITAT Year-round resident in some central and W areas, summer visitor to N, winter visitor to S Europe. Breeds on marshland beside large fresh waters; winters in similar areas and on estuaries and sheltered coastal waters.

NEST Well-concealed, down-lined grass cup on ground.

VOICE Rare; drake whistles softly, duck quacks.

GENERAL Widespread, rarely numerous, but increasing.

Teal

Anas crecca

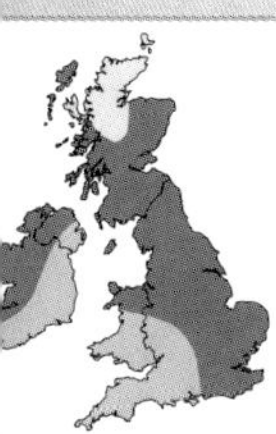

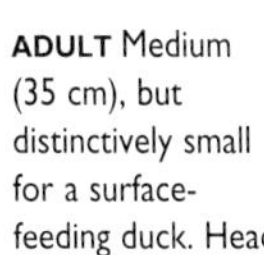

ADULT Medium (35 cm), but distinctively small for a surface-feeding duck. Head pattern of drake clear only at close range. Duck finely streaked grey-brown. Both sexes have white-bordered dark black and green speculum.

JUVENILE Resembles female, as does eclipse male.

HABITAT Year-round resident over much of Europe, summer migrant in far N and winter visitor in extreme S. Breeds on marshland with pools; winters on well-vegetated fresh waters, and on estuaries and sheltered coasts.

NEST Well-concealed in waterside vegetation.

VOICE Drake has distinctive bell-like call and harsh ***krit***; duck a harsh quack.

GENERAL Widespread, often common. Fast and agile, jinking flight is useful guide.

Mallard

Anas platyrhynchos

ADULT Large (58 cm), familiar, surface-feeding duck, the drake brightly coloured, the duck well camouflaged in browns and fawns. In flight, both sexes show purple speculum, bordered in white, on trailing edge of inner half of wing.

JUVENILE Resembles female, as does eclipse male.

HABITAT Year-round resident over most of Europe, summer migrant in far N. Seen on all types of fresh waters anywhere; estuaries and coastal seas, especially in winter.

NEST Of grass, lined with dark down, well concealed in ground vegetation, often close to water.

VOICE Drake whistles quietly; duck quacks harshly.

GENERAL Widespread and common, one of the most adaptable of all birds, associates readily with man.

adult male

adult female

Shoveler

Anas clypeata 45

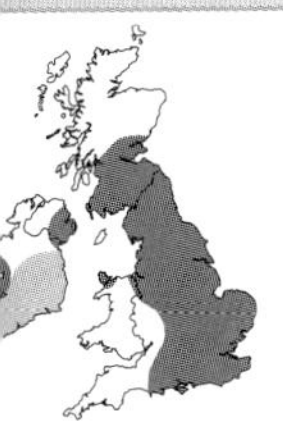

ADULT Medium (50 cm), surface-feeding duck, swimming low in the water, head tilted down because of massive spoon-shaped beak. Green head of drake looks black at a distance. Duck pale brown with darker speckling. In flight, watch for rapid wingbeats and head-up, tail-down attitude in both sexes, and pale grey forewing patches.

JUVENILE Resembles female, as does eclipse male.

HABITAT Summer visitor to N and E Europe, year-round resident in W, winter visitor to S. Breeds and winters on marshes with shallow muddy lakes, also on reservoirs and sheltered coasts.

NEST Well-concealed, down-lined grass cup on ground.

VOICE Drake ***tuk-tuk***; duck a quiet quack.

GENERAL Widespread and fairly common.

adult female

adult male

Garganey

Anas querquedula

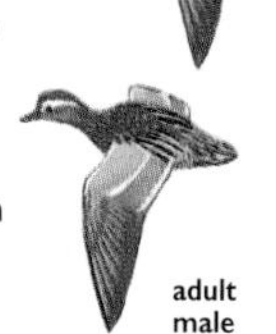

adult female

adult male

ADULT Medium (38 cm), surface-feeding duck, only slightly larger than Teal (p.43). Drake striking, watch for bold white eyestripe, duck camouflaged in browns, but has striped face pattern (distinguishes from Teal). In flight, both sexes show distinctive pale blue-grey forewing and white-bordered green speculum.

JUVENILE Resembles female, as does eclipse male.

HABITAT Summer visitor to extensive reedy freshwater wetlands in central and N Europe.

NEST On ground near water, concealed in dense vegetation.

VOICE Drake has distinctive crackling rattle; duck a short quack.

GENERAL Widespread, rarely numerous: unlike Teal, occasional on brackish water and rare on salt waters.

Pintail

Anas acuta

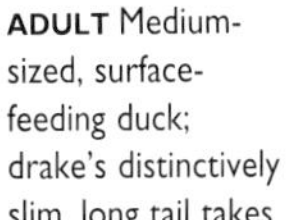

ADULT Medium-sized, surface-feeding duck; drake's distinctively slim, long tail takes the overall length to 70 cm. Watch for white neck mark, prominent even at a distance. Duck pale grey-brown with bold, dark brown markings. Both sexes slim and elongated in flight, with inconspicuous brown speculum on trailing edge of narrow wings.

JUVENILE Resembles female, as does eclipse male.

HABITAT Year-round resident in central and W Europe, summer visitor to N and winter visitor to S. Breeds beside moorland and tundra pools, winters on sheltered coastal waters, estuaries and marshes, occasionally on fresh waters.

NEST Well-concealed, down-lined grass cup on ground.

VOICE Rare; drake whistles, duck growls.

GENERAL Widespread, but rarely very numerous.

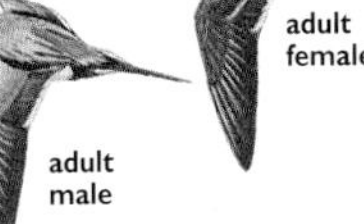

Scaup

48 *Aythya marila*

adult female

adult male

ADULT Medium (45 cm) diving duck. Watch for finely-marked grey back of drake. Duck brown above, shading to white on belly; rich brown head with large white face-patch at base of beak. Note golden eyes and grey beak in both sexes. In flight, both sexes show bold white wingbar.

JUVENILE Resembles female, as does eclipse male, lacking white face patch.

HABITAT Summer visitor breeding on N tundra; in winter favours NW coastal seas, occasionally on fresh waters.

NEST Well-concealed down-lined grass cup on ground.

VOICE Rarely vocal; drake uses low whistle, duck a double quack.

GENERAL Generally scarce, but locally common in winter.

Tufted Duck

Aythya fuligula

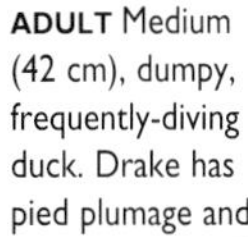

ADULT Medium (42 cm), dumpy, frequently-diving duck. Drake has pied plumage and drooping crest. Duck also compactly built, dark brown above, paler on belly, sometimes with slight crest and small white patch at base of beak. Watch for narrow white wingbar in flight.

JUVENILE Resembles female, as does eclipse male.

HABITAT Summer visitor to N Europe, year-round resident in W, winter visitor in S. Breeds beside reedy lakes and ponds, winters on many types of still, fresh waters.

NEST Well-concealed, down-lined grass cup on ground.

VOICE Rarely vocal; drake uses soft whistle, duck a growl.

GENERAL Widespread, familiar and often common.

Common Scoter

50 *Melanitta nigra*

adult female

adult male

ADULT Medium (50 cm), heavily-built sea duck. Watch for heavy beak, slightly knobbed and black and yellow in summer drake. Unique among wildfowl in its all-black plumage. Duck dark brown with paler buff cheeks. Flies in straggling lines low over sea, showing no wing markings.

JUVENILE Resembles female, cheeks less marked.

HABITAT Breeds beside lakes and rivers on moorland and tundra in N and NW Europe, winters at sea on Atlantic coasts.

NEST Well-concealed, down-lined cup on ground.

VOICE Croons and growls on breeding grounds.

GENERAL Regular, locally common. Scarce Velvet Scoter (*M. fusca*): similar in most respects, but in flight both sexes show bold white patch on wing.

Goldeneye

Bucephala clangula 51

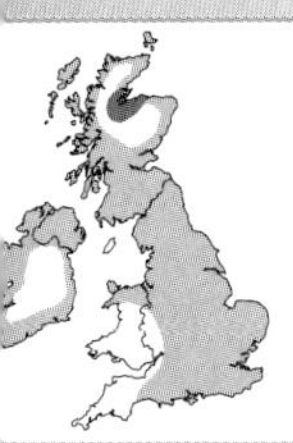

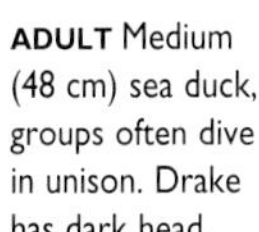

ADULT Medium (48 cm) sea duck, groups often dive in unison. Drake has dark head, white face spot. Duck brown above, dark brown head and white belly. Watch for bulky, angular head profile in both sexes. In flight, whirring noisy wingbeats and white wing patches are conspicuous.

JUVENILE Resembles female, as does eclipse male.

HABITAT Summer visitor or year-round resident in N Europe, winter visitor elsewhere. Favours marshy forests for breeding; winters at sea or on larger fresh waters.

NEST Down-lined cup in old burrow or hollow tree; uses nestboxes well above ground level.

VOICE Rarely vocal; nasal quacks or low growls.

GENERAL Regular in both winter and summer, but never numerous.

Long-tailed Duck

Clangula hyemalis

ADULT Distinctive medium (50 cm) sea duck – but one third of this is tail. Winter drake is largely white with brown patches (note two-tone beak); summer drake largely chocolate brown with white cheeks and flanks. Duck in summer is brown above, white below, with white face patches; winter duck has more white on head and neck.

JUVENILE Resembles winter female.

HABITAT Breeds beside lakes in tundra of far N Europe, wintering on N and W coastal seas, very occasionally on larger fresh waters inland.

NEST Well-concealed, down-lined grass cup on ground.

VOICE Noisy; high-pitched goose-like honks.

GENERAL Locally regular, in places fairly common.

Eider

Somateria mollissima

ADULT Large (60 cm), sea duck with wedge-shaped head profile. Dives for shellfish. Drake strikingly pied in flight, with black belly; duck well camouflaged in browns, shows white underside to forewing. Immature drakes blotched black and white. Flies heavily and low over the sea.

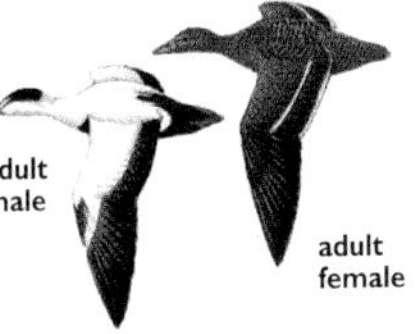

JUVENILE Resembles female; eclipse and young males gradually acquire white plumage.

HABITAT Breeds on N coasts, winters S to Biscay.

NEST Grassy cup with copious downy lining, on ground.

VOICE Vocal; drake uses loud moaning crooning, duck harsh ***corrr***.

GENERAL A typical N coastal bird; fairly widespread and locally common.

54

Red-crested Pochard

Netta rufina

DISTRIBUTION Scarce resident; wild birds sometimes visit from mainland Europe

adult male

ADULT Large (55 cm) diving duck, but dives infrequently and behaves like a surface-feeder. Drake striking, duck brown, paler on belly; watch for dark brown crown contrasting with distinctive pale grey cheeks. In flight, both sexes show bold broad white wingbar running the length of the wing.

JUVENILE Resembles female, as does eclipse male, but pale cheeks less prominent.

HABITAT Year-round resident and winter visitor to reed-fringed fresh or brackish wetlands in S Europe, scarce visitor or vagrant further N.

adult female

NEST Well-concealed, down-lined grass cup on ground.

VOICE Harsh ***kurr***.

GENERAL Uncommon, sometimes plentiful in winter.

Pochard

Aythya ferina

adult male

ADULT Medium (45 cm) diving duck. Watch for characteristic wedge-shaped head profile. Drake sombre but distinctive, in grey, black and chestnut; duck rufous-brown above, paler on face, throat and belly. In flight, both sexes show greyish wings with indistinct paler grey wingbars.

JUVENILE Resembles female, as does eclipse male.

HABITAT Summer visitor to N and E Europe, resident year-round in some W areas, winter visitor further S.

NEST Well-concealed, down-lined grass cup on ground.

VOICE Rarely vocal; duck uses hoarse growl in flight.

GENERAL Widespread, locally common.

adult female

Smew

Mergus albellus

ADULT Small sawbill duck (41cm). Adult male white with a large head and small, silver beak; narrow black lines over back and a black mask over the eyes. Black markings are much more striking in flight. Female grey with maroon head and white cheeks.

JUVENILE As adult female.

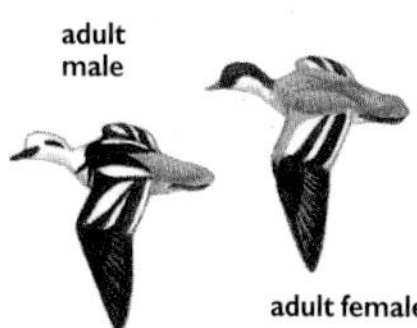

HABITATS Breeds by lakes and ponds in northern forests.

NEST Tree hole lined with feathers and down.

VOICE Grunts while courting.

GENERAL Occasional visitor to Britain in winter. Female may be confused with Red-crested Pochard *(Netta rufina)* or Slavonian Grebe *(Podiceps auritus)*.

Red-breasted Merganser

Mergus serrator

ADULT Large (55 cm) sawbill duck with slim, cigar-shaped body, long slim beak (with serrated edges to grip fish) and untidy bristling crest. Dives frequently. Drake subtly elegant, duck has brown head. In flight, both sexes look elongated, showing white patches on inner wings.

JUVENILE Resembles dull female, as does eclipse male.

HABITAT Summer visitor to far N Europe, year-round resident in W. Breeds along coasts and beside fast-moving fresh waters; winters in similar areas, at sea, and on larger inland fresh waters such as reservoirs.

NEST Down-lined in burrow or hollow.

VOICE Normally silent.

GENERAL Fairly widespread, regular, but rarely numerous.

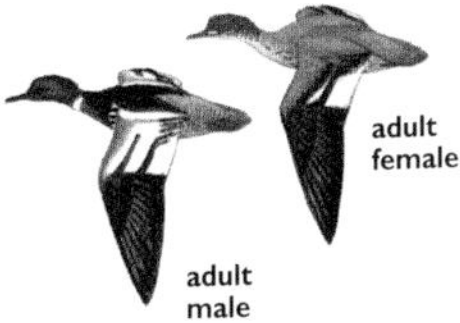

adult female

adult male

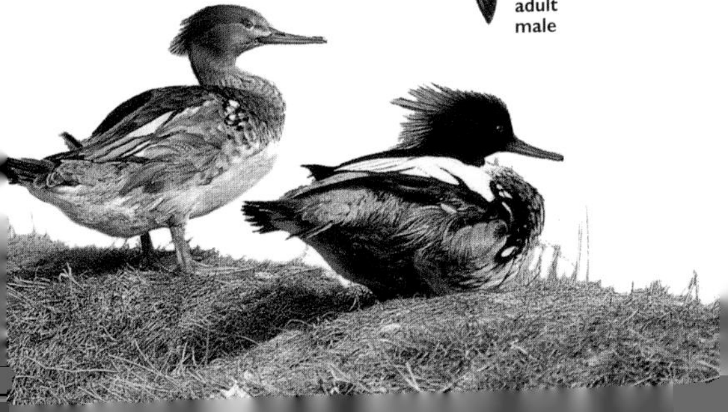

Goosander

Mergus merganser

adult female

adult male

ADULT Large (65 cm) sawbill duck, slim-beaked with a streamlined, cigar-shaped body. Dives frequently. Drake strikingly white at a distance, often tinged pink at close range. Both sexes have bulky but smooth crests, giving angular head profiles. Duck has silver-grey body, white on belly, and chestnut head. Both show white on inner wing in flight.

JUVENILE Resembles dull female, as does eclipse male.

HABITAT Summer visitor to far N Europe, wintering in NW. Breeds beside fast-moving rivers, winters on larger fresh waters inland, rarely on salt waters.

NEST Down-lined, in burrow or hollow tree. Normally silent.

GENERAL Fairly widespread, regular, but rarely numerous.

Honey Buzzard

Pernis apivorus

ADULT Large (52 cm), buzzard-like raptor. Plumage variable. Watch for small grey head with inconspicuous beak and, in flight, boldly barred underwing and black 'wrist' patches. Tail usually held closed, looking long and narrow with three bold bars, one at tip, two near base. Sexes similar.

JUVENILE Variable (as adult), but browner.

HABITAT Summer visitor to forests and woodland over much of Europe except extreme W; migrant or vagrant elsewhere.

NEST Bulky structure of sticks high in tree.

VOICE Rapid squeaky ***kee-kee*** or ***kee-aa***.

GENERAL Widespread, but never numerous. Usually solitary, but occurs in groups along migration routes.

adult

Hen Harrier

60 *Circus cyaneus*

adult male

adult fem

ADULT Medium (48 cm), long-winged raptor. Watch for large, white rump patch on generally brown female. Male pale grey with white rump and black wing tips. Hunts low, gliding on stiff wings held in shallow V, tail long, usually held unfanned, looking narrow.

JUVENILE Browner than female, more dark streaks.

HABITAT Summer visitor to N and NE Europe, year-round resident or winter visitor elsewhere. Breeds in dense ground vegetation (eg heather). Favours open landscapes including moorland, young forestry plantations, marshland (especially in winter). Roosts communally in winter.

NEST Rough grassy platform on ground.

VOICE Chattering ***kee-kee-kee***, but rarely vocal.

GENERAL Widespread, rarely numerous.

Marsh Harrier

Circus aeruginosus

ADULT Large (53 cm), broad-winged raptor; male brown above, chestnut below, with distinctive long grey tail and grey, brown and black wing pattern in flight. Female has uniformly rich brown body and wings, with pale creamy-white crown and throat. Usually hunts low, gliding over reedbeds, wings held stiffly in a shallow V.

JUVENILE Paler brown with heavy darker streaks.

HABITAT Summer visitor to central and E Europe, year-round resident in S. Favours extensive wetlands with reedbeds.

NEST Platform of reeds deep in reedbed.

VOICE Rarely heard ***kee-yah***.

GENERAL Broader-winged and more small-eagle-like than most harriers. Widespread, locally quite common.

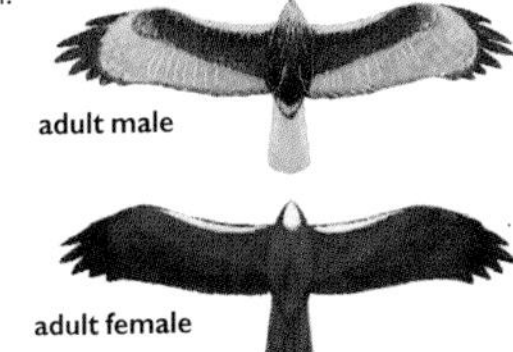

Red Kite

Milvus milvus

ADULT Large (62 cm), long-winged raptor with long, deeply forked, reddish tail distinctive in flight. Watch for pale head when perched. In flight, underwings show large whitish patches near tips, contrasting with black primary feathers. Often soars. Sexes similar.

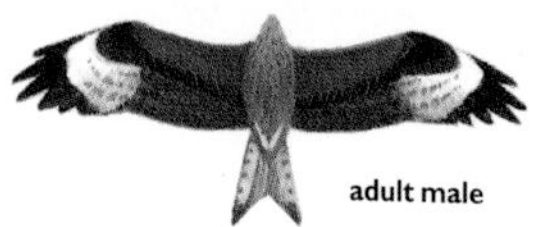

adult male

JUVENILE Resembles adult, but duller and browner.

HABITAT Widespread summer visitor to central Europe, year-round resident in S regions and extreme W (Wales). Favours open woodland and farmland, often in hills.

NEST Bulky, untidy structure of twigs etc., high in a tree.

VOICE Repetitive buzzard-like ***tee-tee-teear***.

GENERAL Though widespread, usually solitary and rarely numerous.

Montagu's Harrier

Circus pygargus

ADULT Medium (40 cm), but small and slim for a harrier. Male like Hen Harrier (p.60), but note black bar on trailing edge of wing, chestnut streaks on flanks and no white rump. Female similar to female Hen Harrier, but white rump patch smaller; has distinctive owl-like face markings. Flight more buoyant than other harriers, wings narrower and more pointed.

JUVENILE As female, but richer-brown, less boldly marked.

HABITAT Summer visitor to S and central Europe; breeds in open habitats from farmland to marshes, moors and sand-dunes.

NEST Grassy platform on ground.

VOICE Shrill ***keck-keck-keck***.

GENERAL Widespread, but erratic, rarely common.

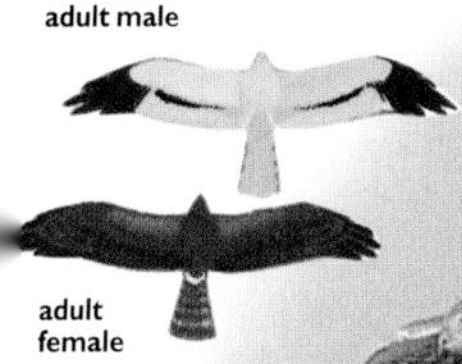

adult male

adult female

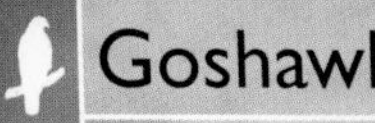

Goshawk

64 *Accipiter gentilis*

ADULT Large (55 cm), heavily-built, but fast-flying hawk, larger female almost buzzard-sized. Watch for prominent eyestripes meeting on nape to give capped appearance, and fluffy white undertail coverts. In flight, note long, broad rounded wings and long tail. Usually among trees, but soars in tight circles at height in spring.

juvenile

JUVENILE Resembles adult, but browner and more scaly above, buff below with heavy streaking.

HABITAT Year-round resident over much of Europe. Favours extensive forests or woodlands.

NEST Platform of twigs high in tree.

VOICE Chattering ***kek-kek-kek*** or geck.

GENERAL Widespread, but generally scarce. Easiest seen in spring when displaying.

Sparrowhawk

ADULT Medium (35 cm), fast-flying hawk. Watch for short, rounded wings, long four-barred tail and distinct eyestripes. Upright perching stance. Smaller male greyish above, barred reddish on breast, larger female barred dark brown on breast, grey-brown back.

JUVENILE As female, but streaked (not barred) on breast.

HABITAT Year-round resident over most of Europe, summer visitor to far N. Favours farmland with trees and woodland/forest of all types.

NEST Platform of twigs, high in tree.

VOICE Sharp, fast ***keck-keck-keck***.

GENERAL Widespread, locally fairly common, increasing after recent pesticide-induced drastic decline.

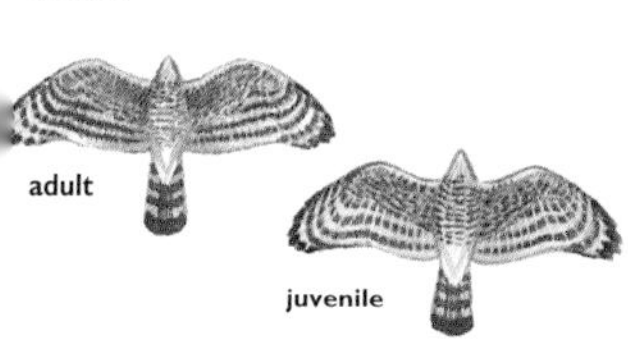

66 Buzzard

Buteo buteo

ADULT Large (55 cm) raptor with long, broad, heavily fingered wings. Plumage very variable, usually dark brown above, paler with dark streaks below. Soars: watch for short fanned and rounded tail, black patches in paler areas of underwing at 'wrist'. Sexes similar.

JUVENILE Similar to adult.

HABITAT Year-round resident over much of Europe, summer visitor to far N. Favours open country including mountains and moorland, often with tracts of woodland.

NEST Bulky twig structure in tree or occasionally on ground.

VOICE Distinctive far-carrying cat-like mewing.

GENERAL Widespread, locally fairly common. Perches solid and upright, on posts or telegraph poles. Visits carrion.

Golden Eagle

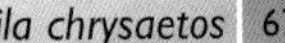

Aquila chrysaetos

adult

ADULT Huge (85 cm) raptor with big beak and long, broad, heavily fingered wings. Adult brown, golden feathers on head and neck visible at close range. Soars frequently; watch for long, broad tail, prominent head, and wings held slightly above horizontal with upcurled tips. Sexes similar.

JUVENILE As adult, but with white patches in wing and black-tipped white tail.

HABITAT Remote and extensive mountain areas, often with forest, throughout Europe, down to sea level in N.

NEST Enormous structure of branches, used year after year, in tree or on high rocky ledge.

VOICE Rarely vocal; ***kaah***.

GENERAL Though widespread, always scarce. Often confused with much smaller Buzzard (p.66).

Peregrine

Falco peregrinus

ADULT Medium (45 cm), but largest European falcon. Grey above, with finely, dark-barred, white underparts; black moustache and white cheeks. In flight, watch for relatively short, broad-based pointed wings. Circles high waiting for prey to fly below, then plunges at high speed in pursuit (stoop).

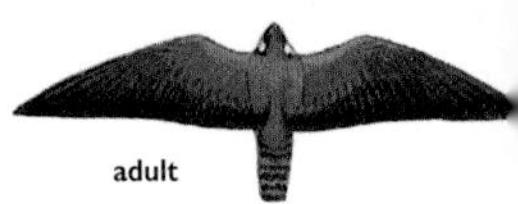

adult

JUVENILE Brown and scaly above, buff below with dark streaks not bars.

HABITAT Year-round resident or winter visitor over much of Europe, summer visitor to far N. Breeds on mountains, moors or coasts with cliffs; winters on moors and coastal marshes.

NEST Eggs laid in bare scrape on cliff ledge.

VOICE Harsh ***keck-keck***.

GENERAL Widespread, never numerous, but range and numbers increasing.

Osprey

Pandion haliaetus

ADULT Large (58 cm) brown and white raptor. Watch for pale underparts and white head with dark eye patches. Carries wings in a distinctive open M in flight, hovers clumsily over water, then plunges spectacularly for fish prey. Sexes similar.

JUVENILE As adult, but less distinctly marked.

HABITAT Summer visitor breeding beside N European lakes, rivers and coasts; also year-round resident or winter visitor to extreme S Europe. Migrates over almost any water.

NEST Bulky, of branches, usually in tree.

adult

VOICE Rarely vocal; whistling ***tchew***.

GENERAL Widespread, but never numerous.

Kestrel

70 *Falco tinnunculus*

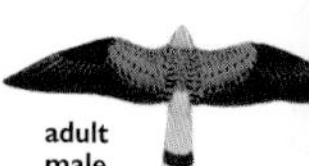

adult male

adult female

ADULT Medium (35 cm) falcon, long-winged and long-tailed, distinctively hovers before diving onto prey. Female brown with multi-barred tail; male has black-spotted chestnut back, grey head, grey tail with black terminal bar. Usually solitary.

JUVENILE As female, but duller.

HABITAT Widespread and common resident year-round except in far N, where is summer visitor. Almost any habitat.

NEST Lays eggs on bare ledge or in hole.

VOICE Shrill ***kee-kee-kee***, usually when breeding.

GENERAL Lesser Kestrel *(F. naumanni)*: gregarious, locally common summer visitor to S Europe, breeding colonially. Male has unspotted chestnut back and pale appearance; rarely hovers.

Merlin

Falco columbarius

ADULT Medium (30 cm) falcon, compact and low-flying, catches prey (usually birds) by surprise and speed. Watch for dark slate-grey back and tail of male, female dark brown, paler below, copiously streaked. In flight, wings heavily barred on undersides, powerful and pointed; tail long, multi-barred in female, with single terminal bar in male.

JUVENILE As female, but more rufous.

HABITAT Summer visitor to N Europe, winter visitor or year-round resident elsewhere. Breeds on moors, tundra and rough grassland, often winters on coastal marshes.

NEST Shallow depression on ground.

VOICE Chattering ***kee-kee-kee***.

GENERAL Widespread, but always scarce. Can occur almost anywhere on migration.

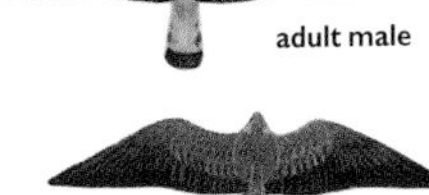

Hobby

Falco subbuteo

ADULT Medium (28 cm), fast-flying falcon. Watch for distinctive flight silhouette like giant swift with long sickle-shaped wings. White collar prominent at a distance, black moustaches, heavily barred underwings and chestnut undertail only clear at close range.

JUVENILE Brown, not grey above; buff, with dark streaks below, lacking chestnut.

HABITAT Summer visitor to European heathland and farmland except in far N. Often hunts over water.

NEST Usually lays in abandoned crow's nest.

VOICE Sharp ***kew*** and repetitive ***ki-ki-ki***.

GENERAL Widespread, locally fairly common especially in warmer S areas with plentiful large insect prey.

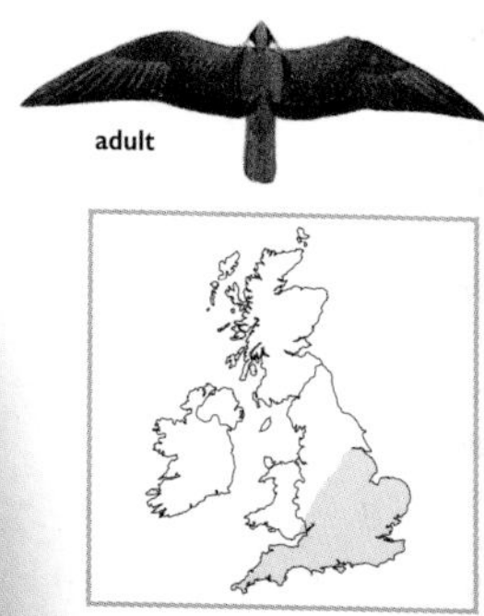

Willow Grouse

Lagopus lagopus

stribution
rcumpolar,
rough most of
:ndinavia except
wland areas

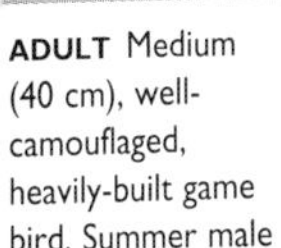

ADULT Medium (40 cm), well-camouflaged, heavily-built game bird. Summer male mottled dark chestnut, red wattles over eyes, striking white wings in flight. Female also white-winged, duller and greyer, no wattles. Both sexes are white in winter except black tail. Remains still until danger close, then whirrs off on noisy, downcurved wings.

JUVENILE Much as female.

HABITAT Year-round resident of moorland, tundra and birch scrub across N Europe.

NEST Well-concealed grassy cup on ground.

VOICE Loud and distinctive ***go-back-urrr***.

GENERAL Locally common, as is British and Irish subspecies, Red Grouse: lacks white plumage year-round.

adult

Ptarmigan

Lagopus mutus

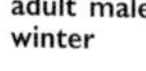

adult male winter

ADULT Medium (35 cm), high-altitude game bird. Summer adult richly mottled brown and grey above, with white belly and wings. In winter, largely white except black tail. Watch for distinctive dark mark through eye and feathered feet, well insulated from snow. Usually run from danger rather than flying. Sexes similar except male has red wattles over eyes.

JUVENILE As summer adult, but duller.

HABITAT Year-round resident of N tundra and isolated mountain areas elsewhere in Europe.

NEST Well-concealed grassy cup on ground.

VOICE Croaking ***arr-arr-kar-kar-kar***.

GENERAL Restricted by habitat, rarely numerous.

Black Grouse

Tetrao tetrix 75

adult female

ADULT Large (50 cm), bulky game bird. Male glossy black with white wingbar and white underside to lyre-shaped tail. Bright red wattles over eyes. Female mottled grey-brown, with longish slightly forked tail. Gathers at dawn and dusk on communal display grounds (leks). Flies high, fast and far when disturbed.

JUVENILE As female.

HABITAT Year-round resident across N and NW Europe. Favours heaths, rough grass, moorland and open woodland. Locally common.

NEST Well-concealed grass cup on ground.

VOICE Cacophonic croons and bubblings at lek.

GENERAL Capercaillie *(T. urogallus):* black turkey-like male (85 cm) with shaggy throat feathers and white beak. Female smaller and chestnut.

Quail

Coturnix coturnix

adult male

ADULT Small (18 cm), vocal, but secretive and well-camouflaged game bird, smaller than a thrush. Underparts sandy buff, upperparts mottled browns, fawns and chestnuts, white streaked. Watch for broader buff stripes on crown and small black bib of male, otherwise sexes similar. Flies only as last resort.

JUVENILE As adult, but duller.

HABITAT Summer visitor to much of Europe except far N, sometimes year-round resident in extreme SW. Favours open farmland, grassland and heath.

NEST Well-concealed grassy cup on ground.

VOICE Ventriloquial ***wet-my-lips*** call.

GENERAL Widespread, variable from year to year, rarely numerous.

Red-legged Partridge

Alectoris rufa

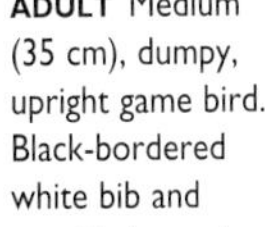

ADULT Medium (35 cm), dumpy, upright game bird. Black-bordered white bib and speckled gorget; white eyestripe and striking black, white and chestnut bars on flanks. Plain rich brown back. Beak and legs deep pinkish red. Sexes similar.

JUVENILE Sandy brown, lacks head and flank patterns.

HABITAT Year-round resident in W and SW Europe. Favours drier farmland, heath, downland and scrub.

NEST Well-concealed grassy cup on ground.

VOICE Distinctive ***chuck***, ***chuck-arr***.

GENERAL Locally common, often in small flocks. Sometimes artificially introduced. Rock Partridge *(A. graeca)* of rocky Mediterranean hillsides is similar, as is Chukar *(A. chukar)* of extreme SE. Both lack the speckled gorget.

Grey Partridge

Perdix perdix

ADULT Medium (30 cm), dumpy, upright game bird. Finely mottled and white-streaked grey, buff and chestnut upperparts, grey breast and dark brown horseshoe mark on belly. Erratically barred chestnut flanks. Crouches, well-camouflaged, flying at last moment. Whirrs off fast and low on downcurved wings, shows chestnut sides to tail. Sexes broadly similar: female has less marked horseshoe.

JUVENILE Sandy and streaked brown, lacks marks.

HABITAT Year-round resident over much of Europe except N and SW. Favours farmland, grassland, heath and scrub.

NEST Well-concealed grassy cup on ground.

VOICE Distinctive, rusty ***kirrrr-ick***.

GENERAL Widespread, once fairly common, but locally declining. Often in small flocks (coveys).

adult

adult

Pheasant

Phasianus colchicus

ADULT Large (85 cm, but half is long tail) distinctive game bird. Male unmistakable, rich gold and chestnut, with green head and scarlet, fleshy face patch. Female smaller, well camouflaged in mottled browns and buffs, with long central tail feathers.

adult female

adult male

JUVENILE As female, but shorter-tailed.

HABITAT Introduced centuries ago, widespread year-round resident across much of Europe except far N. Favours farmland, heath, scrub and open woodland.

NEST Well-concealed grassy cup on ground.

VOICE Ringing, far-carrying ***kok-kok***, followed by explosive wing claps.

GENERAL Numbers variable as stocks artificially augmented for shooting; locally common.

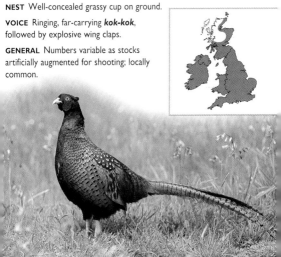

Water Rail

80 *Rallus aquaticus*

adult

ADULT Medium (28 cm) skulking crake. Watch for dull grey breast, black-barred flanks, and white underside to frequently flicked tail. Beak long, downcurved, deep red with black tip. Long legs and spidery toes pinkish. Slips silently through reeds. Flies weakly and low, legs trailing. Sexes similar.

JUVENILE Darker and duller, more speckled and barred than adult.

HABITAT Widespread across much of Europe year-round, summer visitor in N. Favours densely vegetated wetlands, swamps and reedbeds.

NEST Well-concealed cup on ground, deep in cover.

VOICE Often noisy; pig-like grunts and squeals.

GENERAL Difficult to see; commoner than it seems.

Corn Crake

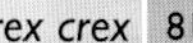

Crex crex

ADULT Stocky water bird (27cm), spends most of its time hidden. Resembles other rails but wings are rich chestnut and head and front of neck are grey. Bill is short and pale. Chestnut wings particularly noticeable in flight. Females show less grey.

JUVENILE Shows no grey; reddish flanks

HABITAT Low, wet marshland, and high grass and hay meadows.

NEST Flat, made of grass and hidden in vegetation

adult

VOICE Loud, grating '***crek-crek***', heard early morning and late evening

GENERAL Now very rare and very hard to see, does breed Ireland and west of Scotland. Mostly known by its call.

Crane

 Grus grus

DISTRIBUTION Breeds across N Palearctic, and migrates through Holland and France to Spain

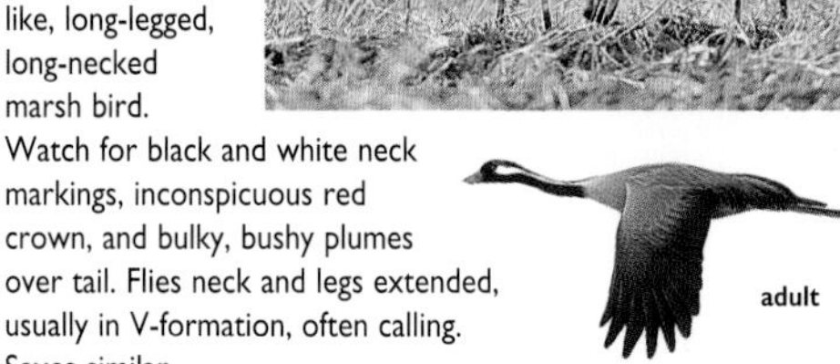

ADULT Huge (110 cm), stork-like, long-legged, long-necked marsh bird. Watch for black and white neck markings, inconspicuous red crown, and bulky, bushy plumes over tail. Flies neck and legs extended, usually in V-formation, often calling. Sexes similar.

adult

JUVENILE Grey brown, paler on underside, lacking head markings and plumes.

HABITAT Summer visitor breeding on far N marshes and tundra; migrates via established staging posts on farmland or marshland.

NEST Huge reed platform rising above swamp.

VOICE Fabulous wild trumpeting in flight, whooping calls on breeding grounds.

GENERAL Generally scarce, flocks on migration.

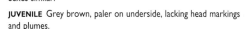

Moorhen

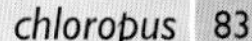

Gallinula chloropus 83

ADULT Medium (33 cm) familiar crake. Watch for dull-black plumage with white flank streak and white underside to frequently flicked tail; short yellow beak and red fleshy forehead shield. Legs greenish with distinctive red 'garter', toes spidery. Sexes similar.

JUVENILE Nestling has black fluffy down; immature brown above, fawn below, lacks frontal shield.

HABITAT Year-round resident over most of Europe, summer visitor to N and NE. Favours fresh waters from smallest pond to largest lake.

NEST Bulky mound of waterweed, often in or over water.

VOICE Varied ringing calls, including ***whittuck***.

GENERAL Widespread, often common.

Coot

84 *Fulica atra*

adult

ADULT Medium (38 cm), familiar, dumpy all-black rail. Watch for grey-green legs with lobed toes, white beak and frontal shield. Aggressive, often fluffs out feathers and fights. Flies low, legs trailing, showing white trailing edge to wing. Dives frequently. Sexes similar.

JUVENILE Downy young fluffy and black; immature dark grey above, whitish throat and belly, lacks frontal shield.

HABITAT Year-round resident over much of Europe, summer visitor to N and NE. Favours larger fresh waters, occasionally on sheltered estuaries.

NEST Conspicuous mound of waterweed, usually in or over water.

VOICE Metallic and strident ***kook*** or ***kowk***.

GENERAL Widespread, conspicuous and generally common.

Stone-curlew

Burhinus oedicnemus

ADULT Large, brown wader (41cm). Large head and yellow, staring eye. Long yellow legs, and yellow bill with black tip. Strong, slow flight, strong black and white wing pattern. Well-camouflaged against stony ground, will stand very still.

JUVENILE Less obvious wing bar, markings generally less well-defined.

HABITAT Open ground with sparse vegetation.

NEST Eggs laid on bare scrape.

VOICE Whining ***coor-lee***.

GENERAL Summer visitor in Britain, winters in SW Europe and Africa.

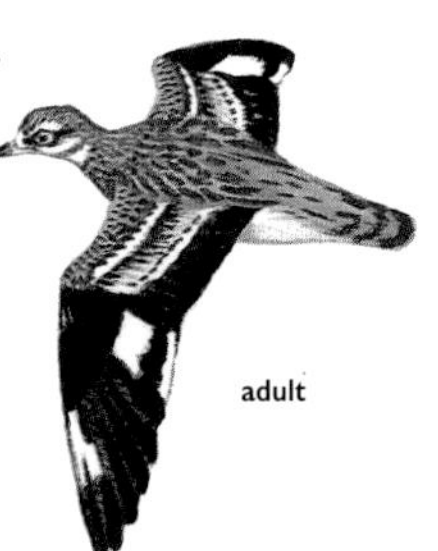

adult

Oystercatcher

Haematopus ostralegus

ADULT Medium (43 cm), but among the larger, more robust waders. Watch for strikingly pied plumage, stout, straight orange beak and thick, fleshy pink legs. In winter, has inconspicuous white collar. In flight shows bold white wingbars and black and white rump and tail pattern. Sexes similar.

JUVENILE Dull, sooty version of adult.

HABITAT Year-round resident, usually coastal, but also on damp meadows in W Europe; summer visitor breeding on N coasts and marshes; winter visitor to S shores.

NEST Shallow scrape lined with pebbles, seaweed or grass.

VOICE Strident pipings and ***kleep*** calls.

GENERAL Comparatively widespread, often common; usually in flocks, sometimes large.

adult

Black-winged Stilt

Himantopus himantopus

adult

ADULT Medium (38 cm) wader, unmistakable if full length of pink legs can be seen. Watch for jet black back and wings contrasting with white body and needle-slim, straight black beak. In winter has smoky crown and nape. Flies with long legs trailing distinctively. Sexes similar.

JUVENILE Duller and browner than adult, with long brownish legs.

HABITAT Summer visitor (occasionally year-round resident) in extreme S Europe; vagrant elsewhere. Breeds by saltpans, brackish lagoons and freshwater marsh pools.

NEST Shallow scrape on ground, lined with pebbles, shells or fragments of vegetation.

VOICE Vocal; strident yelping ***kyip***.

GENERAL Locally fairly common, often in flocks.

Avocet

Recurvirostra avosetta

adult

ADULT Medium (43 cm), unmistakable wader. Watch for boldly patterned pied plumage and unique long, finely-pointed, upturned black beak. Legs long, blue grey. Feeds by sweeping beak from side to side through shallow water. Sexes similar.

JUVENILE Greyer version of adult.

HABITAT Summer visitor to a few N coastal marshes, winter visitor to others and to sheltered estuaries, year-round resident on S marshes, saltpans and lagoons.

NEST Shallow scrape on ground, lined with fragments of shell or nearby vegetation.

VOICE Vocal; distinctive ***kloo-oot*** and ***kloo-eet***.

GENERAL Locally common, generally increasing. Breeds colonially, often feeds in flocks in winter.

Kentish Plover

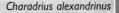

Charadrius alexandrinus

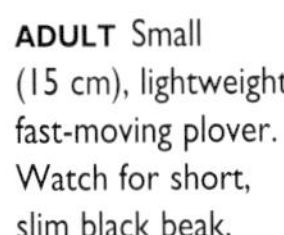

ADULT Small (15 cm), lightweight, fast-moving plover. Watch for short, slim black beak, slender black legs, black and white forehead, pale chestnut crown. Black marks on shoulders. Female and winter birds paler, lack chestnut cap. In flight shows white sides to tail and white wingbar.

JUVENILE Scaly, sandy back; inconspicuous head and collar markings.

HABITAT Year-round resident or winter visitor to Mediterranean coasts, summer visitor to W European coasts. Favours saltpans, muddy lagoons and sandy beaches.

adult

NEST Shallow scrape lined with shell fragments.

VOICE Melodious ***choo-wit***, soft ***wit-wit-wit***.

GENERAL Locally common in S, scarcer on W coast, vagrant elsewhere.

Ringed Plover

Charadrius hiaticula

adult

ADULT Small (20 cm), fast-moving plover. Watch for stubby black-tipped orange-yellow beak, black and white forehead, broad, black collar band, and orange legs. In flight shows broadly white-bordered tail and striking white wingbars. Sexes similar.

JUVENILE Sandier and scaly above, lacks black markings, has brown collar.

HABITAT Summer visitor to N coasts, year-round resident on W coasts; winter visitor to S shores. Favours sandy coasts and saltpans, occasionally inland excavations.

NEST Shallow scrape lined with fragments of local material, on ground and well camouflaged.

VOICE Melodious ***too-lee***; trilling song near nest.

GENERAL Widespread and fairly common.

Little Ringed Plover

Charadrius dubius

adult

ADULT Small (15 cm), fast-moving plover. Short black beak and complex head pattern, with white stripe between crown and black face and forehead bar; yellowish legs and yellow eye-ring. In flight shows slim black collar, white nape, white sides to tail and lack of wingbar. Sexes similar.

JUVENILE Scaly brown above, with greyish collar, pale yellow eye-ring.

HABITAT Summer visitor to most of Europe. Favours sandy coasts, lagoons and saltpans, and inland sandpits, quarries and other excavations.

NEST Shallow scrape on ground, lined with fragments of local material. Very well concealed.

VOICE Quiet, piping ***tee-you***; trills near nest.

GENERAL Widespread, locally fairly common in S, scarce elsewhere.

Golden Plover

Pluvialis apricaria

ADULT Medium (28 cm), but largish among plovers. In summer, watch for striking black-speckled gold back and white-bordered black belly. In winter, dull brown-speckled golden buff upperparts, buff breast and white belly. Flight swift, showing indistinct wingbar. Sexes similar.

adult non-breeding

JUVENILE As winter adult, but drabber.

HABITAT Summer visitor breeding on N moorland and tundra, winters on W wet grassland, farmland and marshes.

NEST Well-concealed grass-lined scrape on ground.

VOICE Sad but melodious ***tloo-eee***.

GENERAL Widespread, but not numerous as a breeding bird, regular and locally fairly common in winter, often in large flocks.

Grey Plover

Pluvialis squatarola

ADULT Medium (28 cm), bulky plover. In summer, black-speckled silver back and white-bordered striking black belly. In winter, dull blackish-speckled grey back and white underparts. In flight watch for black 'armpits', white wingbar, white rump and dark-barred tail. Sexes similar.

JUVENILE As winter adult, but drabber.

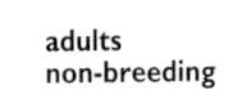

adults non-breeding

HABITAT Scarce summer visitor breeding in extreme N; more numerous on migration or as winter visitor to estuaries and sheltered sandy or muddy coasts along Atlantic and Mediterranean seaboards.

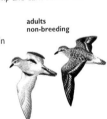

NEST Shallow scrape on tundra.

VOICE Plaintive ***tee-loo-eee***.

GENERAL Widespread, but rarely numerous, often solitary.

Lapwing

Vanellus vanellus

ADULT Medium (30 cm), distinctive plover, predominantly black and white, at close range black areas shot with iridescent purple and green. Watch for conspicuous long slender black crest, chestnut undertail, floppy flight on markedly rounded black and white wings. Sexes broadly similar.

JUVENILE Drabber, scaly-backed with short crest.

HABITAT Summer visitor to N and E Europe, year-round resident, migrant or winter visitor elsewhere. Breeds on fields, moorland and marshes; winters on similar areas, also estuaries and arable farmland.

NEST Grass-lined scrape on ground.

VOICE Very distinctive *pee-wit*.

adult

GENERAL Widespread, often common, often in substantial flocks.

Knot

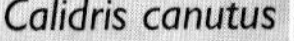

Calidris canutus

ADULT Small–medium (25 cm) wader. Summer adult chestnut with mottled gold and brown back. In winter, lacks distinction: dull grey, with medium beak, medium legs and indistinct wingbar. Watch for bulky build and whitish eyestripe. Sexes similar.

JUVENILE As winter adult, but browner on back.

HABITAT Breeds on Arctic tundra. Brief spring migration up European coasts, but most in autumn or winter. Favours estuaries and sheltered sandy or muddy bays.

adult breeding

NEST Well-concealed grass-lined scrape on ground.

VOICE Occasional but distinctive grunt.

GENERAL Regularly in enormous flocks. Packs close together on ground and in flight, wheeling and turning as one.

Sanderling

Calidris alba

ADULT Small (20 cm), fast-running wader. Summer adult rich rufous cinnamon. In winter, distinctively pale: watch for short dark beak, black smudge through eye. In flight shows bold white wingbar. Chases waves in and out on the sand.

JUVENILE As winter adult, but with brown mottled back.

HABITAT Breeds on Arctic tundra. Brief spring migration on W coasts, but most in autumn or winter on sandy beaches and bays.

NEST Well-concealed grassy cup on ground.

VOICE Repeated short sharp ***quick***.

GENERAL Widespread and regular, locally fairly common though rarely in large flocks.

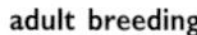

adult breeding

Little Stint

Calidris minuta

adult breeding

ADULT Tiny (13 cm) wader. Short fine beak, black legs and grey outer tail feathers in flight. In summer, rich mottled brown above, with double V marking on back. In winter, pale dull grey, with traces of the V. Sexes similar.

JUVENILE Much as summer adult.

HABITAT Migrant or summer visitor breeding on far N tundra. Some overwinter in W and S. Favours saline lagoons and creeks, freshwater pools and swamps.

NEST Well-concealed grass-lined cup on ground.

VOICE Terse ***chiff***.

GENERAL Widespread, but rarely numerous. Similar-sized but drabber Temminck's Stint *(C. temminckii)* scarcer, yellow legs, white outer tail feathers and rattling ***tirrrr*** call.

Curlew Sandpiper

98 *Calidris ferruginea*

adult non-breeding

ADULT Small (20 cm) wader with distinctive downcurved beak. Summer adult mottled brown above, rich chestnut below. Winter birds pale grey above, white below. Watch for eyestripe and, in flight, square white rump contrasting with black tail. Sexes similar.

JUVENILE As winter adult, slightly buffer, with scaly pattern on back.

HABITAT Summer visitor breeding on Arctic tundra. Regular spring and autumn migrant and occasional overwintering visitor to W and S coasts. Favours sheltered bays, estuaries, lagoons and freshwater marshes.

NEST Well-concealed grassy cup on ground.

VOICE Distinctive trilling ***chirrup***.

GENERAL Regular, but yearly numbers vary greatly.

Purple Sandpiper

Calidris maritima

ADULT Small (21 cm), squat wader. In summer, mottled chestnut above, pale with dark markings below. In winter, dull, purplish, leaden-grey above, paler and grey-spotted below. Short yellow legs, black-tipped yellow beak, and white edges to black rump and tail in flight. Sexes similar.

JUVENILE As winter adult, but with some darker mottling on back.

HABITAT Breeds on Arctic tundra, winters (immature birds may be present all year) on rocky W and NW coasts.

NEST Well-concealed grassy cup on ground.

VOICE Normally silent, occasional ***wit-wit***.

GENERAL Scampers among breaking waves on seaweed-clad rocky shores. Inconspicuous but approachable. Regular and locally fairly common.

adult breeding

Dunlin

100 *Calidris alpina*

ADULT Small (18 cm) wader with long downcurved beak. Summer adult speckled bronze and chestnut above, white below with distinctive black belly patch. In winter, nondescript grey above, white below. In flight, watch for white wingbar and white-edged black rump and tail. Sexes similar.

JUVENILE As winter adult, but generally buffer, with brown mottling on back.

HABITAT Summer visitor or year-round resident breeding on N tundra, moorland and coastal marshes. Winter visitor or migrant to lagoons, estuaries and sheltered bays along entire European coast, inland on marshes.

NEST Well-concealed grassy cup on ground.

VOICE Purring trill in flight; nasal ***shreeep*** call.

GENERAL Common, often numerous, often in flocks.

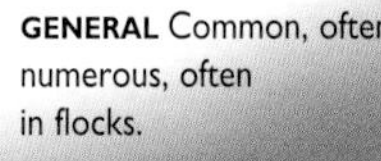

Woodcock

Scolopax rusticola

ADULT Medium (35 cm), bulky, long-beaked wader, with mottled plumage. Pale forehead and cross-wise buff stripes on angular head. Note large eyes, rounded wings and moth-like flight showing no wing markings. Sexes similar.

JUVENILE As adult, but duller.

HABITAT Summer visitor to N Europe, year-round resident or winter visitor to S. Aberrant for a wader in favouring damp woodland year-round.

adult

NEST Scrape in leaf litter on ground.

VOICE Usually silent, but in evening calls a frog-like ***orrrt-orrrt*** and a sneezing high-pitched ***tswick***.

GENERAL Widespread and regular, difficult to see as relies on camouflage until danger very close.

Jack Snipe

Lymnocryptes minimus

ADULT Small, brown wader (19cm). Well camouflaged in brown, black and creamy-white; black on crown and in stripes on head. Bill only slightly larger than the head. Underparts white with dark streaking. Brown and white streaking on the breast. Flies only rarely when disturbed; underwings half black and white.

JUVENILE As adult

HABITAT Breeds in bogs in northern Europe; winters around muddy pools and inland marshes

adult

NEST Cup-shaped, in grass

VOICE Usually silent

GENERAL Smaller than Common Snipe *(Gallinago gallinago)*, with shorter bill

Common Snipe

Gallinago gallinago

adult

ADULT Medium (28 cm), squat, well-camouflaged wader with long beak. Longitudinal buff stripes on crown and back. Legs green, relatively short. Zig-zag flight. Sexes similar.

JUVENILE As adult, but duller.

HABITAT Summer visitor to N Europe, year-round resident in central and W areas, winter visitor further S. Favours saline lagoons, swamps, reedbeds and wet grassland.

NEST Well-concealed deep cup in grass.

VOICE Repeated ***tick-er*** in breeding season, harsh scarp when flushed. Tail feathers produce vibrant 'drumming' noise in diving display flight.

GENERAL Widespread, local. Smaller, scarcer, shorter-beaked Jack Snipe *(Lymnocryptes minimus)*: difficult to flush, silent, flies low and straight for short distance, showing no white on tail.

Ruff

Philomachus pugnax

ADULT Medium (30 cm), long-legged wader. Larger summer male has large bright ruff of feathers. Female and winter male duller and scaly. In flight, watch for white oval patches on each side of rump and tail; long, usually orange, legs extend beyond tail. Beak orange and black in male, blackish in female.

JUVENILE Buff head and neck, scaly brown back, white belly.

HABITAT Summer visitor to N Europe, breeding on tundra and marshland; year-round resident or winter visitor in S. Favours coastal lagoons or inland marshes.

NEST Well-concealed deep cup in grass.

VOICE Usually silent, sometimes ***chuk-uk***.

GENERAL Widespread, but scattered, rarely numerous.

adult male

adult female

Black-tailed Godwit

Limosa limosa

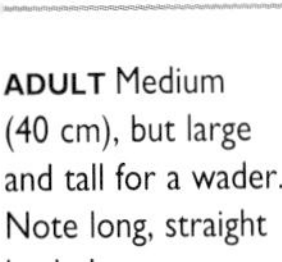

ADULT Medium (40 cm), but large and tall for a wader. Note long, straight beak. In summer, has chestnut head and neck; in winter, dull pale grey with white belly. In flight, watch for striking black and white wingbars, white rump and black tail. Sexes similar.

JUVENILE As winter adult, but buffer, with scaly back pattern.

adult

HABITAT Summer visitor or year-round resident to north-central and NW Europe, winter visitor to S coasts. Breeds on damp grassland and marshes, winters on sheltered estuaries and bays.

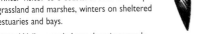

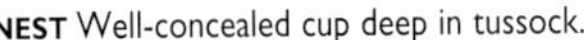

NEST Well-concealed cup deep in tussock.

VOICE Noisy ***wicka-wicka-wicka*** when breeding.

GENERAL Locally fairly common, may flock in winter.

Bar-tailed Godwit

Limosa lapponica

ADULT Medium (40 cm), but large and long-legged for a wader. Note long, slightly upturned beak. In summer, bright chestnut with brown-mottled back; in winter, brown with darker streaks above, whitish below. In flight, note lack of wingbar, white rump and dark-barred white tail. Sexes similar.

JUVENILE As winter adult, with chestnut mottling on back.

HABITAT Summer visitor breeding on Arctic tundra, migrant or winter visitor to W and S European coasts. Favours estuaries and sheltered muddy or sandy bays.

NEST Well-concealed scrape on ground.

VOICE Rare; harsh ***kirrick*** when breeding.

GENERAL Widespread and gregarious, locally common, often in large flocks.

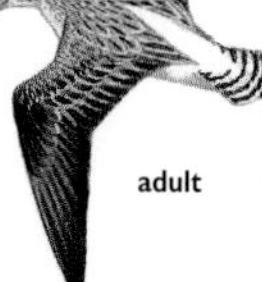

adult

Whimbrel

Numenius phaeopus 107

adult

ADULT Medium (40 cm), mottled brown, long-legged, long-necked wader. Long, downcurved, black beak appreciably shorter than Curlew (p.108). Watch for broad buff stripes on brown crown. In flight, note lack of wingbar, white rump and barred tail. Sexes similar.

JUVENILE Resembles adult.

HABITAT Summer visitor breeding on N moors, marshes and tundra, migrant (often, but not always, on coast) elsewhere.

NEST Well-concealed grassy cup on ground.

VOICE Far-carrying piping whistle, several times in rapid succession: ***pee-pee-pee-pee-pee-pee-pee***.

GENERAL Widespread, regular on migration, rarely numerous.

Curlew

108 *Numenius arquata*

adult

ADULT Large (58 cm), mottled brown and buff, long-legged, long- necked wader. Extremely long, downcurved beak. In flight, note lack of wing markings, pale rump extending well up back, and narrow, dark-barred white tail. Sexes similar.

JUVENILE Resembles adult.

HABITAT Summer visitor to N and north-central Europe, year-round resident, migrant or winter visitor to W and on S coasts. Breeds on moors, wet grassland and marshes; winters on sheltered sandy or muddy coasts and estuaries.

NEST Well-concealed grassy cup on ground.

VOICE ***Coor-lee*** at all times; bubbling song in display flight over breeding territory.

GENERAL Widespread; solitary or in flocks; locally fairly common.

Spotted Redshank

Tringa erythropus

adult

ADULT Medium (30 cm), long-legged, long-necked wader. In summer, unmistakable, uniformly sooty black with white spots. In winter, scaly silver-grey above, white below. In flight, watch for trailing dark red legs, lack of wingbar, white rump and barred tail. Sexes similar.

JUVENILE As winter adult, but buffer on shoulders.

HABITAT Summer visitor breeding on Arctic tundra; migrant or winter visitor on coasts of W and S Europe. Favours tundra areas close to tree limit, winters on marshes, estuaries and sheltered coasts.

NEST Well-concealed grassy scrape on ground.

VOICE Explosive ***chew-it***.

GENERAL Regular, but rarely numerous. Often solitary.

Redshank

Tringa totanus

ADULT Medium (28 cm), wary wader. Rich brown above, streaked blackish in summer, whitish scaly marks in winter. White below, heavily brown speckled and streaked in summer, less so in winter. Note long scarlet legs, and, in flight, broad white trailing edges to wings. Sexes similar.

JUVENILE As winter adult, but buffer overall.

HABITAT Summer visitor to N and NE marshes. Year-round resident, migrant or winter visitor to W and S coasts. Breeds in marshes; winters on estuaries and coasts.

adult

NEST Concealed deep cup in grass tussock.

VOICE Stridently vociferous 'sentinel of the marshes', shrieking calls and melodious variants on ***tu-lee-lee***.

GENERAL Widespread, locally fairly common; solitary, sometimes in small flocks.

Greenshank

Tringa nebularia

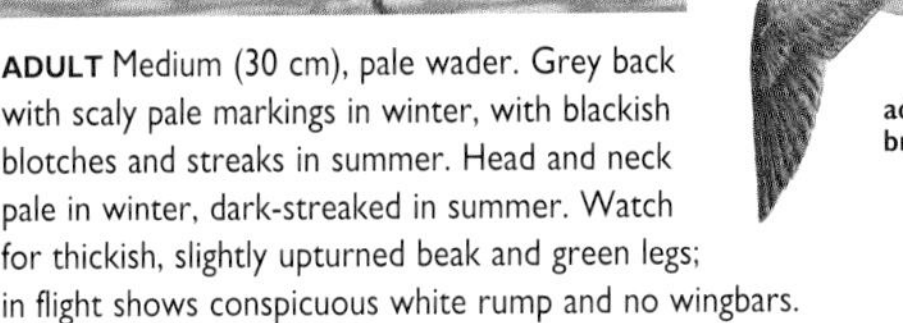

adult breeding

ADULT Medium (30 cm), pale wader. Grey back with scaly pale markings in winter, with blackish blotches and streaks in summer. Head and neck pale in winter, dark-streaked in summer. Watch for thickish, slightly upturned beak and green legs; in flight shows conspicuous white rump and no wingbars. Sexes similar.

JUVENILE As winter adult, but buffer.

HABITAT Summer visitor to N tundra and moorland. Migrant or winter visitor to W and S coasts and marshes. Favours lagoons and sheltered bays and estuaries.

NEST Well-concealed scrape on ground.

VOICE Characteristically trisyllabic ***tu-tu-tu***.

GENERAL Widespread, but rarely numerous.

Green Sandpiper

Tringa ochropus

ADULT Small (23 cm), dark wader. Dark, greenish-grey back speckled white, underparts white. Short, dark green legs. Often bobs. In flight, watch for dark underwings, lack of wingbars, bold white rump and heavily dark-barred tail. Sexes similar.

adult non-breeding

JUVENILE As adult, but more heavily speckled.

HABITAT Summer visitor to N Europe; winter visitor or migrant to coastal and inland marshes elsewhere. Breeds in swampy forest, muddy pools and creeks.

NEST Grassy scrape on ground, occasionally in deserted nest in tree.

VOICE ***Tloot-weet-wit*** on take-off; trilling song.

GENERAL Widespread and regular, but rarely numerous. Often solitary.

Turnstone

Arenaria interpres 113

adult non-breeding

ADULT Small (23 cm), stocky wader. Harlequin plumage, mainly browns and white in winter; black, white and chestnut in summer. Short orange legs and short, dark, wide beak (used to turn over seaweed and pebbles). In flight, watch for complex black and white pattern on back, wings and tail. Sexes similar.

JUVENILE Similar to winter adult.

HABITAT Summer visitor breeding on N rocky coasts and tundra; migrant, winter visitor (or year-round) on coasts further S. Generally maritime, favours rocky, surf-washed coasts with dense seaweed.

NEST Shallow scrape on ground.

VOICE Distinctive staccato ***tuk-uk-tuk***.

GENERAL Widespread, locally common; rare inland.

Common Sandpiper

114 *Actitis hypoleucos*

adult non-breeding

ADULT Small (20 cm), dumpy wader, perpetually bobbing. Sandy brown upperparts flecked with white in summer. Short greenish legs. Watch for whirring flight interrupted by glides on downcurved wings, low over water. Shows white wingbar and white edges to buff rump and tail. Sexes similar.

JUVENILE As adult, but duller and chequered.

HABITAT Summer visitor or migrant to much of Europe, winter visitor to S, may overwinter elsewhere. Breeds beside lakes, rivers and streams; winters on fresh and salt marshes, occasionally along coasts.

NEST Shallow scrape on ground close to water.

VOICE Trilling ***twee-wee-wee*** call; high-pitched song based on ***tittyweety*** phrases.

GENERAL Widespread and regular; often solitary.

Wood Sandpiper

Tringa glareola

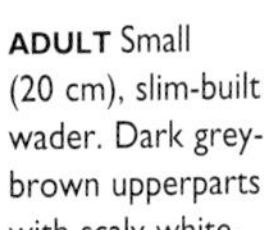

ADULT Small (20 cm), slim-built wader. Dark grey-brown upperparts with scaly white-edged feathers. Head and neck white with darker streaks, note clear eyestripe and yellowish legs. In flight, unmarked wings with pale undersides, white rump with faintly barred tail. Sexes similar.

JUVENILE As adult, but warmer colour and more mottled.

HABITAT Summer visitor breeding on N marshes and tundra, migrant elsewhere visiting inland and coastal pools, marshes and lagoons. May overwinter in S.

NEST Shallow scrape on ground.

VOICE ***Chiff-if-if*** on take-off; yodelling song.

GENERAL Widespread and regular, but rarely numerous. Often solitary, occasionally in small flocks.

adult non-breeding

Red-necked Phalarope

Phalaropus lobatus

ADULT Small, dainty, brownish-grey wader (18cm), with a needle-sharp bill. Adult breeding birds characterised by orange-brown streaking running from behind the eye down the side of the neck. Back is streaked with the same colour. Non-breeding birds grey and white.

JUVENILE As non-breeding male, but brown and white.

HABITAT Breeds in tundra far north of Europe, rarely in north of Scotland around shallow pools, winters in Middle East

NEST Marshland tussocks.

adult non-breeding

VOICE A throaty, clucking ***check*** or ***tyit***.

GENERAL Arrives in Britain in May on passage for summer, and returns in mid-July.

Black-headed Gull

Larus ridibundus

ADULT Medium (35 cm) gull. In summer, watch for dark chocolate hood, red beak and leg s. In winter, head white with black smudge behind eye. In flight shows all-black wingtips and diagnostic white leading edge to wing. Sexes similar.

JUVENILE As winter adult, but with brown W mark across wings and black tip to tail.

HABITAT Summer visitor to N and NE, year-round resident or winter visitor elsewhere. Breeds colonially on islands, dunes, sheltered coasts and beside moorland lakes. Occurs in almost any habitat.

NEST Tall mound of grass and flotsam.

VOICE Yelping ***keeer*** and laughing ***kwaar*** calls.

GENERAL Widespread, common. Scarcer Mediterranean Gull (*L. melanocephalus*): black hood and all-white wingtips, more robust.

adult
winter

Arctic Skua

Stercorarius parasiticus

ADULT Medium (50 cm), gull-like seabird, slim-winged, agile in flight. Two phases: brownish-grey with darker cap or brown above with white underparts and collar. In flight, watch for long-pointed, central tail feathers, conspicuous white patches near tips of brownish wings. Sexes similar.

JUVENILE Brown, speckled and barred buff, without elongated tail feathers.

HABITAT Summer visitor breeding colonially on N coasts, islands and tundra; migrant elsewhere. Maritime, except nesting; favours inshore waters.

NEST Grass cup on ground.

VOICE Harsh ***kee-aar*** over colonies.

GENERAL Widespread, but numerous only near colonies. Pirates fish from other seabirds.

Great Skua

Stercorarius skua

ADULT Large (60 cm) skua, uniformly dark brown flecked and streaked white and buff. In flight, is piratical (even chases Gannets (p.21)); has striking white patches at base of primaries. Sexes similar.

JUVENILE Similar to adult.

HABITAT Summer visitor breeding colonially on N islands, moors and tundra. Migrant or occasional winter visitor elsewhere. Maritime, favours coastal seas.

NEST Bulky grass cup on ground, fiercely defended.

VOICE At colony only, barking tuk or ***uk-uk-uk***, nasal ***skeer***.

GENERAL Locally numerous only at colonies, which are few. Regular but quite scarce except near breeding colonies.

adult

Lesser Black-backed Gull

120 *Larus fuscus*

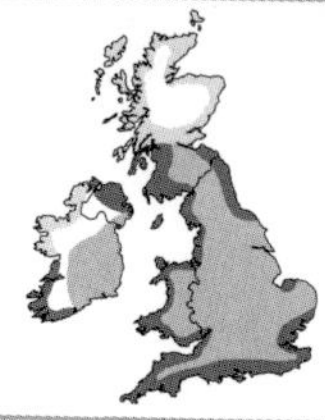

ADULT Large (53 cm) gull. Watch for yellow legs and, in flight, for black and white tips to dark grey wings. Head and neck flecked with grey in winter. Sexes similar.

JUVENILE Speckled dark brown above, paler below, all-dark primaries. Adult plumage after 3 years.

HABITAT Summer visitor breeding colonially on far N cliff-tops, islands, dunes and moors. Year-round resident or migrant along W coasts, winter visitor in S. Occurs in almost any habitat.

NEST Bulky mound of grass and flotsam on ground.

VOICE Powerful throaty ***kay-ow*** and laughing cries.

GENERAL Widespread, often common, increasingly wintering further N.

adult summer

Herring Gull

Larus argentatus 121

adult
summer

ADULT Large (55 cm) diagnostically silver-backed gull. Watch for pink legs (but S race has yellow legs) and, in flight, for black and white tips to pale grey wings. Head and neck flecked with grey in winter. Sexes similar.

JUVENILE Speckled dark brown above, paler below, pale inner primaries in flight. Adult plumage after 3 years.

HABITAT Year-round resident or winter visitor almost throughout Europe. Breeds colonially on all types of coast, moorland and town buildings. Occurs in almost any habitat. Favours refuse dumps.

NEST Bulky mound of grass and flotsam on ground.

VOICE Noisy, familar laughing ***kay-ow*** or ***yah-yah-yah*** and mewing calls.

GENERAL Widespread, often very numerous.

Great Black-backed Gull

Larus marinus

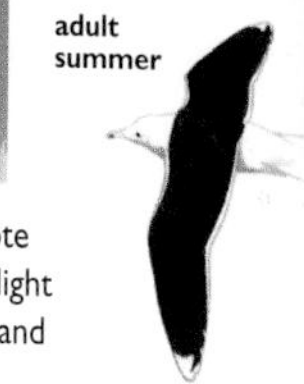

adult summer

ADULT The largest European gull (68 cm). Note massive beak, jet black back and pink legs. In flight shows all-black wings with white trailing edge and white spots at tips of primaries. Sexes similar.

JUVENILE Speckled brown above, paler below. Note dark trailing edge and paler inner primaries in flight. Adult plumage after 4 years.

HABITAT The most maritime gull. Breeds in N and W on islands and cliffs. Year-round resident in most areas, some disperse far out to sea.

NEST Seaweed and flotsam nest on ledge.

VOICE Gruff, powerful ***kow-kow-kow***.

GENERAL Widespread, not as numerous as other gulls. Rare Glaucous Gull *(L. hyperboreus)* adult has white wingtips, immature uniformly pale brown.

Common Gull

Larus canus

ADULT Medium (40 cm), grey-backed gull with rounded head and smallish yellow beak. Watch for greenish yellow legs and, in flight, black wingtips with white spots. In winter, has heavy grey flecking on head. Sexes similar.

JUVENILE Has speckled head, grey back, blackish wings and black-tipped white tail.

HABITAT Summer visitor breeding on N coasts, hillsides and moors. Year-round resident, migrant or winter visitor in S. Primarily coastal, but often on grassland and fields on migration.

NEST Grassy cup on ground.

VOICE High-pitched ***key-yaa*** and nasal ***gah-gah-gah***.

GENERAL Widespread in many habitats, often fairly common.

adult summer

Kittiwake

124 *Rissa tridactyla*

ADULT Medium (40 cm), slender-winged gull. Watch for crimson-lined yellow beak, black legs. Wings long and slim, held angled in buoyant flight, grey with black tips and no white spots. Sexes similar.

adult summer

JUVENILE As adult, but with black spot behind eye, black collar mark, black-tipped, slightly forked white tail and bold, black M on upper surface of wings.

HABITAT A maritime gull, many disperse widely across Atlantic in winter. Nests colonially on cliff ledges, occasionally on buildings on W and N coasts.

NEST Guano, mud and seaweed glued to sheer cliff, often under overhang.

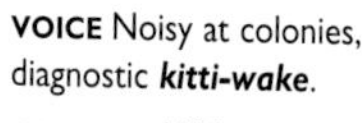

VOICE Noisy at colonies, diagnostic ***kitti-wake***.

GENERAL Widespread, locally numerous.

Little Gull

Larus minutus 125

adult summer

ADULT Medium (27 cm), but small and dainty for a gull. Watch for jet black cap, short dark red bill and legs. In flight shows pale grey upperside to wings, note dark grey underside and rounded white tips. In winter, loses black hood, has dark spot behind eye. Sexes similar.

JUVENILE As winter adult, with striking black M across wings.

HABITAT Summer visitor breeding on Baltic marshes, year-round resident, migrant, or winter visitor to W and S coasts. Most winter at sea, occurs on large inland fresh waters on migration.

NEST Grassy mound on swampy ground.

VOICE High-pitched ***kar-eee*** and ***kek-kek-kek***.

GENERAL Regular, locally fairly common, increasing. Note dipping feeding flight.

adult summer

Sandwich Tern

126 *Sterna sandvicensis*

ADULT Medium (40 cm), large for a tern, and heavy in flight. Watch for long yellow-tipped black beak, bristling black crest. In flight, grey wings show darker primaries; rump white, tail white and slightly forked. Forehead white in autumn. Sexes similar.

JUVENILE As autumn adult, with more white on crown and scaly blackish markings on back.

HABITAT Summer visitor or migrant along coasts. Breeds on isolated beaches and islands.

NEST Simple scrape in sand.

VOICE Distinctive and loud ***kay-reck*** or ***kirr-ick***.

GENERAL Widespread coastally, erratic but locally common as breeding bird. Gull-billed Tern (*Gelochelidon nilotica*): similar, shorter black beak and grey rump. Often occurs inland.

adult

Common Tern

Sterna hirundo

ADULT Medium (35 cm) sea tern. Note deeply forked tail with long streamers. Watch for black cap and black-tipped red beak. Wings uniformly pale grey, primaries with blackish border. Forehead white in autumn. Sexes similar.

JUVENILE As autumn adult, with brown markings across back and black forewing edge.

HABITAT Migrant summer visitor, breeding coastally and occasionally inland over much of Europe. Nests colonially on beaches and on coastal, estuarine and freshwater islands.

NEST Scrape in grass or sand.

VOICE Swift ***kirri-kirri-kirri***; harsh ***kee-aarh*** with emphasis on second syllable.

adult

GENERAL Widespread and fairly common, often numerous around colonies.

Arctic Tern

 Sterna paradisaea

adult

ADULT Medium (37 cm) sea tern, shorter-legged and more grey-bellied than Common Tern (p.124). All-red beak. In flight, watch for forked tail with long streamers, and translucent primaries. Forehead white in autumn. Sexes similar.

JUVENILE As autumn adult, with grey-brown markings across back and grey forewing edges contrasting with white trailing edge.

HABITAT Migrant along W coasts, breeding colonially on N islands. Unusual inland.

NEST Shallow scrape in sand or grass.

VOICE Short sharp ***kee-aah***.

GENERAL Widespread, locally common. Rare Roseate Tern (*S. dougallii*) very pale, with extremely long tail streamers, almost all-black beak.

Little Tern

Sterna albifrons

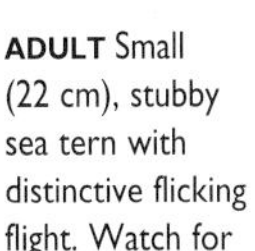

ADULT Small (22 cm), stubby sea tern with distinctive flicking flight. Watch for shallowly forked tail, black-tipped yellow beak, yellow legs and white forehead patch. In flight shows conspicuously black outer primaries. Sexes similar.

JUVENILE Scaly-backed version of autumn adult.

HABITAT Migrant along W and S coasts and lagoons, breeds in loose colonies on sandy beaches.

NEST Shallow scrape in sand.

VOICE High-pitched kitick, hurried ***kirri-kirri-kirrick***.

GENERAL Widespread and regular, but nowhere numerous.

adult

Black Tern

Chlidonias niger

ADULT Small (25 cm), unmistakable when breeding, grey-winged, sooty black-bodied marsh tern. Note white undertail coverts. Watch for black beak and legs and shallowly forked tail. In flight, dips to pick food off water. In autumn and winter, white body, nape and forehead, black crown and dark vertical half-collar marks. Sexes similar.

adult

JUVENILE As winter adult, but scaly above.

HABITAT Migrant and summer visitor to S, central and E Europe, breeds colonially on freshwater swamps and marshes. Migrates along coasts and over inland waters.

NEST Semi-floating platform of waterweed.

VOICE Rarely heard ***krit*** or ***kreek***.

GENERAL Reasonably widespread, regular, locally fairly common.

Guillemot

Uria aalge

adult

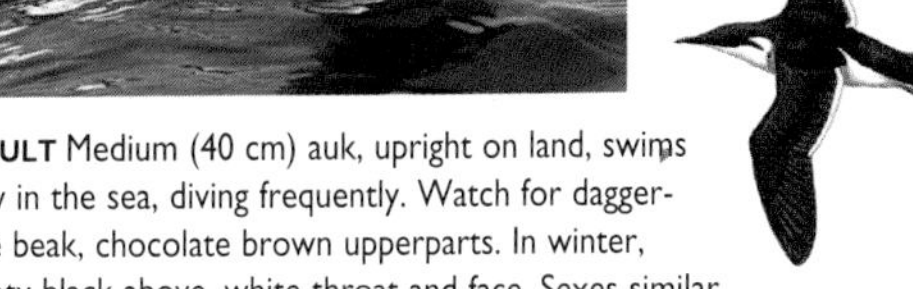

ADULT Medium (40 cm) auk, upright on land, swims low in the sea, diving frequently. Watch for dagger-like beak, chocolate brown upperparts. In winter, sooty black above, white throat and face. Sexes similar.

JUVENILE Resembles winter adult.

HABITAT At sea for much of year off N and W Europe; breeds colonially on cliff ledges.

NEST Single egg laid on bare open rock ledge.

VOICE Grumbling growls and croons on ledges, silent elsewhere.

GENERAL Locally common along rocky breeding coasts in summer, scarce and erratic elsewhere. Black Guillemot (*Cepphus grylle*) of NW coasts and adjacent seas is all-black with striking white wing patches in summer; grey backed, white elsewhere in winter. Note vermillion legs.

Razorbill

Alca torda

ADULT Medium (40 cm), squat, thick-necked auk, jet black above, white below. Dives frequently. Watch for deep flat beak with white vertical line and fine white stripe leading from beak to eye. Winter birds duller, with white face and throat. Flight whirring low over sea. Sexes similar.

JUVENILE As winter adult, greyer with slimmer beak.

HABITAT Summer visitor breeding in loose colonies on W and N cliffs, winters at sea.

NEST Single egg laid on bare rock in cavity.

VOICE Low growls.

GENERAL Locally common along rocky coasts in summer, scarce and erratic elsewhere. Arctic-breeding Little Auk *(Plautus alle)*: half the size of Razorbill, black above and on throat, white on belly, small triangular beak. Irregular in winter.

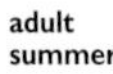

adult summer

Puffin

Fratercula arctica

ADULT Medium (30 cm), squat, upright and familiar auk. Watch for black back, white belly and face patch, bright orange legs and webbed feet, and colourful parrot-like beak. Winter birds duller, with grey face and smaller, dark beak. Sexes similar.

JUVENILE Greyer version of winter adult with slimmer dark beak.

HABITAT Summer visitor breeding colonially on remote headlands and islands in W and N Europe, winters out at sea.

NEST Single egg laid down burrow.

VOICE Low growls.

GENERAL Locally common, sometimes numerous, on breeding coasts in summer. Scarce and erratic elsewhere.

adult

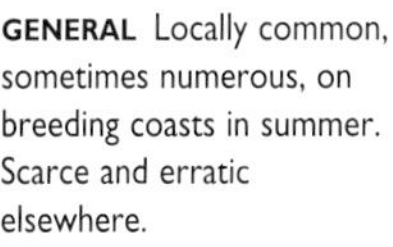

Cuckoo

Cuculus canorus

adult female

ADULT Medium (33 cm), slim, short-legged and long-tailed, heard more than seen. Watch for grey body, barred underparts and white-tipped black tail. Beak tiny; legs yellow. Falcon-like flight on fluttering curved wings; tail looks spoon-ended. Sexes normally similar, female rarely chestnut.

JUVENILE Mottled dark brown above, white with blackish barring below.

HABITAT Migrant and summer visitor to all of Europe except far N, occurs in woodland, on heaths, moors, marshes and farmland.

NEST Parasitic, lays eggs in foster parent nests.

VOICE Cuck-oo and variants, throaty chuckle; female uses bubbling trill.

GENERAL Widespread, often fairly common.

Turtle Dove

Streptopelia turtur

ADULT Medium (28 cm), slim, fast-flying pigeon. Watch for pink breast, scaly bronze back and shoulders, black and white-barred collar patches. In flight shows bronze wings with grey diagonal bars, longish black tail with narrow white borders. Sexes similar.

JUVENILE Duller, browner version of adult, lacking collar marks.

HABITAT Migrant and summer visitor, breeding over much of Europe except N. Essentially a woodland, scrub and farmland bird.

NEST Flimsy platform of twigs in bush.

VOICE Far-carrying monotonous and prolonged purring.

GENERAL Widespread, locally fairly common.

adult

Woodpigeon

136 *Columba palumbus*

ADULT Medium (40 cm), cumbersome pigeon. Watch for pink breast, white collar marks and diagnostic white bar visible in closed wing, conspicuous in flight. Flight fast, but noisy and clumsy, often colliding with vegetation. Gregarious. Sexes similar.

JUVENILE As adult, but lacks collar marks.

adult

HABITAT Widespread year-round resident, summer visitor to N and NE Europe. Breeds in woodland and scrub, feeds in woodland, on all farmland and in urban areas.

NEST Flimsy platform of twigs in bush or tree.

VOICE Monotonously repetitive **coo-coo, coo-coo**.

GENERAL Widespread, often common, often in flocks. Can damage crops.

Stock Dove

Columba oenas

ADULT Medium (33 cm), dull-grey pigeon. Watch for pinkish flush on breast and metallic green collar marks. Swift, direct flight showing triangular black-bordered grey wings and dark-tipped grey tail. Sexes similar.

JUVENILE As adult, but duller, lacking collar marks.

adult

HABITAT Year-round resident over much of Europe, summer visitor to N and NE. Mainly on farmland and woodland, occasionally on coasts and marshes.

NEST In hollow tree or burrow.

VOICE Booming ***coo-oo*** or ***coo-roo-oo***.

GENERAL Widespread, locally fairly common. Rock Dove (*C. livia*, ancestor of town and racing pigeons): similar, with double black wingbars and conspicuous white rump. On remote rocky N coasts and S mountains; scarce.

Collared Dove

138 *Streptopelia decaocto*

adult

ADULT Medium (30 cm), sandy pigeon. Pinkish head and neck with white-edged black band round nape. In flight looks long-tailed and hawk-like, shows buff and grey wings with blackish primaries. Long tail buff above, black below, showing much white on underside. Gregarious. Sexes similar.

JUVENILE Dull version of adult, lacking collar mark.

HABITAT Westward-spreading, post-1940 newcomer to Europe from Asia, colonising Ireland in 1970s. Year-round resident of Europe, except N, in farmland, parks and towns.

NEST Flimsy twig platform in bush, tree, ledge.

VOICE Distinctive dry ***aaah*** in flight; song strident and persistent **coo-coo-coo**.

GENERAL Widespread, comparatively common.

Barn Owl

Tyto alba

ADULT Medium (35 cm), pale, upright owl. Watch for finely mottled orange-buff upperparts and heart-shaped white facial disc with large dark eyes. Legs long, knock-kneed and feathered. Underparts white in NW Europe, dark-speckled rich buff elsewhere. Long-winged in flight, legs dangling.

JUVENILE Much as adult.

HABITAT Widespread year-round resident except in N and NE Europe. Favours open woodland, farmland, heath and marshes.

adult

NEST In hollow tree or deserted building.

VOICE Usually quiet; snoring noises near nest, occasional strident shriek elsewhere.

GENERAL Widespread, nowhere numerous. Usually nocturnal, but in winter may hunt in daylight.

Hawk Owl

Surnia ulula

ADULT Medium (38 cm), long-tailed owl, active daylight hunter. Watch for speckled back and finely barred underparts, and for rectangular white facial disc with striking black vertical margins. Hawk-like posture emphasized by long tail and short, rounded wings in flight. Sexes similar.

JUVENILE Much as adult.

HABITAT Year-round resident in N birch and conifer forests.

NEST In tree hole.

VOICE Distinctive rapid series of short whistles.

GENERAL Helpfully chooses prominent perches. Locally fairly common.

DISTRIBUTION
N Scandinavia and Finland, not found in Iceland and Greenland

adult

Little Owl

Athene noctua

ADULT Small (23 cm), squat, upright owl, perches prominently in daylight. Watch for rectangular facial disc with white 'spectacles', and 'fierce' white eyebrows. Sexes similar.

JUVENILE As adult, but paler, heavily streaked.

HABITAT Year-round resident over much of Europe except N and NW. Broad choice of habitats from woodland, farm and heath to suburban areas and coasts.

adult

NEST In hollow in building, bank or tree.

VOICE Penetrating yelps and ***poop*** whistles.

GENERAL Widespread, fairly common. Pygmy Owl *(Glaucidium passerinum)*: comparatively tiny, with rounded head and pale facial disc. Hunts in daylight through N conifer forests.

Tawny Owl

142 *Strix aluco*

ADULT Medium (38 cm), plump and distinctively round-headed owl. Plumage finely marked grey-brown to reddish brown. Watch for circular facial disc, narrowly bordered black and buff, with two central prominent buff stripes up onto crown. Large all-dark eyes. Sexes similar.

adult

JUVENILE Much as adult.

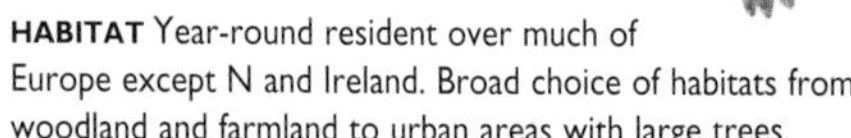

HABITAT Year-round resident over much of Europe except N and Ireland. Broad choice of habitats from woodland and farmland to urban areas with large trees.

NEST Usually in hollow tree.

VOICE Well-known trembling ***whoo-hoo-hoooo*** and sharp ***kew-wit***.

GENERAL Widespread and familiar despite nocturnal habits. The most numerous owl.

Long-eared Owl

Asio otus

adult

ADULT Medium (35 cm), slim and upright owl, comparatively long-winged in flight. Plumage finely marked rich browns giving excellent camouflage. Watch for rounded head, circular facial disc with buff lateral margins and paired white central stripes. Conspicuous long ear-tufts. Eyes strikingly yellow or flame. Sexes similar.

JUVENILE As adult, but duller.

HABITAT Year-round resident or migrant over much of Europe, summer visitor in N. Favours woodlands of many types.

NEST Often in old crow's nest or squirrel drey.

VOICE Repetitive deep ***poop*** calls when breeding.

GENERAL Nocturnal, widespread, but inconspicuous, even secretive. Probably commoner than seems.

Short-eared Owl

144 *Asio flammeus*

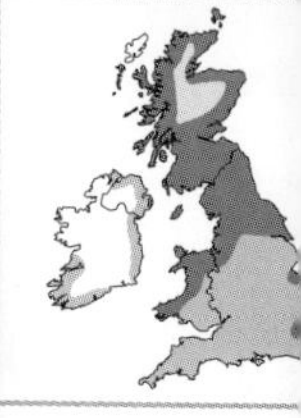

adult

ADULT Medium (38 cm), pale sandy-brown, daylight-hunting owl. Watch for short indistinct ear-tufts; clear roughly circular facial disc, bright yellow eyes. Distinctive bouncing flight; note pale undersides to wings and conspicuous dark patches at wrist. Sexes similar.

JUVENILE Much as adult.

HABITAT Year-round resident or migrant in central and W Europe. Summer visitor in N and winter visitor to S. Favours tundra, moor, rough grassland and marshes.

NEST Rough scrape on ground.

VOICE Normally silent.

GENERAL Widespread, but erratic in distribution and numbers, sometimes locally numerous..

Tengmalm's Owl

Aegolius funereus

DISTRIBUTION N Scandinavia and Finland, not found in Iceland and Greenland

ADULT Small (25 cm), squat, large-headed owl. Brown above, boldly spotted; whitish below with brown mottling and streaking. Watch for rectangular facial disc with pale then dark borders, and for conspicuous 'raised eyebrow' appearance. Eyes yellow. Sexes similar.

adult

JUVENILE Much as adult.

HABITAT Year-round resident in N and E. Favours woodland and forest, often montane and often predominantly coniferous.

NEST Usually hollow trees or old nests.

VOICE Repetitive abrupt whistle.

GENERAL Largely nocturnal; variable in both distribution and numbers, as in several other owls depending on availability of suitable prey.

Nightjar

Caprimulgus europaeus

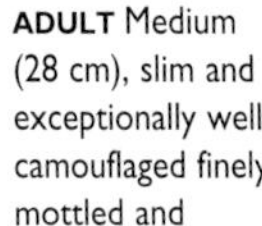

ADULT Medium (28 cm), slim and exceptionally well camouflaged finely mottled and streaked brown, buff and grey plumage. Note short-legged horizontal stance. In silent, moth-like flight, watch for long tail and pointed wings. Males show white patches in wingtips and at tip of tail.

JUVENILE Much as adult female.

HABITAT Summer visitor or migrant to much of Europe except far N. Favours dry heaths, open (often recently cleared) woodland and scrub.

NEST Well-concealed simple scrape on ground.

VOICE Listen for extended ***churring***, with wing-claps in display flight. Best heard at dusk.

GENERAL Widespread, but only locally regular, rarely numerous.

adult male

Swift

Apus apus

adult male

ADULT Small (18 cm), highly aerial bird with familiar long, slim sickle-shaped wings. Note solid, but well-streamlined, sooty-black body, short shallowly forked tail, and large head with smoky white throat patch. Often gregarious, flying at high speed in noisy groups. Sexes similar.

JUVENILE As adult, but with scaly markings.

HABITAT Summer visitor or migrant over most of Europe except far N. Usually breeds in urban areas, feeds over any habitat, often over fresh water.

NEST Rough crudely lined scrape in roof cavity.

VOICE Distinctive shrill high-pitched scream.

GENERAL Widespread, often common. Pallid Swift *(A. pallida)* of Mediterranean: similar but stockier, slower in flight, slightly paler with larger throat patch.

Alpine Swift

 Apus melba

DISTRIBUTION
Summer visitor to S Europe and N Africa; winters in S Africa

ADULT Small (20 cm), but detectably larger than Swift (p.147). Shares Swift flight silhouette and long, narrow sickle-shaped wings, but watch for sandy brown upperparts, throat and undertail contrasting with white belly. Flight more powerful and faster even than Swift. Sexes similar.

JUVENILE As adult, but duller with scaly back markings.

HABITAT Summer visitor to S Europe, breeding in mountain areas, towns and on coastal cliffs. Ranges widely when feeding.

NEST Cavity in rocks or building; breeds colonially.

VOICE Surprisingly loud, far-carrying and distinctive musical trill.

GENERAL Fairly widespread, locally common.

adult male

Swallow

Hirundo rustica

ADULT Small (20 cm including tail streamers) and familiar. Watch for dark purplish upperparts, white underparts and chestnut face patch. Swift, swooping flight on long curved wings. Shows white in deeply forked tail in flight. Male has longer streamers, otherwise sexes similar.

adult male

JUVENILE Duller, with short tail streamers.

HABITAT Summer visitor to most of Europe. Breeds in buildings, ranges widely when feeding, often over water.

NEST Open cup of mud and grass.

VOICE Extended musical twittering; sharp chirrup of alarm indicates presence of a raptor.

GENERAL Widespread. Scarcer Red-rumped Swallow *(H. daurica)*, of Mediterranean: blackish cap, chestnut cheeks, nape and rump contrasting with dark back.

Sand Martin

Riparia riparia

ADULT Tiny (12 cm) hirundine. Largely aerial; watch for longish curved, pointed wings. Sandy brown above, whitish below with brown collar. Gregarious. Sexes similar.

adult male

JUVENILE As adult, but sandy scaly markings on back.

HABITAT Summer visitor and migrant to all Europe except farthest N. Breeds colonially in sandy banks, usually feeds in flight over nearby fresh waters.

NEST Excavates burrow in bank.

VOICE Soft rattling trill, sharp chirrup of alarm.

GENERAL Widespread, locally numerous. Has declined dramatically in some areas recently. Similar Crag Martin *(Hirundo rupestris)*: grey-brown above, grey-buff below. Heavier-built and broader-winged than Sand Martin, year-round resident in Mediterranean mountains and occasionally towns.

House Martin

Delichon urbica

ADULT Tiny (12 cm) hirundine with distinctive purplish black and white plumage. In flight, watch for relatively short broad-based curved wings, white rump and short shallowly forked tail. From beneath, black cap contrasting with white undersides gives capped appearance. On ground, watch for white legs feathered to toes. Sexes similar.

JUVENILE Much as adult, but duller.

HABITAT Summer visitor or migrant over most of Europe except furthest N. Breeds on buildings, occasionally cliffs. Ranges widely when feeding, often over water.

adult male

NEST Very distinctive quarter-sphere of mud pellets, fixed under overhang. Often colonial.

VOICE Harsh chirrup; unmusical twittering.

GENERAL Widespread, often fairly numerous.

Kingfisher

 Alcedo atthis

ADULT Small (17 cm), but unmistakable. Upperparts electric blue-green, underparts chestnut. Crown blue, cheek stripe chestnut and white. Arrow-like rapid flight, usually low over water. Tiny scarlet-orange feet and large dagger-shaped black or black and orange beak. Sexes broadly similar.

adult

JUVENILE As adult, but duller, with heavily dark-flecked crown.

HABITAT Year-round resident over much of Europe, migrant or summer visitor in N. Favours rivers, lakes and streams; occasionally coasts in winter.

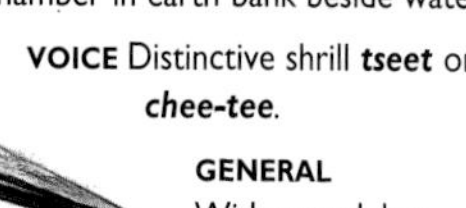

NEST Excavates burrow and nest chamber in earth bank beside water.

VOICE Distinctive shrill ***tseet*** or ***chee-tee***.

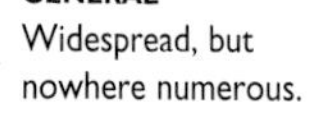

GENERAL Widespread, but nowhere numerous.

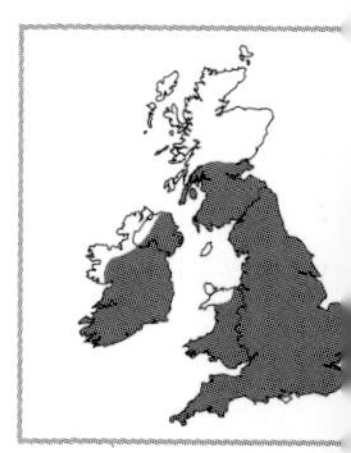

Bee-eater

Merops apiaster

ISTRIBUTION
ummer visitor to
pain, S. France,
aly, Greece,
urkey

ADULT Medium (28 cm), slim, swallow-like and unmistakably colourful. No other European bird shows such dazzling plumage. Watch for long-winged, swooping flight and slim, extended, central tail feathers, longish, dark, downcurved and pointed beak. Gregarious. Sexes similar.

JUVENILE Muted-colour version of adult.

HABITAT Favours open dry country. Often feeds over lakes and marshes with high insect populations.

NEST Colonial, excavates burrow in sandy soil or banks.

VOICE Listen for distinctive bell-like trilling ***prrewit***, often audible when birds are out of sight.

GENERAL Only locally common.

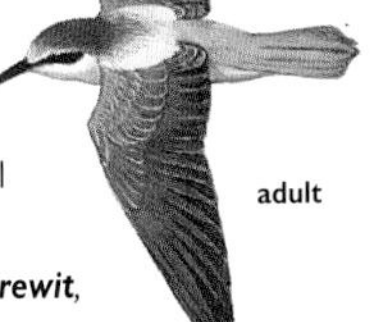
adult

Hoopoe

154 *Upupa epops*

ADULT Medium (28 cm) and unmistakable. Watch for black and white striped back and wings, unusual pinkish-fawn body, long black and ginger crest (erected when excited or often on landing), long, slender, slightly downcurved beak. Distinctive floppy flight, black and white pattern prominent on rounded, fingered wings. Sexes similar.

JUVENILE As adult, duller and greyer, with tiny crest.

HABITAT Summer visitor or migrant to much of Europe except N and NW, where occasional vagrant. Favours dry open country with trees, including orchards, cork oak and olive groves.

NEST Notoriously smelly; in tree hole.

VOICE Soft, but penetrating, repeated ***poo***.

GENERAL Widespread, but only locally common.

adult

Wryneck

Jynx torquilla

ADULT Small (18 cm) relative of woodpeckers. Short-legged, with relatively long body. Looks drab brown at a distance, but close to note beautiful finely marked plumage. Watch for striped head and grey and buff V markings on back. Beak short and strong. Tail long, soft (not stiff as in woodpeckers), finely barred. Often feeds on ground. Sexes similar.

adult

JUVENILE As adult, but duller.

HABITAT Summer visitor or migrant to most of Europe except far N and NW. Favours open land with old trees.

NEST Excavates hole in tree.

VOICE Persistent laughing ***kee-kee-kee***.

GENERAL Widespread, but erratic and inconspicuous, never numerous.

Green Woodpecker

 Picus viridis

juveni

ADULT Medium (30 cm) woodpecker, often feeds on ground. Distinctive greenish-gold upperparts, gold rump, greenish buff below. Watch for stout dagger-like beak, red crown and black face. Male has red and black moustachial stripe, female has black stripe. Flight undulating.

JUVENILE Duller, with dense darker barring.

HABITAT Year-round resident over much of Europe except N and Ireland. Favours dry heath, grassland and open woodlands.

NEST Makes oval-opening hole in tree.

VOICE Distinctive ringing laugh ***yah-yah-yah***.

GENERAL Widespread, locally fairly common. Grey-headed Woodpecker *(P. canus)* of E Europe: browner, grey head and small scarlet patch on crown of male only.

Black Woodpecker

Sterna albifrons

ISTRIBUTION
:, E and N Europe. opulation growing NW Europe

ADULT Medium (45 cm), but the largest and most striking of European woodpeckers. Plumage almost entirely glossy black, with crimson crown, more extensive in male than female. Golden eye. Watch for long-necked, long-tailed 'stretched' appearance in undulating flight.

JUVENILE Only slightly duller than adult, eye pale.

HABITAT Primarily a bird of E Europe, but does occur in the Pyrenees. Favours extensive areas of old forest of all types.

NEST Excavates hole in tree.

VOICE Harsh, far-carrying ***klee-oh***. Drums frequently, loud and slow rhythm.

GENERAL Fairly widespread and locally not uncommon.

juvenile

Great Spotted Woodpecker

 Dendrocopos major

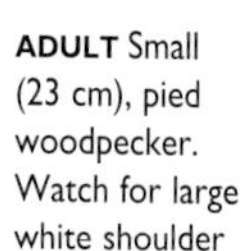

ADULT Small (23 cm), pied woodpecker. Watch for large white shoulder patch, multiple white wingbars, conspicuous scarlet undertail. Complex head pattern; crown black in female, with red nape patch in male. Undulating flight, perches head-up on trees.

JUVENILE Duller version of adult, note red crown.

HABITAT Widespread year-round across much of Europe except Ireland and farthest N regions.

NEST Excavates hole in tree.

VOICE Explosive ***chack***; drums frequently.

GENERAL Widespread, often common. Middle Spotted Woodpecker *(D. medius)* of central Europe is smaller, with all-red crown and dull pink undertail, streaked buff underparts.

juvenile

Lesser Spotted Woodpecker

juvenile

ADULT Small (15 cm), sparrow-sized woodpecker. Watch for black and white 'ladder' markings on back and wings. Male has white forehead and red crown, female buffish white.

JUVENILE Much as adult, but with reddish crown.

HABITAT Year-round resident over much of Europe except extreme N and NW, including Ireland. Favours deciduous woodland, parks, orchards.

NEST Excavates hole in tree.

VOICE Usefully distinctive high-pitched, repetitive ***kee-kee-kee***. Extended high-pitched drumming frequent when breeding.

GENERAL Widespread, but often inconspicuous.

Crested Lark

Galerida cristata

DISTRIBUTIOI
Found througho
Europe apart fro
far north and we

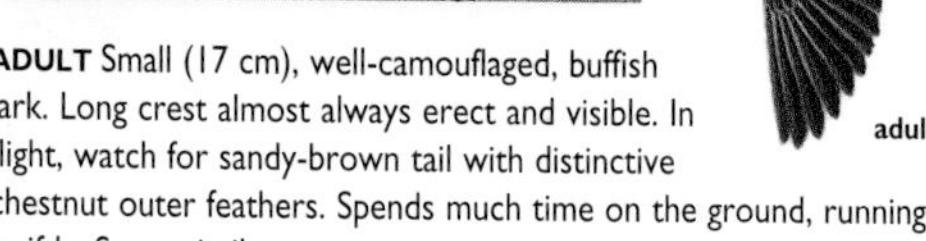

adult

ADULT Small (17 cm), well-camouflaged, buffish lark. Long crest almost always erect and visible. In flight, watch for sandy-brown tail with distinctive chestnut outer feathers. Spends much time on the ground, running swiftly. Sexes similar.

JUVENILE As adult, but often more rufous, with smaller crest.

HABITAT Year-round resident across S and central Europe, absent from N and (unexpectedly) from Britain and Ireland. Favours open land, frequently farmland and roadsides, often near habitation.

NEST Well-concealed grassy cup on ground.

VOICE ***Doo-dee-doo***; varied melodious song with mimicry, usually from ground or a post.

GENERAL Widespread, frequently common.

Woodlark

Lullula arborea

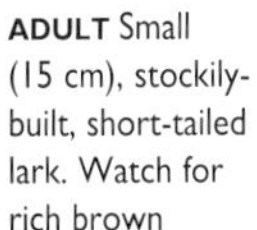

ADULT Small (15 cm), stockily-built, short-tailed lark. Watch for rich brown appearance and bold whitish eyestripes, which with chestnut cheek patches give capped appearance. In flight shows black and white patch on wing shoulder and white tips to outer tail feathers. Sexes similar.

JUVENILE Much as adult.

HABITAT Resident or migrant in SW and S Europe, less common as summer visitor to central and W areas. Favours dry open woodland and heaths.

adult

NEST Well-concealed grassy cup on ground.

VOICE Listen for distinctive flight call ***tee-loo-ee***; melodious song (in spiralling song flight) based on ***loo-loo-yaa*** phrases.

GENERAL Widespread, locally fairly common.

Skylark

162 *Alanda arvensis*

adult

ADULT Small (18 cm), long-bodied, well-camouflaged lark. Watch for short but often visible crest. In flight shows white outer tail feathers and characteristic white trailing edges to markedly triangular wings. Sexes similar.

JUVENILE Much as adult.

HABITAT Year-round resident and migrant in S, central and W Europe, summer visitor in N. Frequents open landscapes of all types.

NEST Well-concealed grassy cup on ground.

VOICE Flight call a liquid chirrup; varied musical song rich in mimicry, usually while hovering or circling high.

GENERAL Widespread, often common. Rare Shore Lark *(Eremophila alpestris)* breeds on Arctic tundra, winters on remote coastal marshes, has yellow and black face and bib.

Tree Pipit

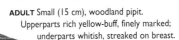

Anthus trivialis 163

juvenile

ADULT Small (15 cm), woodland pipit. Upperparts rich yellow-buff, finely marked; underparts whitish, streaked on breast. Watch for pale pinkish legs, white outer tail feathers in flight. Sexes similar.

JUVENILE Much as adult.

HABITAT Summer visitor or migrant to most of Europe. Favours heaths with trees and woodland with substantial clearings.

NEST Well-concealed grassy cup on ground.

VOICE Distinctive ***teees*** flight call. Descending trilling song, ending in repeated ***see-ar*** notes, in parachute song flight.

GENERAL Widespread, locally fairly common.

Meadow Pipit

Anthus pratensis

ADULT Small (15 cm), undistinguished, streaky pipit, largely terrestrial in behaviour. Plumage variable from yellowish, through olive to greenish-buff or brown, whitish below, copiously streaked. Watch for pale brown legs, white outer tail feathers. Sexes similar.

JUVENILE Much as adult.

HABITAT Year-round resident, winter visitor or migrant over much of Europe, summer visitor to N. Favours open landscapes: moorland, heath, grassland, farmland and marshes.

NEST Well-concealed grassy cup on ground.

juvenile

VOICE Flight call a thin ***tisseep*** or ***tseep;*** song an accelerating descending trill, weaker than Tree Pipit (p.159).

GENERAL Widespread, locally common.

Tawny Pipit

Anthus campestris

ADULT Small (17 cm), pale pipit. Upperparts pale sandy-buff, only faintly marked, underparts whitish, flushed with pink in spring. Watch for conspicuous pale eyestripe, and pinkish legs. Relatively long-tailed, behaves almost more like a wagtail than a pipit. Sexes similar.

JUVENILE Rather darker and more heavily streaked.

HABITAT Summer visitor to S and central Europe, vagrant further N. Favours arid open areas: heaths, saltpans, dunes and marshland.

NEST Well-concealed grassy cup on ground.

juvenile

VOICE Characteristic broad ***tseep*** flight call; song repetitive, reeling ***seely-seely-seely***.

GENERAL Widespread, locally fairly common.

DISTRIBUTION
Summer visitor to C and S Europe; not seen in Britain, Iceland and Scandinavia

Rock Pipit

Anthus petrosus

ADULT Small (17 cm) pipit, darker and greyer overall than Meadow Pipit (p.164), longer in the tail. Watch for longish dark legs and smoky grey outer tail feathers. Sexes similar.

JUVENILE Much as adult.

HABITAT Year-round resident, winter visitor or migrant along much of W coast of Europe, summer visitor to Scandinavian coasts. Favours rocky coasts.

NEST Well-concealed grassy cup.

VOICE Strident ***zeep***; loud descending trill song in parachute display flight.

GENERAL Widespread. Scarcer Water Pipit *(A. spinoletta)*: paler, with unstreaked back, unstreaked pink breast in spring (whitish, boldly streaked at other times); breeds in S and E mountainous areas, winters in S marshlands, vagrant elsewhere.

Yellow Wagtail

Motacilla flava

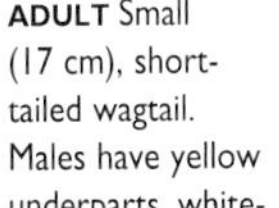

ADULT Small (17 cm), short-tailed wagtail. Males have yellow underparts, white-edged black tails; heads vary. Blue-headed (W, central): blue head, white eyestripe; Yellow (NW, Britain and Ireland): olive head, yellow eyestripe; Spanish (Iberia): grey head, white bib, white behind eye; Grey-headed (N): dark grey head, black cheeks, no eyestripe; Black-headed (SE): jet black head, no eyestripe. All females olive above, dull yellow below. In winter, duller and paler.

JUVENILE As winter adult, with scaly wing markings.

HABITAT Widespread summer visitor and migrant. Favours open land: farmland, marshes, grassland.

NEST Well-concealed grassy cup on ground.

VOICE ***Tseep*** flight call; twittering song.

GENERAL Locally fairly common.

Grey Wagtail

 Motacilla cinerea

ADULT Small (18 cm). Slimmest and longest-tailed of European wagtails. Watch for grey back and crown, white eyestripe, yellow underparts, brilliant yellow rump and undertail. Wags white-edged, blackish tail non-stop. Male is brighter yellow, has black bib in summer.

JUVENILE Paler, duller version of female.

HABITAT Year-round resident over much of Europe, summer visitor to N and NE, and to some mountain areas. Favours fast-moving fresh water, streams, rapids, weirs and sluices.

NEST Grassy cup hidden in cavity near water.

VOICE Characteristic ***chee-seek*** call; trilling song resembles Blue Tit (p.218).

GENERAL Widespread, never numerous.

adult male summer

White Wagtail

Motacilla alba

ADULT Small (18 cm), pied wagtail with silver-grey back and incessantly wagging, white-edged black tail. Grey crown, white cheeks, black bib. Female duller and less clearly marked than male. Often gregarious. Undulating flight.

adult female winter Pied

adult female summer Pied

adult male summer Pied

JUVENILE As female, but with smoky-yellow tinge.

HABITAT Year-round resident or migrant over much of Europe, summer visitor in N. Favours open grassland, farmland, marshland and waterside, and urban areas.

NEST Grassy cup concealed in cavity.

DISTRIBUTION
Resident in W and S Europe; summer visitor in Scandinavia and E Europe

VOICE Soft disyllabic ***swee-eep***; twittering song.

GENERAL Widespread, locally common. Pied Wagtail of Britain and Ireland is dark subspecies, male with jet black crown and back. Sharp ***chissick*** call.

Waxwing

 Bombycilla garrulus

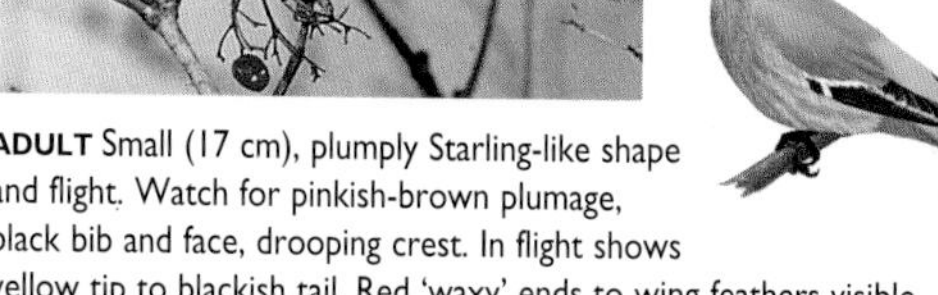

juvenile

ADULT Small (17 cm), plumply Starling-like shape and flight. Watch for pinkish-brown plumage, black bib and face, drooping crest. In flight shows yellow tip to blackish tail. Red 'waxy' ends to wing feathers visible only at close range. Sexes similar.

JUVENILE As adult, but duller, lacking red feather tips.

HABITAT Year-round resident or winter visitor to N Europe, summer visitor to far N. Breeds in conifer woodland or boreal scrub, winters where berries plentiful.

NEST Grassy cup in tree fork.

VOICE Characteristic bell-like trill.

GENERAL Locally common in breeding areas. Erratic wanderer elsewhere.

Dipper

Cinclus cinclus

ADULT Small (17 cm) and dumpy, like a gigantic aquatic Wren (p.171). Bobs, tail-cocked, on rocks before walking into fast moving water. Large white bib, belly chestnut (Britain and Ireland) or blackish (rest of Europe). Sexes similar.

JUVENILE Duller and scaly.

HABITAT Year-round resident in N, NW and S Europe. Favours fast-moving rivers and streams, often in hilly or mountainous country. Vagrant elsewhere.

NEST Grassy cup, concealed in cavity or under overhang, always beside or over water.

VOICE Loud, distinctive ***zit*** or ***zit-zit*** call; both sexes produce warbling song.

GENERAL Fairly common in appropriate habitat.

adult
British race

Wren

 Troglodytes troglodytes

juvenile

ADULT Tiny (10 cm) but familiar despite its mouse-like, largely terrestrial habits. Watch for crouched-stance, dark-barred rich brown plumage, pale eyestripe, cocked tail and pointed, downcurved beak. Flight whirring on rounded wings, usually low and direct. Sexes similar.

JUVENILE Much as adult.

HABITAT Year-round resident over much of Europe, summer visitor in far N. Favours dense vegetation, also rocky mountains and sea cliffs.

NEST Domed grassy structure with side entrance, well-concealed in vegetation or cavity.

VOICE Scolding ***churr*** call; amazingly loud boisterously musical song.

GENERAL Widespread, often common.

Dunnock

Prunella modularis

juvenile

ADULT Small (15 cm), dull bird, lead-grey on head and breast, dark brown back and wings. Beak straight and pointed, legs pinkish, strong; spends much time hopping on ground or in vegetation. Sexes similar.

JUVENILE Duller and scaly.

HABITAT Year-round resident over much of Europe, summer visitor to far N and NE, winter visitor to far S. Favours woodland and scrub of all types, farmland and urban gardens.

NEST Well-concealed grass cup in shrub.

VOICE Strident piping **seek** call; brief but melodious snatches of song.

GENERAL Widespread, locally fairly common. Scarce Alpine Accentor *(P.collaris)*: of high mountain areas in S Europe, broadly similar, but with speckled grey bib and chestnut breast and flanks.

Nightingale

174 *Luscinia megarhynchos*

juvenile

ADULT Small (17 cm), drab thrush. Watch for warm brown back, paler underside, relatively long rufous tail. Long, strong, pinkish-brown legs. Keeps under cover. Sexes similar.

JUVENILE Paler, heavily speckled.

HABITAT Summer visitor or migrant to S and central Europe. Prefers woodland with dense undergrowth, scrub, and swampy thickets.

NEST Well-concealed leafy cup near ground.

VOICE Fluid ***hoo-eet*** call; song rich and varied, long and melodious; listen for opening pee-ooo notes.

GENERAL Widespread, locally quite common. Similar Thrush Nightingale *(L. luscinia)* in same habitats further N, greyish below, faint speckling.

Bluethroat

Luscinia svecica

adult

ADULT Small (15 cm), often secretive thrush. Male has electric blue throat with red or white central spot, much duller in autumn and winter. Female has black-fringed white throat. Watch for brown tail, darker at tip, chestnut patches on either side at base – often all that is seen as darts for cover.

JUVENILE Sandy brown and speckled, with characteristic tail pattern.

HABITAT Summer visitor to N and NE Europe, migrant or vagrant elsewhere. Prefers dense, low, swampy scrub or heathland.

NEST Well-concealed grassy cup on ground.

VOICE Sharp ***tack*** call; extended high-pitched melodious warbling song.

GENERAL Locally fairly common.

Robin

176 *Erithacus rubecula*

adult

ADULT Tiny (13 cm), familiar, plump, long-legged thrush. Watch for rich orange-red face and breast with grey margin. Back brown, underparts whitish. Perky stance showing short brown tail, hops rapidly. Often terrestrial, flights usually short and low. Sexes similar.

JUVENILE Reddish-brown above with buff markings, whitish below heavily scaled with brown.

HABITAT Year-round resident, migrant or winter visitor over much of Europe, summer visitor to N and NE. Varied habitat from woodland, parks and gardens to offshore islands in winter.

NEST Well-concealed grassy cup on or near the ground, often in cavity.

VOICE Sharp ***tick*** call; high-pitched warbling song.

GENERAL Widespread, often common.

Redstart

Phoenicurus phoenicurus

ADULT Small (15 cm), slim, red-tailed chat. Watch for grey back, white forehead, black face and chestnut underparts of summer male, colours partly concealed by buff markings at other times. Female brown above, pale buff below, but with characteristic brown-centred chestnut-red tail. Both sexes show plain brown wings in flight.

JUVENILE Speckled, with brown-centred red tail.

adult

HABITAT Summer visitor or migrant across Europe. Favours woodland, parks and occasionally heaths.

NEST Well-concealed grassy cup, usually concealed in cavity.

VOICE Fluting **too-eet** call; brief, scratchy, but melodious song, ending in a rattle.

GENERAL Widespread, locally fairly common.

Black Redstart

Phoenicurus ochruros

juvenile

ADULT Small (15 cm), distinctively dark, red-tailed chat. Summer male sooty black, paler in winter. Watch for white wing patches. Female uniformly sooty buff. Both sexes have characteristic brown-centred chestnut-red tail. Often feeds on ground. Flicks and shivers tail.

JUVENILE As female, but heavily speckled buff.

HABITAT Year-round resident, migrant or winter visitor to W, SW and S Europe, summer visitor to N and E. Varied habitat including mountain screes, town roofs and major buildings.

NEST Grassy cup, well concealed in cavity.

VOICE Sharp ***tack*** call; brief rattling fast warbling song.

GENERAL Widespread, locally common in S.

Whinchat

Saxicola rubetra

ADULT Tiny (13 cm), upright chat. Watch for bold white eyestripe separating dark crown from equally dark cheeks, white moustachial streak, and orange-flushed breast of male. Female paler and duller. Chooses prominent perches, continuously flicks wings and tail. In flight shows white patches in wings and distinctive white sides to base of tail.

JUVENILE As female, but drabber, heavily speckled.

HABITAT Summer visitor or migrant over most of Europe. Favours open rough grassland, heath and scrub.

NEST Well-concealed grassy cup beneath bush.

VOICE Harsh ***teck*** call; brief high-pitched warble of song, usually produced in song flight.

GENERAL Though widespread, scarce in many areas.

adult female

Stonechat

180 *Saxicola torquata*

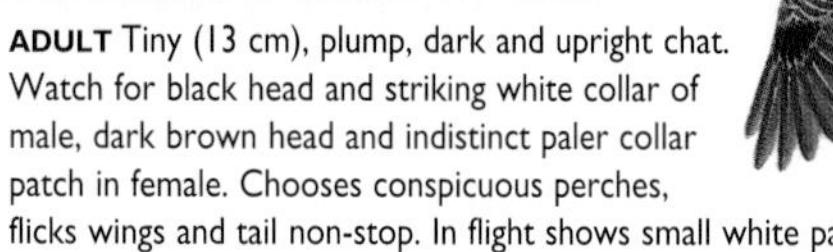

ADULT Tiny (13 cm), plump, dark and upright chat. Watch for black head and striking white collar of male, dark brown head and indistinct paler collar patch in female. Chooses conspicuous perches, flicks wings and tail non-stop. In flight shows small white patch in wings and white rump.

JUVENILE As female, but drabber, heavily speckled.

HABITAT Year-round resident, migrant or winter visitor to S and W Europe, summer visitor to central and some N areas. Favours heath and scrub (often gorse).

NEST Grassy cup well-concealed on ground at base of bush.

VOICE Frequent ***tchack*** call; brief high-pitched scratchy warble song, often in song flight.

GENERAL Widespread, sometimes locally common.

Wheatear

Oenanthe oenanthe

ADULT Small (15 cm), pale, terrestrial chat. Watch for grey back, bold black eyepatch and wings of male; female browner and duller. Striking white rump and tail ending in an inverted black T mark conspicuous in flight. Fast bouncing hop across ground, flicks wings and tail frequently.

JUVENILE As female, but drabber, heavily speckled.

HABITAT Summer visitor or migrant to much of Europe. Favours open areas of heath, grass or moor, even coastal sand or shingle, rarely with tall vegetation.

adult

NEST Grassy cup usually concealed in hole, old burrow, or crevice in the ground.

VOICE Harsh ***tack***; brief scratchy warble of song, often produced in flight.

GENERAL Widespread, but only locally common.

Black-eared Wheatear

 Oenanthe hispanica

ADULT Small (15 cm), terrestrial chat. Male upperparts whitish, washed cinnamon, underparts richer cinnamon, contrasting black wings. Black patch through eye, or black face and throat. Winter male much duller. Female as Wheatear (p.181), but darker head and wings. All have black T mark on white rump and tail, as Wheatear.

DISTRIBUTION Summer visitor to Mediterranean, east to Turkey amd Middle East

JUVENILE Similar to Wheatear, but darker-headed.

HABITAT Summer visitor or migrant to S and SW Europe. Favours open arid stony heath and scrub.

NEST Grassy cup in cavity, usually on ground.

VOICE ***Tchack*** call; brief high-pitched scratchy warbling song.

GENERAL Locally fairly common.

adult female

Ring Ousel

Turdus torquatus

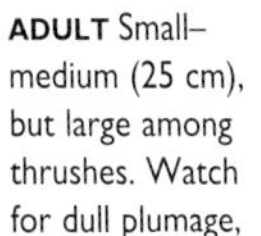

ADULT Small–medium (25 cm), but large among thrushes. Watch for dull plumage, sooty black in male, sooty brown with scaly markings in female. White crescentic throat patch clear in male, often obscure in female. In flight, look for silver-grey wings.

JUVENILE Rich brown, pale scaly markings, lacks bib.

HABITAT Summer visitor to N, W and central mountain areas, migrant almost anywhere. Favours upland grassland, moors, rocky mountainsides in breeding season.

juvenile

NEST Well-concealed grassy cup on ground.

VOICE ***Chack*** or ***chack-chack*** calls; song loud, simple, but melodious ***chew-you, chew-you***.

GENERAL Though widespread, never numerous.

Blackbird

184 *Turdus merula*

ADULT Small–medium (25 cm), but large among thrushes. Adult male unmistakable in glossy jet black with orange beak and eye-ring. Female rich brown, with dark-bordered whitish throat, often faintly speckled on breast. Looks long-tailed in powerful direct flight.

JUVENILE Reddish brown above, slightly paler and spotted below.

juvenile

HABITAT Year-round resident, migrant and winter visitor over much of Europe, summer visitor to far N. Familiar in farmland, heath, woodland and urban areas.

NEST Grassy cup in tree or bush.

VOICE Penetrating ***pink*** or ***chink*** calls; extended fluting and melodious song. Chooses prominent song-posts.

GENERAL Widespread, frequently common.

Blue Rock Thrush

Monticola solitarius

DISTRIBUTION Resident around Mediterranean along coasts; widespread in Spain

ADULT Small (20 cm), dark thrush. Summer male unmistakable: slate-blue body, blackish wings. Winter male duller and slaty. Female duller, brown above, fawn below with darker streaks. Shy – creeps inconspicuously around rocky areas.

adult female

JUVENILE Similar to female.

HABITAT Year-round resident in rocky, often mountainous areas in S Europe, occasionally in towns.

NEST Grassy cup, usually concealed in crevice.

VOICE Sharp ***tchick*** call; loud musical song, often from prominent rocky song-post.

GENERAL Widespread, but rarely numerous. Rock Thrush *(M. saxatilis):* summer visitor to higher altitudes. Male blue above, orange below with white back, black wings. Female brown above, buff below.

Fieldfare

Turdus pilaris

ADULT Small–medium (25 cm), long-tailed thrush. Adult has grey head, chestnut-bronze back, dark-speckled ginger-buff breast. Beak yellow, tipped black. Watch for black tail and grey rump in flight. Sexes similar.

JUVENILE Browner above, fawn below, heavily speckled.

HABITAT Winter visitor or migrant to much of Europe, year-round resident in north-central areas, summer visitor to far N. Breeds in woodland, forests, gardens. Winters in woodland, often on open farmland and grass.

NEST Grassy cup in tree fork.

VOICE Distinctive laughing ***chack-chack-chack*** calls; song a scratchy poorly-formed warble.

GENERAL Widespread, often quite common as breeding bird, migrant, and winter visitor.

Song Thrush

Turdus philomelos

ADULT Small (23 cm), short-tailed, upright thrush. Familiar sandy-brown back, boldly black-speckled whitish underparts, tinged buff on breast. Medium-length and strength, pointed thrush beak. Often terrestrial, runs rather than hops. Flight direct, shows buff underwing. Sexes similar.

JUVENILE As adult, but heavily buff-speckled back.

HABITAT Year-round resident and migrant over central and S areas, winter visitor to SW Europe, summer visitor in N. Favours woodland, parks, gardens and other open landscapes with trees.

NEST Distinctive mud-lined grass cup in shrub.

VOICE Thin ***seep*** call; song usually a series of musical notes characteristically each repeated two or three times. Perches prominently to sing.

GENERAL Widespread, often common.

Redwing

 Turdus iliacus

ADULT Small (20 cm), dark, short-tailed thrush. Watch for buff eyestripe and moustachial streak on either side of dark cheek. Belly whitish, brown speckled, characteristic red flanks, red on underwings in flight. Sexes similar.

JUVENILE Duller than adult, heavily buff speckled on back.

HABITAT Summer visitor to N Europe, breeding in forests and gardens; migrant or winter visitor elsewhere. Favours woodland, open fields and grassland.

NEST Grassy cup in tree or shrub.

VOICE Extended ***see-eep*** flight call, especially migration. Song, fluting notes in slow tempo.

GENERAL Widespread, but erratic. Often locally numerous in winter.

Mistle Thrush

Turdus viscivorus

juvenile

ADULT Medium (27 cm), largest and palest of the European thrushes. Note pale sandy-brown upperparts and boldly brown-spotted pale buffish breast. In swooping flight, watch for whitish edges to tail. Sexes similar.

JUVENILE Paler, greyer, grey scaly pattern on back.

HABITAT Year-round resident and occasional migrant over much of Europe, summer visitor to N and NE. Favours open woodland, farmland with trees, parks and gardens. Often on open fields in winter.

NEST Bulky and untidy cup of grass and litter, usually high in a tree.

VOICE Extended and angry-sounding churring rattle. Song melodious, simple and measured, often in early spring, uses prominent perches.

GENERAL Widespread, but rarely numerous.

Cetti's Warbler

190 *Cettia cetti*

ADULT Small (15 cm) warbler, unstreaked reddish-brown back and pale buffish underparts. Watch for buff eyestripe and characteristically longish rounded tail, often held fanned. Secretive, heard more than seen. Sexes similar.

JUVENILE Much as adult.

HABITAT Unusual among warblers in being year-round resident, occurring in damp, heavily vegetated marshes, ditches and scrub in S, SW and (erratically) W Europe.

NEST Well-concealed grass cup deep in thick low vegetation.

VOICE Very distinctive, explosive ***chink, cher-chink*** notes and tack calls.

GENERAL Widespread, locally common.

adult

Grasshopper Warbler

Locustella naevia

ADULT Tiny (13 cm), skulking, dark grey-brown, heavily streaked warbler. Watch for dark-flecked crown and throat, unstreaked grey-buff underparts with pale whitish throat. Obscure grey-brown eyestripe. Sexes similar.

JUVENILE Much as adult.

HABITAT Summer visitor to much of Europe. Favours dense low shrubby vegetation.

NEST Well-concealed grass cup.

VOICE Characteristic high-pitched extended trill, often lasting for minutes, similar to an unreeling fishing line.

GENERAL Widespread, rarely numerous. Fan-tailed Warbler *(Cisticola juncidis)*: smaller (10 cm), year-round resident of S Europe, reddish-brown, heavily streaked plumage, short cocked tail and plaintive **zee-eek** song flight.

Savi's Warbler

Locustella luscinioides

adult

ADULT Small (15 cm), unstreaked reedbed warbler. Watch for reddish-brown upperparts and longish distinctively wedge-shaped tail. Note insectivorous beak, buff eyestripe, white underparts with buff flanks. Sexes similar.

JUVENILE Much as adult.

HABITAT Summer visitor and migrant to extensive reedbed areas across S and central Europe, less frequent in W.

NEST Cup concealed deep in reedy vegetation.

VOICE Reeling ***churr*** similar to Grasshopper Warbler (p.191), but lower-pitched and in shorter bursts. Ventriloquial, sings from reed stems.

GENERAL Restricted by habitat choice, but locally common in suitable areas.

Sedge Warbler

Acrocephalus schoenobaenus

ADULT Tiny (13 cm), noisy, heavily streaked warbler. Watch for boldly streaked back and unstreaked chestnut rump, pale-flecked dark crown, chestnut-buff eyestripe, short wedge-shaped tail. Inquisitive. Rarely flies far in open. Sexes similar.

JUVENILE As adult.

HABITAT Summer visitor and migrant over much of Europe except extreme S, SW and extreme N. Favours reedbeds and shrubby swamps.

NEST Well-concealed cup.

VOICE Vocal; rapid metallic repetitive jingling, twangy and chattering notes. ***Tuck*** alarm call.

GENERAL Widespread, often common.

adult

Reed Warbler

194 *Acrocephalus scirpaceus*

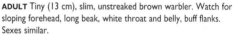

ADULT Tiny (13 cm), slim, unstreaked brown warbler. Watch for sloping forehead, long beak, white throat and belly, buff flanks. Sexes similar.

JUVENILE Much as adult.

HABITAT Summer visitor to marshes and reedbeds across S, SW, central and W Europe.

NEST Cup suspended on several reed stems.

VOICE ***Churr*** of alarm. Song extended, repetitive, more musical than Sedge Warbler (p.193). Similar Marsh Warbler *(A. palustris)* of central, N and NE Europe best identified by fluid musical song with much mimicry; often in bushy habitat.

GENERAL Widespread, often locally common.

Great Reed Warbler

Acrocephalus arundinaceus

DISTRIBUTION Summer visitor to mainland Europe, not Britain Scandinavia and Iceland

ADULT Small (20 cm), but thrush-sized and among the larger warblers. Watch for unstreaked grey-brown upperparts, whitish underparts, bulky build and relatively large, angular head with buff eye-stripe and longish powerful beak. Long tail wedge-shaped at tip. Sexes similar.

JUVENILE Much as adult, buffer on underparts.

HABITAT Summer visitor or migrant to much of Europe except far W and N. Favours extensive reedbeds.

NEST Bulky cup suspended from reeds.

VOICE Noisy; repetitive grating and metallic ***gurk-gurk- gurk, karra-karra-karra*** etc. Sings from reed stems.

adult

GENERAL Widespread, but rarely numerous; usually heard before seen.

Icterine Warbler

Hippolais icterina

ADULT Tiny (14 cm), warbler. Bright yellow breast and belly, yellow eyestripe, long beak and sloping forehead. Watch for blue legs, pale panel in closed wing, wingtips extending halfway along tail when perched. Sexes similar.

adult spring

JUVENILE Much as adult.

HABITAT Summer visitor or migrant to central and N Europe, occasional elsewhere. Favours scrubby growth in woods, gardens, heath etc.

NEST Neat grassy cup, well-concealed in bush.

VOICE Hard ***tack*** call; extended jingling song.

GENERAL Widespread, locally common. Replaced by Melodious Warbler *(H. polyglotta)* in S Europe: brown legs, no wing panel, closed wings only reach base of tail, gradually accelerating song.

Dartford Warbler

Sylvia undata

adult female

ADULT Tiny (13 cm), very dark, very long-tailed warbler. Watch for grey back, dark red-brown breast and speckled throat. Often cocks white-edged tail. Secretive. Female slightly paler, duller and browner, pinker on breast.

JUVENILE As female.

HABITAT Year-round resident in W, SW and S Europe. Favours dense dry heath, gorse or maquis.

NEST Well-concealed cup low in vegetation.

VOICE Loud ***chuck*** or ***churr***; brief soft scratchy warbling song.

GENERAL Locally common, but in variable numbers depending on winter weather. Subalpine Warbler *(S. cantillans)*: similar summer visitor to S Europe. Red throat and breast, white moustachial streak, brown wings and tail. Brief musical warbling song flight over heath and maquis.

Sardinian Warbler

198 *Sylvia melanocephala*

DISTRIBUTION Resident around Mediterranean and N Africa

adult female

ADULT Tiny (13 cm), dark-capped warbler. Male pale grey below, darker grey above, with distinctive black hood. Female similar, but browner. In both sexes watch for characteristic white throat and red eye-ring. Skulking, but active.

JUVENILE As female, but duller and browner.

HABITAT Year-round resident in maquis and similar scrub-covered areas across extreme S Europe.

NEST Neat grass cup concealed low in vegetation.

VOICE Scolding chattering call; song a mixture of scratchy and melodious phrases, usually in bouncing song flight over scrub.

GENERAL Widespread, often locally common. As with other *Sylvia* warblers, inquisitive and can be drawn from cover by making soft squeaking noises.

Orphean Warbler

Sylvia hortensis

ADULT Small (15 cm), but largish for a warbler. Dull grey-brown, paler below, dark grey head, blackish cheeks and white eye. Tail has white outer feathers. Sexes broadly similar.

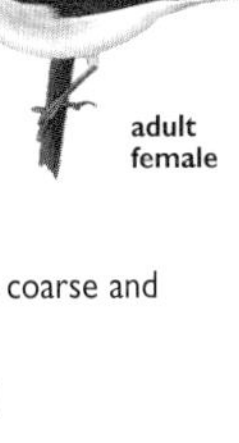
adult female

JUVENILE As adult, paler and scaly with duller eye.

HABITAT Summer visitor or migrant to S Europe. Favours open woodland, orchards, groves, parks.

NEST Well-concealed grass cup in bush.

VOICE Sharp ***tchack*** call; song in SW race repetitive, coarse and unmelodious, in SE race loud, fluting and melodious.

GENERAL Widespread, locally fairly common. Barred Warbler *(S. nisoria)* of similar habitats in north-central and E Europe: same size, drab grey-brown, white eyes, but dark cap. At close range, dark crescentic bars on underparts. Melodious song.

DISTRIBUTION
Summer visitor to Mediterranean, east to Turkey and Middle East

Lesser Whitethroat

200 *Sylvia curruca*

ADULT Tiny (13 cm), neat but dull warbler, whitish below with chestnut white throat, grey-brown above with white-edged tail. Watch for grey cap and blackish patches around eyes. Legs dark blue-grey. Sexes similar.

JUVENILE As adult, but browner.

HABITAT Summer visitor or migrant to central, W, N and NE Europe. Favours farmland with hedges and trees, woodland margins, scrubby hillsides.

NEST Neat grass cup concealed low in bush.

fresh adult

VOICE Abrupt ***tack*** call; distinctive song: a brief warble followed by a repetitive single-note rattle similar to Yellowhammer (p.249).

GENERAL Widespread, but rarely numerous.

Whitethroat

Sylvia communis 201

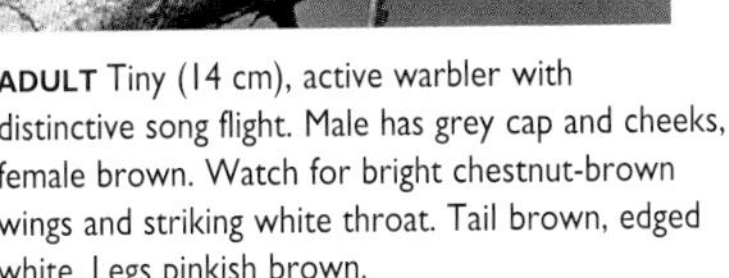

adult female

ADULT Tiny (14 cm), active warbler with distinctive song flight. Male has grey cap and cheeks, female brown. Watch for bright chestnut-brown wings and striking white throat. Tail brown, edged white. Legs pinkish brown.

JUVENILE As female, but duller.

HABITAT Summer visitor or migrant to much of Europe except far N. Favours heath, scrub, maquis and woodland margins or clearings.

NEST Neat grass cup concealed in vegetation near ground.

VOICE Harsh ***tzchack*** call; distinctive song, produced in song flight above vegetation: a rapid but cheerfully scratchy warble.

GENERAL Widespread, locally fairly common, reduced in W after droughts in African wintering grounds.

Garden Warbler

202 *Sylvia borin*

juvenile

ADULT Small (15 cm), robust warbler, almost best identified by its lack of distinctive features, but note voice and habitat. Upperparts drab olive-grey, underparts pale grey-buff. Uniformly olive-brown tail. Beak comparatively short and thick for a warbler. Legs blue. Sexes similar.

JUVENILE Much as adult.

HABITAT Summer visitor or migrant to much of Europe, not breeding in extreme S, W and N. Favours thick scrub or dense woodland undergrowth.

NEST Neat grass cup, concealed low in bush.

VOICE Abrupt ***tack*** call; distinctive song: an extended very melodious warble, sometimes considered second only to Nightingale (p.174).

GENERAL Widespread, occasionally fairly common.

Blackcap

Sylvia atricapilla

ADULT Small (15 cm), plump, distinctive warbler. Upperparts brownish-grey, browner in female; underparts whitish tinged grey in male, buff in female. Watch for jet black cap of male, brown in female. Legs bluish.

adult female

JUVENILE As female, but with ginger-brown cap.

HABITAT Summer visitor and migrant over much of Europe, increasingly through the winter in W and S. Favours parks, gardens and woodlands with both thick undergrowth and mature, tall trees.

NEST Neat grass cup concealed low in bush.

VOICE Abrupt ***tack*** call; distinctive song: a melodious warble, briefer than Garden Warbler (p.202), usually ending with a phrase rising in pitch.

GENERAL Widespread, locally fairly common, scarce in winter.

Bonelli's Warbler

204 *Phylloscopus bonelli*

DISTRIBUTION
Resident SW Europe, Spain, Portugal, France

adult spring

ADULT Tiny (10 cm) leaf warbler. Upperparts greenish-olive with indistinct pale eyestripe. Watch for characteristic silvery-white underparts, golden panel in wing and yellow rump conspicuous in flight. Active, usually in canopy. Legs brownish. Sexes similar.

JUVENILE Much as adult.

HABITAT Summer visitor and migrant in SW, S and south-central Europe. Favours mixed or coniferous woodland, frequently in hill country.

NEST Well-concealed grass cup, usually on or near ground.

VOICE Soft plaintive ***who-eet*** call; song a slow, measured trill.

GENERAL Widespread, locally fairly common.

Wood Warbler

Phyllloscopus sibilatrix

adult spring

ADULT Tiny (13 cm), but large among leaf warblers. Watch for bright yellow-green upperparts and canary-yellow eyestripe, throat and breast, and strikingly white belly. Legs pale pinkish. Active high in canopy. Sexes similar.

JUVENILE Much as adult.

HABITAT Summer visitor or migrant in central, W and N Europe, and to some mountain regions further S. Favours mature deciduous woodland with scanty undergrowth.

NEST Grassy cup, well concealed on or near ground.

VOICE Call ***peeu*** or ***deeoo***; distinctive song: opens with a couple of ***pee-oo*** notes, accelerates into a cascading torrent of sip notes, often during song flight.

GENERAL Though widespread, only locally numerous.

Chiffchaff

206 *Phylloscopus collybita*

ADULT Tiny (10 cm) leaf warbler. Plump, brownish-olive above, whitish-buff below, dark legs. Best distinguished from Willow Warbler (p.207) by song. Sexes similar.

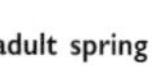

adult spring

JUVENILE As adult, but yellower.

HABITAT Summer visitor, migrant or year-round resident except in far N Europe. Favours woodland with mature trees.

NEST Grassy dome on or near ground.

VOICE ***Hoo-eet*** call; song an unmistakable series of explosive ***chiff*** and ***chaff*** notes.

GENERAL Widespread, often common.

Willow Warbler

Phylloscopus trochilus 207

ADULT Tiny (10 cm) leaf warbler. Yellow-olive above, yellower below, pale brown legs. Best distinguished from Chiffchaff (p.206) by song. Sexes similar.

JUVENILE As adult, but yellower.

HABITAT Summer visitor or migrant to much of Europe, breeding in far N, but not in far S. Favours woodland with dense undergrowth or scrub without trees.

adult spring

NEST Grassy dome on or near ground.

VOICE ***Hoo-eet*** call; song distinctive, a melodious, sparkling, descending, warbling trill ending in a flourish.

GENERAL Widespread, often common.

Goldcrest

Regulus regulus

adult female

ADULT Tiny (9 cm): joint-smallest European bird. Plump and warbler-like, active in foliage. Olive-green back, white double wingbars in blackish wings. Watch for faint black moustachial streak, black-bordered gold crown stripe, and paler patch round large dark eye. Sexes similar (displaying male shows flame bases to crown feathers).

JUVENILE As adult, but lacking crown stripe.

HABITAT Year-round resident, migrant or winter visitor to much of Europe, summer visitor in N. Favours all woodland, also parks, gardens and farmland.

NEST Delicate mossy hammock high in tree.

VOICE Very high-pitched **tseee** call; song a series of high-pitched descending **see** notes ending in a flourish.

GENERAL Widespread, often common.

Firecrest

Regulus ignicapillus

ADULT Tiny (9 cm): joint-smallest European bird. Plump and warbler-like, active in foliage. Yellow-green above, with golden-bronze shoulders. Watch for diagnostic head pattern of black bar through eye, bold white stripe between this and black-bordered fiery crest. Sexes similar.

JUVENILE Duller than adult, with faint white eyestripe.

HABITAT Year-round resident, migrant or winter visitor to S and W Europe, summer visitor to central areas. Favours all woodland, and scrub on migration.

NEST Mossy hammock high in tree.

VOICE Very shrill, high-pitched **tzee** call; song a monotonous, accelerating series of **see** notes, lacking final flourish of Goldcrest (p.208).

GENERAL Widespread, locally common, scarcer in W.

adult male

Spotted Flycatcher FLYCATCHERS

Muscicapa striata

juvenile

ADULT Small (15 cm), drab, rather short-legged, elongated-bodied flycatcher. Dull brown upperparts, paler underparts streaked on breast. Watch for broad, but fine, black beak. Hunts by flying out on long wings to snap up insects, often returning to same perch. Flicks wings and tail incessantly. Sexes similar.

JUVENILE As adult, but speckled on back

HABITAT Summer visitor to most of Europe. Favours woodland clearings, farmland, parks and gardens.

NEST Well-concealed shallow cup in vegetation.

VOICE Listen for distinctive **zzit** call; short squeaky song.

GENERAL Widespread, but not numerous; often inconspicuous.

Pied Flycatcher

Ficedula hypoleuca

ADULT Tiny (12 cm), compactly plump and distinctive flycatcher. Boldly pied summer plumage of male striking, but watch for subtler olive browns of autumn male and female. In all plumages shows broad white bar on dark wing, and white sides to base of dark tail (best seen in flight).

JUVENILE Much as female.

adult female

HABITAT Summer visitor or migrant to parts of SW, W and much of central and N Europe. Favours woodland (usually deciduous) with little undergrowth.

NEST Usually in tree hole.

VOICE Brisk ***witt*** call; brief, unmelodious rattling song.

GENERAL Widespread, locally fairly common.

Long-tailed Tit

 Aegithalos caudatus

ADULT Small (15 cm) with long, thin, black and white tail. Watch for fluffy appearance, black and white striped head pattern (all-white in far N birds), pink eye-ring, pinkish-buff shoulders and undertail. Flight feeble and whirring, calling constantly. Usually in groups. Sexes similar.

JUVENILE Much as adult, but duller and browner.

HABITAT Year-round resident in woodland, scrub, heath, farmland and gardens throughout Europe.

adult northern European

NEST Flask-shaped domed nest of hair, feathers and moss, camouflaged with flakes of lichen.

VOICE Noisy: thin **see-see-see** and low ***tupp*** calls between flock members. Rarely-heard jangling song.

GENERAL Widespread, often common.

Bearded Tit

Panurus biarmicus

ADULT Small (15 cm), tit-like, but not a true tit. Note rich chestnut-brown upperparts and long broad tail. Watch for grey head, conspicuous black 'drooping moustaches' and white throat of male. Female has brown head. Agilely clambers about reed stems. Often in groups.

JUVENILE Pale, drab version of female.

HABITAT Confined to extensive reedbeds, mostly in S and W Europe.

NEST Well-concealed cup in reeds.

adult male summer

VOICE Listen for frequent characteristic ***ping*** calls. Rarely-heard song an undistinguished rattle.

GENERAL Erratic in occurrence and numbers, sensitive to severe weather, but locally fairly common.

Marsh Tit

214 *Parus palustris*

juvenile

ADULT Tiny (12 cm), black-capped tit, dull brown above, pale buffish below. Watch for neat appearance, small black bib. Best distinguished from Willow Tit (p.215) by call. Sexes similar.

JUVENILE Much as adult.

HABITAT Year-round resident over much of central and W Europe. Favours woodland, scrub and gardens.

NEST Deserted tree hole.

VOICE Explosive ***pit-choo*** call; song a bell-like ***pitchawee-oo***.

GENERAL Widespread, but rarely numerous.

Willow Tit

Parus montanus

ADULT Tiny (12 cm), black-capped tit, brownish above, pale buffish below. Watch for scruffy appearance, heavy head and neck, large dull cap and (sometimes) pale panel in wing. Best distinguished from Marsh Tit (p.214) by call. Sexes similar.

juvenile

JUVENILE Much as adult.

HABITAT Year-round resident over much of central, W and N Europe. Favours woodland, scrub and gardens.

NEST Excavates hole in rotten stump, hence thick neck muscles.

VOICE Repetitive ***dee***, ***chay*** or ***eez*** notes in call; song a musical warble.

GENERAL Widespread, but rarely numerous.

Crested Tit

Parus cristatus

ADULT Tiny (12 cm) tit with distinctive black and white chequered crest. Body brown above, buff below; watch for white face and cheeks with black 'fish-hook' marking on cheek and black bib. Sexes similar.

JUVENILE As adult, but poorly marked with little crest.

HABITAT Year-round resident over much of Europe except extreme W and SE, in mature mixed or coniferous woodland. In Scotland confined to relict ancient pine forest.

NEST Excavates tree hole.

juvenile

VOICE Call characteristic purring ***chirr***; song a high-pitched, repeated series of **tsee** notes.

GENERAL Widespread; occasionally fairly common. Usually solitary or with other tits.

Coal Tit

Parus ater 217

juvenile

ADULT Tiny (12 cm) tit, active in canopy. Plump body olive or olive-grey above, pale buff below. Note white double wingbar. Watch for characteristic glossy black head with white cheeks and white patch on nape. Sexes similar.

JUVENILE As adult, duller, with grey head markings.

HABITAT Year-round resident, sometimes migrant, in European woodlands of all types, but favours mature conifers. Also gardens, parks, farmland, especially in winter.

NEST In hole or crevice in tree or bank.

VOICE High-pitched **zeet** call; song a distinctive repeated series of ***wheat-zee*** phrases.

GENERAL Widespread, often common. Solitary or with other tits.

Blue Tit

218 *Parus caeruleus*

ADULT Tiny (12 cm), familiar tit, active in canopy. Back green, with cobalt-blue tail and dark blue wings with a single white wingbar. Underparts yellow. Watch for distinctive head pattern of pale blue crown, white eyestripe, black stripe through eye, white cheeks and black bib. Males usually brighter than females.

JUVENILE Duller, greenish-grey instead of blue.

HABITAT Year-round resident and migrant over much of Europe except far N. Seen almost anywhere except on mountains, moors and at sea.

juvenile

NEST In hole or crevice in tree, bank or building.

VOICE ***See-see-see-sit*** call; song an accelerating trill after **see-see-see** notes.

GENERAL Widespread, often common, frequently gregarious.

Great Tit

Parus major

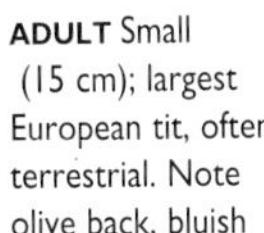

ADULT Small (15 cm); largest European tit, often terrestrial. Note olive back, bluish wings with white wingbar. Watch for glossy black head with white cheeks, relatively long robust beak. Black bib extends in line down middle of yellow underparts; darker and more extensive in male.

JUVENILE Duller, greenish-grey instead of black.

HABITAT Year-round resident or migrant over much of Europe, summer visitor to far N. Wide habitat, but favours woodlands, parks, gardens and farmland.

juvenile

NEST In hole or crevice in tree, bank or building.

VOICE Vocal, calls very varied: ***chink*** most common. Song also varied, characteristic ***teacher-teacher*** and ***see-saw*** phrases.

GENERAL Widespread, often common.

Nuthatch

220 *Sitta europaea*

adult male
northern Europe

adult female

ADULT Small (15 cm), woodpecker-like. Moves head-up or head-down on branch (unlike woodpeckers). Watch for blue-grey back, white throat, black stripe through eye, longish dagger-like beak. Underparts buff, tinged deep chestnut on flanks of male. Tail short and square, white-tipped.

JUVENILE As adult, but duller.

HABITAT Year-round resident over much of Europe except far N and W. Favours deciduous woodland and parkland, occasionally gardens, especially in winter.

NEST In cavity, often in tree, usually with entrance hole plastered with mud to correct diameter.

VOICE Distinctive ringing ***chwit***; whistling ***too-wee, too-wee*** song.

GENERAL Widespread, locally fairly common.

Treecreeper

Certhia familiaris

ADULT Tiny (12 cm) mouse like, creeps up tree-trunks. Mottled brown back, white underparts. Watch for bold frowning eyestripe, downcurved beak, long stiff tail, buff wingbars distinctive in undulating flight. Sexes similar.

JUVENILE As adult, but more heavily buff-speckled.

HABITAT Resident in W, central, N and NE Europe; in mature woodland favouring conifers except in Britain and Ireland.

NEST Usually in crevice behind flap of bark.

VOICE Sharp, shrill **zeee** call; song distinctive descending trill with final flourish.

GENERAL Widespread, rarely numerous. Short-toed Treecreeper *(C. brachydactyla)*: almost identical, widespread in central and S Europe. Favours deciduous woods. Subtly different **zeet** call.

juvenile

Golden Oriole

Oriolus oriolus

ADULT Medium (25 cm) and starling-like. Male brilliant gold and black, with shortish pink beak. Female golden-olive above, whitish below with faint streaks: watch for yellow rump and yellow-tipped dark tail in flight.

JUVENILE As female, but duller, more olive.

HABITAT Summer visitor or migrant to much of Europe except N and far W. Favours mature open deciduous woodland and parkland, also orchards and groves.

NEST Grassy hammock slung between twigs.

VOICE Very characteristic fluting ***wheela-wee-oo*** and ***too-loo-ee*** calls.

GENERAL Widespread, not numerous, heard more than seen. Despite bright plumage, remarkably inconspicuous in canopy.

adult male

Jay

Garrulus glandarius

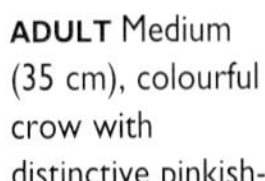

ADULT Medium (35 cm), colourful crow with distinctive pinkish-buff plumage. Watch for dark-flecked crown and black moustachial streaks. Flight looks floppy and hesitant on rounded wings: look for contrasting white rump and black tail, and for blue and white wing patches. Distinctive and unusual pale pink eye. Sexes similar.

JUVENILE As adult, but duller.

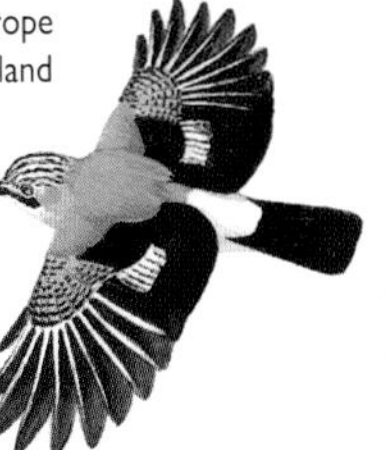

adult

HABITAT Year-round resident over much of Europe except far N. Favours woodland, parks and farmland with plentiful mature trees.

NEST Untidy twiggy shallow cup in tree fork.

VOICE Vocal; harsh ***skaark*** call; rarely heard soft chattering song.

GENERAL Widespread, often fairly common.

Red-back Shrike

224 *Lănius collurio*

adult female

ADULT Small (18 cm) shrike. Watch for male's stubby hooked beak, rufous back, grey crown, black eyestripe and white-edged black tail. Female greyer and duller, scaly marks on breast, dark brown smudge through eye, tail brown.

JUVENILE As female, duller and heavier marks on breast.

HABITAT Summer visitor or migrant to much of Europe except far W. Favours dry open country with bushes, heath, scrub, also farmland.

NEST Neat grassy cup in bush.

VOICE Harsh ***chack*** call; unexpected melodious warbling song.

GENERAL Widespread, rarely numerous. Woodchat Shrike *(L. senator)*, summer visitor to S Europe: white underparts, black back, chestnut and black head, bold white wingbar.

Great Grey Shrike

Lanius excubitor

ADULT Medium (25 cm); the largest shrike. Distinctively pale and long-tailed, uses prominent perches. Watch for hooked beak, black patch through eye, white on forehead and over eye. In deeply swooping flight shows grey rump, long white-edged black tail and broad white bars in black wings. Sexes similar.

JUVENILE Similar, but browner, barred on underparts.

HABITAT Year-round resident across central Europe, winter visitor to W and S, summer visitor to N. Favours open countryside with plentiful bushes, trees and scrub.

adult female

NEST Grass cup in bush.

VOICE Harsh ***chek*** call; jangling song.

GENERAL Widespread, never numerous.

Nutcracker

Nucifraga caryocatactes

DISTRIBUTION Resident of N and E Europe from S Sweden E to Bering Straits, and SC Europe

ADULT Medium (33 cm), dull-plumaged crow. Watch for straight, dark, dagger-like beak, brown cap, white-flecked body plumage. Bold white undertail coverts. In flight shows dark, rounded wings and white-tipped black tail. Sexes similar.

JUVENILE Similar to adult, but duller.

HABITAT Year-round resident in conifer or mixed forests, often mountainous, in N, central and E Europe. Occasionally occurs almost anywhere in W when food short.

adult

NEST Shallow twiggy cup in tree fork.

VOICE Vocal; harsh ***skaark*** and growling calls; jangling squeaky song.

GENERAL Locally fairly common.

Magpie

adult

ADULT Medium (45 cm), unmistakable and familiar long-tailed pied crow. Watch for floppy flight on black and white rounded wings, long iridescent tapered tail cocked on landing. Often terrestrial. Sexes similar.

JUVENILE As adult, but duller, initially with shorter tail.

HABITAT Year-round resident over most of Europe. Wide habitat: woodland, farmland, scrub, parks and gardens.

NEST Football-size dome of twigs, high in tree.

VOICE Harsh ***chack*** calls and chuckles; rarely heard quiet musical warbling song.

GENERAL Widespread, locally common. Azure-winged Magpie *(Cyanopica cyanea)* of extreme SW Europe: pinkish-beige body, blue wings, long blue tail, black hood, whitish throat and collar.

Alpine Chough

 Pyrrhocorax graculus

ADULT Medium (37 cm), slim, glossy-black crow. Watch for shortish, yellow, slightly downcurved beak, pink legs. Often aerobatic in flight, swooping and tumbling characteristically on rounded fingered wings. Sexes similar.

JUVENILE Sooty, with grey legs and dull beak.

DISTRIBUTION From N Spain E, through Pyrenees, Corsica, Alps, to Greece, Turkey ar beyond

HABITAT Resident at high altitudes in mountains of S Europe, often near cable-car stations.

NEST Twiggy platform in cave or crevice.

VOICE Vocal; far-carrying ***chee-up*** or ***skreee***.

GENERAL Locally fairly common. Red-billed Chough *(P. pyrrhocorax)*: iridescent black with slim, downcurved crimson beak and red legs. At lower altitudes in S, on coastal cliffs in far W. ***Kee-ow*** call.

redbilled chough

Jackdaw

Corvus monedula

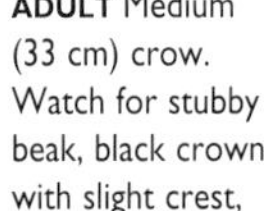

ADULT Medium (33 cm) crow. Watch for stubby beak, black crown with slight crest, contrasting grey nape and striking white eye. In flight, has quicker wingbeats than other crows, wings rounded. Sexes similar.

JUVENILE As adult, but duller, lacking grey nape.

HABITAT Widespread resident except in N Europe. Wide habitat: woodland, farmland, city centres and coastal cliffs.

adult

NEST Usually in tree hole, rocky cleft or building.

VOICE Metallic ***jack***, also high-pitched ***keeaa***.

GENERAL Widespread, often common, often gregarious. Occasionally sunbathes with seeming total relaxation, as do some other birds.

Rook

230 *Corvus frugilegus*

adult

ADULT Medium (45 cm) crow. Watch for long, grey, dagger-like beak and bare white fleshy face contrasting with glossy iridescent black plumage. Loose feathers of upper leg give baggy-trousered appearance. Usually gregarious, often aerobatic, showing fingered wingtips. Sexes similar.

JUVENILE As adult, but duller, lacks face patch, has bristly base to straight-sided beak (see Carrion Crow, p.231).

HABITAT Year-round resident, sometimes migrant, over much of Europe, summer visitor in N, winter visitor to S. Favours farmland and open countryside with plentiful trees.

NEST Colonial, bulky twig nest high in tree.

VOICE Vocal; raucous ***kaar***.

GENERAL Widespread, often common.

Carrion / Hooded Crow

ADULT Medium (45 cm) crow. All-black (Carrion) or grey with black head, wings and tail (Hooded) with intermediates where ranges overlap. Watch for black feathered base and curved ridge to beak, and neat, tight feathering to upper leg. Often solitary, in pairs or family groups, occasionally in flocks in winter. Sexes similar.

JUVENILE Much as adult, but duller.

HABITAT Carrion: year-round resident in W and SW Europe; Hooded: wider ranging through E and SE, central, N and NW, summer visitor to far N. Substantial overlap in central and S Europe. Favours all open countryside, also urban areas.

NEST Solitary bulky twig structure high in tree.

VOICE Deep harsh ***korr***.

GENERAL Widespread.

adults

Raven

232 *Corvus corax*

adult

ADULT Largest (63 cm) of the crows. Note thick neck, heavy head with bristling throat feathers, and massive angular beak. In flight, watch for broad heavily-fingered wings and distinctive wedge-shaped tail tip. Often solitary, in pairs or family groups. Sexes similar.

JUVENILE Similar to adult.

HABITAT Widespread year-round resident in coastal, moorland and mountain areas of W, S, E and N Europe, largely absent from central areas.

NEST Very bulky twig structure in tree, or on rocky ledge.

VOICE Gruff ***pruuk*** and resonant ***gronk***.

GENERAL Though widespread, rarely numerous.

Starling

Sturnus vulgaris

ADULT Small (22 cm) and familiar. Watch for iridescent black plumage with buff speckling, denser in winter. Male sings from prominent perch, throat feathers bristling, wings flapping slowly. Beak yellow in summer, black in winter. Gregarious. Fast and direct flight on triangular wings. Sexes similar.

JUVENILE Dull pale brown, darker above than below.

HABITAT Year-round resident or migrant over much of Europe, summer visitor in N, winter visitor to SW. Occurs in almost all terrestrial habitats.

adult winter

NEST Untidy straw and feathers in cavity.

VOICE Vocal; harsh shrieking calls, song full of chattering notes and mimicry of other birds.

GENERAL Widespread and common.

House Sparrow

 Passer domesticus

adult femal

ADULT Small (15 cm) and familiar. Watch for typical black triangular beak and head pattern of male, with grey crown, white cheeks, brown nape and black bib. Female pale fawn on underparts, mottled browns above; note pale eyestripe.

JUVENILE Much as female.

HABITAT Year-round resident throughout Europe except extreme N. Often near habitation, favours farmland and urban areas.

NEST Untidy spherical grassy structure in dense vegetation or hole.

VOICE Harsh ***chirrup***, often repetitive.

GENERAL Widespread, often common. Male Spanish Sparrow *(P. hispaniolensis)* from extreme S Europe: chestnut crown, white eyestripe, black-blotched breast; female indistinguishable from House Sparrow.

Tree Sparrow

Passer montanus

ADULT Tiny (13 cm), but chunky, sparrow. Both sexes show head pattern of brown crown and narrow white collar. Watch for white cheeks with bold black spot and small black bib.

JUVENILE As adult, but duller and browner.

juvenile

HABITAT Resident, sometimes migrant, except in far N Europe. Favours woodland, farmland and scrub.

NEST Domed grass structure, often in cavity.

VOICE Distinctively liquid ***tek*** and ***tchup*** calls.

GENERAL Widespread, sometimes fairly common. Drabber Rock Sparrow *(Petronia petronia)*: sexes similar, resembles female House Sparrow. Has indistinct yellow spot on throat, distinctive white-tipped tail. Confined to rocky areas in extreme S.

Chaffinch

Fringilla coelebs

ADULT Small (15 cm) finch. Pink breast, grey hood and black forehead in summer male, duller and masked by buff feather fringes in winter. Female olive-brown above, buff below. In flight, watch for white-edged blackish tail and bold, white, double wingbars in both sexes.

JUVENILE Much as female.

HABITAT Widespread year-round resident across Europe, summer visitor in N and E. Numbers in W and N augmented by migrants and winter visitors. Favours woodlands, farmland, parks and gardens. Often gregarious in winter.

NEST Neat, well-camouflaged cup in tree fork.

VOICE Ringing ***pink*** call; song a powerful cascade of rich notes ending in a flourish.

GENERAL Widespread, often common.

Brambling

Fringilla montifringilla

ADULT Small (15 cm) finch. Glossy black head and back contrast with orange on breast and wings in summer male. At other times, black is partly concealed by broad orange-buff feather fringes. Female browner, but still orange on face and breast. In flight, watch for orange-white double wingbars and distinctive white rump.

JUVENILE Much as female.

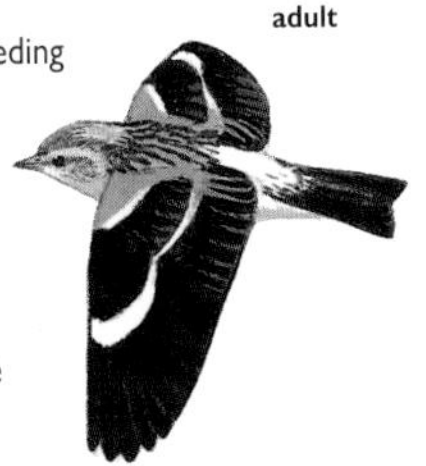

adult

HABITAT Summer visitor to N Europe, breeding in forest and woodland. Migrant or winter visitor to rest of Europe, favouring woodland, parks, gardens and farmland.

NEST Neat, well-camouflaged cup in tree fork.

VOICE Drawn-out ***chwaay*** flight call; simple slow repetitive song based on **twee** notes.

GENERAL Widespread, but erratic.

Serin

238 *Serinus serinus*

adult female

ADULT Tiny (10 cm) yellowish finch. Watch for streaked yellow- brown upperparts, bright yellow breast of male. Female duller and buffer. In flight, note yellow double wingbars and characteristic yellow rump contrasting with dark tail. Beak distinctively tiny and stubby, yet triangular.

JUVENILE Much as female.

HABITAT Summer visitor to W and central Europe, year-round resident further S. Favours open woodland, and farmland, parks and gardens with plenty of mature trees.

NEST Tiny neat moss and grass cup, usually high in tree.

VOICE ***Churr-lit*** flight call and distinctive but monotonous jingling song.

GENERAL Widespread, locally fairly common.

Greenfinch

Carduelis chloris

ADULT Small (15 cm) yellowish finch with relatively heavy, pale triangular beak. Male olive-green above, rich yellow below. Shows yellow edge to folded wing, and grey shoulders. Female duller, buffish yellow on underparts with darker streaks. In flight, fanned, slightly forked tail shows yellow patches at either side of base.

JUVENILE Much as female.

adult

HABITAT Year-round resident or migrant over much of Europe, summer visitor to far N. Favours scrub, open woodlands, parks, gardens and farmland.

NEST Cup of twigs, moss and grass in tree or bush.

VOICE Drawn-out **dweeee** call; purring song in display flight with exaggerated wing beats.

GENERAL Widespread, often common.

Goldfinch

240 *Carduelis carduelis*

ADULT Tiny (13 cm) colourful finch. Watch for diagnostic red face, white cheeks, black crown and nape in adult. In flight, note forked tail, white rump, black wings with distinctively broad, full-length golden wingbar. Sexes similar.

JUVENILE Dull buff, lacking head pattern, but with white rump and broad gold wingbar.

adult

HABITAT Year-round resident or migrant over much of Europe, summer visitor to parts of N and NE. Favours heath and scrub, but also open woodland, farmland, parks and gardens.

NEST Neat, well-camouflaged hair and rootlet nest, usually high in canopy.

VOICE Sharp ***dee-dee-lit*** call; prolonged tinkling jingle of a song.

GENERAL Widespread, often common.

Siskin

Carduelis spinus

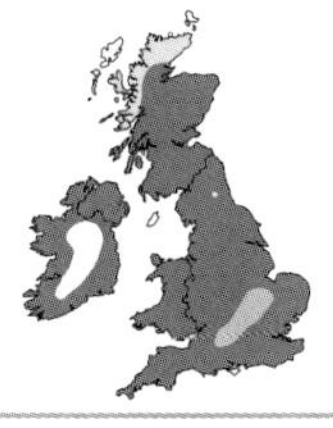

adult

ADULT Tiny (12 cm), dark, agile finch. Upperparts olive, tinged yellow and heavily dark streaked. Male has black cap and bib, yellow cheeks and upper breast; female lacks black, has paler streaked breast. In flight, watch for striking yellow wingbars, yellow rump and yellow patches at base of blackish forked tail.

JUVENILE As adult female, but duller.

HABITAT Year-round resident, migrant or winter visitor to much of Europe, summer visitor in far N. Breeds in woodlands and forest, in winter favours birch and alder, sometimes on farmland or in parks and gardens.

NEST Twiggy cup high in canopy, often in conifer.

VOICE Flight call extended ***chwee-ooo***; prolonged twittering song.

GENERAL Widespread, erratic, locally fairly common.

Linnet

Carduelis cannabina

ADULT Tiny (13 cm), brownish finch. Male rich chestnut-brown on back, with white-edged dark tail, blackish wings with white panel. Watch for rich pink cap to buff head and pink breast, most conspicuous in summer. Winter male and female dull brown above, with paler streaked breast. Flight weakly fluttering, deeply undulating.

JUVENILE Much as female.

HABITAT Year-round resident or migrant over much of Europe, summer visitor in N. Favours heath, scrub and farmland, sometimes parks and gardens.

NEST Neat, well-concealed grassy cup in shrub.

VOICE Loud sweet call; twittering song.

GENERAL Widespread, locally common.

female

Twite

Carduelis flavirostris

ADULT Tiny (13 cm) finch, aptly called the mountain linnet. Streaked dull brown above, buff with brown streaks below. Triangular beak, grey in summer, yellow in winter. Watch for single whitish wingbar and pink flush on breast and rump of summer male, sexes otherwise similar.

JUVENILE Much as female.

HABITAT Year-round resident or winter visitor to NW coastal heath, hills and moorland, summer visitor further N. May winter on coastal marshes and rough grassland.

adult female

NEST Well-concealed grassy cup low in shrub or on ground.

VOICE Nasal ***chway*** or ***chweet***; musical jingling song.

GENERAL Local, sometimes gregarious.

Redpoll

 Carduelis flammea

ADULT Tiny (12 cm), compact, dark finch. Dark brown, heavily streaked above, paler buff below, streaked brown on breast. In summer, has dark red cap (poll), small black bib and male may have pink flush on breast. Note indistinct buff wingbar. Sexes similar in winter.

JUVENILE As winter female, lacking bib.

HABITAT Year-round resident, winter visitor or migrant to N, central and W Europe, summer visitor to far N. Favours mixed woodland, especially with birch, also scrub and open fields in winter in mixed flocks with other finches.

NEST Neat cup, usually high in tree.

VOICE ***Chee-chee-chit*** call; purring trill of song as circles high over trees.

GENERAL Widespread, locally common, in places increasing.

adult

Crossbill

Loxia curvirostra

ADULT Small (15–17 cm), heavily-built finch with distinctively bulky, parrot-like crossed beak. Males orange-brown or crimson-brown, females greenish-olive. Note swooping flight showing notched tail and parrot-like acrobatics, feeding on conifer cones.

JUVENILEMuch as female.

adult

HABITAT Widespread year-round resident over much of Europe, irregular visitor elsewhere, sometimes staying to breed if food supplies allow. Favours conifers, particularly spruce.

NEST Flattish twiggy platform high in canopy.

VOICE Metallic ***jip*** or ***jup*** call; abrupt twittering song.

GENERAL Widespread, erratic, locally fairly common.

Bullfinch

246 *Pyrrhula pyrrhula*

ADULT Small (15 cm), thick-set finch. Male has black cap, grey back and red underparts. Female has black cap, but is suede-brown above, pinkish-fawn below. Looks heavy-headed and slow in undulating flight. Watch for white rump and purplish-black tail.

JUVENILE As female, but lacking black cap.

HABITAT Widespread year-round resident, sometimes migrant, over much of Europe except far SW and SE. Favours woodlands with dense undergrowth, scrub, farmland with hedges, occasionally parks and gardens.

NEST Fragile shallow twiggy platform in shrub.

VOICE Whistling ***peeeuu***. Song a very quiet warble.

GENERAL Though widespread, rarely numerous. Usually solitary or in pairs.

adult

Hawfinch

Coccothraustes coccothraustes 247

adult

ADULT Small (18 cm), but one of the larger finches. Large chestnut head and huge, silvery, wedge-shaped beak with grey nape, brown back and pinkish-buff underparts. In deeply undulating flight watch for white-tipped tail and broad white wingbars. Sexes broadly similar.

JUVENILE Much as adult, but browner and duller.

HABITAT Year-round resident or occasional migrant over much of Europe except far N and NW. Favours mature, usually deciduous, woodland with seeding trees.

NEST Bulky twiggy platform, high in canopy.

VOICE Explosive Robin-like ***zik*** call. Song a rarely-heard twittering warble.

GENERAL Widespread, rarely numerous. Secretive.

Snow Bunting

248 *Plectrophenax nivalis*

ADULT Small (17 cm) bunting. Summer male unmistakably black and white. Female and winter male streaked brown above, paler and buffer below; black-tipped yellow beak. Always shows white in closed wing and conspicuous white mid-wing triangle and white sides to tail in flight.

JUVENILE Similar to female.

HABITAT Summer visitor breeding in far N Europe, migrant or winter visitor to NW and north-central areas. Breeds on tundra and mountainsides, winters on weedy fields and marshes.

NEST Grassy cup, concealed in rocky crevice.

VOICE Plaintive ***sweet*** and ***tew*** calls; fast-moving Skylark-like song.

GENERAL Irregular, rarely numerous.

adult

Yellowhammer

Emberiza citrinella

adult

ADULT Small (18 cm), familiar yellowish bunting. Summer male brilliantly yellow-breasted, with yellow head showing few darker markings. Female and winter male duller and browner, but still with yellow on head and underparts. Note dark-streaked rich chestnut mantle and rump.

JUVENILE Similar to female, but duller.

HABITAT Widespread year-round resident over much of Europe, summer visitor in far N, winter visitor in extreme S. Favours heath, scrub, farmland and grassland with bushes.

NEST Grassy cup low in shrub.

VOICE Abrupt ***twick*** call; familiar song, a rattle of **zit** notes ending in a drawn-out wheezing **tzeeee**.

GENERAL Widespread, often fairly common.

Cirl Bunting

 Emberiza cirlus

adult

ADULT Small (16 cm) southern bunting. Male has grey-green hood with black and yellow markings, dark-streaked chestnut back, chestnut flanks and yellow belly. Female and winter male duller and browner, similar to female Yellowhammer (p.249). All show distinctive olive rump in flight.

JUVENILE Similar to female.

HABITAT Resident in W, SW and S Europe. Favours dry heath and scrub.

NEST Grassy cup concealed low in shrub.

VOICE High-pitched soft ***tsip*** call; song a monotonous rattle of ***zit*** notes, lacking final ***tzeee*** of Yellowhammer.

GENERAL Locally fairly common. Uses prominent bush-top song-posts.

Ortolan Bunting

Emberiza hortulana

DISTRIBUTION Summer visitor to mainland Europe

ADULT Small (15 cm), drab bunting. Summer male has grey hood and breast, with yellow throat and eye-ring, dull chestnut underparts. Female and winter male duller, streaked dull brown above, with buff throat and cinnamon breast. Watch for distinctive pale eye-ring and pale pinkish beak. Shows white-edged tail in flight.

JUVENILE Similar to female, but more uniformly buff.

HABITAT Summer visitor or migrant over much of Europe, scarcer in W and N. Favours dry open country and farmland with scattered scrub, often on hillsides.

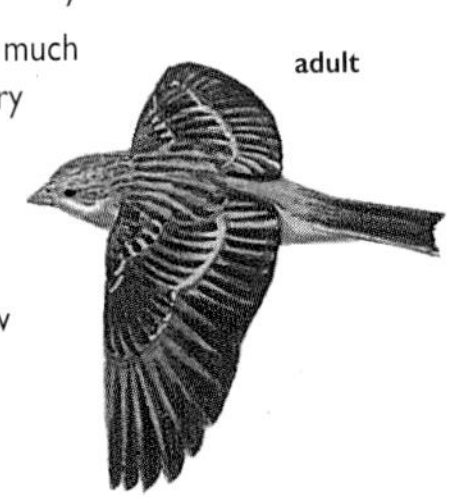

adult

NEST Well-concealed grassy cup.

VOICE Pwit, ***tlip*** and ***chew*** flight calls; slow rasping song of several **zeeu** notes.

GENERAL Though widespread, rarely numerous.

Reed Bunting

 Emberiza schoeniclus

adult female

ADULT Small (15 cm) bunting. Summer male has striking black and white head pattern. Female and winter male browner, streaked; dark head with pale eyestripe, and blackish moustachial streaks. Tail black, white-edged.

JUVENILE Similar to female.

HABITAT Resident over much of Europe. Usually in marshy areas, occasionally elsewhere.

NEST Grassy cup concealed low in vegetation.

VOICE ***Seep*** and measured ***see-you*** calls; song a short, harsh and disjointed jangle.

GENERAL Widespread, locally common. Scarce Lapland Bunting *(Calcarius lapponicus)*: chestnut nape, pale crown stripe, ***ticky-tick-teeu call***; winters on coastal marshes.

Corn Bunting

Miliaria calandra

ADULT Small (18 cm), but the largest bunting, and also the least distinctive in plumage. Upperparts brown, heavily darker streaked, underparts pale buff with brown streaking. Note thick-set appearance, bulky stubby beak. Shows no white in wings or tail in flight. Sexes similar, winter and summer.

adult

JUVENILE Similar to adult.

HABITAT Erratically distributed across much of Europe except N. Favours open, dryish farmland, heath and grassland.

NEST Well-concealed grassy cup on ground.

VOICE ***Tsip*** or quit call; song unmistakable grating metallic harsh jangle, from prominent perch.

GENERAL Though widespread, numbers very variable.

Index